Work, Society, and the Ethical Self

Max Planck Studies in Anthropology and Economy
Series editors:
Stephen Gudeman, University of Minnesota
Chris Hann, Max Planck Institute for Social Anthropology

Definitions of economy and society, and their proper relationship to each other, have been the perennial concerns of social philosophers. In the early decades of the twenty-first century these became and remain matters of urgent political debate. At the forefront of this series are the approaches to these connections by anthropologists, whose explorations of the local ideas and institutions underpinning social and economic relations illuminate large fields ignored in other disciplines.

Volume 7
Work, Society, and the Ethical Self: Chimeras of Freedom in the Neoliberal Era
Edited by Chris Hann

Volume 6
Financialization: Relational Approaches
Edited by Chris Hann and Don Kalb

Volume 5
Market Frictions: Trade and Urbanization at the Vietnam–China Border
Kirsten W. Endres

Volume 4
Industrial Labor on the Margins of Capitalism: Precarity, Class, and the Neoliberal Subject
Edited by Chris Hann and Jonathan Parry

Volume 3
When Things Become Property: Land Reform, Authority and Value in Postsocialist Europe and Asia
Thomas Sikor, Stefan Dorondel, Johannes Stahl, and Phuc Xuan To

Volume 2
Oikos and Market: Explorations in Self-Sufficiency after Socialism
Edited by Stephen Gudeman and Chris Hann

Volume 1
Economy and Ritual: Studies of Postsocialist Transformations
Edited by Stephen Gudeman and Chris Hann

Work, Society, and the Ethical Self

Chimeras of Freedom in the Neoliberal Era

Edited by

CHRIS HANN

berghahn
NEW YORK • OXFORD
www.berghahnbooks.com

First published in 2021 by
Berghahn Books
www.berghahnbooks.com

Library of Congress Cataloging-in-Publication Data

Names: Hann, C. M., 1953- editor.
Title: Work, society, and the ethical self : chimeras of freedom in the neoliberal era / edited by Chris Hann.
Description: New York : Berghahn Books, 2021. | Series: Max Planck studies in anthropology and economy ; volume 7 | Includes bibliographical references and index.
Identifiers: LCCN 2021017507 (print) | LCCN 2021017508 (ebook) | ISBN 9781800732254 (hardback) | ISBN 9781800732261 (ebook)
Subjects: LCSH: Work--Moral and ethical aspects. | Freedom. | Neoliberalism.
Classification: LCC HD4905 .W666 2021 (print) | LCC HD4905 (ebook) | DDC 174--dc23
LC record available at https://lccn.loc.gov/2021017507
LC ebook record available at https://lccn.loc.gov/2021017508

British Library Cataloguing in Publication Data

A catalogue record for this book is available from the British Library

ISBN 978-1-80073-225-4 hardback
ISBN 978-1-80073-226-1 ebook

Contents

Preface vii
Chris Hann

Introduction. Work and Ethics in Anthropology 1
Chris Hann

Chapter 1. The Meaning of "Free" Work: Service as a Gift, and Labor as a Commodity for Ni-Vanuatu Labor Migrants 27
Rachel E. Smith

Chapter 2. On the Meanings of Pleasure: Work, Ethics, and Freedom in the Hunza Valley 49
Katherine J. L. Miller

Chapter 3. Ethics of Work and Freedom in the Argentinean Andes: Value Creation and Virtuous Self-Crafting through Miniature Production 70
Olivia Angé

Chapter 4. Pursuing Pleasure at Work: Friendship and Precarity at North Indian Call Centers 89
Akanksha Awal

Chapter 5. More Than Money: Work as Self-Realization in Accra's Private Media 108
Anna-Riikka Kauppinen

Chapter 6. Capitalism, Overwork, and Polanyi's Dialectics of Freedom: Emerging Visions of Work–Life Balance in Contemporary Urban China 132
Gonçalo Santos, Yichen Rao, Jack L. Xing, and Jun Zhang

Chapter 7. From Freedom to Loaf to Freedom to Work: The Late Socialist Countermovement and Liberalization from Below in Yugoslavia 158
Ivan Rajković

Chapter 8. Max Weber's Heirs? Work and Ethics among Small Business Owners in East Germany 182
Sylvia Terpe

Chapter 9. Click for Work: Rethinking Freedom through Online Work Distribution Platforms 201
Ilana Gershon and Melissa Cefkin

Chapter 10. Unicorn-Makers Working for Freedom (and Monopolies): The Work of Venture Capital Investors 221
Johannes Lenhard

Chapter 11. Individuality, Teamwork, and Work Processes in a Financial Services Center in Germany 240
Magdalena Dąbkowska

Chapter 12. Writing without Fear—or Bylines: Freedom and Frustration among US American Ghostwriters 258
Deborah A. Jones

Afterword 278
Gerd Spittler

Index 285

Preface

Chris Hann

This volume is a product of research cooperation between the Max Planck Society and the Department of Social Anthropology at the University of Cambridge. Launched in 2017, the Max Planck–Cambridge Centre for Ethics, Economy and Social Change (MAX-CAM) has two bases in Germany: the Max Planck Institute for Social Anthropology in Halle (Saale) and the Max Planck Institute for the Study of Religious and Ethnic Diversity in Göttingen. The majority of our postdoctoral researchers are based in Cambridge, but there is continuous communication and considerable mobility between the three institutions.

With the phase of fresh data collection behind us, during 2019–21 each institution has been initiating collective exploration and debate of a subject of particular interest to its own members. The first such topic was work. We set out to investigate how the study of work in the contemporary world, conventionally located in the subdiscipline of economic anthropology and connecting with other social sciences, might cross-fertilize with the new anthropology of ethics, with its interest in culturally specific notions of personhood and close links to the study of religion and ritual. Following discussions within the core of MAX-CAM, in December 2019 Johannes Lenhard and I organized a meeting in Halle which marked an important stage in the gestation of this volume. Special thanks go to Wolfgang Streeck, who delivered a rousing keynote lecture, and Stephen Gudeman and Gerd Spittler, who helped us tie everything together at the end. Other colleagues and guests who made valuable contributions (either as presenters or discussants) but who are not visible in the final collection included Jennifer Cash, Ruth Dukes, Kirsten Endres, Jiazhi Fengjiang, Miriam Glucksmann, Chris Gregory, Mark Harvey, Patrice Ladwig, James Laidlaw, Susan MacDougall, Scott MacLochlainn, Patrick McKearney, Nikolaos Olma, Peter van der Veer, Samuel Williams and Lale Yalçın-Heckmann.

This is the first collective output of the MAX-CAM initiative, but it is simultaneously the last in a series of collaborations in Halle stretching back over more than a decade, the results of which have all been published in this series. The pattern has been the same throughout: a core group of postdoctoral researchers carries out fresh empirical research, individually but as members of a team, before drawing in other researchers (by invitation and/or via open calls) when the project has matured. Sharing responsibility for these earlier teams with Stephen Gudeman, Catherine Alexander, Jonathan Parry and Don Kalb has greatly enriched my own understanding of economic anthropology.

This is also an appropriate place to record my thanks to my co-directors in MAX-CAM, from whom I am continuing to learn much about other areas of anthropology: James Laidlaw, Joel Robbins, and Peter van der Veer.

Finally, as always it is a pleasure to acknowledge the assistance of Anke Meyer in every phase of preparing this work for publication.

Introduction

Work and Ethics in Anthropology

CHRIS HANN

Producing this volume has required a lot of work from a lot of people. For the editor, it has meant quite a few hours of tedium, including long stretches at weekends which ate into his normal leisure time but allowed for better concentration than he finds possible in his regular office hours. Along the way there have been moments of satisfaction and even genuine excitement, which I hope readers will recognize and share. The work of a journeyman academic differs from that of, say, a seasonal worker in the construction sector as much as it does from that of an artist or craftsman. Its rhythms and the nature of the product change during the life course. In anthropology, an edited volume is very different from a single-authored monograph. But it has attractions, especially if it can generate sentiments of solidarity with co-authors as well as a kind of identity with the final product. Even if much of the work on this book has been solitary, ties of collegiality to a creative bunch of authors have made the project pleasurable in distinctive ways.

From Monday to Friday, I habitually leave my comfortable home and walk to a separate building to carry out routine tasks. My work ethic can be gauged from the fact that I often arrive early in the morning, when the cleaners are just finishing their early shift. Since neoliberal reforms were introduced by the Max Planck Society, this section of our workforce has not been employed by the organization but by a subcontractor, which pays its staff the prescribed minimum wage. Most co-workers known as "non-scientific staff" (including administrative and secretarial employees) also reach their offices early. Without the help of Anke Meyer, the task of preparing the manuscript of this book to the standard expected by the publisher would have taken much longer. The secretaries have more flexibility than the cleaning staff, but for most of the time that we have worked together Anke Meyer has been required to clock in and out, so that her fulfillment of the requisite number of working hours each month can be controlled.

As for researchers like myself, so far no one counts the hours we work. Most arrive on the late side. All have well-equipped offices, though some prefer to work from home whenever there is no necessity to come to the institute to participate in a seminar or to use the library. Nowadays, most activities can be undertaken online. In the wake of the Covid-19 epidemic, it is widely anticipated that (as in many other sectors) what Germans call "home office" will become even more popular among academics. It is hard to predict the impact this will have on their academic productivity or work-life balance. Researchers at our Max Planck Institute enjoy a lot of freedom in performing their work. But in comparison with the non-scientific staff, the time budgets of the academics are likely to remain fuzzy. The former find it easier to switch off from the concerns of their employment during evenings and weekends (at least I hope they do). Perhaps Covid-induced working from home will force all of us to rethink our work ethics and the meaning of productivity.

Distinctions between work and leisure are often blurred, more so for some than for others. An explicit concept of leisure is relatively new in human history. Another distinction that interests us is the one the English language draws between work and labor. In the course of the industrial revolution, large sections of the population were drawn into paid employment and subjected to factory discipline for the first time. The new wage-laborers did not necessarily cease performing other kinds of work outside the factory or the mine. Work is the broader term and significant forms of sociality can be expected to develop wherever it is undertaken, even in highly regimented, automated "Taylorist" conditions. Feminist scholars have investigated the unpaid work that takes place in the home and is oriented more to reproduction than to production. Studies of the "informal sector" have demonstrated that, in both developing and in highly industrialized economies, a lot of manual work takes place in conditions utterly unlike the Fordist factory. Standard white-collar office work has always been supplemented by freelancing and consultancies. Most forms of work depend in one way or another on time-consuming investments in social networks. If the expansion of digital technologies accelerates the shift towards working from home, the archetypal household of the industrial age in which the breadwinner(s) were subject to direct external discipline will be consigned to history. With no need to trek out to the fields as in the preindustrial era, and with online delivery services readily available, the digitalized household has unprecedented control over its rhythms of production and consumption. Economic anthropologists might be tempted to theorize an era in which the economy of the house is again preeminent—were it not for the overwhelming constraints of markets and financialization (see Gudeman 2016).

Worlds of work are changing rapidly. Many humans have too few options for paid employment and are compelled to take jobs under precarious conditions. They might be more than willing to work longer hours in return for a secure contract. The proportion of "contingent workers" has risen sharply in recent decades (Herod 2018: 81–84). Everywhere, many are obliged to work longer and harder than they would wish. Some unions in Europe are campaigning for a general shift to a four-day working week, which they claim will lead to a significant rise in economic productivity as well as diffuse social benefits. The shock occasioned by the pandemic shutdown has drawn attention to the *social* in the most graphic ways: some groups are much more vulnerable than others, and societies fall apart without their "key workers." What can the concept of work-life balance mean when work is so deeply embedded into one's existence? The activity that is arduous and alienating for some can be pleasurable and a source of identity for others; and even for the same individual in different phases of the life course. Should every human activity be considered as work, at least potentially? Can the concept of work be extended to other forms of life, or even to spirits and inanimate objects? These are just a few of the questions that anthropologists have raised in connection with work, and they cannot all be pursued in this book. Our particular focus is on the ethical dimension: on "work ethics" in the popular sense, but also on the tension between work as a key aspect of social organization and its subjective experience by individuals—by what scholars have come to call the "ethical self." We are especially interested in the relationship between work and freedom, and how this is changing under the impact of new technologies and neoliberal political economy. In this Introduction, I set the scene by examining contested keywords and reviewing how work has been studied in earlier generations, especially by anthropologists. I will suggest that it is no accident that questions of freedom, both personal and social, have come to the fore at our moment in history.

Definitions, Semantic Fields

Work is conventionally defined as activity to secure the livelihood and reproduction of the human group. Usually formulated as purposeful activity to satisfy needs (including the need for money), for the economist it generally entails costs, such as physical and/or mental discomfort and giving up leisure time. In an elegant introduction to a rich collection of case studies, Sandra Wallman (1979) rejected every form of reductionism, from the biological and ecological to the economic and technological. Each of these factors is significant, and they must be pursued together. She begins with energy:

> Work is the application of human energy to things; which application converts, maintains, or adds value to the worker, the thing worked on, and the system in which the work is performed. (Wallman 1979: 4)

Note the use here of "value", rather than a more prosaic "utility." A few pages later, she explains why, for an understanding of work, moral criteria are as important as the material:

> [W]ork is the performance of necessary tasks, and the production of necessary values – moral as well as economic. The task[s] of meeting obligations, securing identity, status and structure, are as fundamental to livelihood as bread and shelter. On this basis, work may be defined as the production, management or conversion of the resources necessary to livelihood. (Ibid.: 7)

Philosophers have reflected on work for millennia (thereby performing philosophical work). The authors of Wallman's volume are more concerned with the empirical social scientific analysis of work. This did not begin in a systematic way until after the combined impact of the industrial revolution and the European Enlightenment. The dominant academic discipline was a new one called sociology. Its practitioners investigated new processes of work, more concentrated in factories than ever before, and their consequences for social structure and organization. It was assumed that the patterns found in the economically most advanced countries would eventually be replicated elsewhere. From Dickensian sweatshops to Fordist mass production, many parts of the globalized economy of the twenty-first century do indeed exhibit affinities to precedents set in the North Atlantic region. The old heartlands of the working classes have changed greatly, but even here most citizens are still obliged to sell their labor-power in order to secure their livelihood. An industrial proletariat has expanded enormously in the Global South, albeit in precarious forms that Marx and Engels failed to anticipate.

Anthropologists have also played a role in the modern academic division of work on work. By exploring various forms of preindustrial work they established its universality: no society is free of work. The male hunter who pursues forest prey in encounters animated and enabled by spirits is working. Typically, the gathering activities of the females of the band provide a more reliable source of food. In terms of effort and drudgery, gathering is closer than hunting to the painstaking forms of work that dominate in agrarian and industrial societies. Herders work too, sometimes in more isolated ways than hunters, but with similarly rich cosmologies that shape their economic action. The rhythms of preindustrial work tend to follow the seasons. Early ethnographers were interested in whether or not "savages" and "primitive tribesmen" worked efficiently, for example by minimizing the effort they invested in their gardens. It was soon realized that they did not, at least not according to the European criteria. More was going on. The social significance of work could not be reduced to calorific efficiency or the models of an industrial engineer. Work was universal, but understood in a social context it was endlessly diverse (Spittler 2008).

In the course of globalization, anthropologists' efforts to study work have tended to converge with those of sociologists. Both have been influenced by feminist theory, and nowadays give appropriate recognition to unpaid housework and the work of care—emotional as well as material. Sociologists have joined anthropologists in using qualitative ethnographic methods to give insight into worlds of work, such as the informal (or black or grey) economy, that are not captured in official economic statistics. Anthropologists have been reluctant to adopt the quantitative methods still favored by most sociologists, but the results of their fieldwork on factory floors and on contemporary digital platforms are often indistinguishable. Most of the authors contributing to this book have been trained in anthropology. Some of the more remote settings and some of the theories on which they draw are strongly associated with that discipline. But for the most part, in the study of contemporary work the boundary with sociology has become porous if not fully irrelevant.

The English language offers "labor" as an alternative to "work," whereas German knows only *Arbeit*. I am not the first to wonder what difference this makes: for example, if it had been the Work Party that had frequently formed the government of Great Britain during the last century, or if a "work theory of value" had been a key component of Marxist theory (Firth 1979: 178–79). Labor is more closely associated with waged employment and with an industrial heyday that is receding into history, at least in some parts of the world. Labor is typically thought of a *resource*, one that is transacted in the market as a commodity, albeit a "fictitious" one (see Polanyi 1944). Work, as defined above by Sandra Wallman, is better grasped as an *activity*. In this volume we are mostly concerned with working to make money, though the opening chapters illustrate broader possibilities. Working for money subsumes not only blue-collar employment in capitalist factories and white-collar office work that is similarly disciplined, but also the expert knowledge-work of managers, owners, and consultants. Alongside standard forms of employment contract, several contributors to this volume are particularly interested in changing forms of self-employment.

Freedom is another word with large semantic fields that have changed considerably in recent centuries—parallel to the transformations of material conditions, though the connections are not always easy to disentangle. Certain philosophers of the Enlightenment proposed freedom or "liberty" as a new moral (political) absolute. In the twentieth century it was coupled with notions such as "open society" to define the core of pluralist liberal democracy, in opposition to the unfreedom of socialism and fascism. But Karl Popper and other proponents of the open society could never explain why this imaginary should be freely embraced by all groups in the pluralist society to which they aspired (see Ignatieff and Roch 2018). The paradox of freedom intensifies when neoliberal economic institutions effectively exclude, atomize and *degrade* large sections of the population (Rakowski 2016). The contributors to this volume explore freedom in ways that open up to usages beyond Western individualism and the version of human rights that has been derived from it since the 1940s (Moyn 2010). Freedom in this anthropological sense is inherently social, as only in specific social conditions can libertarian notions of free individuals take root. In practice, as I will outline below, freedom is always accompanied by constraints and responsibilities.

In addition to defining their etic (analytic) concepts like any other researcher, when anthropologists carry out ethnographic field research they attend to emic (vernacular) concepts. They cannot expect to find words neatly congruent with work and freedom, the key English terms for this volume. The semantic fields of the vernacular concepts may not be stable, just as local meanings of work and freedom have changed in our own societies, reflecting ideological as well as technological trends. We can try as neutrally as possible to identify the local ideas that correspond most closely to the terms we attempt to operationalize in comparative analysis, but the pitfalls are legion. For example, we may define freedom analytically in terms of a concept that prioritizes an individual's scope to make choices, and then proceed to identify the space for making such choices and the vocabulary used to describe this space in the societies we investigate. But what if the society has a more collective approach as to what constitutes "true freedom"? Similar difficulties arise in the case of work. Some societies may not make a clear distinction between work (effort) and leisure (or play). This does not obviate the fact that at least some members of these societies engage in forms of physical work. Others may perform activities that are not classified as work at all, though the ethnographer notes the indispensability of this toil. The contributors to this book are concerned with local understandings of work—mental as well as manual, individual as well as collective, tedious and unrewarding as well as pleasurable and emotionally fulfilling. Problems in the precise demarcation of work from other human activities exemplify the difficulties of cross-cultural translation, including the problem of how to theorize (the) economy itself (Hann and Hart 2011).

Work in Anthropology

From Raymond Firth in the 1920s to Gerd Spittler nearly a century later, it has frequently been lamented that anthropologists have neglected the topic of work (Firth 1929; Spittler 2008). It is not necessary to subscribe to strong theories of economic determination, such as Marxist historical materialism, to recognize the importance of work in shaping human evolution. Yet within the subdiscipline of economic anthropology, topics such as markets, trade, gifts, and consumption have received more attention over the years.[1] Spittler suggests various possible reasons for the neglect. Work often involves long periods of tedious, repetitive, and strenuous effort. Ethnographers are usually short of time and likely to prefer participation in other activities where the dividends appear greater, such as political assemblies or rituals performed on special occasions. The significance of waged employment in shaping the personal and collective identities of so many human beings in recent generations has perhaps encouraged anthropologists to focus their studies of precapitalist societies on what makes them *different*, and thereby to overlook work altogether. Spittler suggests that the attraction of more exotic themes has impoverished studies of work in modern conditions as well. The discipline would be better equipped to investigate industrial and postindustrial forms of work if early ethnographers had paid more attention to its preindustrial forms (Spittler 2008, 2017).

If the picture is not entirely dire, this has a lot to do with contributions from the German-speaking world dating back to the early nineteenth century. Many anthropologists have drawn inspiration from Karl Marx, who in early philosophical writings envisaged a radical dissolution of the very concept of work (in his native language *Arbeit*). Outside capitalism there could be no boundary between work and other activities: "[Marx] imagined labor as it would be, had it not been formulated by capitalism, and saw that it would then be merely an aspect of the total business of living, unseparated from such activities as recreation, consumption, family life: that it would be just part of existence" (Bloch 1983: 91). Bloch confirms this insight with reference to the people with whom he did field research in Madagascar. Rural Malagasy had no word that could be translated as "work" or "labor," as their daily activities did not differentiate "production activities" from other activities they undertook. Everything was intertwined and a part of living, thus supporting the Marxist proposition "that the conceptualization of productive activity is totally integrated with other social relations in pre-capitalist societies, and that the sharp boundary that we draw between labor and other activities is absent" (ibid.: 91).

This interpretation (denying the very possibility of a "work-life balance") is perhaps over-drawn. The young Marx was strongly influenced by the utopian ideas of Charles Fourier. However, his later contributions to political economy suggest that some aspects of the discipline imposed by capitalism would have to be retained in a future communist order. Even if work is conceptualized as a "free" activity submerged in the flows of everyday life, most preindustrial societies have a substantial vocabulary for the more or less specialized activities essential to their subsistence. The tasks fluctuate with the seasons, and impose burdens of coordination as well as physical effort. And even where we do not find much by way of a special vocabulary, the romantic tones of European utopian socialism find scant confirmation in the ethnographic record.

Etic definitions of work must also include activities such as the work of ritual specialists when these are considered to be just as necessary (often even more vital) for successful economic outcomes as manual exertion and dexterity. Ethnographers can probe attitudes towards different kinds of work, using an analytic spectrum ranging from alienation and drudgery to identity and satisfaction. Early ethnographic approaches to work were influenced by philosophical assumptions as well as evolutionist speculation. The economic stages posited by economic historian Karl Bücher found little corroboration in ethnographic work. His concept of the "closed household economy" oriented towards self-sufficiency echoed Aristotle's concern with the *oikos* in ancient Greece (from which our word for economy derives). It turned out that the autarkic farm or estate was always imperfect; elements of trade and market were seldom if ever completely absent. Nonetheless, work in such societies was overwhelmingly regulated by domestic groups, with age and sex the main axes of differentiation. This applied as much to the yam gardeners of the Trobriand Islands studied by Bronislaw Malinowski (1935) as it did to the peasant households of late imperial Russia, whose economic behavior was investigated by Alexander Chayanov (1986). Both Malinowski and Chayanov studied with Bücher in Leipzig before the First World War.

From the beginning, ethnographers drew attention to the ways in which work was embedded in social organization. Karl Bücher was obsessed with understanding how people could be motivated to participate in the grind of physical work (he was brought up on a farm in Hessen). One vital consideration was the sociality of working together, exemplified by singing during the activity as well as sharing refreshments and celebrating when the task was completed. According to Bücher's contemporary, American sociologist Thorstein Veblen, an innate sense of "workmanship" motivated humans toward superior technical solutions (Veblen 1899). Like the stages put forward by Bücher, Veblen's evolutionism was soon dismissed. But his demonstrations of how the making and consuming of objects invariably reflect status preoccupations and the aesthetics of a society have stood the test of time.

Work was simultaneously a matter of practical effort and an activity regulated by beliefs about the supernatural and by rituals that supplemented (but did not replace) technical knowledge. This duality was a recurring theme in the first triumphant crop of ethnographic studies of work, in which Malinowski and younger members of his seminar were the pioneers (Malinowski 1935; Firth 1939; Richards 1939). The Trobriand Islanders, studied by Malinowski himself, cared about the appearance of their gardens and sought to raise their personal standing through generous, publicly displayed gifts of yams to their in-laws. The Bemba, investigated by Audrey Richards, did not work as hard, in spite of the threat of hunger; they were matrilocal as well as matrilineal, and their institutions did not enable them to produce a surplus that could be protected from appropriation by other households. Forty years after these pioneering studies of work in non-market settings, Raymond Firth, Malinowski's successor at the London School of Economics, returned to his Polynesian materials to demonstrate the limitations of the "work theory of value." He did not doubt, however, that Marxist approaches to alienation and exploitation could be fruitfully extended to non-capitalist societies. A diagnosis of exploitation could be refuted if it could be shown that "positive surplus labor" was performed on the basis of free choices. While modern plantations certainly had the potential for exploitation, work for chiefs in the traditional non-monetary economy of the island of Tikopia was a different matter altogether (Firth 1979: 198–99; see Rachel Smith, Chapter 1, this volume).

After the Second World War, as the principle of market exchange expanded rapidly all over the world, cash cropping and migrant labor disrupted earlier forms of subsistence-oriented work. Documenting this was a major preoccupation of the field that became known as "peasant studies," to which anthropologists made important contributions. They also studied the impact of capitalist wage-labor in mines and in factories, illuminating culturally specific forms of resistance to new forms of exploitation and managerial power (Nash 1979; Ong 1987). The ethical dimension was captured most effectively through adaptations of the concept of "moral economy" (Scott 1976). Structuralist varieties of Marxism were popular in these decades, and both Marxists and non-Marxists drew attention to the importance of ideological factors in reproducing hierarchy. Even those who used the concept of a mode of production often neglected the actual processes of work in order to focus on its social organization (e.g., Meillassoux 1981, Donham 1985), or on marketing and price formation (e.g., Cook 1982).

In the North Atlantic world and its offshoots, where Keynesian economic policies ensured stability and new forms of welfare state embeddedness, anthropological contributions remained rare in the postwar decades. Sociologists documented divisions within the working classes (Goldthorpe et al. 1969). Some maintained that, due to a combination of sociological and technological factors, it was time to bid farewell to this class altogether (Gorz 1982).

Meanwhile, most of the Eurasian landmass was dominated by Marxist-Leninist-Maoist socialism. In collectivized systems of agriculture, thanks to the so-called private plot, the household continued to function as simultaneously a unit of production as well as consumption. The modernist agenda of Fordist capitalism was emulated under socialism: Lenin was an admirer of Taylorist technological efficiency. Over a century has passed since he proclaimed the necessity of comprehensive electrification to secure the economic development and "enlightenment" of the infant Soviet Union. But that polity collapsed in the early 1990s. From the evidence available, the socialist alternative to capitalist modernity did not make for more attractive workplaces. Retrospectively, there was nostalgia for the cozy social relations of the brigade, in which the rhythms of work were more humane than under the successor enterprises (Dunn 2004; Müller 2007). But piece-rate work in a Hungarian tractor factory in the 1960s was dehumanizing (Haraszti 1977). Monica Heintz, in a study carried out after the collapse of socialism, found that service sector employees were critical of the poor work ethics, both of socialism and of their nation (Heintz 2004; see also Ivan Rajković, Chapter 7, this volume).

The Era of Neoliberalism

The concept of neoliberalism is as contested as any of the terms introduced above. Many anthropologists are inherently suspicious of periodization. Like historians, they tend to play down the sharpness of the temporal divide between preindustrial and industrial by detecting continuities, for example in terms of values or ethics. The establishment of factories in India did not mean that workers adopted the work ethic of a textbook Fordist assembly-line worker, in which the world of paid work was radically separated from the rest of life (see Mollona, De Neve and Parry 2009). The same can be said of state farm employees and collective farm members under socialism. Even in Western Europe, where change began earlier and the rupture appears sharper, proto-industrial working from home, skilled and unskilled, had lasting effects on later industrial divisions of labor (Kalb 1997; Narotzky and Smith 2006). Continuities also manifest themselves in phases of deindustrialization, when the household re-assumes prominence as the prime frame for work (Mollona 2009).

Yet for all the continuities in the social organization of work, spreading out around the globe from the North Atlantic region, there is no mistaking the impact of intensified pro-market ideology from the 1970s onwards. Since the collapse of the Soviet bloc, neoliberal constellations have dominated globally and precarity has become a pervasive theme in anthropological research (Procoli 2004). The working classes have expanded numerically, while job security and protective benefits have declined, and activity of an informal or underground (not to say criminal) character has increased. The role of finance has continued to expand, despite the crisis that shook the global economy in 2007–8. The age of neoliberalism is also the age of acute environmental concerns and popular movements to address the causes of climate change, which lie in unsustainable economic growth models. It is an age of looting collective property to facilitate the gains of a few. At the time of writing in 2020, the Covid-19 pandemic is accentuating these polarizing trends, strengthening the power of tech giants and plunging almost all states further into debt.

Many anthropologists have struggled with the term "neoliberalism" (Hilgers 2013; Venkatesan et al. 2015). Some, however, have joined other social scientists and historians to investigate this new phase of capitalism from the perspective of a distinctively anthropological political economy. Marxist approaches have been reinvigorated to focus more concretely on the extraction of surplus value in global chains of exploitation. Building on earlier contributions from sociology (Burawoy 1979), anthropologists have investigated how owners and managers secure consent at the workplace and inhibit effective collective action by the exploited class (Kasmir and Carbonella 2014; Kalb and Mollona 2018). The organization of protest and resistance is vitiated by hegemonic ideas and dynamic patterns of class segmentation that require multiscalar relational analysis (Kalb 2020). For example, the affluent worker phenomenon, first diagnosed in the West, takes on new forms in the Global South. While ever more workers experience precarity, some enjoy secure contracts and privileges. Some blue-collar workers enjoy not only higher wages but a range of benefits that differentiate them from co-workers and push them into the middle classes (Hann and Parry 2018; Parry 2020).

Another conspicuous feature of the neoliberal era is the expansion of the service sector. Anthropologists have tended to lag behind their sociologist colleagues in studying white-collar professionals. The contributions to this volume by Akanksha Awal (Chapter 4) and Anna-Riikka Kauppinen (Chapter 5) indicate the pleasure and fulfillment that well-educated young persons find in new forms of work that are rich in sociality. Such rewards are not so prominent in the financial center investigated by Magdalena Dąbkowska (Chapter 11); and they may be missing altogether in work that is organized through digital platforms. The break-up of firms due to the encroachments of the gig economy highlights the dilemmas facing capital. How far can digital technologies permit work tasks to be redistributed around the shrinking planet such that those who want more work can find it without needing to cross borders? We know from economic and social science theory (and also from common sense in everyday life) that the principles of market and contract are never sufficient in practice to secure the maximization of private profit, let alone the public good. These problems are addressed in several chapters of this volume, especially that of Ilana Gershon and Melissa Cefkin (Chapter 9).

I have suggested already that some trends in the neoliberal era appear to be enabling households to return to preindustrial patterns of the house economy. For some workers in "home office", such as the ghostwriters discussed by Deborah Jones (Chapter 12), productive activities take place primarily in front of the laptop. But for others, such as the Chinese Uber-type drivers investigated by Gonçalo Santos and his co-authors Yichen Rao, Jack L. Xing, and Jun Zhang (Chapter 6), the appearance of control over one's labor is part of a wider neoliberal fantasy—that digital technologies can assure a market-based optimization that is transparent and fair to all participants.

Work and Freedom

The notion of fairness brings us back to ethical dimensions. These have always been central for the philosophers. In the social science literature, including anthropology, ethical justifications have usually been treated as an aspect of social organization. Adapting Karl Polanyi's (1944) metaphor, we might say that this dimension was "embedded." Often, especially in the revival of Marxist approaches, it is represented in terms of ideology, hegemony, or mystification (Narotzky and Smith 2006).

Marxist theory itself has ancient roots. Raymond Firth (1979) notes the similarities between Marxist value theory and medieval notions of just price. Marx admired Adam Smith's conceptualization of abstract labor, and adapted it in his later work. But in his philosophical manuscripts of the early 1840s (and later in the *Grundrisse*, 1857–58), he feared that the division of work, applauded by Smith, posed a threat to the freedom of the human being in terms of self-realization. For his notions of freedom and work, Marx looked to German philosophy and French engineers respectively (here I am following the exposition of Spittler 2008). In merging them, he was inspired particularly by Fourier. The focus shifted in Marx's later work: away from romantic notions that portrayed work as the satisfying activity of an artist, and toward an emphasis on the exploitation of work-power (*Arbeitskraft*) in processes of factory production. Truly free work was the only possible basis for the communist society of the future. In later writings, Marx stressed the social character of this self-realization, without offering much guidance as to how it could be operationalized. The "childishly naive" ideas of Fourier would not suffice (Spittler 2008: 58).

The incoherent formulations of the later Marx on value (critiqued by Firth) and the codification of an overly determinist historical materialism by Friedrich Engels do not invalidate the lasting significance of Marx's earlier contributions. In the 1920s, just as Malinowski was setting new standards for ethnographic research, a Hegelian version of Marxism that celebrated man's self-realization through work was advanced by Georg Lukács ([1923] 1971). This strand was later taken up by Karl Polanyi, a friend of the philosopher from their student days in Budapest. Even before the publication of Marx's philosophical manuscripts in 1932, Polanyi was developing similar themes in Vienna. Polanyi rejected the determinism of Marxism-Leninism. In an essay written in 1927, he laid out his own Hegelian-Marxist vision of freedom, rooted in anthropocentric notions of emancipation through work, by insisting on the primacy of the social and *responsibility* (Polanyi 2018). Polanyi's later theorizing of the embeddedness of economic phenomena in society gave rise to a "substantivist" school in economic anthropology in the second half of the twentieth century, in opposition to the "formalists" who maintained that the paradigms of mainstream (neoclassical) economics had universal validity (see Hann and Hart 2011).

From the pure formalist point of view, every decision (whether or not to work legally, whether or not to send one's children to work, etc.) is subject to calculations of utility maximization. Alongside the English utilitarians, such approaches had their strongest roots in the Austrian School of economics, generally acknowledged as the most influential forerunners of neoliberalism. Their most distinguished exponent is Friedrich August Hayek (1960), an interlocutor of both Polanyi and Karl Popper in the interwar decades. Hayek believed that liberty was the basis of civilizational progress and that this liberty could only be assured by private property and market competition. In this volume, his libertarian values turn up most conspicuously among the venture capitalists studied by Johannes Lenhard (Chapter 10).

In Hayek's lifetime (he died in 1992), reviving laissez-faire capitalism meant strengthening capitalist corporations against states. The firm was taken for granted. Its central role in capitalist economic organization had been reappraised by scholars who emphasized how, beyond the compelling logic of market competition, the trust established within the firm reduced "transaction costs" and thus facilitated coordination (Coase 1937). This "institutionalist" theory was still predicated on notions of efficiency and profit-maximization. It was attractive to some economic anthropologists, who adopted the institutionalist language to explain patterns of work and trade in preindustrial conditions, and even their evolutionary emergence (Acheson 1994). In recent decades, however, digital technologies have undermined the theories of Coase by calling the boundaries of firms into question. In particular, platforms have vastly extended the scope for task-individualization, as Gershon and Cefkin show in their chapter. The anthropologist asks: if trust was a crucial lubricant of efficient performance in Fordist days, for management and blue-collar workers alike, what happens to human social life in a world of entrepreneurial selves? What does "work ethic" come to mean for those whose personhood is defined in this way? Can we imagine a society in which working becomes a facet of human life that is *not* valued as the prime basis for entitlements, but instead gives way to vistas of free time as imagined by utopian socialists from Fourier to Gorz?

In the modern social sciences, it is above all the tradition of Max Weber that approaches social action in terms of meanings. His study of the links between the economic ethic of Protestantism and the "spirit of capitalism" is particularly pertinent (Weber [1904–5/1920] 2011). It forms the baseline for Sylvia Terpe's investigation (Chapter 8) of the self-employed in a postsocialist German city, in which she demonstrates that a very positive identification with work can conflict with a profit-maximizing approach to the business. Neoliberal subjectivities that have emerged more gradually elsewhere appear in sharper relief among populations in which entrepreneurialism was previously suppressed by socialist planning; so too does social critique of the new "entrepreneurial self" (see also Makovicky 2014).

Most scholarly invocation of the ethical self in recent anthropological writings has little or no connection with work, or with other activities that would conventionally be classified as economic. The bias in anthropology's recent "ethical turn" is toward the religious component of the relationship that intrigued Weber, and (in our more secular age) toward multiple cultural elements of personhood. One major source of inspiration is Michel Foucault's focus on the techniques of an individualized self (Foucault 1997; Laidlaw 2014). It is assumed that, however great the cultural variation, the individual always has scope to craft personhood and thus express freedom.

Critics question such notions of individualized personhood and stress the need to re-embed individuals in social organization. In the context of neoliberalism, they ask whether ubiquitous discourses of aspiration and entrepreneurship do in fact lead persons to see themselves as bundles of assets and to internalize new dispositions of agency (Hilgers 2013; Parry 2018).

The Foucauldian approach to these questions runs against the grain of the social sciences. Attention is focused not on structural constraints, not on unequal power relations and the ideologies that support them, but on free individuals. For most social scientists, this is an illusion, an ideological construct. A "free" wage-laborer differs from an indentured worker, a serf, or a slave, but he or she is not truly free; not when entering ostensibly free labor contracts, nor when engaging in other work tasks, nor in any other existential moment. Their employers are not free either, though the power they dispose of is likely to be vastly greater. Karl Polanyi builds on the work of Marx, Weber and Durkheim by applying a communitarian notion of responsibility across the board: not just to one's family or some narrower community but to Society with a capital letter, perhaps even to humanity. This is not to cast Foucault as an apologist for economic neoliberalism (see Rajković's chapter in this volume). But just as Polanyi's notion of freedom was a reaction to the grave threats of "disembedded" market economy and fascism in the interwar decades, Foucault's reception in the neoliberal era is best assessed in the context of the "embedded liberalism" (Ruggie 1982) on which the capitalist world embarked after the Second World War.

The point is elaborated by Rajković with respect to socialist Yugoslavia, where large bureaucratic enterprises nourished corruption and resentments. More generally, the Keynesian compromises that stabilized the world economy between the 1940s and the 1970s left many citizens disappointed, even frustrated. Their individual freedoms were curtailed by high taxation, recurrent strike action, affirmative action programs, and the perception of excessive bureaucratization. Neoliberal ideology fell on fertile terrain. Precisely because its individualism was so brazen, it needed ethical support. With a lag of some decades, the Foucauldian perspective on self-realization and "freedom from" discipline and constraint met this need. Anthropology was not immune, and these currents eventually resonated productively in economic anthropology (Browne and Milgram 2009).

At this point it would seem that we have two schools unable to communicate with each other. In the one camp are those anthropologists who see themselves as social scientists and engage primarily with sociologists—for example, in pursuing Marxist approaches to work and labor relations. In the other camp are those who find the social science approaches ethically dehumanizing and so opt instead for more cultural approaches and engagement with moral philosophers. But these apparently irreconcilable currents can be brought together. In this book we attempt such a cross-fertilization. We insist on the social (relational, political) determinants of the distribution and performance of work tasks, but we are no less interested in the subjective experience of a work ethic, and how work contributes to the ethical self in a larger sense. Foucauldian influence is strong in the chapters of Olivia Angé, Akanksha Awal, and Anna-Riikka Kauppinnen (Chapters 3, 4, and 5 respectively). Polanyian insights are pursued most explicitly by Katherine Miller (Chapter 2) and Sylvia Terpe (Chapter 8). The contributions of Gonçalo Santos et al. (Chapter 6) and Ivan Rajković (Chapter 7) suggest how Polanyian and Foucauldian approaches can fruitfully be combined to grasp the life courses of individuals and the historical dialectic of a population, respectively.

A Hungarian Case

To conclude this brief discussion of self-realization through work in the age of neoliberalism, let me shift the register to the concrete realities of ethnography. Most of my field research in recent years has taken place in provincial Hungary, which happens to be the homeland of both Karl Polanyi and Georg Lukacs. One of the most powerful planks in the ideology of the Fidesz Party, in power since 2010, has been to create a "work-based society" (Hann 2018; Szombati forthcoming). After twenty years of postsocialist turmoil, Fidesz promised stability on a firm ethical foundation, consisting of the spiritual values of Christian civilization in tandem with the values of work. The strength of the latter in Hungary's preindustrial rural society was richly documented by ethnographers in the twentieth century. The emphasis on work, especially manual work, persisted throughout the decades of rapid industrialization under socialism. Prime Minister Viktor Orbán has drawn upon these traditions. Having introduced huge cuts in social benefits (especially for the unemployed), his government boosted the rate of employment by means of a massive workfare scheme. Western social scientists tend to condemn such schemes as punitive neoliberalism, yet workfare has been received positively by large sections of the Hungarian population. It was only to be expected that those who held more or less secure jobs favored restricting state support to those who had made themselves morally eligible by virtue of their work. It was more surprising that many of those now forced to get up early to perform tedious manual tasks to provide for their households (Roma prominent among them) also welcomed the new policy. This work puts more money in their pockets than the state benefits they had received previously. Moreover, public work is seldom solitary, and so new forms of camaraderie develop. Few Hungarians would endorse universal income schemes of the kind increasingly touted elsewhere in recent years. They are rejected for the same ethical reasons that lead them to approve of workfare.

Karl Polanyi would be appalled by the xenophobic intolerance of Viktor Orbán. But he would understand and sympathize with the appeal to work as the supreme ethical basis of value and freedom in society (not to be confused with naive utopian celebration of communal or collective work). Polanyi teaches that the populist politics of our age have their roots in the application of market models to both the economic organization of society (nowadays world society) and the realization of the self. The dissident East European intellectuals who rejected socialism before 1990 thought they could replace it with a liberal utopia consisting of free individuals and their associations in an open society. They reckoned without neoliberal political economy. The outcomes have been devastating, economically and ethically. In the third decade of postsocialism, Viktor Orbán has led a paradoxical "countermovement" to market domination that is profoundly illiberal but has strong ethical roots in Hungarian society.[2]

The Chapters

Most of the following chapters are based on fieldwork; those of Rachel Smith and Ivan Rajković also draw on historical data. In Chapter 1, Smith starts out from the Maussian notion of "prestation," famous in anthropology due to its prominence in *The Gift* (Mauss [1923–24] 2016), but replete with ambivalences. To begin with, the concept disguised coercive French colonial practices in an era when new forms of labor commodification mingled with unfree forms of plantation work. In independent Vanuatu, collective work for the benefit of the community contrasts with the contractual basis on which many individuals spend much of the year working in New Zealand agribusiness. These migrants show a reluctance to engage in collective tasks when back in their villages, where the rhythms of work and perceptions of time have remained quite different. Smith shows that, even in the colonial era, it was possible to avoid this work by means of a monetary payment. The equivalent fee today is not high, but the pressure to pay it is resented by returnees. They are prepared to give generously only in contexts where the act of giving, in this case through work, retains its voluntary character.

In Chapter 2, Katherine Miller explores work in the Hunza Valley (northern Pakistan). Long after the demise of a feudal regime that is remembered as harsh and exploitative, collective work in recent decades has been systematically fostered by development initiatives that link volunteering to work with Islamic ideals of service and love, and ultimately to the cosmos. Outside such communal activities, various forms of mutual aid are practiced with kin, neighbors and others. The constellations reflect the social structure of the community and they evoke a range of emotions. Miller found physical pleasure and satisfaction to be pervasive in carrying out agricultural tasks yet to be transformed by mechanization. Emotional and bodily experiences through the performance of work constitute a form of ethical reflexivity, which leads Miller to reject the individualist and intellectual bias in Foucault's "techniques of the self" in favor of a Polanyian emphasis on the social.

Other kinds of work are investigated against a different religious background by Olivia Angé in Chapter 3. Indigenous Kolla in the Argentinian Andes combine devotion to the Christian God and his pantheon with more specifically Latin American ideas about the flow of vital force and spirit. In annual fairs to celebrate Saint Anne, admired for her industry, believers craft a wide range of familiar objects in miniature in order to demonstrate both their aesthetics and their dexterity. They thereby impress other participants and please the saint they strive to emulate. Much has changed in recent decades: the social structure of the town has been transformed, miniatures are no longer bartered, some are produced quite crudely, and some stallholders at the fair sell industrial goods. Yet according to Angé, the cosmology has remained largely intact. The intensive work necessary to produce pleasing miniatures reflects both utilitarian considerations (such as minimizing effort, and going home with a profit) and ethicized notions of what it takes to lead a successful human life. Angé concludes that those who craft and transact these Andean objects challenge the Aristotelian distinction between doing and making. Their work is a technique that is transformative of the self, in the Foucauldian sense.

Finding pleasure through work is also important for the young middle-class Indian women discussed by Akanksha Awal in Chapter 4. Although parents would prefer their daughters to obtain government jobs that pay quite well and offer long-term security, these jobs have become scarce. In any case, the women themselves disdain the emotional work that is required by the entrenched hierarchies of government schools. Irrespective of social background (caste or class), they prefer the "affective practices" of call-center work, where they can experience conviviality with their co-workers, both men and women. Working hours are flexible and the women enjoy considerable autonomy, including the freedom to flirt with clients and managers alike. In these high-turnover jobs, the boundary between work and leisure is fuzzy. Freedom has its limits, notably with regard to sexualization and harassment. It is significant that these women do not expect to continue working to earn money after they marry.

Anna-Riikka Kauppinen (Chapter 5) investigates professional men in a similar "young adult" phase of the life course in Ghana's capital, Accra. Unlike the call-center workers studied by Awal, these men take their work with the utmost seriousness, and aspire to make it a career. They owe their qualifications to long-term family investment and so experience moral pressure to contribute to supporting their lower-middle-class households. They are also expected to conform to public expectations that educated white-collar workers should be the "drivers" of national development. This imaginary dates back to an ideology implanted in the era of colonial struggle, though Nkrumah's socialist rejection of private accumulation ran counter to the norms of local societies. Despite these pervasive collectivist discourses (and the prominence of social obligations in much Africanist ethnography), Kauppinen finds that the young professionals with whom she worked hold very different values. The jobs they do are badly paid, if compared to blue-collar employees. What money they earn is more likely to be spent selfishly (e.g., on the purchase of a car) than in supporting their families. Nonetheless, with the help of notions of self-realization (Foucault) and authorship (Jane Guyer), Kauppinen shows that their dedication to excellent work is sincere and deserving of respect. Personhood has changed, as it has in India, permitting more room for friendship and contracting the traditional bonds of kinship. According to Kauppinen, the concern with professional excellence is not so much a reflection of generic neoliberalism, but rather a key component of contemporary Ghanaian "middle classes in the making."

Gonçalo Santos and his co-authors (Chapter 6) explore how pressures to increase working hours affect different segments of the workforce in contemporary urban China. Working twelve-hour days, six days a week, is a prerequisite for success and "ownership" among IT developers, the majority of whom consider the sacrifice to be justified: this hard work is good for their companies, good for their country, and good for themselves. Taxi drivers, by contrast, have low status and it has become increasingly difficult to make a decent living due to competition from Didi (the Chinese version of Uber). Didi drivers enjoy more autonomy but they end up working extremely long hours for dwindling rewards. There is variation among the drivers, as there is in the IT sector. For some, "financial freedom" is the motivation for signing up at Didi. This would appear to suggest that they value personal freedom more highly than the social model of freedom outlined by Karl Polanyi. But closer inspection leads the authors to identify a dialectic: greater financial freedom is not an end in itself, but rather a means to achieve the more complete forms of social freedom that workers in both occupational communities crave.

The contrasts between traditional taxi firms and e-hailing drivers are picked up by Ivan Rajković in his opening discussion in Chapter 7. The body of the chapter illuminates the history of socialist Yugoslavia by training a sharp light on the Zastava car plant in Kragujevac, Serbia. Karl Polanyi proposed the concept of "countermovement" to capture how workers resisted the domination of the market by carving out new forms of self-protection (and thereby *social* forms of freedom). However, the system of self-management institutionalized in federal Yugoslavia gave rise to a different dialectic. Blue-collar workers (for the most part migrants whose families had previously known only agricultural work) were initially celebrated as the heroic builders of a socialist civilization. Before long, however, the proliferation of managers and a lack of market discipline led to problems. Work remained the moral basis of value, but under self-management it became impossible to discern who was really working and who was loafing. In this context, the countermovement ended up taking the form of more liberal, individualist notions of personhood. In the absence of an effective collective work ethic, collective demands for wage increases were perceived as excessive. Eventually, following the break-up of the country, the combined economic and ethical difficulties became insuperable; neoliberal privatization and takeover by foreign capital were by and large welcomed by the workforce.

In Chapter 8, sociologist Sylvia Terpe takes her inspiration from Max Weber's celebrated account of how the work ethic associated with Protestantism gave rise to an unprecedented *Wirtschaftsethik* (economic ethic). In this transformation, steady-state householding gives way to "acquisition" and the maximization of profits. Terpe amends Weber's account by noting that the dynamic of mature capitalism is sustained by the creation of new needs (or wants), rather than by slavish adherence to a work ethic. In her empirical materials, stemming from a study of the owners of small businesses in the postsocialist city of Halle, she finds patterns not anticipated by either Martin Luther or Weber. One businessman continues to work hard and identify strongly with his craft, while rejecting the logic of mass production. He has trimmed his workforce such that his economic ethic is nowadays closer to householding than profit maximization. In the second case discussed by Terpe, work does not involve handicraft skills but consists in an exciting buzz as money is made through launching new companies. For this entrepreneur, work merges with his leisure time, which (when he is not enjoying foreign holidays) he spends with customers and potential business partners. Terpe shows that both individuals have a social ethic inasmuch as they feel responsibility for their family and workforce. The one who is driven by profits practices a form of *soziales Engagement* by supporting a private school, the aim of which is to produce entrepreneurs like himself. Both are unsympathetic to state support for those who do not work hard enough to *deserve* public support. According to Terpe, they thus fall well short of Karl Polanyi's notion of "true freedom."

Ilana Gershon and Melissa Cefkin (Chapter 9) investigate the impact of the platform economy on the distribution of work and the nature of working relations. At first sight, if the worker is free to select the task, then hierarchies melt away and a neoliberal utopia is brought within reach. The reality is quite different, not least due to the role played by the same digital technologies in evaluation and the ensuing "reputational effects." The tacit knowledge of an experienced worker cannot be adequately captured in open calls. The authors highlight a deeper contradiction of neoliberalism: the intensification of a market model *inside* firms as well as between them undermines the evolved coordination of cumulative institutions that economists of neoliberal disposition had previously theorized with the concept of transaction costs.

Johannes Lenhard (Chapter 10) has worked in Europe and North America with venture capitalists, most of whom focus their work on start-ups seeking to implement platform technologies of the kind discussed by Gershon and Cefkin. Without ever losing sight of the financial bottom line, namely the "fiduciary duty" to maximize profits for investors, the men and women who decide in which companies to place the funds they control do so primarily on the basis of gut feelings and ideological affinities. The investors perform the mission statements of their firms, which articulate what Lenhard identifies as a "soaring" libertarianism. This worldview is congenial to entrepreneurs whose aim is to reshape entire economic landscapes, and for whom any form of state regulation is anathema. Lenhard pinpoints the paradox whereby embracing notions of "creative destruction" (in the spirit of Schumpeter) camouflages the imperative to achieve quasi-monopolistic power in order to meet the investors' bottom line.

In Chapter 11, Magdalena Dąbkowska investigates cosmopolitan young professionals who carry out less glamourous forms of financial work for an international bank that established a new center in Berlin in the wake of the international crisis of 2007–8. Jobs of relatively low complexity (compared to work at the major hubs) depend on efficient teamwork, and there is little scope for creativity. Yet Dąbkowska finds that the entrepreneurial self is resistant to the deskilling of process-driven work. The bank runs formal schemes to promote original thinking, but those who stray too far outside mainstream expectations are likely to experience disappointment and to diagnose hypocrisy among their managers. Some individuals strive to attain greater freedom, but it is hard (perhaps impossible) to reconcile professional ambition with collegiality and trust.

That anthropologists should develop an interest in the work of ghost-writers would probably have surprised the pioneers of the study of work in non-monetized societies a century ago. However, writing more or less creatively for a client can be seen as a continuation of a tradition that dates back millennia, to when scribes commoditized their expertise in societies in which literacy was still highly restricted. In Chapter 12, Deborah Jones reviews the many kinds of projects undertaken by contemporary US ghostwriters. She focuses on two individuals, one of whom has successfully established her own brand and bylines, while the other struggles in anonymous precarity. Even when their authorship is entirely invisible, this work is satisfying and meaningful; it might even generate forms of freedom. Apart from exchanges with clients, limited forms of sociality with other writers are made possible by the internet. But, for the most part, ghostwriting exemplifies the digitally-enabled "return to the household" that will also impact dramatically on academic work in the twenty-first century.

Acknowledgments

This Introduction has benefited from the comments of several contributors to this volume and two anonymous reviewers.

Chris Hann is a director at the Max Planck Institute for Social Anthropology, Halle/Saale, and also of the Max Planck–Cambridge Centre for Ethics, Economy and Social Change. In Cambridge he is a Fellow of Corpus Christi College. His publications include *Economic Anthropology: History, Theory, Ethnography* (with Keith Hart, Polity Press, 2011); *Repatriating Polanyi: Market Society in the Visegrád States* (Central European University Press, 2019); and *The Great Dispossession: Uyghurs between Civilizations* (with Ildikó Bellér-Hann, LIT Verlag, 2020).

Notes

1. The situation improved towards the end of the twentieth century. A Society for the Study of Work has existed within the American Anthropological Association since 1980. It publishes the *Anthropology of Work Review*. From 1984, June Nash edited a lively series titled *Anthropology of Work* for the State University of New York Press, but this was discontinued in the new century.
2. This is not the place to delve deeper into the tensions and paradoxes of Orbán's Hungary. The labor market has improved in recent years thanks to investments by transnational capital, but also to the rise of a national bourgeoisie supported by transfers from the EU and endemic cronyism. Wage levels have remained low. Trade unions (which struggle to make an impact) allege new forms of exploitation and even a modern form of slavery. See Hann 2018, 2019; Scheiring 2020; Hann and Scheiring forthcoming.

References

Acheson, James M., ed. 1994. *Anthropology and Institutional Economics*. Lanham, MD: University Press of America.

Bloch, Maurice. 1983. *Marxism and Anthropology*. London: Oxford University Press.

Browne, Katherine E., and B. Lynne Milgram, eds. 2009. *Economics and Morality: Anthropological Approaches*. Lanham, MD: Rowman & Littlefield.

Burawoy, Michael. 1979. *Manufacturing Consent*. Chicago: University of Chicago Press.

Chayanov, Alexander. 1986. *The Theory of Peasant Economy*. Manchester: Manchester University Press.

Coase, Ronald. 1937. "The Nature of the Firm." *Economica* 4(16): 386–405.

Cook, Scott. 1982. *Zapotec Stoneworkers: The Dynamics of Rural Simple Commodity Production in Modern Mexican Capitalism*. Lanham, MD: University Press of America.

Donham, Donald L. 1985. *Work and Power in Maale, Ethiopia*. Ann Arbor: UMI Research Press.

Dunn, Elizabeth. 2004. *Privatizing Poland: Baby Food, Big Business and the Remaking of Labor*. Ithaca, NY: Cornell University Press.

Firth, Raymond. 1929. *Primitive Economics of the New Zealand Maori*. London: George Routledge.

———. 1939. *Primitive Polynesian Economy*. London: Routledge.

———. 1979. "Work and Value: Reflections on Ideas of Karl Marx." In *Social Anthropology of Work*, ed. Sandra Wallman, 177–206. London: Academic Press.

Foucault, Michel. 1997. "The Ethics of the Concern of the Self as a Practice of Freedom." In *Essential Works of Michel Foucault, Vol. 1: Ethics: Subjectivity and Truth*, ed. Paul Rabinow, 281–301. London: Allen Lane.

Goldthorpe, John, et al. 1969. *The Affluent Worker in the Class Structure*. Cambridge: Cambridge University Press.

Gorz, André. 1982. *Farewell to the Working Class: An Essay on Post-Industrial Socialism*. London: Pluto.

Gudeman, Stephen. 2016. *Anthropology and Economy*. Cambridge: Cambridge University Press.

Hann, Chris. 2018. "Moral(ity and) Economy: Work, Workfare and Fairness in Provincial Hungary." *European Journal of Sociology* 59(2): 225–54.

———. 2019. *Repatriating Polanyi: Market Society in the Visegrád States*. Budapest: Central European University Press.

Hann, Chris, and Keith Hart. 2011. *Economic Anthropology: History, Theory, Ethnography*. Cambridge: Polity.

Hann, Chris, and Jonathan Parry, eds. 2018. *Industrial Labor on the Margins of Capitalism: Precarity, Class and the Neoliberal Subject*. New York: Berghahn Books.

Hann, Chris, and Gábor Scheiring, eds. Forthcoming, 2021. Special Issue of *Europe-Asia Studies*, "Neoliberal Capitalism and Visegrád Countermovements".

Haraszti, Miklós. 1977. *A Worker in a Workers' State*. Harmondsworth: Penguin.

Hayek, Friedrich August. 1960. *The Constitution of Liberty*. Chicago: The University of Chicago Press.

Heintz, Monica. 2004. *"Be European, Recycle Yourself!": The Changing Work Ethic in Romania*. Münster: LIT.

Herod, Andrew. 2018. *Labor*. Cambridge: Polity.

Hilgers, Mathieu. 2013. "Embodying Neoliberalism: Thoughts and Responses to Critics." *Social Anthropology* 21(1): 75–89.

Ignatieff, Michael and Stefan Roch, eds. 2018 *Rethinking Open Society: New Adversaries and New Opportunities*. Budapest: Central European University Press.

Kalb, Don. 1997. *Power and Everyday Politics in Industrial Communities, The Netherlands, 1850–1950*. Durham, NC: Duke University Press.

———. 2020. "Introduction. Transitions to What? On the Social Relations of Financialization in Anthropology and History." In *Financialization: Relational Approaches*, ed. Chris Hann and Don Kalb, 1–41. New York: Berghahn Books.

Kalb, Don, and Massimiliano Mollona, eds. 2018. *Worldwide Mobilizations: Class Struggles and Urban Commoning*. New York: Berghahn Books.

Kasmir, Sharryn, and August Carbonella, eds. 2014. *Blood and Fire: Toward a Global Anthropology of Labor*. New York: Berghahn Books.

Laidlaw, James. 2014. *The Subject of Virtue*. Cambridge: Cambridge University Press.

Lukács, Georg. (1923) 1971. *History and Class Consciousness: Studies in Marxist Dialectics*. London: Merlin Press.

Makovicky, Nicolette, ed. 2014. *Neoliberalism, Personhood, and Postsocialism: Enterprising Selves in Changing Economies*. Farnham: Ashgate.

Malinowski, Bronislaw. 1935. *Coral Gardens and Their Magic*. London: Allen & Unwin.

Mauss, Marcel. (1923–24) 2016. *The Gift. Expanded Edition*. Chicago: Hau Books.

Meillassoux, Claude. 1981. *Maidens, Meal and Money. Capitalism and the Domestic Community*. Cambridge: Cambridge University Press.

Mollona, Massimiliano. 2009. *Made in Sheffield: An Ethnography of Industrial Work and Politics*. Oxford: Berghahn Books.

Mollona, Massimiliano, Geert De Neve, and Jonathan Parry, eds. 2009. *Industrial Work and Life: An Anthropological Reader*. Oxford: Berg.

Moyn, Samuel. 2010. *The Last Utopia: Human Rights in History*. Cambridge, MA: Belknap/Harvard University Press.

Müller, Birgit. 2007. *Disenchantment with Market Economics: East Germans and Western Capitalism*. New York: Berghahn Books.

Narotzky, Susana, and Gavin Smith. 2006. *Immediate Struggles: People, Power, and Place in Rural Spain*. Berkeley: University of California Press.

Nash, June. 1979. *We Eat the Mines and the Mines Eat Us: Dependency and Exploitation in Bolivian Tin Mines*. New York: Columbia University Press.

Ong, Aihwa. 1987. *Spirits of Resistance and Capitalist Discipline: Factory Women in Malaysia*. Albany, NY: State University of New York Press.

Parry, Jonathan P. 2018. "Introduction: Precarity, Class, and the Neoliberal Subject." In *Industrial Labor on the Margins of Capitalism: Precarity, Class, and the Neoliberal Subject*, ed. Chris Hann and Jonathan Parry, 1–38. New York: Berghahn Books.

———. 2020. *Classes of Labour: Work and Life in a Central Indian Steel Town*. London: Routledge.

Polanyi, Karl. 1944. *The Great Transformation: The Political and Economic Origins of Our Times*. New York: Rinehart.

———. (1927) 2018. "On Freedom." In *Economy and Society: Selected Writings*, ed. Claus Thomasberger and Michele Cangiani. Cambridge: Polity Press.

Procoli, Angela, ed. 2004. *Workers and Narratives of Survival in Europe: The Management of Precariousness at the End of the Twentieth Century*. Albany, NY: State University of New York Press.

Rakowski, Tomasz. 2016. *Hunters, Gatherers, and Practitioners of Powerlessness: An Ethnography of the Degraded in Postsocialist Poland*. New York: Berghahn Books.

Richards, Audrey. 1939. *Land, Labour and Diet in Northern Rhodesia: An Economic Study of the Bemba Tribe*. Oxford: Oxford University Press.

Ruggie, John. 1982. "International Regimes, Transactions, and Change: Embedded Liberalism in the Postwar Economic Order." *International Organization* 36(2): 379–415.

Scheiring, Gábor. 2020. *The Retreat of Liberal Democracy: Authoritarian Capitalism and the Accumulative State in Hungary*. London: Palgrave Macmillan.

Scott, James C. 1976. *The Moral Economy of the Peasant*. New Haven, CT: Yale University Press.

Spittler, Gerd. 2008. *Founders of the Anthropology of Work: German Social Scientists of the 19th and early 20th Centuries and the First Ethnographers*. Münster: LIT.

———. 2017. *Anthropologie der Arbeit: Ein ethnographischer Vergleich*. Wiesbaden: Springer VS.

Szombati, Kristóf. Forthcoming, 2021. "The Consolidation of Authoritarian Rule in Rural Hungary: Workfare and the Shift from Penal Populist to Illiberal Paternalist Poverty Governance." *Europe-Asia Studies*.

Veblen, Thorstein. 1899. *The Theory of the Leisure Class: An Economic Study of the Evolution of Institutions*. New York: Macmillan.

Venkatesan, Soumhya, et al. 2015. "The Concept of Neoliberalism Has Become an Obstacle to the Anthropological Understanding of the Twenty-First Century." *Journal of the Royal Anthropological Institute* 21(4): 911–23.

Wallman, Sandra. 1979. "Introduction." In *Social Anthropology of Work*, ed. Sandra Wallman, 1–24. London: Academic Press.

Weber, Max. (1904–5/1920) 2011. *The Protestant Ethic and the Spirit of Capitalism*. Oxford: Oxford University Press.

1

The Meaning of "Free" Work

Service as a Gift, and Labor as a Commodity for Ni-Vanuatu Labor Migrants

Rachel E. Smith

Introduction

Marcel Mauss's famous essay "The Gift," written in the early 1920s, discussed the social phenomenon he termed the *prestation*, tentatively translatable as "provision of a service" (Mauss [1925] 2016). Whereas in liberal economic thought, "services"—and thus people, and their actions—are often treated as commoditized "things," in Mauss's analysis even the exchange of objects could be seen as transfers of "total services" with a personal character. For Mauss (ibid.: 61), the prestation was a general and lasting contract, in which are exchanged not only material and movable wealth but a wide range of services and courtesies. While there has been much discussion of the exchange of "things-as-gifts," less attention has been paid to human actions, performances, services, or work given voluntarily, or in the expectation that it will be reciprocated in kind.

Work in small-scale agricultural societies was often arranged as a rendering of personal services, at once economic, political, and religious; it could be voluntary, but sometimes it was compelled by an authority (Godelier 1972: 266). Work was often regulated by institutional arrangements, norms, and expectations. While assistance was often freely given as mutual help, larger tasks such as the construction of buildings, and ritual tasks, often required more formal reciprocal arrangements, and coordination by leaders. Malinowski (1921: 6–7) discussed how work in the Trobriands was guided by respect for the chief and the magician. Trobrianders had a range of categories of communal or cooperative work, some of which carried expectations that workers would be fed by the chief or organizer of the tasks. It seems common throughout Melanesia that meals were provided in return for tasks such as garden work. The food was not considered as "payment" akin to a wage. Rather, work parties would expect the garden owner to reciprocate in kind when they needed assistance. As Gregory ([1982] 2015: 62) summarizes, "Labor-time is often given as a gift, and it creates the obligation to return a work-gift at some future time."

Anthropologists have long argued that motivations for work cannot be reduced to subsistence and necessity, or utility and gain, as had been supposed by earlier economic theories of "natural economy" (Mauss 2016: 185; Malinowski 1921). A variety of social and political motivations and incentives should be taken into account, including prestige, obligation and satisfaction (Firth 1951: 141–47). Malinowski (1921: 7) discussed Trobrianders' enjoyment of work, showing that they had a "keen interest in their gardens, work with spirit, and can do sustained and efficient work, both when they do it individually and communally." Different forms of "work ethic" and satisfaction in work can be found across Melanesia (Spittler 2009: 172). For instance, Fajans (1997) wrote of the value that the Baining people place on work and "sweat."

Despite early ethnographers' depictions of pristine social activity, islanders in the Western Pacific have been engaged in forms of commoditized and wage labor since mid-nineteenth century. In this chapter, I explore how meanings and values of work in rural Vanuatu have been transformed in the process of European colonization, and by the imposition of indentured and wage labor regimes. I focus on the rural communities of Lamen and Lamen Bay, on the island of Epi, who have had a high degree of engagement in New Zealand's Recognized Seasonal Employer (RSE) Pacific seasonal worker program. Workers are issued with seasonal contracts and visas for up to seven months to work in orchards and vineyards. Although Epi has a long history of labor engagements, this has been sporadic, and during my fieldwork many adults were experiencing formal wage labor for the first time in their generation.

Mauss (2016: 57–58) wanted to connect contractual law and ethics[1] with the forms and ideas that guide exchange, including the ties between people and things. In order "to construct a kind of prehistory of our modern kind of legal and economic contract," he focused on the obligation to return (Parry 1986: 457). For Mauss, total *prestations* were irreducible to calculative market logics and legal frameworks, and had to be approached as "wholes" in which human actions were guided by a mixture of self-interest and generosity, freedom and obligation (Mauss 2016: 194; see also Hart 2007).

The term *prestation* features frequently in Mauss's text, alongside *don*, *cadeau*, and *present*, and indigenous terms such as *potlatch*. *Prestation* is emphasized in the introduction and conclusion, where its relevance to contemporary Europe, to ideas of contract, and to the multidimensional aspects of "total" returns are foregrounded (Guyer 2016: 19). Mauss was particularly interested in exploring the *prestation*'s "voluntary character, so to speak, apparently free and without cost, and yet constrained and interested" (Mauss 2016: 58). The term has an ambivalent history. Guyer (2016: 13, 19) writes that *prestation* suggests status differentiation and an upward movement, suggestive of feudal arrangements or a kind of tax. Hart (2007: 480) interprets *prestation* as "community service," which may appear volitional, but he too describes it in feudal terms and likens it to labor performed as an alternative to imprisonment. Mauss himself was interested in semantic ambiguity. In another essay, he discusses the slippage between "gift" and "poison" in old German, and how the origins of the wage (in *gage, wadium, vadi*) "is at the same time good and dangerous" (Mauss 1997: 30). This is true of *prestation* too: as I will show, the ambiguity of the term was exploited by colonial powers in imposing work regimes.

Mauss (2016: 179) suggested that through the introduction of modern European legal arrangements and forms of market exchange, this multidimensional form of social contract had become increasingly abstracted, attenuated, individuated, and reduced to naked calculation in the market: "Exchanges between groups [that] had an aesthetic, religious, moral, legal, and economic aspect have been stripped down to leave purely economic exchanges between individuals" (Parry 1986: 457). As for Marx before him, for Mauss this process implied not only increasing individualism but also calculation and logical abstraction (Hart 1982: 47). The attention paid by Mauss to different types of exchange and contractual theory is an intriguing starting place to investigate questions of freedom and obligation, voluntarism and coercion, with reference to work. In the first section of this chapter, I summarize debates around different work regimes from the colonial era to the present day. I contrast the Maussian approach with free market theories that treat labor as a commodity (Guyer 2012: 495).

In the second section I explore why some forms of work in the colonial era were experienced as coercive and exploitative. Although promoted as voluntary (and legally distinguished from slavery), nineteenth-century indentured labor regimes were markedly "unfree." While the plantation economy extended the commodification of labor, colonial officers appropriated and extended communal work practices to fit their economic and political interests. Communal labor under colonialism was often more coercive than "voluntary," though it was frequently described in gift-like language of *prestation* and mutual assistance.

Finally, I look at values and meanings of work in a contemporary rural Vanuatu community that has a high degree of engagement in New

Zealand's Pacific seasonal worker program. I will contrast work figured as a gift—either as a "voluntary" contribution towards the community as a whole, or with expectation of reciprocity—with work conceived as a commodity under capitalism (i.e., labor performed with expectation of payment). I do not intend to insinuate that commodity and gift correspond to an "us" (West) and "them" divide. Gift and commodity exchanges have long coexisted and interacted in Melanesia.[2] In European metropoles, much if not most work—especially in the home—has never been commodified (Spittler 2009: 173). Gift-like characteristics can be found in the heart of commercial centers and industrial workplaces (Carrier 1992; Martin 2015).[3] Mauss (2016: 178–82) identified gift-like practices in many arenas of twentieth-century European life and work.

My discussion of free work in contemporary Vanuatu addresses both the sense of experiencing autonomy in one's work (rather than feeling "like a slave"), and the giving of work free of charge. There were growing anxieties within the communities of Lamen Island and Lamen Bay about a decline in cooperative and sharing behaviors, as seasonal wage workers were said to be increasingly reluctant to "work for free" or "work for others." But calculative reasoning in which time is treated as a scarce resource appeared to be altering people's attitude to community work at home, including the attitudes of those who were not performing wage labor.

Free Contracts and the Commodification of Work

It is conventional in liberal theory to assume that, if a contractual agreement to work is deemed free from fraud or coercion, then it is just. If on the other hand the worker is compelled to sell labor power by coercion, necessity, or deception, then the free or voluntary basis of a just price or "ethical value" for labor is no longer given; it is a "voluntarium imperfection" (Ryan 1916: 329). This is the realm of "Freedom, Equality, Property, and Bentham" that Marx (1990: 280) derides, because under capitalism the free laborer, devoid of any other means to make a living, has no choice but to sell his labor-power. Thus, the formal equality presupposed in the free contract masks the deeply unequal relations between buyer and seller of labor in capitalism's "hidden abode."

Durkheim (Mauss's maternal uncle) was similarly concerned to critique liberal economic and political assumptions about the rise of individualism and the role of the market, but he did so by focusing on contract and solidarity. For Durkheim (1958: 174), "all exchange is a contract, explicit or implicit," and this is the basis of social bonds. A contract expresses cooperation and binds parties in mutual agreement. Thus, by definition, it should be free and consensual, and based on agreement over "just value." Labor contracts should not contravene the worker's interests (ibid.: 211). The contract transforms economic interests into morally binding, enduring relations of interdependence, demanding mutual sacrifice, and it is subject to moral obligations as well as law (Durkheim [1893] 1984: 160, 173). Contrary to the assumptions of free-market theorists, he stressed that the privatization of contracts required *more* state intervention (cf. Graeber 2001: 152).

Like his uncle, Mauss (2016: 57–58) was interested in the "archaic forms of contract" and the "non-contractual elements" that form the moral basis of social solidarity. Mauss refuses the oppositions between freedom and obligation, self-interest and generosity, individual and society, that underpinned much political and economic thinking (Parry 1986: 456; Graeber 2001: 153; Hart 2007: 481). The gift is the paradigmatic example of how a voluntary act creates a sense of obligation, with a mutual and open-ended quality. Mauss (2016: 179) detected the continuation of custom and moral obligation in many aspects of French society at the time he was writing, when many legal and economic ideas had become impersonal (even inhuman) abstractions.

Although some concept of "work" can generally be found across a great many languages and historical contexts, for Marx (1990), its abstraction as quantities of commodified "labor(-time)" is specific to (and a defining feature of) capitalism—a mode of production in which the market is dominant. Earlier, in his Paris manuscripts, he had written that work "produces not only commodities: it produces itself and the worker as a commodity" (Marx 1988: 71). The life and free activity of the worker are abstracted and appropriated, resulting in his estrangement and alienation.

Mauss saw industrial alienation similarly, but took a more legal approach by concentrating on the transfer of rights (Graeber 2001: 162). In his conclusions, Mauss wrote of an incompatibility between industrial and commercial law, and living morality: "One might even say that an entire section of the law (*droit*), that relating to industrialists and merchants, is presently in conflict with morality. The economic presumptions of the people, the producers, come from their firm desire to follow the thing they have produced, and from the acute sense that their work is being sold without their sharing in the profit" (Mauss 2016: 179). In comparison to the "total *prestation*" of the kind Mauss saw in gift relationships, "a relation of wage labor was a miserable and impoverished form of contract" (Graeber 2001: 162).

Mauss welcomed echoes of the gift in the emergence of institutions such as social insurance, mutual societies, family assistance funds, and other forms of social protection (Mauss 2016: 179–81). He was a guild socialist, sympathetic to voluntarism and the cooperative movement, though not to the Bolshevik revolution (Hart 2007: 478). What mattered for contemporary society was to counter abstractions such as the legal distinction between persons and things, and to add rights beyond the "bare" commoditization of services.

Mauss was one of many to contend that work/labor is not a commodity. Lujo Brentano had written in 1877 "that labor power is nothing but the person itself and, hence, labor is essentially different from all other commodities" (quoted in Evju 2013: 225). Three years later, Irish economist John Kells Ingram complained to the British TUC that "Labor is spoken of as if it were an independent entity, separable from the personality of a workman." In fact, the worker was a "free man" (quoted in Evju 2013: 225; see also O'Higgins 1997: 226). In 1919, the phrase "labor is not a commodity" was inserted into Article 427 of the Treaty of Versailles. In 1944, a century after Karl Marx had drafted his Paris Manuscripts, "Labor is not a Commodity" was the opening statement in the "declaration of aims and purpose" of the ILO.[4]

For Karl Polanyi, labor was a "fictitious commodity" in the sense that work is a human activity inseparable from life, not a thing produced for sale on the market (Polanyi [1944] 2001: 75). Ethnographic accounts of work in non-market societies had shown that work was not primarily motivated by economic gain or necessity, but by "reciprocity, competition, joy of work, and social approbation" (ibid.: 277).[5] Polanyi valued freedom highly—not the liberal bourgeois concept based on individual self-responsibility, private property, contractual relations, and "free" enterprise, but "social freedom", to be free through social responsibility and interconnectedness (see also Hann, Miller, Santos et al., this volume). This collective capacity to lead an ethical life and to shape society could only be achieved when people were no longer dominated by opaque political and economic forces (Baum 1996: 27; Polanyi 2001: 265–66; Polanyi 2018: 22). Polanyi recognized the contradiction that in order to extend "freedom of contract" in colonized regions, people were "forced to make a living by selling their labor" and "freed" from non-contractual social relations (Polanyi 2001: 171). In the next section I consider the complex processes through which labor markets were established in Vanuatu.

Vanuatu's Unfree Labor History

Melanesia has a long history of commoditized labor. Vanuatu (formerly New Hebrides) broadly fits the pattern that Gregory (2015: 127) classifies into four phases: forced (overseas plantations 1860s–1903), semi-forced (domestic plantations, 1880s–1950), "semi-free" (agreement labor,

1950s–1970s), and "free" wage labor (since 1920s). In the nineteenth century the archipelago was treated as a labor reserve for indentured labor, known as "blackbirding." Most went to plantations: at least forty thousand Ni-Vanuatu were taken to Queensland, fourteen thousand to Fiji, ten thousand to New Caledonia, and others to Samoa and Tahiti (Adams 1986: 59).

The extent to which Ni-Vanuatu could be said to have entered into freely negotiated agreements, first for overseas labor and then for domestic plantations, has been hotly debated.[6] In the nineteenth-century labor trade, recruitment practices deviated from legal conventions for indentured labor.[7] Melanesians usually received no written contract outlining reciprocal obligations and conditions, and in any case, would likely be unable to interpret written or verbal contracts in English or French (Hoefte 2017: 368).

Although blackbirding is legally distinct from the chattel slavery that characterized the Atlantic slave trade, much of the nineteenth-century Pacific labor trade fits the conventional definition of modern slavery as a term covering trafficked, forced, and bonded labor.[8] Especially in the early phases, deception and kidnapping were common practice (Saunders 1982; Mortensen 2000). Activist descendants of trafficked laborers in Queensland object to the term "indentured" as a weak euphemism, preferring "Sugar Slave" (Davis 2017). And even in cases where islanders appear to have accepted their passage (such as those recruiting for a second time), they were often subject to exploitation, disease, and violence in poor working and living conditions (e.g., Saunders 1982; Shineberg 1991).

One of the reasons I chose Epi as a field-site is its long history as a "labor frontier" (after Gregory 2015: 127). Epi was one of, if not the most, blackbirded islands in the region (Price and Baker 1976: 114; Siegel 1985: 48). In the nineteenth-century labor trade, there were numerous abuses and violent incidents involving Epi islanders (e.g., Saunders 1982: 20; Mortensen 2000). Later, west Epi became a primary location for plantations during a "land grab," especially by a French chartered company, in the late nineteenth and early twentieth century (Smith 2017). As labor was difficult to obtain on the island where the plantations were located, most workers were brought in from elsewhere. Planters sold and gambled workers, sometimes in the currency of "years of work"—an example of "extreme commodification" (Jones 2019: 549, 552). Workers often suffered brutality at the hands of the planters (Jacomb 1920; Adams 1986: 54, 61; Panoff 1991). This is particularly true of French-owned plantations, in part due to the fact they were not regulated until the 1910s, and even then, regulators usually sided with planters (Adams 1986: 56; Panoff 1991; Jones 2019: 545).[9] People on Epi today recall horrific abuses and punishments on the plantations (see also Rodman 1998).

On Australian and Pacific island plantations alike, Melanesian workers were paid little, and typically given trade goods or truck,[10] in lieu of (cash) wages. This was also the case on Epi (Jones 2019: 546), where planters often distributed poor quality alcohol. Goods were often sold at inflated prices, offering further profits for planters and traders (Graves 1983). Over time, more and more islanders refused indentured work, often preferring to sell their own copra, or would negotiate short-term contracts, and better pay. Even poorer inland villages were able to command higher wages from local planters suffering labor shortages (Adams 1986: 59; Jones 2019: 551).

The residents of Lamen experienced a range of contractual labor in the later decades of the twentieth century. World War II brought compulsory conscription of adult males in 1942 (Haberkorn 1990: 155). Conditions were poor, and many died from dysentery. The establishment of military bases accelerated urban development. Rural islanders continued to engage in wage labor, but they mostly returned to the village at the end of short-term engagements. Throughout the 1950s and early 1960s, most able-bodied Lamen men worked at a fishery at Palikula, on Espiritu Santo island. The owners were notoriously duplicitous, and Lamen workers were promised fortunes. A former Palikula worker on Lamen told me of his former boss's deception: "He said, 'This is your number. When it's time to give you your money, you will need your number. Big money! You can buy a ship, or you can marry a white woman.' They lied so much!" (recorded interview).

Later, in the 1960s and 1970s, after the departure of Vietnamese laborers from New Caledonia, Lamen men were engaged to fill labor shortages in the expanding nickel mines. Urbanization accelerated, but opportunities for international migration dried up after Independence in 1980, except for work on foreign fishing vessels. It was not until the launch of New Zealand's seasonal labor program in 2008 that large numbers of rural Ni-Vanuatu once again had an opportunity for international migration. As in the past, in this new phase workers are issued temporary contracts, are tied to particular employers, and have the costs of their reproduction borne largely by their home communities (Smith 2015).

These forms of commoditized contractual labor were not the only kind of work arrangements experienced by islanders during the colonial period. As in many colonized regions, a range of non-commoditized labor arrangements were in operation. And while these regimes were artefacts of colonial administration, they were often figured by administrators as customary, communal, and "voluntary" in nature.

Prestations and Communal Work

While Mauss used *prestation* in a positive sense in his essay "The Gift," he was aware that the term had an ambivalent history (Mallard 2018: 188, 196). In the early 1900s, Mauss was involved with the "Committee for the Protection and Defence of Indigenous Populations" (Comité de protection et de défense des indigènes). The committee, conscious of abuses in often violent extraction of labor by chartered companies (including in New Caledonia), had written to the minister of colonies to request that in-kind payments should be prohibited, and that women should be exempted from some heavy labor. At the same time, they advocated that the term *prestation* (or *requisition*) should replace *corvée*. For, while *corvée* was associated with coercion and forced labor, *prestations* should be premised on consent, although such arrangements did not need to take the form of a wage contract (Mallard 2018: 187–89). But, as Grégoire Mallard (ibid.: 198) suggests, perhaps Mauss also deceived himself when he naively considered the possibility for a more "giving" and reciprocal relationship between France and her colonies in his later work, *The Nation*.

A system of *prestations* was implemented across many of France's colonies. But the connotations of volition and reciprocity can be read as a fiction (Mallard 2018: 189), or a facade, masking the exploitation of a cheap labor force in extending colonial infrastructure: "French colonial governments in Central Africa created a system of forced labor that they disguised rather thinly as in-kind contributions 'for the common good': that is, they claimed that building roads . . . would benefit everyone, including Africans, and then made Africans do all of the work" (Freed 2010: 213).

Due to the relatively late institution of a colonial government, and the fact that it was a condominium with Britain, it seems doubtful that a formal conscripted labor system was imposed centrally in Vanuatu (then New Hebrides). However, when recruitment of New Hebrideans for labor in New Caledonia ceased, a system of *prestations* was introduced in the latter. In 1924, around the time Mauss wrote his famous essay, "*Les Prestations*"—a labor tax requiring compulsory labor from adult men—was instituted on the Grand Terre, and extended to the whole colony by 1929. This labor was restricted to "public works," mostly for road works. Men could buy out their liability for *prestations* with a payment known as *rachat* (redemption). French colonial officers were instructed to convince the indigenous Kanaks that the system was in their own best interest, and had to document Kanak compliance (Muckle 2015).

Unpaid communal labor appears to have been a routine part of colonial administration in the colonial New Hebrides, albeit in a more informal, decentralized form. In 1934 a British district agent wrote to the resident commissioner to request legal power to enforce communal labor for young men evading road maintenance obligations (specified as a task for communal work since 1917). The commissioner's response was negative: enforcement would be contrary to the International Labor Convention of 1930 (WPA, 1953 (1934) 295/201/34). This convention was the result of protracted efforts by the ILO to ban forced labor. Mauss was acquainted with its French socialist director general, Albert Thomas, who had long campaigned against abuses by French companies (Mallard 2018: 189). However, the ban did not extend to work fulfilling "normal civic obligations of citizens," or "minor communal services of a kind which, being performed by the members of the community, [were] in the direct interest of the said community" (ILO, n.d.). France officially prohibited forced labor practices in 1937 (Mallard 2018: 192), but it took several more years before the measures were implemented in the colonies (Freed 2010: 220; Okia 2012: 18).

Communal labor—that is, labor deemed to be in the interests of the local community—continued in the postwar years in both French and British colonies. These practices were often overseen by a chief or headman, and legitimated as a continuation of traditional communal labor practices (Okia 2012: 16–22). Like the French *prestations*, collective labor systems in the British Empire were often described in the language of the gift, or of mutual aid.[11] In the New Hebrides, the British commissioner assumed communal work was "customary," and that it was the job of the chief or headman to ensure that all participated. In 1940, a district officer provided a list of communal tasks that the headman could instigate, summarized here:

1. Cleaning public spaces in the village
2. Building houses (including gendered tasks) in return for food from the owner
3. Communal pig fences
4. Yam planting (including gendered tasks) in return for food from the garden owner
5. Cleaning paths or roads (usually on Tuesdays)

It is likely that house construction and yam planting were continuations of traditional practices, while cleaning tasks (including the fencing of pigs) are remembered on Epi as having been promoted by missionaries and colonial officers. A notion of monetary equivalence appears to have been introduced, even for the traditional tasks. The agent for the southern district added that "[w]here a villager is in regular employment he must pay his headman a forfeit for days lost, otherwise he will get no help for the construction of his garden or home" (WPA, 1953 (1940) 2/40).

In 1953, the agent for the southern district again corresponded with the resident commissioner regarding the ILO's regulations on forced labor. The commissioner appeared to know that communal unpaid labor was routinely used to perform tasks such as clearing roads. The district agent replied:

> There appears to be general agreement that communal work is necessary, and especially so on Tanna, where some hundreds of miles of road have for decades been kept in a just-passable state by communal labor. In France local roads are maintained by a system of communal work without protest from the International Labor Organization, to which the fact is reported with full explanation annually.[12] Is there any reason why communal work should not be enforced—by means of suitable legislation [*this comment was added later*]—on Tanna in order to spread the burden of road maintenance (which is in the general interest) over the whole population instead of letting it fall, as it now does, on the few whom the District Agents can persuade to do some work? (WPA, 1953 F. 1/8)

The commissioner responded to the agent that, although he did not consider "customary" communal work to contravene the ILO's Forced Labor Convention (No.29/1930), "the admittedly loose control at present exercised through Government 'work' days is as far as we can go" (WPA, 1953/327 F201). In this way the "voluntary" nature of custom and communal work was appropriated by the colonial power.

Perhaps in response to the ILO's 1957 Convention, which had sought to complement the 1930 Convention by adding certain conditions that had become concerns following World War II, on 30 June 1958 both the French and British resident commissioners wrote to all district agents to "remind" them that all communal labor must be reported beforehand—including any offers of remuneration; "the use of communal labor, whether such labor is obtained through the intermediary of Chiefs or otherwise, is permitted only where the work is of direct utility to the community and those who will be employed have freely consented to give their labor and are not acting under duress of any kind" (WPA, 1953 (1958) 24/58). The British and French district agents for the southern district replied that communal labor had been deployed to clear roads since 1917, and that the use of paid government labor had been resisted by local people, who preferred to do it themselves (WPA, 1953 (1958) F.1: 8).

While the above exchanges are drawn from a file concerning the island of Tanna in the south, it is likely similar arrangements pertained on Epi during the colonial period. Missionaries too commanded communal labor projects: from the first missionaries in the area in late nineteenth century, who arranged the construction of churches, up to Graham Horwell, the missionary resident on Lamen Island from 1948 until 1968. When it came to building the district school on Lamen, nearly all the able-bodied men were working at the Palikula fishery, and so it was the women and children who did the brunt of the construction work (Horwell 2006: 21). To this day, influenced by missionary and colonial interventions, community work has remained an important part of weekly routines across Epi. Days are set aside for it, including one day for chiefs to suggest tasks, and another for the church. However, one increasingly hears that communal work is in decline, and older people remember a golden age prior to Independence, when paths and avenues were free of leaves, and grass was frequently cut.

Labor as Gift and Commodity in Contemporary Vanuatu

It has been argued that managed migration programs, including the RSE scheme mentioned in the introduction to this chapter, represent a greater commodification of labor, because they treat the workers in terms of labor capacities before discarding them (Connell 2010: 120; Rosewarne 2010). The temporary migrant is doubly exploited and excluded because the costs of reproduction and the duties of protection are borne by their home community, and the "left behind" (Smith 2015). These programs are unfree even by liberal free market standards, as workers are typically tied to one employer (Smith 2019: 362). They are vulnerable to the threat of deportation or of not being hired again in the following season, and therefore become compliant workers, willing to accept low wages and poor conditions, and unable to protest or unionize (Basok 2002; Bailey 2009). On top of these perfectly legal constraints, workers allege that their wage rates and deductions are manipulated (Smith 2019: 357). When discussing abuses, Ni-Vanuatu sometimes recall the history of blackbirding and indenture, and subordination to white masters. They may even compare their situation to slavery, although they undertake these hardships willingly, in the hope of a better future. As one team leader stated: "Sometimes we feel like slaves, but we believe there is a Judge God that will turn these hardships into a blessing in many of our children's lives, if this scheme continues."

Perhaps because seasonal workers combine wage labor with a range of household, subsistence, and communal work, they are acutely aware of differences in work rhythm and their underlying ethics. RSE officials often imply that time management and in particular a work ethic are foreign values to Pacific islanders, who need to be educated accordingly. For their part, Ni-Vanuatu described their experience of working as wage laborers in terms of feeling subordinate to a calculative temporal and profit-making regime, in which "time is money" (Smith 2019: 357–58).[13] But they readily acknowledge the contrast between the temporal regime in wage work (particularly in the packhouses, which run at a factory pace) and the pace of life at home, where people tend to fit work around the rhythms of health and energy, daily life, the seasonal cycle of crops, and ritual obligations. In their gardens, they are free to work at their own pace, socialize, eat and drink, and rest frequently, often phrased as "Vanuatu time," or "island time." As one Lamen man put it, "In New Zealand, time is the boss of you, but here we are the boss of time." People distinguish between centers of wage labor where "everything is money" (*evri samting hemi mani*), and village life where one can "live for free" (*liv fri nomo*), or "eat for free" (*kakae fri nomo*). Such distinctions function as a way to valorize rural identities and ways of life. Living for "free" in terms of not relying on money is associated with "freedom" in a broader sense of being one's own boss.

However, calculative reasoning based on "time is money" seems to be altering people's attitude to working for the community (such as tasks related to the kindergarten, church, or meeting houses, generically referred to as *komiuniti wok*, and organized either by the chiefs and council, or by the church). Many residents of Lamen perceived a decline in these forms of work, which they associated with a rise in individualism, foreign and urban lifestyles, diminished respect for traditional authority, and the availability of money and wage work. One seasonal worker told me, "Before [the village] chief would call everyone and they would all go. But now many people visit town and they think they know it all; they just do their own work." Another, a youth worker, said bluntly, "People don't cooperate to discuss [community work]. They are too individualistic." A third told me, "Everyone has a lot of money—they don't want to be bothered by all the chiefs now." The chief of Lamen Bay said that regular overseas workers tend to come back "different," as if they have become "greedy". A prominent ex-MP told me that she believed that the new houses springing up in Lamen Bay, dispersed and with private yards hedged off from the road, were conducive to villagers "hiding away," and not taking part in community work. People even deployed the English terms "human resources" and "manpower" when discussing these problems.

On Kindergarten Day in 2012, the kindergarten committee in Lamen Bay organized a parade and gifts for the children. Following this, a church elder came to dedicate the newly completed kindergarten building. He read the parable of the Good Samaritan and, after a prayer, he explained to the onlooking parents that the kindergarten was like the injured man in the biblical passage: "How many people walked past after the building was falling down in disrepair, but did nothing to help? God honors the 'few' who came to assist."

The chairman of the kindergarten committee blamed New Zealand as the main "excuse" for people not coming to work: "The people who go to New Zealand, they work for their money, they don't work for all of us. That's the problem . . . They never work for free. You have to pay them now." This corresponds to the common perception that members of the Lamen community increasingly expect money in return for work that in the past would have been given freely, as part of a generalized reciprocity or mutual help. This applied not only to community work, but also to tasks like washing for another household, helping with the garden, or assisting with house construction. It was remarked upon that more and more residents were transacting food for cash, whereas in the past that food would have been shared.

Both the council and the church have attempted to oblige seasonal workers to contribute financially to the community on their return, as compensation for their extended absence from community activities. Such demands for monetary contributions echo the norms surrounding communal labor in the colonial era: community work has its monetary equivalent, or can at least be substituted.

Seasonal workers resisted the payment of such a fee. Some argued that government workers did not have to pay, so why should they? Others said that their families contributed enough to community work in their absence. This was not primarily an issue about onerous financial obligations. The monies requested by the council were modest compared with the sums that seasonal workers typically accumulate overseas. The demands for community work were not particularly burdensome; most weeks went by without any community work at all. Moreover, many workers made generous gifts to the community, such as purchasing materials for community projects, or sponsoring boat trips for annual New Year festivities (*ponane*). Workers were more willing to give money to the community if this was represented as a voluntary gift, rather than a mandatory fee. Commands to work or share tend to be less successful than exhortations to give time and labor voluntarily, freely. Workers were often generous in donating to the church, and supporting "fundraisings" where the donation was ostensibly voluntary (even though chiefs stressed that every household was obliged to offer support). Returnees preferred to affirm their autonomy and enhance their reputation than submit to demands by an authority, whether secular or religious (cf. Miller, this volume).

Community leaders often berated seasonal workers for only "working for money," or working for themselves, and refusing to "work for free," and for the benefit of others. Those who remain represent themselves as performing disproportionate amounts of communal labor. They are increasingly suggesting it is *they* who are treated like slaves. The chief of Lamen Bay told me that "[t]hose that go over there, they do not recognize our struggle to keep the community in place . . . [The seasonal worker] works over there for his own money, but those of us who stay here, we stay as 'slaves' working for free for the community." Complaints about "working for free" or working "like slaves" restate the conceptual links between calculations of work, time, and money. Statements invoking "slavery" suggest that "working for free" is exploitative in itself. The "time is money" equation of commoditized labor regimes is transforming attitudes to non-commoditized, communal work, even as people explicitly denounce the calculative ethos of the former.

Conclusion

Mauss's holistic concept of *prestation*, encompassing religious, aesthetic legal, and moral elements is a useful framework in which to examine the social character of work across time and space. The *prestation* resists reductive definition, and calculation. It can shapeshift between freedom and obligation, self-interest and generosity, and person and thing. Language and gestures conveying its apparently voluntary character often disguise that underlying it is "a fiction, a formality, a social falsehood" (Mauss 2016: 1). Mauss's analysis points to the paradox that the *prestation* is "essentially ambiguous and always evoking the contrary of each definition" (Gasché 1997: 100).

The division between service and freedom is a "Gordian knot" in Abrahamic religions, one from which the Protestants have sought to tease out ideas of freedom, individual consent, and personal responsibility (Guyer 2016: 17, 20). The particular Western liberal ethic of "freedom" is of relatively recent origin. Outside of modern European traditions, mutual implication of freedom and service is often the norm.

The question of freedom in different labor arrangements and work ethics is similarly complex. Can work ever be entirely free? Is free work limited to a self-actualizing *homo faber*? In preindustrial Europe, the "free man" was the man who did not need to work, and arrangements resembling wage labor were likened to slavery (Graeber 2006). Only with the rise of industrial capitalism and the Protestant work ethic does wage labor become a cornerstone of "freedom" and independence in liberal thought (Fraser and Gordon 1994: 316). Marx, Mauss, and Polanyi all pointed to how the (mis-) characterization of the "free" wage labor contract as an exchange between equals in the marketplace belies forms of alienation and exploitation that subordinate human life and dignity to a calculating regime. Labor is not a commodity, they agree.

But neither is work given without expectation of payment necessarily a (free) gift. Work is often motivated by a mixture of interest and obligation, competition and reciprocity. Some unpaid labor arrangements are very obviously unfree. Colonial arrangements, even when disguised in the language of gifts, mutual aid, and community service, were routinely based on coercion and extraction. I have shown this to be the case in the deployment of the term *prestation* itself in colonial settings, which disguised arrangements that can be seen as quasi-feudal. This shows how the ambiguity, "social falsehood," and even the "poison" that Mauss (1997: 30; 2016: 1) recognized in the gesture of gift could be exploited by colonial powers.

While Mauss saw continuities with the gift in modern contracts; he criticized the ways in which formal labor contracts and free-market theories reduced ethical values and motivations to the cold logic of utilitarian calculation: "*Homo oeconomicus* is not behind us, he is in front of us; like the moral man and the man of duty . . . Man . . . has not long been a machine, made complicated by a calculating machine" (Mauss 2016: 190; also, Graeber 2001: 163). This calculative reason could also be destructive: "The brutal pursuit of individual goals is harmful to the purposes and the peace of the whole, to the rhythm of its work and its joys, and—by feedback effect—to the individual himself" (Mauss 2016: 191). Rather than accepting at face value formal legal and economic definitions of labor, we would do well to return to a broader concept of work as a total social phenomenon, and to question the voluntary character of all of its forms.

If Mauss is right that the conceptual division between self-interest and obligation is entrenched within commercial and industrial law and economistic understandings of the market (Parry 1986: 458, 466), then the binaries of gift/commodity and altruism/self-interest can be expected to become more pronounced in Vanuatu as the market-based economy expands and the division of labor becomes more elaborate. The experience of wage-labor regimes in which "time is money" is affecting attitudes to work, even in the supposedly non-commodified sphere of communal work in rural Vanuatu. This is not a straightforward matter of a "disembedding" of economy from society. Rather it is a redefinition of the terrain for debate and critique. The people of Epi continue both to assert autonomy and to make claims on others in terms of obligations to the community. What it means to work for free or work for money, to work autonomously or to work for others, depends a lot on where you stand in the workplace or the village, and their inherent social and political relationships.

Acknowledgments

This research was funded by an ESRC-UK PhD scholarship (fieldwork), and the Max Planck–Cambridge Centre for Ethics, Economy and Social Change (archival work). I am grateful to editor Chris Hann, and discussant (and former mentor) Chris Gregory, for their incisive comments on this chapter. I would also like to thank Karen Sykes, Keir Martin, and Madeleine Reeves, and collaborators on the ESRC-funded "Domestic Moral Economy" project for guidance during my doctoral work.

Rachel E. Smith is a research fellow at the Max Planck–Cambridge Centre for Ethics, Economy and Social Change, and a lecturer at the University of Lucerne.

Notes

1. Jane Guyer (2016: 21) translates *la morale* as ethics rather than morality, due to its connotations of guidance, discipline, and teaching.
2. Indeed, Gregory (2015) deployed his much-misunderstood gift/commodity heuristic precisely to show how the market did not displace gift exchange, but led certain forms to flourish.
3. Economist George Akerlof suggests that aspects of wage labor can be considered as a gift: people are motivated by sentiments they develop for institutions, and workers may work harder if they feel the firm has an interest in their welfare. Although Akerlof discusses these exchanges in terms of utility, he approximates Mauss when he argues that "the optimal contract may not set wages at the minimum acceptable: if part of worker effort is a gift, likewise, part of wages paid should be a gift" (Akerlof 1982: 550–51).
4. Known as the 'Declaration of Philadelphia', which can be read here: https://www.ilo.org/legacy/english/inwork/cb-policy-guide/declarationofPhiladelphia1944.pdf. On its centenary, ILO issued a statement evocative of Mauss: "We propose a human-centered agenda for the future of work that strengthens the social contract by placing people and the work they do at the center of economic and social policy and business practice . . . We hope to see explicit recommitment to inclusive social contracts around the world, based on the collective understanding that, in return for their contribution to growth and prosperity, people are protected against the inherent vicissitudes of the market economy and their rights are respected. . . . To be successful, such efforts demand solidarity among people, generations, countries, and international organizations" (ILO 2019: 54).
5. As Spittler (2009: 162) argues, Polanyi contrasts embedded human action with the abstraction and commoditization of labor, but does not foreground work in his analysis.
6. See Adams 1986. Doug Munro (1995b) outlines a historiography of the Labor Trade in Queensland in terms of two main tendencies. Australian "revisionists" (esp. Scarr 1967; Corris 1973) emphasized the agency of the Pacific Islanders. According to them, most laborers were recruited voluntarily and many returned. But "counter-revisionists" (Saunders 1982; Graves 1993) saw the trade in critical political economic terms of coercion and exploitation. Concerning the Fiji

labor trade, there was a similar heated debate between the "market" approach of Shlomowitz (1986; 1991), and the "class" approach of Brass (1991; 1994). Brass has been criticized for a vulgar Marxian analysis (Munro 1995a: 246; Grubb 2001), and Shlomowitz for overemphasizing supply and demand in restrictive conditions that can hardly be seen as a "free market" (Munro 1995a: 246).

7. Indenture has been formally defined as "a contract committing one party to make a series of payments to or on behalf of the other—settlement of transport debt, subsistence over the (negotiable) contract term, and final payment in kind or, less usually, cash at the conclusion of the term. In exchange the payee agrees to be completely at the disposal of the payor, or the payor's assigns, for performance of work, for the term agreed" (Tomlins, in Hoefte 2017: 363).
8. See also Jones 2019. A recent claim by the Australian prime minister that Australia has no history of slavery was met with much resistance, not least from Australian South Sea Islander descendants of blackbirded laborers (see, e.g., Buchanan 2020).
9. Shortly before the Treaty of Versailles, an English lawyer named Edward Jacomb (who had been trying to prosecute abuses on plantations in the then New Hebrides) suggested a League of Nations was required to tackle colonial maltreatment of "native races" (Jacomb 1920). While the clause for racial equality ultimately failed, the treaty did give rise to the ILO and the amelioration of some forced labor practices (Maul 2007).
10. Graves (1983: 87) quotes G.W. Hilton's definition of the truck system as "the name given to a closely related set of arrangements whereby some form of consumption is tied to the employment contract." He adds that "Truck in Queensland was also associated with a system of deferred pay and the consumption by workers of goods on credit from the 'truck' shops."
11. For example, in Malawi, it translated as "help" (*thangata*), while Ugandan *luwalo* and *kasanvu* were named after "traditional" work practices (Hansen 1993; Okia 2012: 16–22).
12. Although *corvée* (unpaid, unfree) labor in French colonies had been formally banned in 1937, labor practices deemed "communal" were allowed until 1946. They were apparently modelled on feudal arrangements in prerevolutionary France, and the allocation of local responsibility for road-building in rural areas in the nineteenth century (Okia 2012: 131n67; Price 2017: 39).
13. Workers and sometimes employers resist treating workers as a "pure commodity," preferring to build enduring moral obligations through gifts and hospitality as "non-contractual elements" in the labor contract (Smith 2019).

References

Published Sources

Adams, R. 1986. "Indentured Labour and the Development of Plantations in Vanuatu: 1867–1922." *Journal de la Société des Océanistes* 42: 41–63.

Akerlof, G. A. 1982. "Labor Contracts as Partial Gift Exchange." *Quarterly Journal of Economics* 97: 543–69.

Bailey, R. 2009. "Unfree Labour? Ni-Vanuatu Workers in New Zealand's Recognised Seasonal Employer Scheme." MA dissertation. Kent: University of Canterbury.

Basok, T. 2002. *Tortillas and Tomatoes: Transmigrant Mexican Harvesters in Canada*. Montreal: McGill-Queen's Press.

Baum, G. 1996. *Karl Polanyi on Ethics and Economics*. Montreal: McGill-Queen's Press.

Brass, T. 1991. "Market Essentialism and the Impermissibility of Unfree Labour: A Reply to Shlomowitz." *Slavery & Abolition* 12: 225–44.

———. 1994. "Contextualizing Sugar Production in Nineteenth-Century Queensland." *Slavery and Abolition* 15(1): 100–17.

Buchanan, K. 2020. "'Mate, Be Respectful of Our History': Morrison's 'No Slavery' Comment Prompts Invite to Cane Regions." Available at: https://www.abc.net.au/news/2020-06-12/call-for-scott-morrison-visit-bundaberg-to-learn-about-slavery/12347686 (last accessed 24 June 2020).

Carrier, J. G. 1992. "Emerging Alienation in Production: A Maussian History." *Man* 27(3): 539–58.

Connell, J. 2010. "From Blackbirds to Guestworkers in the South Pacific. Plus ça Change. . . ?" *Economic and Labour Relations Review* 20: 111–21.

Corris, P. 1973. *Passage, Port and Plantation: A History of Solomon Islands Labour Migration, 1870–1914*. Melbourne: Melbourne University Press.

Davis, (Waskam) E. 2017. "Australia's Hidden History of Slavery: The Government Divides to Conquer." *The Conversation*. Available at: http://theconversation.com/australias-hidden-history-of-slavery-the-government-divides-to-conquer-86140 (last accessed 12 June 2020).

Durkheim, E. 1958. *Professional Ethics and Civic Morals*. Glencoe, IL: Free Press.

———. (1893) 1984. *The Division of Labour in Society*, trans. W. D. Halls. Basingstoke: Palgrave.

Evju, S. 2013. "Labour Is Not a Commodity: Reappraising the Origins of the Maxim." *European Labour Law Journal* 4(3): 222–29.

Fajans, J. 1997. *They Make Themselves: Work and Play among the Baining of Papua New Guinea*. Chicago: University of Chicago Press.

Firth, R. 1951. *Elements of Social Organization*. London: Watts & Co.

Fraser, N., and L. Gordon. 1994. "A Genealogy of Dependency: Tracing a Keyword of the US Welfare State." *Signs* 19: 309–36.

Freed, L. 2010. "Networks of (Colonial) Power: Roads in French Central Africa after World War I." *History and Technology* 26(3): 203–23.

Gasché, R. 1997. "Heliocentric Exchange." In *The Logic of the Gift: Toward an Ethic of Generosity*, ed. A. Schrift, 100–120. New York: Routledge.

Godelier, M. 1972. *Rationality and Irrationality in Economics*. New York: Monthly Review Press.

Graeber, D. 2001. *Toward an Anthropological Theory of Value: The False Coin of Our Own Dreams*. New York: Palgrave.

———. 2006. "Turning Modes of Production Inside Out: Or, Why Capitalism is a Transformation of Slavery." *Critique of Anthropology* 26(1): 61–85.

Graves, A. 1983. "Truck and Gifts: Melanesian Immigrants and the Trade Box System in Colonial Queensland." *Past & Present* 101: 87–124.

———. 1993. *Cane and Labour: The Political Economy of the Queensland Sugar Industry 1862–1906*. Edinburgh: Edinburgh University Press.

Gregory, C. A. (1982) 2015. *Gifts and Commodities*. Chicago: HAU Books.

Grubb, F. 2001. "Methodology and the Pacific Labor Trade to Queensland, Australia." *Historical Methods: A Journal of Quantitative and Interdisciplinary History* 34(1), 5–36.

Guyer, J. I. 2012. "Obligation, Binding, Debt and Responsibility: Provocations about Temporality from Two New Sources." *Social Anthropology* 20(4): 491–501.

———. 2016. "Translator's Introduction." In *The Gift*, M. Mauss, 1–25. Chicago: HAU Books.

Haberkorn, G. 1990. "Paamese in Port Vila: Peasants on Leave, or a Wage Dependent Proletariat?" In *Migration and Development in the South Pacific*, ed. J. Connell, 151–69. Canberra: Australian National University.

Hansen, H. B. 1993. "Forced Labour in a Missionary Context: A Study of Kasanvu in Early Twentieth-Century Uganda." *Slavery & Abolition* 14: 186–206.

Hart, K. 1982. "On Commoditization." In *From Craft to Industry: The Ethnography of Proto-Industrial Cloth Production*, ed. E. Goody, 37–54. Cambridge: Cambridge University Press.

———. 2007. "Marcel Mauss: In Pursuit of the Whole. A Review Essay." *Comparative Studies in Society and History* 49(2): 473–85.

Hoefte, R. 2017. "Indentured Labour." In *Handbook Global History of Work*, ed. K. Hofmeester and M. van der Linden, 363–76. Oldenbourg: de Gruyter.

Horwell, G. 2006. *A Voyage of Discovery: The Presbyterian Church of the New Hebrides 1948–1980*. Christchurch: Horwell Family (Printed by Copy Quality Printers).

ILO (International Labour Organization). 2019. "Work for a brighter future: Global Commission on the Future of Work." https://www.ilo.org/wcmsp5/groups/public/---dgreports/---cabinet/documents/publication/wcms_662410.pdf (last accessed 18 March 2021).

———. n.d. Convention C029 – Forced Labour Convention, 1930 (No. 29) https://www.ilo.org/dyn/normlex/en/f?p=1000:12100:0::NO::P12100_ILO_CODE:C029 (last accessed 1 May 2020).

Jacomb, E. 1920. "The Future of the Kanaka." *The Anti-Slavery Reporter and Aborigines' Friend* 9: 115–17.

Jones, G. 2019. "The Construction of a Slave Identity: An Examination of the Dual Identity of Indentured Labourers across the Western Pacific." *Labor History* 60(5): 540–57.

Malinowski, B. 1921. "The Primitive Economics of the Trobriand Islanders." *The Economic Journal* 31(121): 1–16.

Mallard, G. 2018. "The Gift as Colonial Ideology? Marcel Mauss and the Solidarist Colonial Policy in the Interwar Era." *Journal of International Political Theory* 14(2): 183–202.

Martin, K. 2015. "Afterword." In *Flexible Capitalism: Exchange and Ambiguity at Work*, ed. J. Kjaerulff, 261–76. New York: Berghahn Books.

Marx, K. 1988. *Economic and Philosophic Manuscripts of 1844*. Amherst, NY: Prometheus.

———. 1990. *Capital: A Critique of Political Economy Volume 1*. London: Penguin Classics.
Maul, D. R. 2007. "The International Labour Organization and the Struggle against Forced Labour from 1919 to the Present." *Labor History* 48(4): 477–500.
Mauss, M. 1997. "Gift, Gift." In *The Logic of the Gift: Toward an Ethic of Generosity*, ed. A Schrift, 28–32. New York: Routledge.
———. (1925) 2016. *The Gift: Expanded Edition*. Chicago: HAU Books.
Mortensen, R. 2000. "Slaving in Australian Courts: Blackbirding Cases, 1869–1871." *Journal of South Pacific Law* 4: 7–37.
Muckle, A. 2015. "Putting Kanak to Work: Kanak and the Colonial Labor System in New Caledonia." *Pacific Studies* 38(3): 345–72.
Munro, D. 1995a. "Revisionism and Its Enemies: Debating the Queensland Labour Trade." *Journal of Pacific History* 30(2): 240–49.
———. 1995b. "The Labor Trade in Melanesians to Queensland: An Historiographic Essay." *Journal of Social History*: 609–27.
O'Higgins, P. 1997. "Labour Is Not a Commodity: An Irish Contribution to International Labour Law." *Industrial Law Journal* 26: 225–34.
Okia, O. 2012. *Communal Labor in Colonial Kenya: The Legitimization of Coercion, 1912–1930*. Basingstoke: Palgrave.
Panoff, M. 1991. "The French Way in Plantation Systems." *Journal of Pacific History* 26(2): 206–12.
Parry, J. 1986. "The Gift, the Indian Gift and the 'Indian Gift.'" *Man* 21: 453–73.
Polanyi, K. (1944) 2001. *The Great Transformation: The Political and Economic Origins of Our Time*. Boston: Beacon Press.
———. (1927) 2018. "On Freedom." In *Economy and Society: Selected Writings*, 15–40. Cambridge: Polity Press.
Price, C. A., and E. Baker. 1976. "Origins of Pacific Island Labourers in Queensland, 1863–1904: A Research Note." *Journal of Pacific History* 11(2): 106–21.
Price, R. 2017. *The Modernization of Rural France: Communications Networks and Agricultural Market Structures in Nineteenth-Century France*. London: Routledge.
Rodman, M. C. 1998. "Creating Historic Sites in Vanuatu." *Social Analysis* 42(3): 117–34.
Rosewarne, S. 2010. "Globalisation and the Commodification of Labour: Temporary Labour Migration." *Economic and Labour Relations Review* 20: 99–110.
Ryan, J. A. 1916. *Distributive Justice: The Right and Wrong of Our Present Distribution of Wealth*. New York: Macmillan.
Saunders, K. 1982. *Workers in Bondage: The Origins and Bases of Unfree Labour in Queensland 1824–1916*. St. Lucia: University of Queensland Press.
Scarr, D. 1967. "Recruits and Recruiters: A Portrait of the Pacific Islands Labour Trade." *Journal of Pacific History* 2(1): 5–24.
Shineberg, D. 1991. "'Noumea No Good. Noumea No Pay': 'New Hebridean' Indentured Labour in New Caledonia, 1865–1925." *The Journal of Pacific History* 26(2): 187–205.
Shlomowitz, R. 1986. "The Fiji Labor Trade in Comparative Perspective, 1864–1914." *Pacific Studies* 9(3): 107–52.

———. 1991. "The Latin American Enganche System: A Comment on Brass." *Slavery & Abolition* 12: 217–24.

Siegel, J. 1985. "Origins of Pacific Islands Labourers in Fiji." *The Journal of Pacific History* 20(1): 42–54.

Smith, R. E. 2015. "The 'Hidden Abodes' of Temporary Migration Programs." *Focaalblog.* https://www.focaalblog.com/2015/11/12/rachel-smith-the-hidden-abodes-of-temporary-migration-programs/ (last accessed 17 November 2019).

———. 2017. "From Colonial Intrusions to 'Intimate Exclusions': Contesting Legal Title and 'Chiefly Title' to Land in Epi, Vanuatu." In *Kastom, Property and Ideology*, ed. S. McDonnell, M. Allen, and C. Filer, 327–55. Canberra: ANU Press.

———. 2019. "Be Our Guest/Worker: Reciprocal Dependency and Expressions of Hospitality in Ni-Vanuatu Overseas Labour Migration." *Journal of the Royal Anthropological Institute* 25(2): 349–67.

Spittler, G. 2009. "Contesting the Great Transformation: Work in Comparative Perspective." In *Market and Society: The Great Transformation Today*, ed. C. Hann and K. Hart, 160–74. Cambridge: Cambridge University Press.

Archival Sources

WPA: Administration: Communal Work. 1940–1953. NHBS 15. Western Pacific Archives. MSS & Archives 2003/1. N File 1/41. Special Collections, University of Auckland Libraries and Learning Services.

2

On the Meanings of Pleasure

Work, Ethics, and Freedom in the Hunza Valley

KATHERINE J. L. MILLER

In much of the tradition of liberal thought, the time for pleasure is after work; pleasure, imagined in terms of consumption (Graeber 2011), is a consequence or reward for work rather than part of the experience of working. Freedom refers both to the terms under which one sells one's labor and to the freedom to select among the many commodities one's wages can purchase for the satisfaction of one's needs and desires. But this view of pleasure has its critics. Adam Smith himself, before laying the groundwork for free-market thinking in *The Wealth of Nations* ([1776] 1976), developed in his *The Theory of Moral Sentiments* ([1761] 2002) a view of pleasure rooted in the sympathy we feel for and receive from others. David Graeber points out that the specific pleasures conjured by most liberal thinkers are solitary ones, suggesting that a theory of value that adequately accounts for the ways in which people actually expend their creative energies would center on sociable pleasures derived from the presence, attention, and sympathy of others (Graeber 2001: 260). In this chapter, I draw on this line of thinking about pleasure as a fundamentally social—a moral—experience to ask how we might think about the pleasures people find in work.

Gerd Spittler (2011) has long argued for a comparative anthropology of work that would complicate rather than replicate dichotomous categorizations such as the contrast, derived from Karl Polanyi, of embedded and disembedded economies. It would do so by attending to the experiential aspects of work, which would not be determined by its location on one side or the other of the "great transformation," nor be reducible to the dynamics of exploitation. Spittler finds in the studies of Richard Thurnwald, from whom Karl Polanyi drew much of his evidence, detailed descriptions of the "different aspects of [work's] performance," which include "knowledge and skill, performance and compulsion, care and accuracy . . . devotion and indifference . . . the intertwining of mental and physical elements, *feelings of pleasure*, but also of tedious and dreary burden" (Spittler 2011: 162; emphasis added). Polanyi himself asserted that classical economic theory was always ideological rather than descriptive of people's real motivations for working, which were in fact "remarkably 'mixed,' not excluding those of duty towards [themselves] and others—and maybe, secretly, even enjoying work for its own sake" (Polanyi 2018: 205).

My ethnographic project, for which I conducted seventeen months of ethnographic fieldwork in 2006–8 in central Hunza, northern Pakistan, was supposed to investigate the moral and ethical stakes of international development for its beneficiaries. In the field, however, I found myself spending relatively little time observing activities that matched my ideas about what counted as development, and a great deal of time participating in activities that seemed like ordinary work—sowing potatoes, harvesting apricots and processing a variety of foodstuffs for later consumption or sale. This work was performed in all of the modalities listed by Spittler: from enjoyment to drudgery, necessity to voluntary care. In the midst of the endless seasonal cycle of tasks that remain the foundations of most people's livelihood, there are moments when enjoyment and pleasure come to the fore and are actively sought out and cultivated.

In a terraced field in the dry cold of early spring, I helped the household with whom I was living to sow potatoes. Stooping repetitively and dragging buckets full of seed potatoes along the furrows, the work itself was hard but the conversation was light and teasing, and the children made a game of racing newly filled buckets to the sowers. Not only the members of the household itself but several of their *sukúyo*, close patrilineal kin, were there to lighten the burden as well as the mood. The young men claimed for themselves a supervisory role, carving out straight furrows between the potato mounds with long sticks, and giving orders for which the women, who were left with the harder, slower tasks, mocked them laughingly. At mid-morning we took a break, leaning companionably on one another for support to drink sweet milky tea from a cloth-wrapped thermos and eat chunks of *phiti* (Bu.[1]), a dense wheat bread. Lunch, enjoyed together in the noisy warmth of the house, was *aloo paratha*, a staple in lowland Pakistan but a rarer treat in the mountains.

Months later, in the full warmth of late summer, my neighbors took me with them to harvest apricots in one of their small orchard plots (U: *bagh*). Before we began work, they directed my attention to the beauties of the place: the pleasant shade, the warm gold of the apricots and the sound of water trickling in the irrigation channels. A young cousin scrambled up the tree while my friend Rubina and her sister-in-law laid out a large tarpaulin underneath; shrieking with glee, the girl used her whole body to shake the branches, sending down a hail of ripe fruit. My companions searched out the best and ripest ones for me, watching me attentively for signs of enjoyment. After we had loaded the tall baskets, Rubina took me to see the grave of her father in a sun-dappled corner of the *bagh*, where she said she often came to remember him and to enjoy the peace of the place.

Another day, as I was walking down the main access road from the village of Altit, I was hailed from the passenger seat of a Suzuki minibus by Naseem Bano, the mother of the family with whom I had sown potatoes. Her normally reserved face was lit by a wide smile. She told me that the family had hired the Suzuki for the day (a major expense) to transport themselves and half a dozen adolescent cousins up to their plot in Duikar, a small hamlet perched atop the cliff above Altit, where the family had six large and very old black walnut trees. It was a big job, and they had decided to make a day of it, packing a "picnic" and calling their relatives to join them. "*Mazaq ho ga*" (it will be fun/enjoyable), Naseem Bano told me, urging me to squeeze in beside her. I declined, regretfully, having scheduled interviews that day. Family members later recounted what a good time they had had climbing into the high branches, staining their fingers black with the walnut skins and taking in the sweeping views from *noor tóq* (summit of light), a promontory overlooking the central valley, with its mix of orderly tilled fields and stark, uncultivated mountainsides.

Moments such as these and countless others in which I participated seemed to call for explanation for two reasons. First, they contrasted sharply with depictions of agricultural labor in oral history narratives I had collected on a brief prior visit to Hunza, in which such labor was depicted as unrelenting toil doubly imposed by necessity and by a coercive state regime. Second, closer to the concerns of the present day, both the pleasure and the moral value people found in this kind of quotidian, repetitive and necessary work fit awkwardly alongside ubiquitous narratives of development, in which the goal of social and economic transformation is to make as much work as possible resemble that performed by salaried professionals who ride around the terrain in Land Cruisers.

Livelihoods in Hunza remain centered around intensive agriculture, supplemented by transhumant pastoralism. Hunza lies within a region, Gilgit-Baltistan, that is understood by both residents and outsiders as remote in contrast to the urban centers of lowland Pakistan (Hussein 2015), where much of the produce grown in Hunza is sold and to where many people now migrate. Opportunities for wage work exist in the valley, but are scarce compared to the number of young people seeking them. Partial integration into Pakistan's economy has, over the past fifty years, profoundly changed the way people live and work, but there are notable continuities. In the face of economic pressures and aspirations, households struggle to remain "sites of integration" for a range of economic activities (Gagné 2018: 29), strategically mobilizing the capacities of their members along with networks of extended kin to take advantage of new opportunities, while still maintaining their livelihood and meeting the moral obligations central to village life. These obligations consist principally of collective work and mutual assistance.

One of Spittler's central claims is that the subjective experience of work is not a straightforward reflection of the political economic conditions under which it takes place. My ethnographic material bears this out, but I argue in this chapter that the kind of ethnographic study of work proposed by Spittler *can* tell us something about the way that individuals and communities register broad historical and economic shifts, and about the ethical possibilities that arise. The particular qualities (of both people and collectivities) and experiences cultivated and highlighted in the performance of work depend, in a variety of nondeterminative ways, on the historical moment in which it takes place. In Hunza, a particular kind of attunement to pleasure and enjoyment was an essential practice in constituting work as a "terrain of ethics" (Pandian 2008). These experiences underscore and help to render ethically significant the specific forms of freedom afforded by—and recognized within (see Rajković, this volume)—the organization and wider sociopolitical conditions of work at one moment in time and space. By juxtaposing these experiences with explicit discourses on that history, including the discourse of development, I suggest that we can also see how emotional and bodily experience can themselves be a form of ethical reflexivity.

Transformations of Collective Work in Hunza

In order to contextualize the ethical significance attached to agricultural and household work at the time of my fieldwork it is necessary to provide some historical background. The recent history of Hunza is often narrated as a story of the sudden arrival and rapid uptake of development, beginning with the Aga Khan Rural Support Programme (AKRSP). This followed a series of momentous changes during the half-decade from 1974 to 1982. Prior to 1974, Hunza was one of numerous princely states in the mountainous northern frontier regions of Pakistan. The ruling dynasty retained local sovereignty under British rule (1891–1947), a state of affairs that continued for several decades after the region's incorporation into newly independent Pakistan.

Historians disagree about the age and origins of the Hunza state. The first scholarly account interpreted its rise and consolidation as an instance of Wittfogel's hydraulic hypothesis, according to which state power rests on control over water resources; rule was tied to the ability to marshal the labor required to maintain the extensive system of water channels necessary for agriculture (Sidky 1996). Local oral histories support the notion that the ability to command corvée labor (called *rajaáki*) was central to the state's power and its relationship to its subjects (Holzwarth 2006). Some, however, have questioned whether the princely state was an autochthonous development; its transformation from a relatively weak offshoot of a neighboring dynasty into a genuine state has been attributed to the successful "route politics" of the eighteenth- and nineteenth-century Mirs (Stellrecht 2006). The Mirs used their strategic position along important trade routes between South and Central Asia to establish tributary relationships with distant lowland empires, which allowed them in turn to consolidate power internally. Prior to around 1800, the clans (Bu: *rom*) of each village likely retained considerable autonomy in matters of water management, collective labor, land rights, and dispute resolution (Holzwarth 2006). Following the incorporation of Hunza into the British Empire in 1891, it is likely that taxation and demands for corvée labor intensified cruelly, as elsewhere under Dogra rule (Gagné 2018: 34–35). Memories of deprivation and suffering were still vivid in 2000. Hunza men began to migrate in large numbers, often to serve in the army. The Mirs of Hunza did their best to stem the flow and retain control of the population; according to local memory, manned guard towers were erected to survey the main routes in and out of the valley.

In the 1960s and early 1970s, Prime Minister Zulfikar Ali Bhutto enacted reforms abolishing the princely states and instituting direct administrative rule from Islamabad, with limited local representation. After the Hunza state was dissolved in 1974, villages remained largely self-governing. Clan elders and village leaders (Bu: *trangfa*; U: *lambardar*) coordinated the collective work required to maintain village infrastructure. In the mid-1970s, work began on the construction of the Chinese-funded Karakoram Highway (KKH), a 1,300-kilometer paved road linking Kashgar to Abbotabad, and serving as a conduit for Chinese goods to Pakistan's Indian Ocean ports. Officially opened in 1978, the highway runs the length of the Hunza Valley.[2] In addition to radically expanding the range of manufactured goods available in Hunza, the KKH has allowed for greater contact with "downcountry" Pakistan, facilitating labor migration and travel for education, and enabling a transition to cash-cropping accompanied by increasing reliance on imported food. Many inhabitants now rely on government-subsidized wheat flour, while potatoes are grown in the terraced fields and sold to middlemen for transport to markets in urban Pakistan.

International development efforts in Hunza began with the founding of AKRSP in 1982. AKRSP is one of a number of NGOs making up the Aga Khan Development Network (AKDN), which is active across South and Central Asia and in parts of East Africa. Although avowedly secular, the AKDN was the creation of the 48th and 49th Imams of the Nizari Isma'ili branch of Islam, known to the world as the Aga Khans. The majority of Hunza's people are Isma'ili, and the AKDN institutions enjoy a privileged status there. These NGOs were born out of efforts begun in the nineteenth century by the first Aga Khan to consolidate the Imam's spiritual leadership over widely scattered Isma'ili populations. This involved the creation of parallel bureaucracies aimed at modernizing the poorer and more remote communities along with the Imamate itself (Steinberg 2011). The first community welfare organizations in Hunza were the Diamond Jubilee schools founded 1946–1950. Since 1957, the present Aga Khan has broadened the scope of his predecessors' vision and refashioned these organizations in conformity with the post–World War II model of international development. AKRSP's distinctive model of rural community development reflects the marriage of emerging trends in development theory, such as participation and sustainability, with what were understood to be local forms of village democracy. Although AKRSP was a less visible presence in Hunza during my 2006–8 fieldwork, its model for securing local participation in development, building on indigenous traditions of collective labor augmented by Isma'ili ideals of voluntary service, had left a mark on the way Hunza people engaged in development, as well as on the ethical significance of the most ordinary acts of daily household work.

As a response to competing imperatives to let local communities shape development while acting as a "catalyst" and contributing technical expertise and experience (Wood 2006), AKRSP required participating villages to form representative bodies through which to agree on and articulate their development needs. Village Organizations (VOs) and Women's Organizations (WOs) were to include members from at least 75 percent of households as a condition of AKRSP's assistance. AKRSP would then help the VOs in establishing a savings program, with AKRSP acting as banker. The pedagogical or, in the language of development, "capacity-building" functions of these savings programs were a significant part of their rationale. In addition to the savings program, AKRSP inaugurated its relationship with each new VO by providing monetary and technical support for a physical infrastructure project chosen by the VO. These commonly took the form of extending water channels to bring more land under cultivation, constructing link roads and bridges to connect villages with the KKH, and, later, the construction of micro-hydroelectric plants (*microhydels*) to harness the power of fast-moving glacial streams (U: *nallah*) for village electrification.

The emphasis on capacity building and on the VOs and WOs as a mode of governance reflected the frequent portrayal of the political situation in Hunza in the 1980s as a "leadership vacuum" (Wood 2006: 41). The dissolution of the princely state in 1974, together with the lack of interest on the part of the state of Pakistan in taking up a substantive role in regional governance, opened up gaps in both inter- and intra-village political life. From its early days, AKRSP saw its projects as not only meeting economic needs but also supplying new forms of leadership. While AKRSP's interventions were framed as filling a vacuum, the developmentalist rhetoric obscured the political and historical dimensions of the conditions they were to ameliorate. In the eyes of many Hunzakuts, the rule of the Mirs was not a source of lost order and stability but the root cause of the scarcity and inefficiency underpinning the rationale for development. Lingering effects of high taxation under the princely state included spring famines that continued into the 1980s (Allan 1990). Allan also argues that corvée labor obligations inhibited villagers from undertaking innovative agricultural projects of their own. At the time of my research, Hunzakuts still recalled *rajaáki* as the most oppressive and burdensome aspect of princely rule. Younger people repeated stories heard from their elders about how people were reduced to eating grass like cattle, and how they bound wide strips of cloth around their waists to stifle the pangs of hunger while they labored in the Mirs' fields.

These details were often woven into a larger account of the recent history of Hunza that depicted the tumultuous period of the late twentieth century as a movement from "darkness to light." The phrase seemed to underscore the temporal logic of development itself: the unilinear, teleological structure of progressive time upon which liberal conceptions of development rely (Ferguson 1999). The focus on capacity-building was influenced by a set of negative assumptions about what held rural populations back. Empowering people to develop themselves meant giving them the knowledge and the tools to work for development. To what end they would engage in development hardly needed stating; the logical result of freeing people from scarcity and ignorance was greater market participation.

Among ordinary Hunzakuts, by contrast, the narrative has clear political and moral dimensions. In their memories of the past, it is not the absence of material wealth or capacity that made their lives so difficult and painful, but violent coercion by a regime that forcibly coopted their labor for its own ends, depriving them of the ability to work toward their own needs. Their narratives describe the transition from oppression to a form of freedom. While many have embraced the possibilities of market participation, one of the most ethically significant exemplifications of this freedom lies in the voluntary gift of labor toward, among other ends, development projects.

By ethically significant, I refer to actions or states of being that are recognized as relevant and available for ethical evaluation (Laidlaw 2014: 3). What makes a particular way of enacting freedom ethically significant? Numerous scholars have presented accounts of freedom as a condition of ethics and, in particular, of the relationship of freedom to moral norms and obligations (Laidlaw 2002, 2014; Mahmood 2005; Robbins 2007; Zigon 2007; Keane 2014, 2016). Laidlaw makes the strongest case that ethics cannot be conceived without freedom, echoing Foucault's definition of ethics as 'the conscious (*réfléchie*) practice of freedom' (Foucault [1984] 2000: 284; cited in Laidlaw 2002: 324). Others, including myself, have argued that an anthropological view of ethics should be centered on the interplay between freedom and its social and cultural conditions, including our relations with others and with moral norms, rules, and obligations (Keane 2014; Miller and Lukes 2020). Polanyi thought of freedom similarly as "based on the real relation of men to men," that is, arising from "the responsibility we bear for our part in mutual human relationships" (Polanyi [1927] 2018: 22). This freedom consists in the "duty one assigns oneself; . . . not a form of releasing oneself from society but the fundamental form of social connectedness" (ibid.).

Freedom must be understood not solely in opposition to the constraints imposed by other people and by moral systems, but as emerging from them; as "inseparable from the ways in which people define situations and describe actions, in a scene of interaction with one another" (Keane 2014: 451). This allows us to ask what particular ways of enacting freedom have an ethical dimension in a given sociocultural context—that is, to explore how they relate to our responsibilities to others and to moral norms. Work is a key domain because through its performance (to say nothing of centuries of theorizing), questions of freedom and domination surface so insistently. Par excellence, work is a form of activity in which we produce and reproduce ourselves, other people, and the material and social world around us.

Both ways of narrating recent history that I summarized above have a form of freedom as their telos, but in the local narratives, freedom is not merely an absence of constraint. In these narratives, people in the present were now freed from coercive obligations of *corvée* to rulers. Equally important was what they were free *to* do: to live up to moral norms governing interpersonal relations, and to work for the shaping of a collective future. As I came to learn, there are both continuities and ruptures with the past in the way that Hunza people narrate and enact this freedom.

Freedom and Volunteerism

Another component of AKRSP's strategy that has had a deep impact on the way development and the ethical dimensions of work have been understood and experienced in Hunza is the practice of requiring communities to provide the non-technical labor for projects they undertake. The original VOs were charged with mobilizing this labor on an equitable basis, contracting with the NGO as to who would provide what. By the mid-2000s such written contracts had become the standard way of inaugurating any development project (or phase of a project) jointly undertaken by a village (or neighborhood) and any development organization or donor.

In securing manual labor from the community in exchange for its technical and monetary assistance, AKRSP drew directly on the practices of mobilizing and organizing collective labor previously employed by the princely state (and possibly by earlier forms of polity). To some extent this was acknowledged. Masood Khan, a senior AKCSP consultant in heritage preservation, used the term *rajaáki* to describe community contributions of labor toward architectural restoration projects in the 1990s, glossing it as "voluntary unskilled labor," without further comment (Khan 2006: 317). The usage of the term *rajaáki* for contemporary practices was not confined to written reports. I first heard it used in the context of a conversation between a village elder and the young female secretary of the Altit Town Management Society (a body formed, in the spirit of the largely defunct VOs, to coordinate between the village and outside agencies) over the coordination of "volunteers" and materials for the construction of a new building to house a library, tea shop and ticket-*ghar* (ticket house) for visitors, a project jointly undertaken by the ATMS and Aga Khan Cultural Services Pakistan. In general, continuities with the past are framed by the AKDN institutions in terms of a vague "tradition" and references to "local skills and knowledge" rather than specific invocation of the rule of the Mirs; however, they often referred to elements (such as built heritage) associated with the Mirs and their rule rather than to the lives of ordinary Hunzakuts (on colonial and postcolonial framings of communal labor as "customary" and "voluntary," see Smith, this volume). And though I could not help but hear a note of irony in the use of the term under the new regime of development, I did not find evidence that my interlocutors intended it.

The use of local village labor for development, particularly for infrastructure projects such as road-building or *microhydel* construction, was not only a cost-saving measure for AKRSP; it was an essential component of its policy-driven mandate to secure the participation of its constituent communities. "Participation" has been a key concept in development policy since the mid-1980s (Mosse 2004). AKRSP was a widely studied and much-emulated exemplar. Others (Mosse 2004; Li 2007) have described how participation confers legitimacy on development regimes by supporting their claims to be responsive to the interests and needs of target populations. As the trend toward participation as a metric for development projects grew, it was linked to other important concepts signifying the values of responsibility and self-governance central to neoliberal frameworks (Settle 2011).

While expert discourse foregrounds familiar neoliberal logics of responsibilization, by making participation in development via collective obligations of work central to the promise of improvement, the AKDN has contributed to making work in general a distinctly vibrant ethical domain. Work, not only in the context of development projects but in a variety of forms, is an activity in which the moral character of both individual subjects and the community at large are at stake. This is not to say that work had no ethical significance in the past – no doubt it was always an important site of formation of ethical selves, and of relationships among individuals and households. But by the 2000s the question of freedom, in the guise of voluntarism, was central to the way that work and its ethical qualities were understood. The transformation of *rajaáki* from corvée to "voluntary collective labor" is illustrative not only of the depoliticization that development so often effects but also of the ubiquity of volunteerism as a framework for understanding and organizing work in Hunza. Across the various of practices of work described in this chapter, obligation and freedom are mixed in varying proportions, often under the label of volunteerism.

The collective work of maintaining common features of the village fabric and its wider infrastructure, including the water channels, involves clearly defined obligations on the part of each household and clan (*rom*) to the village (cf. Smith, this volume). Elders of each *rom* and *kuti* (sublineage) allocate responsibility among their constituent households, based on the number of able-bodied members. There are penalties for failing to contribute.[3] While the obligation was perceived as a binding one, however, it appeared that households had some leeway in deciding when and how to fulfill their obligations.

Given the complex mixture of economic strategies that most households employed, and the frequency with which people, particularly young men, came and went from the valley, this flexibility of collective labor obligations was important. Households like that of Ghulam Hussein and Naseem Bano, who had six unmarried children and were well-off by Hunza standards due to Ghulam Hussein's lucrative career downcountry, could meet their obligations without undue hardship. By mobilizing their comparative wealth and the capacities of their large household in a complex division of labor—purchasing land in Gilgit as an investment, sponsoring their eldest son in a variety of entrepreneurial ventures, and sending three middle children for higher education while holding the youngest daughter back to assist with household tasks—they were largely able to secure their standing in the village while also pursuing income-generating opportunities. Others, like Marina and Manaf, an aging couple who were supporting their two children at downcountry universities, had a harder time. Out-migration simultaneously sustains Hunza's moral economy and leaves those who remain behind to shoulder the burden of maintaining it. The burden, furthermore, is distributed unequally by age, gender, and by growing inequalities of wealth and status. However, while the additional work requirements of village-level collective labor sometimes arose during times when capacities were already stretched, overall people did not appear to find them excessive, especially by comparison to the work of maintaining a household.

If not without its costs, *rajaáki* is understood as a collective endeavor arising from institutions of village self-governance that are generally perceived as legitimate, rather than a duty imposed from above and outside, as in the time of the Mirs. Although the authority of AKDN organizations and the VOs to call on collective labor was often contested through the 2000s, there remained the sense that development constituted a common good, in the name of which such claims could be made. Not all entities were understood to have the standing to call on collective labor; when the Pakistani state insisted that villagers contribute labor for a long-anticipated project to widen and pave the link road connecting Altit to the Karakoram Highway, there was widespread cynicism. My interlocutors insisted that it was the government's responsibility to provide this kind of infrastructure, and that it had the money to pay for the work. The state could be expected to provide such largesse, even to its most marginal citizens, but it lacked the moral legitimacy in villagers' eyes to call on their voluntary labor.

The question of legitimacy is lent an additional dimension by the fact that another form of voluntary work, the Isma'ili duty of voluntary service, or *khidmat*, is central to religious life in the valley. *Khidmat* encompasses everything from individual acts of charity, to making food for the *jummah* (Friday congregational prayer), to teaching religious education classes. Children begin performing *khidmat* early—for instance, minding the shoes of the congregation during prayer. The present Aga Khan articulated his vision of the ethic of service in a 1960 speech: "Islam means not only faith but it means work, it means creating the world in which you can practice your faith to the best of your ability" (quoted in Susumu 2000: 156). Along with the tithes that believers pay to their Imam, *khidmat* can be considered as a "gift to God" (Gregory 1980) by which Isma'ilis repay the unrepayable gift of creation through service to their fellow humans. Modern Isma'ili thought emphasizes the inextricability and complementarity of *din* and *dunya,* religion and the world, resulting in a "strikingly positive evaluation of the potential of the material and the human world" (Bocock 1971: 372). Some of the practices most strictly enjoined on Muslims in other traditions, including observance of a literal fast during Ramadan, are not required for Ismailis, while the duty of service is arguably the most important religious practice in Hunza.

Engaging in *khidmat* is categorically distinct from working for the village or on development projects, and possesses its own moral logic. At the same time, the practices and the infrastructure through which they are organized do overlap: the loudspeaker of the *jamaat khana* (Isma'ili house of worship) was used to broadcast calls for volunteers that might involve construction of the library or rebuilding the old *ghusulkhana* (the structure within the *jamaat khana* grounds where corpses are prepared for burial). Participation in development itself is understood as an expression of religious devotion and identity (cf. participation in Saint Anne's fair in the Andes—see Angé, this volume). Both the religious and the profane forms of work are in some sense collective, inasmuch as they are not undertaken alone or on one's own behalf. The voluntary nature of *khidmat* is if anything more strongly emphasized than that of development-oriented collective work. In fact, the English words "volunteering" and "volunteer" are more frequently used to refer to the activity itself. There is no material sanction for failing to engage in *khidmat,* but one's performance of this religious service is a source of social approbation and moral evaluation.

Although both the nature of the obligation and, by relation, the degree of voluntarism involved in these distinct categories of work vary, volunteerism constitutes a prominent local model of ethical freedom. By this I mean that it includes not only a particular negative vision of freedom (Berlin 1969), of what it is that people should be free from, but also a sense of what that freedom is for, or of what might count as an exercise of that freedom. As I have argued elsewhere, "all actually existing conceptions of freedom include both a particular understanding of the acting subject and some notion of what it is that the subject must be free to do; this helps us to see how any ethnographically describable ethical project is conceived in relation to a particular set of available or imaginable alternatives, from which other possibilities are excluded" (Miller and Lukes 2020: 12–13). Another way to think about this is that particular ways of exercising freedom are only recognizable as such according to particular "*protocol[s] of recognition* of freedom and resistance" (Grewal 2013: 226; emphasis in original). These protocols establish "not only what can be perceived but how perceived things are to be understood and categorized" (ibid.). Volunteerism is a local category of action that can be recognized as both free and ethically significant because it relates to the treatment of others and to moral norms.

Volunteering as Virtue

Voluntarism, then, is the freedom to fulfill one's obligations to others and to the collectivity in whose name one is summoned to work. One way in which people highlight the presence of freedom against a backdrop of obligation is by the manner and spirit in which they undertake their voluntary work. To work willingly and with a light heart when the need arises marks certain people as being of good character (Bu.: *shuasís*) and also, for young people, as potential future leaders of the village (Bu.: *uyunkosís*). When the call goes out for volunteers to help in some collective task, they do not shirk but go of their own accord, readily exceeding their mere obligation. Young men who have paid jobs or are in school full-time are generally excused from criticism on this basis (less so girls, who may be called *gutas* [lazy]); but those who do not engage in volunteering or collective labor willingly, and who perform no other work that might excuse them but instead hang around the public spaces of the village and affect an urban style and concomitant disdain for physical labor, are derided as "loafers" or worse, *badmaash* (U.: miscreant or lowlife).[4]

People frequently lamented what they saw as growing selfishness and a loss of cooperation and closeness among villagers (see similar discourse in Smith, this volume). People often told me that the influence of modern concerns with money, possessions, and status was undermining the love people had for one another in the past and leading them to turn their backs on the close-knit life of the village. This was a favorite theme of my friend Rubina, who said that the hardships of the past brought people together, while people today preferred to sit in their own homes watching television. At the same time, the willingness of Hunzakuts to engage in voluntary work was often mentioned to outsiders like myself as evidence of the fundamentally "cooperative" nature of Hunza people and their culture, especially as compared with neighboring groups. Against the perception of growing atomization and the fraying of social bonds, those who were seen as maintaining the spirit of cooperation and care for others were noticed.

Who labors willingly—exceeding specific obligations and even taking enjoyment in the tasks—and who shirks are matters of public knowledge and discussion (see Mayblin 2010: 34). One young man who was known to have a willing heart when it came to helping others was Safdar, a nephew by marriage of Naseem Bano, who had been fostered by the Hussein family after his mother's death. While women are generally enthusiastic about the forms of work described in this chapter, the attitudes and commitments of men (particularly young men) are more varied. Safdar's reputation in this respect was notable. One day I visited their home, finding only Naseem Bano at home. Explaining the rest of the family's whereabouts, she noted that Safdar had gone to help with the building project undertaken by the Town Management Society mentioned earlier. "*Safdar but shua*" (Safdar is very good/lovely), she said proudly, adding that everyone in the village liked him because he was always ready to help when needed, even without being asked. Moreover, as he did so he was always smiling. Even in the midst of fulfilling their most morally significant obligations, then, freedom is recognized in excess—in going beyond what is expected or required—and in the worker's affectively communicated experience of enjoyment, care, and willingness.

Work and Love

If pleasure surfaces fleetingly in these contexts of organized and obligatory collective labor as a sign of the particular virtue of individuals or of the moral state of the community as whole, it is actively cultivated in the domain of household work. In this section, I turn to the kinds of everyday agricultural work undertaken by households primarily to produce food for their own subsistence and for the market, as illustrated in the three vignettes at the beginning of this chapter. This kind of work is not conceived of as collective: people, primarily adult men, own their fields, orchards, and animals; and the responsibility of working them lies with the household. Unlike the forms of work undertaken within a framework of obligation to the collectivity or to God, this involves a degree of choice about when and whom to help.

Mutual aid is most important at peak periods in the agrarian cycle, notably sowing and harvesting, when completion of a pressing task requires more work than household members can perform alone. Very little of this work is mechanized: a few households in Altit owned tractors that were used to plow the larger and more accessible fields. Inconstant electricity meant few opportunities to streamline the processing of foodstuffs. The relationships created and sustained through this kind of routine work are characterized by mutual affection (U.: *mohabat*). They can take the form of long-term attachments between households, between a single person and another household, or between individuals. The verb *amántse* (Bu.) denotes helping others in the form of ideally mutual but importantly voluntary gifts of labor. I once sought to test my hypothesis that people exchanged acts of helping reciprocally by asking a group of young women who came to me for conversational English practice (and who made an ideal focus-group) whether this was the case. As Mauss might have predicted, my interlocutors downplayed the reciprocal character of the gift, insisting that while two households might indeed help one another in turn, it was not to cancel a debt created by some prior act of assistance, but out of love (U.: *mohabat*). Furthermore, they agreed that a household in need would not have to call, but that those close to them would "just know" when help was needed and would come.

The prototypical figure toward whom such voluntary, affectionate and mutual help is directed is the neighbor (Bu.: *hamál*; U.: *hamsaya*, "one who shares the same shade"). Hunza villagers owe specific obligations of care and assistance to close kin (particularly close patrilateral kin or *sukúyo*, a smaller group within the *rom* encompassing approximately three generations of descendants from a male ancestor). Births, marriages, and deaths activate powerful obligations among *sukúyo*. On ordinary occasions too, people are most likely to exchange help with their closest kin, but patterns varied widely among the households I knew best.

Neighbors, by contrast, are those to whom one is free to form bonds based on personal inclination and unconstrained affection (cf. Awal, this volume). This resonates with the account of Bedouin hospitality given by Andrew Shryock (2008), who, drawing on Derrida and Kant, argues that the "exemplary, moralizing power" of hospitality lies in its "idealized or impossible" location outside the present, in excess of established obligation or expectation, and as an exception to any pre-given rule. In exemplary Bedouin narratives, the paradigmatic recipient of hospitality is the stranger, toward whom a kind of excessive, because wholly voluntary, generosity is possible.

Historical patterns of residence reflecting the scarcity of land suitable for dwelling or cultivation mean that spatial proximity is not tightly correlated with genealogical distance. The village of Altit consists of a densely packed core of structures build against one another (Bu: *khun*), surrounded by a more loosely clustered set of dwellings (the result of a recent boom of new construction spreading into agricultural land), and ringed by fields with orchards at the margins. People whose houses share a wall may therefore be members of the same or a different *rom*, and a neighbor can be anyone who lives in the same loosely defined quarter. In fact, however, those categorized as neighbors may turn out to be more distant patrilineal relatives or maternal kin, as well as people with whom no kinship tie is acknowledged.

Recognizing or declining to recognize a kinship tie is less an indication of their actual genealogical relationship than a way to highlight the dimension of choice in the relationship. Likewise, foregrounding sensory and sociable pleasures of work calls attention to the volition of the act, emerging as it does out of the tangle of obligations, responsibilities, and affective ties that enable it.[5] It sometimes suits people to emphasize the free and affectionate character of the work they do even for their closest kin. For the same reason, they may downplay the importance of close kin as the source of assistance and care, and instead valorize mutual assistance within relationships rhetorically constructed as between non-kin. While *amántse* involves its own normative expectations and judgments, its ethical significance lies in its framing as a choice motivated by love in contrast to the obligatory aspects of kinship relations. People give significant moral weight to the proper performance of their duties to close kin, but it is the distance from mere duty that distinguishes the performative freedom of *amantsé*. This distinction reverberates beyond mundane matters of household economy. I have argued elsewhere that the contrast between assistance owed to kin and freely given to neighbors serves as a local model of the relationship between moral obligation and ethical freedom operating at other scales (Miller and Lukes 2020).

The contrast between the duty to care for kin and the virtue of caring for others finds support in Islamic ethical thought. More than one of my interlocutors referenced a Burushaski proverb that echoes a verse from the Qur'an: "*háale garí néspal, majítulo sénáan*" (first light the house and then the *masjid*). The verb 'to light' connotes care in the sense of providing for others, and the *masjid* (mosque) stands for the community at large. The expression urges people to think first of their own household before attending to the needs of others. Paradoxically, when I heard this injunction in reference to people overzealous in volunteering, the context seemed to confirm the seductive appeal of laboring beyond one's strict obligations, in that the speaker was reminding his hypothetical listeners to look to their own hearths first.

The spatial organization of the village shapes the sociable dimension of work and its pleasures. The fields belonging to a single household are not contiguous, so two separate work parties in adjacent fields may call out to one another and to passers-by in greeting, to flirt or to exchange gossip. In summer, the rooftops of the *khun* present an even more convivial space where household members, neighbors, and kin sit together to talk and sing while splitting apricots for drying and other tasks. This was where Rubina would tell me her stories about the past or patiently help me transcribe the lyrics of Burushaski love songs. Others stopped by to join in the lesson or share a bowl of fresh cherries. Rubina would also fetch me some evenings to walk with her to her family's animal enclosure on the outskirts of the village to milk their cow. On these occasions we could talk without being overheard, and it was from her that I learned that such places are the preferred meeting spots for illicit lovers. Located around the margins of the village, they are also liminal spaces between human habitation and the abode of various non-human beings. Finally, the *bagh* is a place of beauty as well as the source of some of their most highly prized foods (stone fruits, chiefly apricots, are the prototypical "simple" foods considered healthy and sustaining of a virtuous body). As the story of the Suzuki minibus at the beginning of this chapter suggests, work in the *bagh* can occasionally blend into newer practices of picnicking and touring that have begun to be adopted from tourists and from television programs aimed at Pakistan's urban elite.[6] Such practices are sometimes seen as congruent but sometimes as incongruent with local notions of the good life.

Pleasures associated with consumption—from travel and tourism to spicy, oily downcountry foods and the self-making possibilities of style—were increasingly accessible, and were subject to ambivalent desires and contested moral evaluation. Countering the lure of these new forms of enjoyment and of freedom was a discourse celebrating the "simple" life of the village and its pleasures of wholesome food and natural beauty, as well as of love and work. By a variety of gestures—preparing special food to be enjoyed by the work party, attending to one another's emotional states and bodily sensations, noticing the aesthetic qualities of places, joking, singing, and telling stories—work is made into a site where people performatively enact a kind of freedom. It is not the freedom of a satellite television program, a life full of commodities, or a life unburdened by toil; and nor is it a "freedom of duty and responsibility" (Polanyi 2018: 22) that an interlocutor once envisioned in a harried moment, declaring that she would move to the city where no one knew her. It is, rather, the kind of freedom that cannot be disentangled from a fundamental condition of social relatedness and obligation, but surfaces at moments within it.

Conclusion

A densely layered series of events, institutions, and discourses combined to shape ordinary work as a "terrain of ethics" (Pandian 2008) in Hunza in the 2000s. Memories of past scarcity and oppression lingered, reminders of darkness overcome, but also spurs to nostalgic longing for a prior warmth and closeness. Development organizations, drawing on older practices of collective labor, had substituted contract for *corvée* and infused traditional forms of work with a future-oriented sense of purpose, while the fusion of religious and development logics in the AKDN made engagement with such practices a form of devotion. Isma'ili ideals of service and local notions of kinship and neighborliness shaped relations in the village with their distinct but overlapping logics of reciprocity. Intensified participation in the market offered a range of new possibilities for work as well as new challenges to existing patterns, not to mention new forms of mobility and ideals of autonomy. New pleasures linked to consumption threatened to distract from the more austere and unpredictable joys of mountain life.

In Hunza, development offers a readily available language in which to narrate experiences of recent history and to envision possible futures. I argue that emotional and embodied experiences constitute an alternative modality in which people register and realize the possibilities of freedom in their ethical lives, and that pleasure is such an experience. My argument is not that the primary experience of work in this context was one of pleasure. It is that there were moments when people not only experienced but sought out and elaborated the pleasure they found in ordinary acts of work, and that these were a crucial part of the "moral experience" (Rasanayagam 2010) of life there. These moments indexed the presence of a form of "social freedom" in Polanyi's sense.

If the realization of a certain form of freedom through the experience of work was in part a reflection of the historical moment in which I conducted my fieldwork, this has led me to wonder how subsequent events have changed people's experiences and aspirations. Since then, a generation has grown up with expectations shaped by development promises; the memories of their parents and grandparents are no doubt more distant and abstract for them. Since 2008 the region has become more entangled with the state due to a series of reforms in 2009 that promised (and largely failed to deliver) greater political inclusion, as well as the 2010 landslide that activated the bureaucracy of disaster relief (Sökefeld 2020). These entanglements, which have kindled demands for the rights and entitlements of full citizenship and provoked frustrating and often violent responses from the state (Ali 2019), will surely reconfigure the forms of belonging and authority that I have described. Ongoing migration, shifting Pakistan–China relations, and reverberations from the 2010 disaster are no doubt changing the delicate calculus by which the households I knew maintained their footing. I often wonder what possibilities they are finding in these changing configurations.

Acknowledgments

I would like to thank Chris Hann, Zirwat Chowdhury, and two anonymous reviewers for their generosity in reading and commenting on this chapter. Gratitude is also owed to the individuals from Hunza mentioned in this chapter, who shared their work with me.

Katherine J. L. Miller obtained her PhD in cultural anthropology in 2015 from the University of California, San Diego. She is currently visiting assistant professor in the Department of Anthropology at Western Oregon University.

Notes

1. Burushaski is the primary language spoken in central Hunza. Urdu is taught in schools and spoken by all but the oldest generation. Terms in Burushaski will be marked Bu.; U. will denote words in Urdu.
2. In 2010, a catastrophic landslide occurred above the village of Attabad, killing twenty people and blocking the Hunza River. A lake formed above the blockage, submerging several villages in Upper Hunza and a lengthy section of the KKH (Sökefeld 2012). Several villages remain flooded and their residents displaced, but a massive "realignment" project, including the construction of five tunnels, restored transit along the highway in 2015.
3. I was told that monetary fines are more often threatened than enforced, but in one extreme case a man was said to have had his property appropriated by his *rom* as punishment for long-term shirking. More often, sanctions are social and reputational.
4. From Persian and Arabic roots meaning "bad" and "occupation."
5. I see a link here to Angé's analysis (this volume), in which the aesthetic and gustatory pleasures of the *miniaturas* made for the festival of St. Anne play a role in the circulation of ethically—and materially—productive qualities through the social body.
6. While leisure is not a meaningful way of categorizing either time or activity in Hunza, such practices connect to cosmopolitan aspirations and to deeply felt aesthetic sensibilities for the landscape.

References

Ali, Nosheen. 2019. *Delusional States: Feeling Rule and Development in Pakistan's Northern Frontier*. Cambridge: Cambridge University Press.

Allan, Nigel J. R. 1990. "Household Food Supply in Hunza Valley, Pakistan." *Geographical Review* 80(4): 399–415.

Berlin, Isaiah. 1969. "Two Concepts of Liberty." In *Four Essays on Liberty*, 118–72. London: Oxford University Press.

Bocock, Robert T. 1971. "The Ismailis in Tanzania: A Weberian Analysis." *The British Journal of Sociology* 22(4): 365–80.

Ferguson, James. 1999. *Expectations of Modernity: Myths and Meanings of Urban Life on the Zambian Copperbelt*. Berkeley: University of California Press.

Gagné, Karine. 2018. *Caring for Glaciers: Land, Animals and Humanity in the Himalayas*. Seattle: University of Washington Press.

Graeber, David. 2001. *Toward an Anthropological Theory of Value: The False Coin of Our Own Dreams*. New York: Palgrave.

———. 2011. "Consumption." *Current Anthropology*: 52(4): 489–511.
Gregory, Chris A. 1980. "Gifts to Men and Gifts to God: Gift Exchange and Capital Accumulation in Contemporary Papua." *Man* 15(4): 626–52.
Grewal, Zareena. 2013. *Islam is a Foreign Country: American Muslims and the Global Crisis of Authority*. New York: New York University Press.
Holzwarth, Wolfgang. 2006. "Sources of Gilgit, Hunza and Nager History (15001800) and Comments on the Oral Roots of Local Historiography." In *Karakoram in Transition: Culture, Development and Ecology in the Hunza Valley*, ed. H. Kreutzmann, 171–90. Oxford: Oxford University Press.
Hussein, Shafqat. 2015. *Remoteness and Modernity: Transformation and Continuity in Northern Pakistan*. New Haven, CT: Yale University Press.
Keane, Webb. 2014. "Freedom, Reflexivity, and the Sheer Everydayness of Ethics." *HAU: Journal of Ethnographic Theory* 4(1): 443–57.
———. 2016. *Ethical Life: Its Natural and Social Histories*. Princeton, NJ: Princeton University Press.
Khan, Masood A. 2006. "Conceptual Planning in the Karakoram: The Built Heritage and the Dynamics of Institution Building." In *Karakoram in Transition: Culture, Development and Ecology in the Hunza Valley*, ed. H. Kreutzmann, 329–58. Oxford: Oxford University Press.
Laidlaw, James. 2002. "For an Anthropology of Ethics and Freedom." *Journal of the Royal Anthropological Institute* 8: 311–32.
———. 2014. *The Subject of Virtue: An Anthropology of Ethics and Freedom*. Cambridge: Cambridge University Press.
Li, Tania Murray. 2007. *The Will to Improve: Governmentality, Development, and the Practice of Politics*. Durham, NC: Duke University Press.
Mahmood, Saba. 2005. *Politics of Piety: The Islamic Revival and the Feminist Subject*. Princeton, NJ: Princeton University Press.
Mayblin, Maya. 2010. *Gender, Catholicism, and Morality in Brazil: Virtuous Husbands, Powerful Wives*. New York: Palgrave Macmillan.
Miller, Katherine J. L., and Steven Lukes. 2020. "The Other Side of Freedom: On the Sociality of Ethics." *Anthropological Theory* 20(4): 414–37.
Mosse, David. 2004. *Cultivating Development: An Ethnography of Aid Policy and Practice*. London: Pluto Press.
Pandian, Anand. 2008. "Devoted to Development: Moral Progress, Ethical Work and Divine Favor in South India." *Anthropological Theory* 8(2): 159–79.
Polanyi, Karl. 2018. *Economy and Society: Selected Writings*, ed. Claus Thomasberger and Michele Cangiani. Cambridge: Polity Press.
Rasanayagam, Johan. 2010. *Islam in Post-Soviet Uzbekistan: The Morality of Experience*. Cambridge: Cambridge University Press.
Robbins, Joel. 2007. "Between Reproduction and Freedom: Morality, Value and Radical Cultural Change." *Ethnos* 72(3): 293–314.
Settle, Antonia C. 2011. "The New Development Paradigm through the Lens of the Aga Khan Rural Support Programme: Legitimacy, Accountability and the Political Sphere." *Community Development Journal* 47(3): 386–404.

Shryock, Andrew. 2008. "Thinking About Hospitality, with Derrida, Kant, and the Balga Bedouin." *Anthropos* 103: 405–21.

Sidky, H. 1996. *Irrigation and State Formation in Hunza: The Anthropology of a Hydraulic Kingdom*. Lanham, MD: University Press of America.

Smith, Adam. (1761) 2002. *The Theory of Moral Sentiments*, ed. K. Haakonssen. Cambridge: Cambridge University Press.

———. (1776) 1976. *An Inquiry into the Nature and Causes of the Wealth of Nations*. Chicago: University of Chicago Press.

Sökefeld, Martin. 2012. "The Attabad Landslide and the Politics of Disaster in Gojal, Gilgit-Baltistan." In *Negotiating Disasters: Politics, Representation, Meanings*, ed. U. Luig, 175–204. Frankfurt: Peter Lang.

———. 2020. "The Power of Lists: IDPs and Disaster Governmentality after the Attabad Landslide in Northern Pakistan." *Ethnos*. https://doi.org/10.1080/00141844.2020.1765833

Spittler, Gerd. 2011. "Contesting the Great Transformation: Work in Comparative Perspective." In *Market and Society: The Great Transformation Today*, ed. Chris Hann and Keith Hart, 160–74. Cambridge: Cambridge University Press.

Steinberg, Jonah. 2011. *Isma'ili Modern: Globalization and Identity in a Muslim Community*. Durham: The University of North Carolina Press.

Stellrecht, Irmtraud. 2006. "Passage to Hunza: Route Nets and Political Process in a Mountain State." In *Karakoram in Transition: Culture, Development and Ecology in the Hunza Valley*, ed. H. Kreutzmann, 191–216. Oxford: Oxford University Press.

Susumu, Nejima. 2000. "Pir, Waiz, and Imam: The Transformation of Socio-Religious Leadership Among the Isma'ilis in Northern Pakistan." *Islamic Area Studies Working Paper Series* (Vol. 23). Tokyo: National Museum of Ethnology.

Wood, Geof. 2006. "Introduction: The Mutuality of Initiative." In *Valleys in Transition: Twenty Years of AKRSP's Experience in Northern Pakistan*, ed. G. Wood, A. Malik and S. Sagheer, 1–31. Oxford: Oxford University Press.

Zigon, Jarett. 2007. "Moral Breakdown and the Ethical Demand: A Theoretical Framework for the Anthropology of Moralities." *Anthropological Theory* 7(2): 131–50.

3

Ethics of Work and Freedom in the Argentinean Andes

Value Creation and Virtuous Self-Crafting through Miniature Production

Olivia Angé

Argentina is a country of deep Catholic faith, where humans petition support from a wide pantheon featuring God, Jesus, and an array of Virgins and saints in order to enhance success in their daily economic endeavors. In the northern province of Jujuy, where most of the rural population are registered as members of the Kolla indigenous people, popular expressions of Catholicism exhibit commonalities with acts of worship in other Andean contexts.[1] Every year on 26 July, Saint Anne is celebrated with vibrant fairs of items reduced from their usual size, locally known as *miniaturas*. Far from being an isolated case, scaling practices are pervasive throughout this range of the mountains (*cordillera*) (Angé and Pitrou 2016). Because Andean miniatures are usually found in the countryside (*illas*) or bought as commodities (*alsasitas*), the academic literature has concentrated on their exchange and the uses to which they are put (Allen 1997; Molinié 2012; Sillar 2009; Golte and Gabriel 2014). Saint Anne miniatures, however, are ideally produced by her devotees, inviting an ethnographic study of their meaningful craft. Complementing earlier semiotic analyses, which have regarded the circulation and use of miniatures as a request (Sallnow 1987: 201), a text (Allen 1997), a mimetic play (Stensrud 2010), and a representation of a procreative encounter (Golte and Gabriel 2014), a study of miniature crafting illuminates the shifting materialities and embodied gestures that engender prosperity via scaling practices.

The work of crafting miniatures facilitates the circulation not only of small objects and money, but also a contingent and unpredictable flow of vitality. This takes the form of *suerte* and *fuerza*, meaning luck and strength respectively in the Spanish spoken in the Argentinean *cordillera*. Both qualities are auspicious for everyday work in the year to come. The multiple values created at the interface between human and non-human realms demonstrate how this vital flow contributes to the shaping of devotees' flourishing subjectivities. Indeed, Saint Anne's goods are more than physical representations of bigger models: they are exemplary realizations of moral values, in the sense of Joel Robbins (2015). In this light, I will explore the entanglements between the production of commodities and the creation of ethical subjects by showing how worshippers adjust their pursuit of instrumental mundanities to the moral values of community bonds and transcendental devotion.

What follows is an investigation of the multiple values that circulate across the feast day fair and the ordinary economy. By documenting forms of self-reflective engagements tied to petty commercial endeavor, I seek to support Chris Hann's contention that "economic action is continuously shaped by subjective convictions of good and bad" (Hann 2018: 249). As lamented by Hann, however, economics and ethics have come to constitute separate domains within social theory (see also Graeber 2001; Lambek 2013; Laidlaw 2014). Following this cleavage, work is usually defined as a productive practice driven by utility (for critical analysis, see Spittler 2018). My account of entrepreneurs' complicity with Saint Anne outlines productive practices far subtler than those of a hypothetical maximizing *homo oeconomicus*. Yet, as I will show, these entrepreneurs do not conform to the rules of a Christian moral economy either. Delving between the application of collective conventions and egoistic calculation, the chapter opens up a field of self-reflective ethical evaluations entangled with practices of material value creation. While the history of Western work, from unfree forms such as slavery and serfdom to free wage labor, stresses an opposition between productive effort (as constrained and exhausting) and rest (as free and fulfilling) (Spittler 2010: 40), we will see that Saint Anne crafters outline an ethic of work that is both arduous and free at the same time.

Value Creation in a South Andean Town

Humahuaca is a small town located in the eponymous valley in the northwestern Argentinean province of Jujuy, at about 3,000 meters above sea level. Counting some thirteen thousand inhabitants,[2] the town has grown continuously during the past century, due primarily to migrants arriving from surrounding agricultural hamlets in search of a better life in the urban environment. The villages of this region are classified as Kolla communities. Numbering about 70,500, the Kolla are the second largest of the thirty indigenous ethnic groups recognized by a 1994 constitutional amendment, following the state's ratification of the International Labour Organization's Convention 169 on Indigenous and Tribal Peoples.[3] This legal classification should not be confused with the established category of Creoles, which refers to citizens who are not direct descendants of Europeans but who do not identify themselves as indigenous (though some of their ancestors may have done so; see Sturzenegger-Benoist 2006). In town, ethnic identities are highly subjective and blurred. They crystalize in the punctual enactment of practices regarded as indigenous, such as miniature production.

Notions of indigenous belonging have shifted according to the socio-historical context. In the *cordillera* of Jujuy, the 1994 constitutional amendment launched a "re-ethnicization" (*re-ethnicización*) movement. Long-standing urban residents lacking ties to any rural community began to self-identify as Kolla and claim a filiation with indigenous ancestors. Likewise, local elites who formerly despised indigenous culture started to claim filiation with precolonial culture and heritage. The reappraisal of indigeneity was particularly strong in the Humahuaca Valley after it was declared a UNESCO World Heritage site in 2003. The local diffusion of a global hierarchy of value fostered by international heritagization (Herzfeld 2004) involved a reversal of the symbolic status of the Kolla people, now publicly displayed as a cultural emblem of the nation while remaining politically and economically discriminated. A polemic arose over the fact that, while the richness of the heritage was due to the indigenous people, the benefits of the lucrative touristic market fueled by UNESCO's prestigious brand were monopolized by non-indigenous citizens—mostly migrants from the south of the country.

Many townspeople of rural origin maintain strong ties with their home communities, where some still cultivate their plots. Doña Cruz, for instance, brought up nine children in the town of Humahuaca, where she was able to build a house. Yet she still plants maize, beans, and potatoes in her home village of Aparzo, some fifty kilometers away. But even if they continue to cultivate their rural plots, migrants depend on the market for basic goods once they have settled in the town. They make a living from informal street businesses (selling souvenirs, cooking food, driving taxis), while the more successful run their own small businesses, or work for wages in hotels and restaurants, or as public employees in hospitals, schools, and town councils. Another source of income comes in the form of public allowances granted to an array of citizens, including elders, heads of numerous families, and those who are not formally employed. Although they are usually combined with informal work, including petty trade, temporary labor sale, or agricultural production, these allowances are criticized for incentivizing beneficiaries' laziness. Those indulging in sloth and excessive alcohol consumption are reproached indeed. While urban living is aspired to as more comfortable and less laborious than agricultural life in the countryside, idleness is decried as a vice in both sectors. In town and countryside, work is regarded as a moral duty and a means for the expression of subjective accomplishment (Angé 2018a). However, this moral economy of work is being unsettled by the vagaries of urban integration. Lacking access to formal qualifications, and puzzled by the turmoil of the notoriously unstable Argentinean economy, many rural migrants fail to build stable livelihoods.

Even if they own their means of production, these people are not entrepreneurs motivated by capitalist accumulation (see Terpe, this volume). The money they earn is used for domestic provisioning (such as food, housing, and transportation) and for meeting children's educational expenses. Economic activities are enmeshed in a busy calendar of religious gatherings. In towns and hamlets alike, the main purpose in the performance of feast days is to foster auspicious relationships with non-human beings involved in the distribution of vital resources among humans. The whole year round, communities and neighborhoods honor their patron saint with ecclesiastical rites, balls, sporting competitions, and barter fairs (Angé 2018a). Saint Anne's celebration differs from others in the way she is revered through miniatures. According to the Catholic tradition, Anne is the mother of Mary, so Jesus's maternal grandmother; this is agreed by most of her Andean worshippers. Still, when I inquired further into the identity of this saint, I heard many stories. In all of them, Anne was a hardworking woman who knitted clothes for the poor, or for Jesus when he was a child. She has long been recognized as the patron saint of workers, also named Virgen del Trabajo, where *trabajo* (Spanish: "work") refers to creative effort. Although she is known to have conceived her daughter, Anne is commonly referred to as a Virgin, thus resembling many other sanctified females worshipped in the region (these include the Virgen de Candelaria, the Virgen de Inmaculada Concepción, the Virgen de Guadalupe, and the Virgen del Carmen). Some worshippers associate the Virgin with the Pachamama, known as the Virgin of the Earth. Pachamama is celebrated throughout August, but especially on the 1st. Like Saint Anne, she is seen as being responsible for the distribution of human vitality, in its various dimensions. While Pachamama has primary responsibility for the growth and reproduction of all beings dwelling on the earth, including humans, Saint Anne provides the latter with the *suerte* and *fuerza* they need to make their work rewarding.

The *fuerza* at stake is similar to the flows described by Stephen Gudeman in Panama and in the Colombian *cordillera* where the same word is used to describe "the energy that people need and use in all of life's doings. . . . The energy of life—that humans must have to live" (Gudeman 2012: 60).

Strength is ensured daily by ingesting food, particularly local ingredients such as meat, maize, and potatoes, which are considered nourishing for the body that has to toil in the fields. These are contrasted to the industrial food widely consumed by urbanites. Alcohol and coca leaves are seen as most powerful in this regard, and both are key ingredients for offerings. Encapsulated in food, strength stems from the Pachamama. It can also be captured by worshipping the Catholic God, with whom people communicate via sanctified images, including that of Saint Anne. As Sofía, the daughter of Doña Cruz, put it: "All images, it does not matter it being Saint Anne Virgin, Saint Santiago, . . . all the saints we have, they communicate with God, and make him give us strength."[4] I will come back to this vital distribution below. First, I will sketch out the fairs at which worshippers pay tribute to Saint Anne.

Celebrating Saint Anne in Humahuaca

The 26th of July was proclaimed the feast day of Saint Anne by a papal bull in 1481 (Wirth 2003). Her celebration in Humahuaca is said to have been initiated by the Lopez family several centuries ago. Theirs is still the main gathering among the dozens nowadays organized between late July and the middle of August. A statue of Saint Anne stands in the chapel of the family estate on the outskirts of Humahuaca, along with other effigies including Saint Roque and Saint James Apostle. The extended Lopez family gathers to celebrate the feast days of these saints, most travelling all the way from San Salvador de Jujuy, where they have lived for decades. Every year on 26 July, people congregate in their courtyard to celebrate Saint Anne. The assembly is announced on local radio stations, but locals do not need this reminder as many of them are active devotees of the little Virgin (*Virgencita*). In 2013, I arrived at the Lopez family home at noon, bringing a bag of miniature clay pots I intended to sell. The members of the family, who had been working intensively for days, were still busy with the last preparations. These involved cleaning the chapel, cooking food to sell to visitors, and installing the loudspeakers and other infrastructure. The few people who had already arrived were regular traders (*comerciantes*) setting up their stalls in the same strategic places they occupied every year.[5] I was asked to kindly not occupy these myself. Traders continued to arrive until mid-afternoon, along with eager and curious consumers. That year's fair attracted several hundred buyers and some fifty traders, all of us female.[6] Sellers and buyers alike would walk to the altar to "greet the Virgin" (*saludar a la Virgen*) when they arrived. By three o'clock most of the participants had arrived and the chapel was crowded. An organizer used a microphone to invite everyone to gather at the statue for prayers. Before the fair was officially opened, worshippers carried the saint in a procession around the courtyard, burning incense all around her. After this procession, and once the starting signal had been given, the hustle and bustle of the fair became intense.

The majority of the stalls sold bite-size portions of ready-to-eat food, such as cakes, pies (*empanadas*), sandwiches, breads, donuts, jelly, and stuffed cornhusks (*tamales*). My immediate neighbor was selling a range of miniature knitted textiles she had beautifully pinned onto a white lace background. Nowadays, knitwork is the main handicraft, but in the past the range of handcrafted miniatures was much wider: shoemakers used to supply rubber sandals, carpenters made small pieces of furniture, and scrap merchants created agricultural tools. Saint Anne's miniatures nowadays include industrial goods, but according to the participants this is a recent innovation. They include foods such as sweets, popcorn, beer, and lemonade; toys such as small cars, dolls and playing cards; and home utensils such as glasses for drinking alcohol, garlic graters, sewing threads, and hair clips. The later are usual commodities selected by the traders for their small size. Other manufactured items are produced as miniatures in the thriving Bolivian economy of *alasitas*.[7] Cristina, a middle-aged member of the Lopez family, noted: "Nowadays, because everything has changed, some people buy things to resell them. Other people sell their handicrafts. These are not the times of yesterday. Formerly, we used to craft everything."

Nostalgic tropes also deplore the diffusion of new modalities for exchanging the *miniaturas*. Several devotees recalled that in the past they were bartered. Others remember that, prior to the 1950s, miniatures were exchanged for Saint Anne bills (*plata de Santa Ana*), scraps of paper stamped by the organizers. Eager to revive old traditions, some fair organizers have recently reintroduced the use of *plata de Santa Ana*, with an established parity with the peso.[8] This is not the case in some rural communities, where the Saint Anne bills are not exchangeable for the official currency.[9] Yet, in Humahuaca, most *miniaturas* are currently sold for pesos. Each seller is free to set her own prices and they usually calculate as if they were participating in a conventional market. They try to figure out a price that will cover the cost of the raw material and take some account of the amount of labor they have invested. Others proceed by using the prices of normally scaled objects as their yardstick. Buying food "in miniature" is a bit more expensive than purchasing the same quantity in normally scaled portions. For instance, in 2013, a woman who usually sold her cookies at the bus station for 4 pesos each sold them at one-fifth of the usual size for 1 peso each at Saint Anne's fair. Graciela, a gateau baker whose work I describe below, also evaluates her mini pastries as more expensive than the usual ones because they "comprise more meringue and it is hard to make them (*cuesta hacer*)."

Ingested in a mouthful, miniature food does not constitute a proper meal. As pointed out by Maria, a teacher who promotes the organization of a fair at her high school, people eat for "the taste and pleasure of a small pastry that you might not be able to fit into your mouth in its bigger size." While small portions do not nourish hungry people, utensils lose their instrumental efficiency altogether when their scale is reduced. Rather than productive use by adults, many small items are intended for children to play with, which diminishes their lifespan considerably. Still, miniatures produced as toys are admired by people of all ages. The Humahuaca seamstress who every year sells glamourous shiny dresses for Barbie dolls delights girls and their mothers alike. Their manifest delectation suggests that the consumption of *miniaturas* is first and foremost about hedonistic sensual pleasures.[10] Devotees spend the afternoon happily buying, admiring, eating, and handling objects to the sound of *cumbia* and folksongs broadcast by speakers. Alongside the commerce, visitors gather at tables set up in an adjacent courtyard, where traditional dishes are served for a standard 50 soles.[11] Others play *taba*, a game in which they bet oranges and display their human dexterity. Many different kinds of games may feature in Saint Anne celebrations.[12] As usual on saints' feast days, the afternoon passed in an atmosphere of fun, heightened by the joys of consumption. I walked back home at dusk, moved by this laborious religious fervor and cheered up by the many lively conversations I had enjoyed at stalls laden with commodities. I was carrying an array of them for my ethnographic collection, plus just a few unsold clay pots, as my own trade had been quite successful that day.

Scaling Practices and Vital Distribution

Appreciation of the small objects produced for and transacted on the feast day of Saint Anne is attested by the marveling faces and comments uttered by participants when contemplating an object that they are used to handling in another dimension. "Very little, really beautiful!" (*chiquitito bien bonito*), they would say with a loving expression. In his classic work *The Savage Mind*, Lévi-Strauss generalized this aesthetic appreciation, as an "*émotion esthétique très profonde*" (Lévi-Strauss 1962: 37). He attributed this to a cognitive satisfaction in being able to apprehend the object in its entirety and to understand its fabric, without needing to first decompose it into its constituent parts. In the case of miniatures, however, the emotional excitement is also triggered by sensorial satisfaction. This appreciation is in turn projected onto the Virgin who, it is hoped, also takes pleasure in the small objects. While being exchanged among humans, the *miniaturas* are also offered to the Virgin.[13] Beside her reduced size, the distinctive sign of Saint Anne's statue is her little Andean spinning wheel (*piusca*), indexing her capacities for textile industry. When a fair closes, the statue is surrounded by a multitude of spoons, wicker baskets, clay pots, sandals, and clothes, all of which are deposited on her altar as a present (*regalo*). Regardless of whether they are instantaneously ingested, offered, or kept as valuables, all miniatures are intended for the Saint (*son para la Virgen*). This is attested by the elders' instruction to place durable miniatures under the Virgin's altar before they are exchanged. Boxes filled with small goods are therefore piled up in the chapel, where they remain during the liturgy and procession.

Miniatures are offered in gratitude for blessings received in the past but also to petition for further *fuerza* and *suerte* in the transactional spheres that will unfold in the aftermath of the fair. On the one hand, scaling practices are a divinatory gesture concerning one's business. When a stall clears effortlessly, this is interpreted as a promise of success in mundane economic undertakings. This was clearly stated by Doña Juana, who hosted me in her guesthouse during my stay in the village of Santa Ana: "And if they buy everything, and you have nothing left, that's how your business will run. They will buy everything. It's to test your luck; to know how your business will work for the rest of the year. Will you be able to sell? Will you be able to buy? All this . . ." On the other hand, the production, distribution, and consumption of *miniaturas* are propitiatory acts aimed at capturing *suerte*. Luck is not distributed equally among fields or individuals. Some people are known for having more luck than others. The same person can be very lucky in one field of activity but unlucky in another one. Hence, luck does not have the connotation of a hazardous turn of events. It rather refers to divine support for an advantageous outcome to a venture. In other words, devotees distribute and consume miniatures in order to benefit from a divine *suerte* that will enable them to cope with any mundane uncertainty that could hamper fulfillment of an economic project.

To this instrumental end, worshippers establish a relationship between the form of the object and the project they want the Virgin to support them with: a small car for purchasing a motorized vehicle, a clay pot for a constant supply of food to the household, or a small piece of furniture for a large cozy sofa. Likewise, people keep Saint Anne bills blessed at the fair in their wallet so that their pesos will multiply themselves before they are spent. Tiny goods are thus iconic statements presented to "request specific material favors" similar to those examined by Catherine Allen in Peruvian pilgrimages (Allen 1997: 85). For those who have a stall at the fair, expectations may focus on the productive activity itself: a restaurant owner will offer meals to expand her clientele, a baker will sell bread, and a textile artisan her knitwear. Herders may sell beans to cause their livestock to multiply. In the village of Santa Ana, the story of Isabela has become famous as proof of the efficacy of the *miniaturas*. When she opened her grocery, this businesswoman in the making took a range of small commodities to the fair, where they were rapidly purchased. Her neighbors still remember her beautiful stall, decked out with packets of sugar and flour, potato seeds, shots of beer, and other goods they could purchase with Saint Anne's bills. The success of her flourishing store in the village is collectively attributed to Isabela's spectacular participation in the fair. She herself commented as follows on Saint Anne's blessings:

> [The Virgin] helps you. She blesses you so that you achieve [your objective]. You have faith and you work; afterwards you have what you had asked for. You know that sometimes you work, and the money is spent without you being able to save. If you ask Saint Anne, you work and after a while, unwittingly, you already have what you had asked for.

Another cherished value that workers hope to acquire when participating in the fair is the above mentioned *fuerza*, which enables one to perform an activity with assiduity and perseverance. Lack of strength means slackness and incapacity to engage energetically in productive efforts. Andrea remembers a terrible fall that immobilized her for days, after she had refused to contribute to the organization of Anne's celebration; implying that an Anne who is upset can retaliate by absorbing a person's vitality. Sloth is thus an individual vice that entails a dangerous relationship with non-human entities. The moral danger of such laziness also emerges at fairs, because the proliferation of industrial commodities is taken as a sign that people are becoming lazy and not producing handicrafts anymore. While industrial goods are accepted as suitable gifts for the saint (as long as they respect the prescribed reduction in scale), fine handcrafted miniatures raise deeper admiration. Customers often asked me whether I had made the clay pots I was selling myself, confirming that the artisanal process was important to them, even if no longer compulsory. It is noteworthy that all stalls include at least a few items that are handmade. For instance, a young mother complemented the various plastic toys she was selling at the Lopez fair with a series of handmade images of famous soccer players in miniature, together with a scaled-down album in which to stick them. The coexistence of industrial and handcrafted items, exhibiting a wide spectrum of materials, skills, and scales, attest individual creativity in the constitution of the stall. In the next section I look more closely at the work of miniature crafting to explain why artisanal goods are more suited to foster complicity with Anne.

The Work of Miniature Crafting

Preparing a stall requires relentless work, especially in the week preceding the celebration. On the eve of the feast in July 2018, I visited Graciela, a fervent devotee. She guided me to the kitchen where she was cooking with her two daughters. When I commented admiringly on the sight of a kitchen full of resting dough, icing, and freshly baked pastries, they told me to take a look in the living room, where the dining table was being covered with trays and pots of little biscuits and pastries. The three women had started kneading the day before, beginning with the *rosquetes, maizenitas,* and *empanadillas.* The preceding week they had prepared mini *tamales,* which were stored out of sight in the fridge. But there was still a lot to be done. The cooks would barely rest before the fair, by which time the last-minute preparation of the creams and decorations left them exhausted. They would resume cooking in the following week to prepare a stall for a second minor fair, requiring less work. Participating in these two celebrations was a tradition (*tradición*) established by Graciela's mother. "She taught me everything," Graciela asserted with satisfaction. In addition to biscuits baked according to family recipes inherited through her maternal descent, Graciela had innovated by creating meringue-iced cakes, which she stuffed with the richest *moka* or fruit cream, replicating in miniature the finest gâteau usually prepared for celebrating life-cycle rituals.

After proudly summarizing the composition of her stall, Graciela returned to the kitchen to resume the meringue icing of the *rosquetes* with her daughters. I switched off my camera and set my notebook aside to give them a hand, icing the little circular biscuits one by one with a tea spoon. The meticulous and repetitive gestures allowed for a constant flow of conversation. I learned about Graciela's aspiration to open her own bakery and possibly resign her job as a schoolteacher. She had been inquiring about rental opportunities near the market, but she was afraid that the expenses of a central shop would be excessive. She confessed that she needed more *ánimo* before launching a business. *Ánimo* refers to a heightened mood and lively impetus that is essential if one is to engage in challenging endeavors. Throughout the Andes, this notion also alludes to a life-sustaining force that animates all beings endowed with a potential for growth, human or not. I shall come back to this concept below. In the meantime, Graciela baked for a growing informal network. Her skills were well known in town, and even strangers knocked at her door to order treats for weddings, birthdays, and other celebrations. She specialized in gorgeous gateaux—an activity that provided a source of secondary income throughout the year to boost her meagre public salary. The Saint Anne celebration took up all her time and energy from mid-July to the beginning of August.

While food products have to be freshly made, other forms of *miniaturas* are crafted the whole year round. Take, for instance, the case of Eulogia, a schoolteacher in her fifties who works 150 km away from Humahuaca and returns home only at weekends. Commuting by bus, she uses this time to knit tiny clothes for the fair, in homage to her dear Saint. Alejandra, a fair organizer, recalls: "It used to be beautiful, the tools they used to craft: spades, wheelbarrows, identical to the big ones. And the furniture, properly crafted, with leather seats set in the wood. And with carving and everything!" In miniature production it is the detail that counts, where contrasts are produced by bringing together an array of colors, materials, and patterns. Even though such elaborate *miniaturas* are nowadays exceptional, crafters agree that small items are more demanding to produce than bigger homologues.[14] The dexterity required to produce small pieces is obviously greater. Doña Cruz's daughter, Sofía, explained this in words that explicitly posit work as a moral value: "My grandfather used to say that we must value work, making things, taking your time. Because it takes time to make the very small things. It is not the same as making them in large [sizes]. It is much more difficult, much more laborious and much more complicated."

As the Virgin of Work, Saint Anne provides her worshippers with the skills necessary to realize this arduous work. This was explained by Eulogia: "It seems that she gave me this ability. I come [to the fair] to thank her. I knit the whole year round thinking of the Virgin, of what I am going to knit for her. And then I come here, and I leave happy (*contenta*)." Allen observed a similar pattern of transmission at the famous Qoyllur Rity pilgrimage in Peru, where women sit down at the shrine of Virgin of Fatima, the patroness of weaving, to knit reduced-scale clothes that they leave behind as offerings: "They say that as they weave, their hands learn from the Mamacha, and they depart more accomplished in their craft" (Allen 1997: 74).

If Saint Anne is particularly delighted by tiny handicrafts, it is thus not only for the aesthetic qualities mentioned above, but also because miniatures display the fruits of an outstanding ability that she has transmitted. This is attested by the stance of devotion that miniature artisans are expected to take. An experienced miniature crafter, Sofía explained to me how this moral prescription was explicitly transmitted to her by her grandmother:

> It is mostly faith we put into these tiny things. I don't know, my grandmother always instructed me, and she told me this: "If we do something, we must do it with affection. Do it with enthusiasm, because we do it for Saint Anne. She was Jesus's grandmother. She was a person who was very hardworking," she used to say.

Work of this kind resembles the productive efforts documented by Gudeman, whereby "economy performed expresses a belief in God as much as a belief in God is made manifest in economic practices" (Gudeman 2012: 62). Compared with the routines of everyday production, the arduous crafting of *miniaturas* is an outstanding instantiation of piety. In the next section of this chapter, I will show that this laborious enactment of faith transforms the subjectivity of the devotee.

Crafting Smallness as Self-Making

When listing the benefits of crafting *miniaturas*, many participants included *ánimo*—the courage Graciela had said she was missing for opening her bakery. In Andean ethnography, *ánimo* is usually translated as "spirit." It is described as a most intimate component of a living being, which if captured by upset entities in the environment can provoke sickness, or even death (Allen 2002; Angé 2018a; Gose 1994). In Humahuaca, features of the Catholic pantheon also impact on the flourishing of human *ánimo*. Doña Cruz attributed her prosperity to her close relation to Saint Anne. When I participated in the preparation of the fair at her place in 2013, she explained that praising the Virgin made her heart joyful (*alegre*). During a recorded interview, she told me of the significant shift her life course had taken when she brought her father's Saint Anne statue from her home village to Humahuaca: "Here [in town] I celebrate the Virgin. You see, this has helped me a lot. Here I own a house, I am living peacefully. I am happy (*feliz*)." When Doña Cruz's daughter, fifty-year-old Andrea, attributed her recovery from serious illness and harsh poverty to her devotion to Saint Anne, I realized how important miniatures were for the reproduction of the self, both physically and socially. She explained to me that Saint Anne was powerful in fostering her worshippers' prosperity: "She gives you *fuerza* and value." Hence, when zealously crafting little goods, worshippers encapsulate in their *miniaturas* the very values that are provided by the Saint.

A common feature in reduced-scale production (Stewart 1992; Kohring 2011; Foxhall 2015), "arduousness" takes here particular meaning, positing *miniaturas* as exemplary in the sense that they offer an "ontological home for values" (Robbins 2015: 28). Minute size is admired not only for its aesthetic attributes in the Levi-Straussian vein but also as the incarnation of its crafter's virtue as a skillful and diligent worker. These are the very qualities Anne is admired for, as Guillermo, the retired son-in-law of the Lopez matriarch, described: "Saint Anne was a very hardworking woman. She comes to be Jesus's grandmother. At this time, she directly worked. And she was a woman like us, very humble, very poor, but she used to work. And, well, she used to do what we are doing now; but she became a goddess."

When preparing a stall for the fair, the devotees' intention is not to produce objects for human use, but to please Saint Anne, by realizing the value for which she has been sanctified as the Virgin of Work. In fashioning *miniaturas* they gradually acquire her skill, diligence, and virtue. From this perspective, Anne provides an inspiring ideal for leading a virtuous economic life. Just as Caroline Humphrey's (1997) Mongolian interlocutors develop virtuous characters by adjusting their conduct to the acts of historical personages they have chosen as models, so worshippers in Humahuaca aspire to acquire Anne's outstanding qualities.[15] Like the Mongolian exemplars, the little Virgin evokes a moral horizon that is not coupled with explicit rules that must be followed. While the accomplishment of arduous work is fundamental, the procedures and strategies suited to Anne's ideal are left unspecified. The paths to prosperity indicated by the saint are indeed manifold: some strive to run a thriving agricultural domestic economy, others target a juicy business in the burgeoning economy of heritage tourism, or stable wage-labor employment, or some combination of these goals. Saint Anne's support is solicited with much insistence when engaging an ambitious project, typically when pursuing a university diploma, or when starting a new productive activity or trade. When targeting a particularly laborious objective, devotees can "promise themselves" (*apromesarse*) to the Virgin by committing to serve her for the three subsequent years. This involves praying during the *novena*, volunteering in the organization of her feast day, and ideally putting up a stall at her fair. Complicity with Anne thus comes to its crux at the critical points in a person's professional life, when embracing opportunities for an improved position in the economic field.

This diversity of virtuous achievement is also enacted within the fair, where it is visible in the disparate composition of the stalls. While some strive to emulate the fine miniatures of their elders, others are content to produce simpler pieces lacking mastery and diligence, and still others rely heavily on industrial miniatures produced within the urban capitalist economy. Disparities in miniature crafting give rise to debate over the kind of work that is propitious and pleasing to the Saint. The modality of exchange is also discussed. Those keen to revive cultural tradition often advocate using fake bills, although it is accepted that traders would not participate if it were not possible for them to earn pesos. Hence the generalized polemical question: are they motivated by devotion or are they ultimately more concerned with monetary gain? Worshippers face a conundrum: how to reconcile profit making and devotion, individual provisioning and collective sharing? These tensions were vividly expressed by a middle-aged knitter who decided not to produce miniatures for the fair any longer, lamenting that it was being undermined by selfishness and the quest for personal benefit (*beneficio*). Together with the proliferation of industrial items, this generates ethical controversies that unfold on pavements, at the marketplace, or during break time at work. Even though scaling practices maintain *fuerza* as an overarching value, the fair nonetheless offers a space to negotiate how to appreciate, use and distribute this vital flow properly in the contemporary economy.

Conclusion: Working with Miniatures in Andean Capitalism

Argentinean moral economy is haunted by two despised figures, condemned as the plagues of the nation: the idle poor and the idle rich. The thief (*ladrón*) and the lazybones (*vago*) both avoid work, either by making a comfortable livelihood out of corrupted forms of exploitation or by eking out a miserable one through state allowances. Members of indigenous communities are persistently stigmatized for the latter. Striving to secure a decent subsistence out of their skillful, unrelenting efforts, the devotees of Saint Anne avoid these two perversions by enacting arduous work as an overarching human virtue. Clearly, this work ethic departs from the Protestant one outlined by Weber to account for the spirit of early capitalism (Weber [1904] 2003). Weber famously identified instrumental rationality as a prominent asset for a thriving capitalist economy, where rationality refers to increasing benefit with minimum effort. Saint Anne devotees, in contrast, claim participation in local capitalist value creation without being subjected to the discipline of any maximizing rationality. By stressing the necessity of distributing *fuerza* and securing *suerte* to achieve economic prosperity, the crafters of miniatures acknowledge an ineluctable contingency to instrumental achievement, which is always entangled with social and biological flows of vitality than cannot be fully controlled (Gudeman 2012). Furthermore, if the devotees of the Virgin of Work share the Protestant ideal of virtuous labor, they nonetheless depart from the systematic calculating reason of the archetypal European capitalists. Far from being guided by Christian postulates of scarcity and frugality, they compose opulent stalls that instantiate the "postulate of abundance", so vividly captured in Nico Tassi's study of urban indigenous Bolivians in La Paz markets, where "the ascetic and individual renunciation of the material as a pathway to God is . . . paralleled by an exaggerated, collective participation in the production of abundance" (Tassi 2010: 206). Contrary to the Protestant doctrine whereby the ethical scope of work is opposed to amusement and sensuous enjoyment, Saint Anne artisans situate the ethical scope of their acts in joy and pleasure. They do not apply a tedious work regulation to save their souls. Instead of disciplined and painful efforts oriented toward thrifty consumption and stingy saving, Saint Anne's flock flourish through a sense of work as self-fulfillment in their earthly life.

If the way work is collectively perceived and performed in an Andean town like Humahuaca is tainted with this "material theology" (Tassi 2010: 206), the enactment of religious morality leaves plenty of room for self-reflection and individual judgment. Devotees engage in a laborious avenue for value creation not by conforming to specific moral obligations, but rather by developing techniques of the self that are the essence of ethical freedom (Laidlaw 2002, 2014).[16] Through their miniature crafting, Saint Anne devotees flesh out Aristotle's metaphor: the crafting of virtues, like the crafting of objects, requires skills that can only be achieved through enduring exercises and practice (Laidlaw 2014: 72). It is, indeed, by sharpening their craft skills through miniature production that devotees concomitantly shape their ethical subjectivity. Through the arduous choreography of their miniature crafting, artisans become akin to the saint, embodying her dexterous and diligent presence in the world when she was alive.

Drawing on a lively description of woodcarving entanglement with intimate relations of kinship in a Mexican workshop, Alanna Cant suggested that labor is actively made, rather than determined by the ownership of the means of production (Cant 2018). Similarly, Saint Anne worshippers claim freedom to fashion their productive practices by collaborating with human kin and non-human exemplars. When crafting tiny useless objects, however, they are not only shaping local labor hierarchies, they are also "doing work" as an autotelic virtuous activity. Challenging the distinction between doing and making that the Western philosophical tradition inherited from Aristotelian thought (Lambek 2013), Saint Anne workers insist on an ethical dimension inherent to economic practices, including craftwork. They thereby enjoin us to extend the definition of work as an instrumental act oriented toward an external end, and to also consider work as virtuous self-crafting.

Acknowledgments

I am indebted to all the many Saint Anne devotees who shared their faith, skills, and economic aspirations. This research was initiated when I held postdoctoral fellowship at the research department of the Quai Branly museum. I am grateful to this institution, and to my colleagues Julien Clément, Jessica de Largy Healy, Frédéric Keck, Paz Nuñez-Regueiro, and Anne-Christine Taylor for their intellectual guidance and warm hospitality.

I carried out further fieldwork in Humahuaca as an assistant professor at the Université de Bruxelles supported by the Fonds National de la Recherche Scientifique (National Fund for Scientific Research). Parts of this work (pp. 486, 489, and 490) were first published in the *Journal of Anthropological Research* copyright 2016 by the University of New Mexico, available online at: https://doi.org/10.1086/689296; and in *Ethnos* 2018, available online at: https://doi.org/10.1080/00141844.2018.1458042.

Olivia Angé is an associate professor of anthropology at the Université Libre de Bruxelles who specializes in the study of value creation, prosperity, and agriculture in the Andes. She is the author of *Barter and Social Regeneration in the Argentinean Andes* (Berghahn, 2018), and co-editor with David Berliner of *Ecological Nostalgias* (Berghahn, 2021) and *Anthropology and Nostalgia* (Berghahn, 2014). Her research has been published in *Terrain, Social Anthropology*, the *Journal of Latin American and Caribbean Anthropology, Ethnos*, and the *Journal of Anthropological Research.*

Notes

1. I have lived in northwestern Argentina for about eight years. This chapter also draws on ethnographic fieldwork realized after I returned to Belgium, involving both participant observation and recorded conversations.
2. https://www.municipalidad-argentina.com.ar/municipalidad-humahuaca.html (last accessed March 2021).
3. According to the 2004 census: https://www.desarrollosocial.gob.ar/wp-content/uploads/2015/08/8.-INAI-Informacion-estad--stica.pdf (last accessed March 2021).
4. In Gudeman's words, "it is a contingent gift of the Divinity" (2012: 62). Gudeman notes a distinction between power attributed to God and strength circulated by the earthbeings. Further research would be needed to understand how this polarity unfolds in this southern part of the *cordillera*. Sofía is a pseudonym: to respect my interlocutors' privacy, I am not using real names in this chapter.
5. At the 2018 celebration, traders had to pay 70 pesos to secure a stall. This money is intended to contribute to the cost of maintaining the chapel.
6. Some were helped by a son or a husband. Women are the main traders in most Andean markets, but these gender dimensions cannot be pursued in the scope of this chapter.
7. *Alasitas* are miniatures sold during pilgrimages, mostly in Peru and Bolivia, to be used as votive gifts to the Virgin (see Tassi 2010; Molinié 2012; Golte and Gabriel 2014; Allen 2016).
8. In this case, buyers exchange pesos for stamped bills at the desk identified as Saint Anne's Bank in order to purchase tiny goods. When leaving the fair, they can change unused mock money back into the official currency (a commission of 10

to 20 percent is charged). According to the organizers, the money earned "is for the Virgin," as it should in principle be used to enliven her celebration by providing maize beer and other foods for the participants.

9. The fact that Saint Anne money cannot be exchanged for pesos significantly modifies the functioning of the fair, as previously described (Angé 2018b).
10. Miniatures are also used during funerals, when clay pots and other tiny basic goods are buried with the deceased to provide for his/her afterlife needs. Saint Anne *miniaturas* are also used for food offerings to the dead at All Saints.
11. This was worth approximately 5 euros at the time—the price of a basic menu in a restaurant in town.
12. The fair is regarded as an entertainment for the young and old alike. Participants describe their transactions as "playing Saint Anne" (*jugar a la Santa Ana*). Situated at the crossroads of ritual, play, and mundane economic practices, this fair raises many further questions about the intertwining of these modes of action, but regrettably they cannot be pursued within the scope of this chapter.
13. Although I dwell here on transfers between humans and Saint Anne, I have shown elsewhere that the fair is also intended to please closer ancestors (Angé 2016).
14. When it comes to knitting, for instance, women use industrial yarn rather than their own wool. The patterns they use are very basic.
15. While Mongol teachers are personal and individually chosen, Saint Anne is collectively worshipped, and her devotion is transmitted within families.
16. Foucault famously defines these technologies as those that "permit individuals to effect by their own means, or with the help of others, a certain number of operations on their own bodies and souls, thoughts, conduct, and way of being, so as to transform themselves in order to attain a certain state of happiness, purity, wisdom, perfection, or immortality" (Foucault 1997: 225).

References

Allen, Catherine. 1997. "When Pebbles Move Mountains: Iconicity and Symbolism in Quechua Ritual." In *Creating Context in Andean Culture*, ed. R. Howard-Malverde, 73–84. Oxford: Oxford University Press.

Allen, Catherine. 2016. "The Living Ones: Miniatures and Animation in the Andes," *Journal of Anthropological Research* 72(4): 416–41.

Angé, Olivia. 2016. "Materializing Virtues: Crafted Miniatures as Moral Examples in the Argentinean Andes." *Journal of Anthropological Research* 72(4): 483–503.

———. 2018a. *Barter and Social Regeneration in the Argentinean Andes*. Oxford: Berghahn Books.

———. 2018b. "Reproductive Commodities: Work, Joy, and Creativity in Argentinean Miniature Fairs." *Ethnos* 84(2): 241–62.

Angé, Olivia, and Perig Pitrou. 2016. "Miniatures in Mesoamerica and the Andes: Theories of Life, Values, and Relatedness." *Journal of Anthropological Research* 72(44): 408–15.

Cant, Alanna. 2018. "'Making Labor' in Mexican Artisanal Workshops." *Journal of the Royal Anthropological Institute (N.S.)*: 61–74.

Foucault, Michel. 1997. "Technologies of the Self." In *Ethics: Subjectivity and Truth. Essential Works of Foucault 1954–1984. Volume 1*, ed. P. Rabinow, 223–51. New York: The New Press.

Foxhall, Linn. 2015. "Introduction: Miniaturization." *World Archaeology* 47(1): 1–5.

Golte, Jürgen, and Doris León Gabriel. 2014. *Alasitas: Discursos, prácticas y símbolos de un "liberalismo aymara altiplánico" entre la población de origen migrante en Lima.* Lima: Fondo Editorial del Instituto de Estudios Peruanos.

Gose, Peter. 1994. *Deathly Waters and Hungry Mountains: Agrarian Ritual and Class Formation in an Andean Town.* Toronto: University of Toronto Press.

Graeber, David. 2001. *Toward an Anthropological Theory of Value: The False Coin of our Own Dreams.* New York: Palgrave Macmillan.

Gudeman, Stephen. 2012. "Vital Energy: The Current of Relations." *Social Analysis* 56(1): 57–73.

Hann, Chris. 2018. "Morality and Economy: Work, Workfare, and Fairness in Provincial Hungary." *Archives Europénenes de Sociologie* 59(2): 225–54.

Herzfeld, Michael. 2004. *The Body Impolitic: Artisans and Artifice in the Global Hierarchy of Value.* Chicago: University of Chicago Press.

Humphrey, Caroline. 1997. "Exemplars and Rules: Aspects of the Discourse of Moralities in Mongolia." In *The Ethnography of Moralities*, ed. Signe Howell, 25–47. London: Routledge.

Kohring, Sheila. 2011. "Bodily Skill and the Aesthetics of Miniaturisation." *Pallas* 86: 31–50.

Laidlaw, James. 2002. "For an Anthropology of Ethics and Freedom." *Journal of the Royal Anthropological Institute* 8(2): 311–32.

———. 2014. *The Subject of Virtue: An Anthropology of Ethics and Freedom.* Cambridge: Cambridge University Press.

Lambek, Michel. 2013. "The Value of (Performative) Acts." *HAU: Journal of Ethnographic Theory* 3(2): 141–60.

Lévi-Strauss, Claude. 1962. *La pensée sauvage.* Paris: Plon.

Molinié, Antoinette. 2012. "L'argent sauvage: Une énigme andine de la monnaie." In *Monnaie Antique, monnaie moderne, monnaie d'ailleurs . . . Métissage et hybridations*, ed. P. Pion and B. Formoso, 175–87. Paris: Editions De Boccard.

Robbins, Joel. 2015. "Ritual, Value, and Example: On the Perfection of Cultural Representations." *Journal of the Royal Anthropological Institute* 21(S1): 18–29.

Sallnow, Michael. 1987. *Pilgrims of the Andes: Regional Cults in Cuzco.* Washington, DC: Smithsonian Institution Press.

Sillar, Bill. 2009. "The Social Agency of Things? Animism and Materiality in the Andes." *Cambridge Archaeological Journal* 19(3): 367–77.

Spittler, Gerd. 2010. "Beginnings of the Anthropology of Work: Nineteenth-Century Social Scientists and their Influence on Ethnography." In *Work in a Modern Society: The German Historical Experience in Comparative Perspective*, ed. Jürgen Kocka, 37–53. New York: Berghahn Books.

———. 2018. "Work." In *The International Encyclopedia of Anthropology*, ed. Hilary Callan, Vol. XII, 6490–98. Oxford: Wiley Blackwell.
Stensrud, Astrid. 2010. "Los peregrinos urbanos en Qoyllurit'i y el juego mimetico de miniaturas." *Anthropologica* 28: 39–65.
Stewart, Susan. 1992. *On Longing: Narratives of the Miniature, the Gigantic, the Souvenir, the Collection*. Durham, NC: Duke University Press.
Sturzenegger-Benoist, Odile. 2006. *L'Argentine*. Paris: Karthala.
Tassi, Nico. 2010. "The 'Postulate of Abundance': *Cholo* Market and Religion in La Paz, Bolivia." *Social Anthropology* 18(2): 191–209.
Weber, Max. (1904) 2003. *L'éthique protestante et l'esprit du capitalisme*. Paris: Gallimard.
Wirth, Jean. 2003. *Sainte Anne est une sorcière et autres essais*. Geneva: Droz.

4

Pursuing Pleasure at Work

Friendship and Precarity at North Indian Call Centers

Akanksha Awal

In Ghaziabad city, on the outskirts of Delhi, Pushpa, a 24-year-old IT graduate of mid-ranking caste, had given up her job as a manager at a large real estate firm to accept a more junior position—and for less pay—at a call center. This puzzled me: hierarchy at work is taken for granted in India, and Pushpa was at a pinnacle. Why would she give up a senior, more secure position for one with lower pay? Pushpa explained that, in her previous job as a manager, she had been expected to reproach staff who had missed their sales targets. "Show some *attitude*," she was frequently told, even as she struggled to do so. Typically, men missed their sales targets at the real estate company, while women tended to be more successful. Pushpa felt sorry for the men but asked me rhetorically if it was their own fault. She explained that Indian customers often hang up on hearing a man's voice, and the young men at her workplace could hardly be blamed for this. In her view, this was more a reflection of India's sexualized society, where conversations with a woman will be pursued by male customers, even when they have no intention of buying the product on offer. Men often lost jobs because of this kind of discrimination, and she felt sorry for them. She struggled to perform what Arlie Hochschild (2003) calls emotional labor—the outward performance of expected emotions in customer-facing roles. Pushpa refused to perform the "attitude" that was expected of her as a manager. Therefore, she chose a different kind of a job—for less pay and a lower position in the workplace hierarchy.

At her new workplace, Pushpa befriended a number of her peers, including men, whom she went out of her way to help. She joined her new colleagues to visit malls and discos near the call center, preferring this sociality to marginally higher earnings. She thereby engaged in middle-class ideals of intimacy, characteristic of many workplaces in contemporary India.[1]

This chapter interrogates how young women narrated emotional work in their everyday working lives. I first encountered an emotional justification when a young teacher quit her job because of her inability to be angry with her students. Like Pushpa, many women complained about the expectation that they should show anger toward customers. Conversely, they were proud when they succeeded in manipulating a client's emotions to complete a sale. Women like Pushpa refused to perform emotional labor in professions such as teaching or private sector management, yet they readily manipulated emotions when working in call centers in jobs that were more precarious than the alternatives open to them. During ten months of fieldwork in Ghaziabad, I found that young women did not consider all types of emotional labor as subjugation. In this chapter I illustrate how the cultivation of an emotional self and the strategic deployment of "affective practices" allow young women to realize workplace freedoms. Affective practices are cognitive and non-cognitive emotional repertoires that are situated in the broader socioeconomic histories of individuals and relations across generations (Wetherell 2012). In India, emotions such as anger and laughter derive from generalized societal affects, such as caste-based stiffness at hierarchal workplaces and class-based pleasures of leisure. Affective practices connect global affects with localized norms (Dave 2012) and shed light on meanings and practices of workplace freedoms for young women.

Drawing on Foucault, some anthropologists have argued that freedom is found in the thoughts and practices that reflect on habituated patterns of human conduct (Laidlaw 2014). These ideas of freedom shift over time and in different cultural settings, but affective work on the body is constitutive of modern subjectivity and vernacular ideas of freedom. For example, Saba Mahmood (2005) argues that women in Cairo invest considerable energy to develop a pious persona to realize ideals of gendered freedom. In neoliberal Italy, relations with fellow citizens and ideas of freedom are shaped and underpinned by compassion (Muehlebach 2012). In contemporary India, as I will show, pleasure achieved through affective practices at the workplace is, for many young women, fundamental to realizing freedoms of mobility, consumption, and urban sociality.

In post-liberalization India, the predominant affect of middle-class subjectivity derives from leisure practices and concomitant emotions of fun and pleasure (Mazzarella 2003; Brosius 2010). These intersect with Euro-American cultural norms that emphasize the pursuit of happiness and well-being at workplaces and in personal relations (Ahmed 2007). A focus on conviviality emphasizes togetherness, sociability, and festivity rooted in friendship and shared cosmopolitan norms (Nowicka and Vertovec 2014).

These emotional registers mark a break from the emotional restraint and reserve that have characterized notions of civil and respectable behavior in India since colonial times (Chatterjee 1989, 2004). Rather than focus on individual freedom, Indian nationalists reframed freedom in the religious language of *dharma*, and sought to free the soul from the slavery of the senses to produce a new national community (Chakrabarty 1992: 14). Thus, in postcolonial India, the emotional disposition of restraint filters access to individual freedoms guaranteed by the constitution in government offices and civil society. Emotional restraint intersects with upper-caste norms (Rege 1995) and is manifest in the affective quality of respectable interactions among strangers (Froystad 2006), religiosity (Laidlaw 2000), and queer politics (Dave 2012). At industrial workplaces, economic transformations have entrenched masculine cultures of disappointed hope and boredom (Sanchez 2012; Cross 2014; cf. De Neve 2014). However, little attention has been paid to how broader socioemotional transformation affects emotional repertoires in service sector workplaces, such as call centers (but see Mankekar and Gupta 2019), educational institutions or retail stores. I analyze the ethical judgments surrounding young women's affective practices to illuminate the more general emotional transformation of work cultures in India.

Call-center workers strategically perform emotional labor that allows them to challenge existing ideas of desirable, hierarchal workplaces. They reframe personhood in idioms of friendship and thereby generate new, pleasure-based work cultures. While many of the workplaces in my field site required women to be adept in cultivating an approachable persona, they were also expected on occasion to demonstrate the opposite (or to show "attitude"). The latter disposition involved treating customers with indifference, for example by making them wait or by aggressively dissuading them from their pursuit of a refund. The tactical invocation of anger or aggression is considered acceptable at workplaces, indeed respectable, since it is in keeping with the long tradition of reserve, restraint, and indifference. However, the young women I worked with found it hard to deploy anger, as the case of Pushpa demonstrates. Instead, they preferred to seek positions that would enable them to make friends, to get away from their families, and to earn pocket money to go to the cinema with their boyfriends or buy them gifts. Their jobs enabled them to enjoy the liminal phase of their lives before marriage.

Lower-middle-class college graduates on the outskirts of Delhi achieve emancipation through precarious forms of work that challenge evolved South Asian stereotypes, especially concerning sexuality. In their offices, my respondents expected to act as happy and confident workers mingling with their peers in gender-fluid ways. The sexual lives of young women in

India have always been subject to intense scrutiny, and are shot through with fears of prostitution (Mody 2008; Lukose 2009). But my interlocutors rejected moralizing discourses that reduced workplace collegiality to moralizing discourses of transactional sex (cf. Cole 2010), just as they rejected jobs that required them to cultivate emotional practices of aggression and indifference. Instead, they willingly endorsed the sexualization of the female body, on their terms, in order to enjoy workplace freedoms. At the same time, their friendships structured the labor market and allowed them to break with older Indian ideas of restraint in hierarchal workplaces.

Ghaziabad is a city of 1.6 million inhabitants. Call-center workers in this study are "neophyte workers" (Ong 1997). Often from rural backgrounds, they were the first in their families to take up employment outside of the home. Call centers in Ghaziabad serve a largely lower-middle-class Indian clientele. Typically, the work involves selling education courses and life insurance, or recruitment for service sector jobs in Bengaluru or Chennai (South India). Most call centers prefer to hire women (typically 90 percent of all staff), but men and upper-caste women dominate management. Call centers offer the possibility of doubling one's base salary if sales targets are met. The job itself is not considered entirely respectable. Call centers are often located near a mall and require travel away from one's neighborhood. Neighborhood schools, by contrast, offer insecure, poorly paid teaching positions. While a teacher at a private school earns around Rs 2,000 per month and a teacher at a government school up to Rs 40,000, a typical base salary at a call center would be around Rs 10,000.

Few of my respondents were responsible for household expenses. Most were paid a base salary and a commission on sales. While they contributed their salaries to household expenditure—and poorer families would need this money more than richer ones—most did not disclose their commissions to their families. Women would allocate this money toward their dowry, or use it to cover leisure expenditure or education fees. Because they did not have financial responsibilities, many quit their jobs if their workplaces became tiresome, and almost always before marriage. Against the backdrop of local gender norms where young women cook, clean, and do care work around the house, precarious call center work offers a respite from domestic drudgery.

This chapter is structured as follows. I begin by locating debates about emotional labor in global debates concerning precarity, affect, and autonomy. In the second section I show how women conceptualize a good job in emotional terms. I then investigate call center work, drawing attention to creativity and conviviality, but also to the constant threat of sexual harassment. I conclude by explaining how female friendships have given rise to non-unionized forms of workplace bargaining.

Precarity, Affect, and Autonomy

Feminist scholars have long argued that emotional labor is expected particularly from women (Federici 1975; Hochschild 2003). The production and circulation of affect, central to late capitalist economies (Hardt 1999; Bear et al. 2015), can also be approached via the concept of "precarity" (Standing 2011). This term has commonly been used in the analysis of insecure employment and short-term contracts that are exploitative and undesirable.[2] However, I follow Millar (2014: 35), who shows that certain forms of exploitative work can be desired, and uses "the analytic of precarity to conceptualize the labor condition as inseparable from issues of subjectivity, affect, sociality, and desire."

In their studies of call centers in Bengaluru, Purnima Mankekar and Akhil Gupta (2016, 2019) overlook the creativity of call-center workers, preferring to emphasize the Taylorian aspect of task segmentation, deskilling, and time discipline. Call-center employees are required to imagine a version of themselves that is culturally attuned to customers' lifeworlds, learning accents and social mores accordingly (Aneesh 2006; 2015). This imagined self becomes alienated from the rhythms and sociality of her surroundings, and experiences "social death" (ibid.). These scholars emphasize the alienation and exhaustion caused by unrelenting emotional work. Mankekar and Gupta (2016) follow Hochschild (2003) in proposing that affect produces subjectivities, but they fail to explain how different kinds of affects—Fordism, post-Fordism, or precarity—create different subjectivities that may foster creativity and friendship.

Feminist and Marxist approaches also banish imagination from the factory floor (Ong 1997). Aihwa Ong (1997) suggests investigating workers' subjectivities in order to grasp the creativity of their practices. Young women in this study sought jobs in order to get closer to an imagined ideal: typically, a woman who dresses stylishly, speaks confidently, and has knowledge of the world. To develop this persona, they developed emotional repertoires to escape the routine of domestic life. As I will show, call centers are conducive to such imaginings in ways that more hierarchal jobs, such as government sector work, are not. The flexibility of the tasks and the working hours allow women scope to socialize with colleagues outside—and often during—working hours. They looked for companies where they could have "fun" (cf. Mankekar and Gupta 2016).

Precarious labor as a condition is distinct from its lived experience (Millar 2014). Precarious jobs may be preferred to more secure waged work if they enable "relational autonomy"—for example, the maintenance of relationships essential for childcare. Similarly, garment workers in India prefer contract work that allows them to look after their families (De Neve 2014). Even in the era of neoliberalism (and perhaps especially in this era), workers are enmeshed within social worlds and frequently prioritize care for kin over personal preferences. Young women in Ghaziabad, however, sought work as a way to distance themselves from kin. Instead, they worked and helped each other as friends in a liminal phase of their lives. They chose this work not primarily on the basis of its availability or its remuneration, but to have fun. They enjoyed themselves with friends, and frequently formed intimate relations with their bosses. Their sexuality was the subject of intense discussion and suspicion in new circuits of patriarchy (see Ong 1997). Such discussions highlight how workplace freedoms are precariously won.

The Emotional Requirements of a Job

Let me open the empirical discussion with Malika, a Dalit woman aged 27, whose first job as a government schoolteacher was in Gonda district, 400 miles from her home. She stayed with her brother in a small rented apartment while teaching secondary school students in the district. "The students tell me that no one has ever dealt with their questions in the way I do," she told me with pride on the phone. "But Madam [school principal] says that I should show some *attitude*." Attitude, the English word used in Hindi, signaled the performance of calculated indifference. As such, it implied a classed and upper-caste distinction of wariness. In remarking on Malika's practices, the principal of the school was suggesting that Malika was too pally with the students and their families, whereas she should be commanding over students and parents as a government schoolteacher. "*Chakkar ghumao*" (don't act immediately, but make them return over and over again so that they need to wait), the principal instructed her. Waiting structures power relations in South Asia (Chakrabarty 2000; Corbridge 2004). Making people wait, or making them come back repeatedly to complete some small task, is an exercise in establishing social order. Rooted in rituals of circumambulation in temples, such tactics that force people to return over and over again reinforce hierarchy, and make requests appear as prayers. Similar techniques were common in the private schools and retail workplaces I studied. The female receptionists who acted as the first point of contact for irate customers were expected to intimidate them by asking them to return to the office several times or fob them off through diversionary tactics.

Malika, however, preferred not to impose hierarchies through indifference. She was eager to teach and to attend school each day, but this was too much for the school's principal, a woman of mid-ranking caste. Malika found *not* teaching was depressing. Why should she have to show attitude to students who were turning up at school in order to study, Malika constantly wondered. Her inability to enforce discipline was perceived as a sign of her Dalit background, while her willingness to help others was seen as a sign of her sexual availability (Rege 1995). The principal suggested that Malika should informally return home to her family in Ghaziabad, instead of maintaining a separate household in Gonda. For payment of a bribe of Rs 10,000 a month, or a quarter of her salary, the principal would confirm her daily attendance. Malika was powerless to alter caste hierarchy at this school, and returned home shortly thereafter. Although she continued to receive a salary for a job she was no longer doing, having to stay at home restricted her professional growth. She therefore sought creativity and challenge by enrolling in a PhD program at a nearby university. She developed a research proposal with her former MA supervisor, and enrolled with the help of a scholarship available for Dalit students.

Although Malika's research in sociology was mainly desk-based, she frequently hung out at her supervisor's office.[3] This allowed her to access a wider network of contacts, but as hierarchical as the one she had shunned in the government job. However, she explained that the PhD research had inspired a new awareness of the society around her. The research involved observing a tribal group and encouraging its members to send their children to school. She had already been invited to a couple of conferences in different parts of India, and had engaged with men and women of many different caste backgrounds. Her supervisor had been educated at a British university and Malika hoped that she too would be able to visit a university abroad. For Malika, a public sector job as a teacher had sapped her creativity, whereas working for a PhD encouraged lateral thinking.

Many young women preferred the private sector to working in government jobs, even if the latter were more secure because they provided an avenue to be creative. A private sector employee was more likely to have "personality" and "confidence" because she frequently shifted workplaces, travelled to new places, and acquired new skills. She engaged with a wider array of, mostly wealthy, customers in the private sector. The call centers had regional specializations and offered opportunities to improve one's English and knowledge of the whole country. As Vinita, a Dalit call-center worker, explained: "In an interview, they check your personality, the way you walk, talk, and your dress sense." Personality denotes desirable middle-class traits, such as good English and elegant comportment e.g., shoulders that are pulled back and erect spines. It implied the know-how to navigate the local world by adeptly deploying emotional repertoires in tune with the latest requirements of the job market. The emphasis was on learning new, embodied affective dispositions.

In a government job, by contrast, it was often unnecessary to turn up.[4] In government jobs one typically encountered a narrow range of, often poorer, people. Many government services, such as schools, no longer attract large numbers of students; if they do, they are typically from poor households. Women argued that a government job made one lazy, as one got more "secure" (again, the English word is commonly used when speaking Hindi). One does not have to dress up to please a boss or customers at a government job, for example. Neither does one need to learn new skills. The public sector is perceived as antithetical to learning, and government workers are considered slow. They are unable to partake in the new emotional cultures of the Indian society because they are wedded to patterns of indifference when exercising bureaucratic power (Mathur 2019). In contrast, the young women I interviewed aspired to the emotional agility required in call centers, even if this required a cultivation of emotional practices to conform to the emotional culture of call centers. Like the garment workers in Tamil Nadu (De Neve 2014), young women preferred being free and convivial in an insecure workplace to the securities of a regimented Fordist regime or the "attitude" required in a government job.

Women were pragmatic about their working aspirations; while a government job would make them attractive to a prospective partner, it was hard to get such a job—and besides, preparing for the examination in gender-segregated libraries was restrictive and boring. Most women complained that staying at home was "boring" (Islam 2020). Their mothers pushed them to help with household chores. Their brothers monitored their movements in the neighborhood and frequently checked their phones, and tensions with their brothers over television or phones often ended in verbal abuse or physical assaults.

By contrast, precarious work in call centers was easy to obtain, generally paid well enough to cover the costs of their everyday leisure activities, and was away from home. The affective nature of call-center work blurs the distinction between work and leisure, so that employment takes over private leisure time (Mankekar and Gupta 2019). It disrupts rhythms of social life, producing "docile bodies" programed to capitalist discipline (Ong 1997). In my field site, the managers, upper-caste men and women, controlled working hours (often long), pay, and commission earnings. Lateness and missing targets led to deductions. But a seemingly harsh regime was softened by intimate relationships with men, including bosses. Friends of both sexes covered for each other, such that it was possible to visit a mall, for example, during the day without financial penalties. Ritika, an upper-caste call-center worker, explained that upon graduating she had chosen a call center over a teaching job because it offered her greater control over her working hours. Her mobile phone enabled her to do her job—selling insurance for a major Indian bank—from the city's parks and retail malls. Pushpa, with whom I began this chapter, explained that she made sure not to exceed her daily targets and to reserve sufficient time and money for leisure activities. She remarked that even if she did not get time off from work, being with friends at work was more enjoyable than staying at home. In other words, the workplace itself was a kind of leisure. In this way, young women reframed personhood away from their families and towards friendships that nurtured individual sexual and social freedoms through short-term, flexible work at call centers.

The devaluation of government work was both a rejection of stereotypes of a caste-ridden society and a challenge to the gendered nature of service-sector work. The preference for call-center jobs might be explained as a discursive strategy that young women utilized to deal with pervasive job insecurity and the increased scarcity of government jobs. Moreover, the opinions of some women may shift when, later in life, they struggle to find a secure footing in a sexualized job market that privileges younger women.[5] My respondents' families wanted their daughters to obtain a government job, which they might keep after marriage. Yet, the vast majority of the young women I worked with had different ideas: they engaged with the workplace as a way to seek greater freedoms in the here and now. The pursuit of freedom offered my interlocutors a way to inhabit an urban caste-less sensibility. If the demands of a job became onerous, as in the case of Pushpa, they shifted jobs, preferring workplaces that required a different kind of emotional labor, more suited to the leisure-seeking middle-class cultures of contemporary northern India.

Creativity and Conviviality

Many young women emphasized that their work required them to converse creatively with customers, quite unlike teaching or the humdrum tasks of the household. To sustain the necessary creativity, my interlocutors studied the dialogues of Bollywood films, which they would later rehearse with their friends in parks and in the food courts of the malls. They also deployed emotional repertoires learnt from the films on their customers.

Call centers serving American or European customers in India train their workers to imagine a different self (Aneesh 2006; Vora 2010; Mankekar and Gupta 2016). Companies typically take much trouble to train staff in using neutral accents. They use videos to acculturate them to Western lifeworlds. However, the young lower-middle class women of this study did not receive formal training. Their job interviews typically involved a written test on a subject such as "My School Days," followed by a short conversation. They developed their skills later from their colleagues. Often, they imagined their customers' lives from the portrayals of middle-class lives as portrayed on television or in Bollywood films. Some women used Hindi honorifics and practiced not only accents but also a coquettish laugh. It was common practice to glean information about a customer's family. Ritika conjured an imaginary family for herself when egging on customers to divulge more about their own circumstances. As a trained accountant, she knew exactly how to probe a customer's creditworthiness. She and her close friend Vinita shared the information they obtained with their supervisors. These methods, and the access they gave to family networks, were instrumental in expanding their sales.

Some women persuaded their clients by co-producing fantasies of a middle-class life. Nagma, a Muslim respondent and friend of Pushpa, worked in a call center that recruited staff for jobs in multinational corporations in Bengaluru. Their main tasks included convincing IT engineers to move to new companies. They helped clients format their CVs and update the skills required by offering training courses and preparing them for interviews. Nagma was good at persuading software engineers to set their sights higher and apply for new posts. She drew on imaginaries of middle-class success, such as a holiday abroad that a higher salary would make possible, to encourage clients to imagine a better future for themselves. Pushpa was good at procuring CVs but less adept at convincing clients to proceed to interview. Pushpa became angry when men declined to apply for better-paid jobs and rebuked them: how could they be so complacent and not apply for a job with superior potential? Nagma helped Pushpa develop tact. She suggested that Pushpa tell the client that the job might open up new possibilities and urge him to at least go for the interview before making up his mind.

Women were considered more creative than men in being able to hold longer conversations with customers.[6] However, they also suffered from the downsides of using affective practices that hinged on capitalizing on their sexuality: the same emotional skills that drew the customers into longer conversations could also serve as an opening to sexual harassment. One afternoon, I was hanging out with Ritika and Vinita in a park in Ghaziabad city. Both were skipping the workplace that day but taking urgent calls on their mobiles. Ritika had just been on the phone with a wealthy client in Pune, a small city in southern India, who had agreed to buy an insurance policy of Rs 45,000. He had been looking around for something suitable and informed Ritika that, although he was keen to purchase the policy from her, a colleague from her office had offered him a bonus: a train ticket to Delhi upon completion. Vinita and Ritika were both incredulous. What was he suggesting? A liaison with Ritika in Delhi? And who might this mysterious colleague be? In the cut-throat insurance market, they noted, almost anything was possible, but they doubted it would be followed through. The customer insisted that he wanted to buy the insurance policy from Ritika, but that she would need to match that offer of a train ticket.

Hanging up, Ritika mused on how she always passed as a "high class" (or rich) woman on the phone. She would lower the tone of her voice when speaking with men, which usually sufficed to clinch the deal. Ritika consistently met her targets *and* those of her boyfriend. She was so good at her job that she often took time off work to frequent discotheques and cinemas during normal working hours. This time she wondered if she had gone too far in flirting with the client: her boyfriend had grown jealous, and was threatening to delay the bonus payments she was due.

Although angry, Ritika eventually agreed to send a train ticket. If the customer turned up in Delhi, she reasoned, she did not have to meet him, though she had implied that she would. Was it right to sell an insurance policy by spinning lies? She was unmarried, and the train ticket was simply an incentive to make a sale. Besides, flirting with customers was part of the pleasure of the game. She had "character," she asserted. Character indexed a middle-class sensibility of propriety and, for her, a moral way of being. Her boyfriend/boss agreed, authorized the purchase, and Ritika and Vinita went to watch a film that afternoon.

Ritika's case exemplifies the moral dilemmas of using affective practices in a sexualized public sphere. They are precarious morally because they involve misrepresentations, even lies. They are open to misinterpretation by predatory men (both customers and bosses). Women often established relationships with men in order to "enjoy" their time at work, but once established, it was hard to shift the relationships without quitting. Most women said that it was preferable to change workplaces frequently than to seek career progression in one. There was no way they could pursue sexual harassment charges. Worse, if women were to complain at home about sexual harassment, their families would not allow them to go to work. In this context, establishing friendships with women at work was often their best bargaining chip, as I show in the next section.

The sexualization of workplaces in India is linked to caste-based registers of recognition. Many customers assume that all women in call centers and retail shops belong to the lower-castes. But affective practices do not neatly correspond to caste practices. Not all dominant caste women use stronger voices or project aggression, while not all Dalit women crack jokes or give the impression of being sexually available. Pushpa, the call-center worker who quit a managerial role, came from a mid-ranking caste background but she rejected the expectation that she should assert dominance at the workplace. Malika, the government schoolteacher in Gonda, was from a

Dalit background, but she too had to wrestle with the stereotypes in order to perform well at her workplace. Both women rejected the crushing isolation of maintaining hierarchy, while pretending busyness at work (Graeber 2019). Instead, they chose roles that fostered collegiality, giving them more control over their interactions with male superiors, if only temporarily.

Friendship at Work

Most of India's working-age population is employed in the informal sector (Sanchez 2012; Parry 2020). Men use established family networks, often backed up with violence, to secure work in industrial labor, real estate, or education. By contrast, young women in Ghaziabad had no access to such networks. They relied on friendships to secure a job, to learn the ropes after getting it, to negotiate a rise, and even to learn when and how to quit.

Vinita once told me: "You can progress a lot with a friend." Vinita had been dating her supervisor for over three years. On a team-building trip to Shimla, they developed a rapport. She explained that having a boyfriend at work offered protection from the sexual advances of other men, both in the office and from predatory customers. Most of her friends, including Ritika, also had boyfriends at work. Intimate relationships are common, if frowned upon, among colleagues in call centers in Bengaluru (Mankekar and Gupta 2016). However, unlike waged workers in Bengaluru, Ritika and Vinita used intimate relationships to establish their own business or seek a promotion.

In five years at the call center, Vinita had formed a deep bond with her boyfriend that had given her the confidence to start her own business. After saving up her commission in a bank account for over five years (Vinita could isolate this from her contributions to her parents' household), she pooled this sum with the savings of her partner to start a call center. She estimated that although the initial investment was high (around Rs 250,000), her monthly income was sure to double. Her boyfriend managed the setting up of the bank account and the renting of the premises. Vinita recruited her female friends, including some from her previous workplace, promising them a higher rate of commission. The expectation was that long-term clients would also transfer their allegiance.

After three months had passed, Vinita's business was still mired in administrative bottlenecks and Vinita tried to move back to her old workplace. She was turned down because, as Vinita later recognized, the word had gotten around that she had tried to steal data from her previous employer. During this time, Vinita's friend Shiba, who had quit her job to join Vinita's call center, complained that she could not sustain herself while waiting for Vinita's business to generate its first cash flows. Vinita took Shiba out for meals at the mall and provided Rs 1,000 to cover her immediate expenses. She encouraged Shiba to look for jobs elsewhere and we conducted a mock interview in a mall to help her prepare. But Shiba struggled to find a toehold. Eventually, some months later, Vinita was rehired at her old place thanks to the good offices of her friend Ritika. Once back in, she helped Shiba to join that well-established call center.

Although precarious work conditions are economically exploitative, workers can choose to have time to care for their families or to maintain friendships (Millar 2014). In Tamil Nadu, garment workers use the idioms of fictive kinship to secure new work and maintain a cordial workplace atmosphere (De Neve 2014). Yet the family idioms tie workers to exploitative relationships and reproduce hierarchal dynamics along caste and gender lines. However, young women like Vinita maintained that they entered workplaces with their friends. While at work, they sought separation from family and caste-based kinship networks. They spent their free time not doing care work, but enjoying time with their friends watching films or window shopping at the malls. Friendships can be a contradictory resource for advancement and for social sanction (Dyson 2010). Ritika and Vinita competed over their respective clients, but the former was loyal to her friend and threatened to quit her job when Vinita was barred from entering the work premises after she had launched her new firm.

A concern with realizing the self did not turn young people in Ghaziabad away from each other (cf. Gooptu 2013). Although my interlocutors did not join unions, their workplace friendships helped them negotiate better working conditions. Days after joining, I was hanging out with Nagma, her boyfriend and Pushpa at a mall after work. We discussed how Pushpa's salary was far below industry standards for men with a Bachelor's in Technology. Pushpa was unsure about asking her boss for a pay rise shortly after joining, but Nagma reassured her. The next day, when Pushpa discussed her qualifications with her boss, Nagma chimed in. Subsequently, Pushpa secured a pay rise of Rs 2,000 (an increment of 10 percent).

Many employers openly admitted that they hired women at a lower starting salary because women had little sense of the norms and hesitated to negotiate. Young women's families did not rely on their incomes and so did not push them to request more. Moreover, few women stayed long enough to qualify for annual pay rises, and many skipped the appraisals that would alert them to the possibilities for seeking rises. Young women relied on their friends to establish salary benchmarks and negotiate shorter working hours. When Pushpa was given CVs to format just before the end of the day, Nagma intervened on her behalf so that her friend could be home on time. She also ensured that Pushpa could take time off when she asked for it, such as when her period was due.

The more clients a female worker obtained, the greater her bargaining power for herself and for her friends. Ritika and Vinita had successfully negotiated time off to attend law school in Ghaziabad, as part of their career progression at work. Not all women were friends: some were competitors (e.g., the mystery caller in the previous section). Small, non-unionized groups of three or four friends would support each other intensely, to the point of collectively threatening to quit if one of them were placed in an unacceptable situation. If one person in this group was in a relationship with her boss, it would strengthen the bargaining power of the whole group. This solidarity was experienced as empowering.

At work, women often addressed each other by first names, or collectively as "friends". Even as some addressed their superiors as "Sir" or "Ma'am," both in and out of the office, the use of the English words signaled new class-based hierarchies at work rather than caste-based ones. Such hierarchies flourished in malls and parks, where commensality, handholding, and hugging (across castes and between genders) were norms. Among older generations of workers in South Asia, the linguistic registers that index social relationships also establish genealogy. They reiterate a person's connections in a new workplace or the city. By contrast, friendships provide an alternative, non-hierarchal mode of relating, as has already been noted for young men (Nakassis 2016). At call centers, upper-caste women like Ritika interacted with Dalits such as Vinita by deploying the same affective practices with clients and enacting the same class-based leisure activities outside their workplace. Their friendships emphasized pleasure-seeking cultures of Indian modernity.

Even the most successful women in call centers, those who earned the maximum bonuses, earned only about half the salary of a public sector job. A call-center worker who had perfected the necessary affective practices had some bargaining power vis-à-vis her bosses, but it was limited because these women were easily replaceable. Sooner or later, marriage and patriarchy would capture them. By and large, women's friendships formed initially at college and in workplaces were not sustained after marriage. Neither Ritika nor Vinita expected to marry their bosses. Almost all friendships with men were severed in days before marriage—women quit their jobs, changed their phone numbers, and cut off all contact. Sometimes, women would even break with women colleagues before marriage to separate their workplace relationships. This knowledge intensified the conviviality of this interlude in the life course. Both during working hours and when socializing outside them, women valued the self-confidence and relative autonomy they obtained through their employment. Friendship was the crucial institution.

Conclusion: Precarious Pleasures at Workplaces

The feminization of Indian workplaces is accompanied by a socioemotional transformation of the society. In this chapter I have shown that new emotional repertoires shape conceptions of workplace freedoms. Young women cultivate affective practices, including self-confident demeanor, stylish dress, and smart verbal skills in order to avail themselves of the freedoms of India's burgeoning consumer cultures, i.e., the ability to go out and about, have fun with friends. Call-center jobs are precarious, but discourses and practices of agile learning enable women to situate themselves as desirable employees. This work is preferred to more secure, better paid, but "bullshit" jobs for the government, such as teaching.

My interlocutors, with their pleasure-seeking practices and happiness repertoires (see Ahmed 2007), were tapping into global emotional processes. Even as these affective practices were contested as morally incorrect, young women sought to augment their use in their daily work. Their pursuit of sensual pleasure marks a break with nationalist ideals of hierarchy and restraint, as well as with the constraints of kinship and caste. Personhood is being reframed towards individual friendships and conviviality. Women rely on affective bonds to secure their jobs, stay employed, and find new work, even though these friendships are ephemeral. This notion of personhood shapes negotiating tactics at the workplace concerning everything from pay rises to sick leave, and to informal contestation of unfair dismissals. While the structures of capitalism in a patriarchal society keep their wages low, the role played by educated young women as brokers in dynamic sectors of the new economy underscores a feminized transformation of the urban economy. Women are expendable employees in global circuits of capital accumulation, and yet the work I have discussed in this chapter gives them a chance to live out gendered aspirations for a good life. This, rather than anxieties about precariousness of work, is the most powerful aspect of work for them. The friendships they form at work are experienced as empowering, and open up ways to curtail abusive work practices. At the same time, they highlight the precarious nature of workplace freedoms; these freedoms are often only available to those who can financially afford to remain at the bottom of call-center hierarchies. For ambitious young women like Ritika and Vinita, relationships with men offer opportunities for growth, even as they entrench the sexualization of workplaces. Women who refuse to enter into liaisons with men in senior positions often have no choice but to quit their jobs.

As women progressed in their short careers at the call centers, some learnt emotional agility—quickly shifting from smiles to anger, and back again—to progress in their line of work. For the vast majority of young women, these skills seemed difficult. Their lower-middle-class families did not rely on women's income, and did not press their daughters to take up jobs. Given a choice between secure but tedious government employment and a sexualized public sphere, they preferred to enter this public sphere as temporary workers as it gave them greater freedom to choose their friends. It gave them a degree of control over the nature of relationships they had with men. But this was illusory. Eventually, this led most of them to give up their precarious employment altogether, especially before marriage.

Acknowledgments

I would like to thank my respondents for opening up their lives to my constant questioning and observation, even when it sometimes killed the joyous mood. I would also like to thank Ilana Gershon, Chris Hann, James Laidlaw, and Peter van der Veer for challenging my ideas during conversations in Halle, and later. Thanks also to David Mills, Abigail Branford, and members of the Thursday writing group at Oxford for comments on the first draft, and to an anonymous reviewer.

Akanksha Awal has a doctorate in social anthropology from the University of Oxford, where she remains based as a Leverhulme Early Career Fellow at the School of Anthropology and Museum Ethnography. She previously worked as a journalist for the *Financial Times* in London and New Delhi.

Notes

1. This work is based on ten months of ethnographic fieldwork in 2015–16 with young lower-middle-class women in Ghaziabad district, Uttar Pradesh. I interviewed over a hundred respondents (about 80 percent were women), and observed them over a period of time at their places of work, in education, and at leisure. I do not discuss men's perspectives in this chapter. Most women (90 percent) were teaching in some capacity, either a local primary school or home tutoring students after school. Not a conventional workplace ethnography, this chapter specifically focuses on two groups of women working in two different call centers. Although some of my respondents worked at well-established call centers (such as Ritika and Vinita),

some call centers were like mayflies that opened and shut down within three to six months. In addition, I interviewed call-center owners as well as retail store managers and school and college principals to understand how employers recruit staff and perceive women's entry into workplaces. I also interviewed call-center customers. The chapter is an account of the working lives of young women, which includes leisure and unemployment.

My own positionality as someone who grew up in Ghaziabad and went abroad to study might have affected the answers I received. I was often recognized as educated (General Caste), but also (incorrectly) identified as Muslim by some of my respondents. I was frequently a point of comparison, and it is possible that some women exaggerated their own sense of desire and gave me answers that they thought I might have been seeking.

2. For anthropological critique of this term in contexts of industrial labor, see Hann and Parry 2018.
3. I met Malika at her supervisor's office when visiting one day.
4. Joining the police was popular, however, because it legitimized their presence on the streets.
5. Some managers, men or women of high-caste, refused to employ married women, or encouraged them to quit following marriage.
6. It was much easier for women to find jobs than it was for their brothers. Men, I was told over and over again, were less able to initiate conversations. They were abrupt and, when challenged, would often curse and hang up. Women were regarded as less threatening, even when they doggedly repeated their calls, as Pushpa did with her IT clients. As a woman, she could pester them in a way that a man could not.

References

Ahmed, Sara. 2007. "The Happiness Turn." *New Formations* 63: 7–15.

Aneesh, A. 2006. *A Virtual Migration: The Programming of Globalization*. Durham, NC: Duke University Press.

———. 2015. *Neutral Accent: How Language, Labor, and Life Become Global*. Durham, NC: Duke University Press.

Bear, Laura, Karen Ho, Anna Tsing and Sylvia Yanagisako. 2015. "Gens: A Feminist Manifesto for the Study of Capitalism." Theorizing the Contemporary, *Fieldsights*, March 30.

Brosius, Christiane. 2010. *India's Middle Class: New Forms of Urban Leisure, Consumption and Prosperity*. New Delhi: Routledge.

Chakrabarty, Dipesh. 1992. "Postcoloniality and the Artifice of History: Who Speaks for 'Indian' Pasts?" *Representations* 37: 1–26.

———. 2000. *Provincializing Europe: Postcolonial Thought and Historical Difference*. Princeton, NJ: Princeton University Press.

Chatterjee, Partha. 1989. "Colonialism, Nationalism, and Colonialized Women: The Contest in India." *American Anthropological Association* 16(4): 622–33.

———. 2004. *The Politics of the Governed: Reflections on Popular Politics in Most of the World*. New York: Columbia University Press.

Cole, Jennifer. 2010. *Sex and Salvation: Imagining the Future in Madagascar*. Chicago: University of Chicago Press.
Corbridge, Stuart. 2009. "Waiting in Line, or the Moral and Material Geographies of Queue-Jumping." In *Geographies and Moralities*, ed. R. Lee and D. M. Smith, 183–98. Malden, MA: Blackwell Publishing Ltd.
Cross, Jamie. 2014. *Dream Zones: Anticipating Capitalism and Development in India*. London: Pluto Press.
Dave, Nais. 2012. *Queer Activism in India: A Story in the Anthropology of Ethics*. Durham, NC: Duke University Press.
De Neve, Geert. 2014. "Fordism, Flexible Specialization and CSR: How Indian Garment Workers Critique Neoliberal Labour Regimes." *Ethnography* 15(2): 184–207.
Dyson, Jane. 2010. "Friendship in Practice: Girls' Work in the Indian Himalayas." *American Ethnologist* 37(3): 482–98.
Federici, Silvia. 1975. *Wages Against Housework*. London: Power of Women Collective.
Froystad, Kathinka. 2006. "Anonymous Encounters: Class Categorisation and Social Distancing in Public Places." In *The Meaning of the Local: Politics of Place in Urban India*, ed. G. De Neve and H. Donner, 159–81. London: Routledge.
Gooptu, Nandini. 2013. *Enterprise Culture in Neoliberal India: Studies in Youth, Class, Work and Media*. London: Routledge.
Graeber, David. 2019. *Bullshit Jobs: A Theory*. London: Penguin Books.
Hann, Chris, and Jonathan Parry, eds. 2018. *Industrial Labor on the Margins of Capitalism: Precarity, Class, and the Neoliberal Subject*. New York: Berghahn Books.
Hardt, Michael. 1999. "Affective Labor." *Boundary* 26(2): 89–100.
Hochschild, Arlie Russell. 2003. *The Managed Heart: Commercialization of Human Feeling*. Berkeley: University of California Press.
Islam, Asiya. 2020. "It Gets Really Boring if You Stay at Home: Women, Work and Temporalities in Urban India." *Sociology* 54(5): 867–82.
Laidlaw, James. 2000. "A Free Gift Makes No Friends." *The Journal of the Royal Anthropological Institute* 6(4): 617–34.
———. 2014. *The Subject of Virtue: An Anthropology of Ethics and Freedom*. Cambridge: Cambridge University Press.
Lukose, Ritty. 2009. *Liberalization's Children: Gender, Youth, and Consumer Citizenship in Globalizing India*. Durham, NC: Duke University Press.
Mahmood, Saba. 2005. *Politics of Piety: The Islamic Revival and the Feminist Subject*. Princeton, NJ: Princeton University Press.
Mankekar, Purnima, and Akhil Gupta. 2016. "Intimate Encounters: Affective Labor in Call Centers." *positions* 24(1): 17–43.
———. 2019. "The Missed Period: Disjunctive Temporalities and the Work of Capital in an Indian BPO." *American Ethnologist* 46(4): 417–28.
Mathur, Nayanika. 2019. "A Petition to Kill: Efficacious Arzees against Big Cats in India." *Modern Asian Studies* 53(1): 278–311.
Mazzarella, William. 2003. *"Very Bombay": Contending with the Global in an Indian Advertising Agency*. Chicago: University of Chicago Press.

Millar, Kathleen. 2014. "The Precarious Present: Wageless Labor and Disrupted Life in Rio de Janeiro, Brazil." *Cultural Anthropology* 29(1): 32–53.
Mody, Perveez. 2008. *The Intimate State: Love-Marriage and the Law in Delhi*. New Delhi: Routledge.
Muehlebach, Andrea. 2012. *The Moral Neoliberal: Welfare and Citizenship in Italy*. Chicago: University of Chicago Press.
Nakassis, Constantine. 2016. *Doing Style: Youth and Mass Mediation in South India*. Chicago: University of Chicago Press.
Nowicka, Magdalena, and Steven Vertovec. 2014. "Introduction. Comparing Convivialities: Dreams and Realities of Living-with-Difference." *Convivialities of European Journal of Cultural Studies* (Special Issue) 17(4): 341–56.
Ong, Aihwa. 1997. *Spirits of Resistance and Capitalist Discipline*. New York: SUNY Press.
Parry, Jonathan. 2020. *Classes of Labour: Work and Life in a Central Indian Steel Town*. London: Routledge.
Rege, Sharmila. 1995. "The Hegemonic Appropriation of Sexuality: The Case of the Lavani Performers of Maharashtra." *Contributions to Indian Sociology* 29(1–2): 23–38.
Sanchez, Andrew. 2012. "Questioning Success: Dispossession and the Criminal Entrepreneur in Urban India." *Critique of Anthropology* 32(4): 435–57.
Standing, Guy. 2011. *The Precariat: The New Dangerous Class*. London: Bloomsbury Academic.
Vora, Kalindi. 2010. "The Transmission of Care: Affective Economies and Indian Call Centres." In *Intimate Labors: Cultures, Technologies and the Politics of Care*, ed. E. Boris and R. S. Parrenas. Stanford, CA: Stanford University Press.
Wetherell, Margaret. 2012. *Affect and Emotion: A New Social Science Understanding*. London: Sage.

5

More Than Money

Work as Self-Realization in Accra's Private Media

Anna-Riikka Kauppinen

"My family does not understand the nature of my job," Frankie[1] said on one of those late evenings we spent with his colleagues in a popular bar in central Accra after a long day's work. Frankie was an unmarried media professional in his early thirties, working at an Accra-based private television station, TV Central. After years of unpaid internships and temporary contracts, he had become a permanent employee a few months earlier. But that evening in late 2013, Frankie explained he had problems; his managers were refusing to support his ambitions to produce what he called "serious programs." They were not allowing him access to certain equipment, such as good cameras. Frankie was frustrated by their "mediocrity." He had tried to explain this to his mother, who was a trader, but she could not understand Frankie's constant preoccupation with his work. Why did he spend such long hours at the office, and have "so little to show" in return? Frankie could not convey the intricacies of his work or what it meant to pursue "a career" and be a "career person."[2]

On that particular day Frankie and his colleagues had run from one shooting location to the next, and spent hours perfecting shots for a documentary. As we conversed and night fell, some colleagues were still checking the footage on the camera and thinking how to improve the shots. Indeed, even Frankie's mother knew that late nights in bars were not leisure time, but hard work—occasions for "meetings", where new "deals" were struck, new ideas developed, and future career moves plotted. A lot of aspiration was in the air: both aspiration to succeed in terms of material prosperity, and aspiration to become excellent at one's job, dubbed "serious" in everyday speech. Seriousness was an elusive quality of both work and people that may have escaped articulation, but which one could recognize when one "saw it." Serious work would "make a mark" and potentially travel way beyond the borders of Ghana to the global stage.

The main issue between Frankie and his family was the discrepancy between the time Frankie spent at work and his monetary contributions to the family household. According to many mothers, fathers, and siblings of young media professionals I met in Accra, these young people were "killing themselves for nothing"—in other words, toiling at a job that did not pay well. For these families, a "serious person" was someone who had successfully transitioned from childhood and adolescence into adulthood, which was marked by their capacity to contribute to the household. For instance, Frankie's siblings had recently gathered to cement the compound of the family house, but Frankie had only managed to contribute one bag of cement, leaving the bag at the compound and rushing to the next "meeting." This was inconsistent with his status as a professional employee, who Ghanaians had historically perceived as someone with a stable financial standing and thus a capacity to cultivate networks of dependents (Behrends and Lentz 2012: 151). But the Ghanaian private media industry was notorious for its low salaries, which Frankie found difficult to explain to his family. Some months, he was not paid on time and had to rely on "dashes"[3] from colleagues. The employees constantly planned how to make more money through informal means. "A taxi driver earns more than me," Frankie's colleague Kodjo would sometimes say, in a frustrated tone.

This may not have been too far from the truth. Salary grumbling and unmet family expectations were typical problems (called *palava* in Ghanaian pidgin) among young professionals, especially among those from lower-middle-class families who had no history of "professionalism" in the lineage. Many young professionals in Accra were the only members of their families with university degrees and salaried employment. They would start the day carefully ironing a collared shirt before catching a minibus, *trotro,* to the office as early as 5.30 a.m. in order to avoid traffic. The women would wear plastic slippers along sandy roads to catch the bus, and then change into impeccably polished black leather heels before they jumped off to proceed gracefully to the company gates. These children were objects of pride as well as of failed expectations. They had obtained tertiary education and become "somebody," a person with an office job who has colleagues ("my guys"/"office mates"), managers ("my bosses"), "meetings," "salary slips," "contracts," perhaps even "clothing allowances" and "insurance policies." This was the world of professionals, a world that promised not just freedom from daily financial constraints but other types of freedom; the potential to become a different kind of person, though the nature of this personhood was often unclear.

Moral Dimensions of Work: Between Obligation and Self-Realization

White-collar work is a scarce resource in Ghana. Of the three hundred thousand young Ghanaians who enter the labor market annually, a mere 2 percent obtain jobs in the formal sector.[4] Even fewer obtain professional jobs requiring tertiary-level qualifications and/or accredited expert knowledge. Despite these poor prospects, villages are reputed to pool resources to send at least one academically well-performing child to a boarding school, in the hope that this child will eventually become a professional—someone who can bring "development" and "open the eyes" of the entire village (Lentz 1995; Skinner 2009: 482). Lower-middle-class families in Accra with limited resources to educate their children reason similarly. Siblings are expected to make sacrifices for the one who is selected, in the hope that the professional sister or brother will one day help their own children towards a better life. The same basic logic extends to friends: those with office jobs are expected to seek opportunities for unemployed friends, whether in the form of "projects" or minor tasks, like running errands. In a city where unemployment and irregular work in the informal sector are the norm, the status of a professional who receives regular wages and works in an air-conditioned office is high. Working in an office indexes a respectable livelihood and a capacity to contribute to life-cycle rituals, surprise hospital bills, school fees, and other expenses that ordinary Ghanaians struggle with on a daily basis. A professional career is thus an achievement embedded in local moral economies; it emerges from shared investments rather than mere individual hard work. Consequently, professional status is the property of a larger collective that is entitled to its rewards, whether in the form of money, family reputation, or anticipation of future upward mobility.

Young professionals in Accra are deeply enmeshed in these networks of mutual obligation. They aspire to help their financially struggling families, but meeting these expectations is challenging, given their frequently precarious employment situations, which is especially the case in private media companies like TV Central. African urban professional labor markets are changing due to the expansion of the private sector, the broadening of access to higher education, the resulting surplus of educated labor, and the unpredictable movements of global capital (Bolt 2015: 26; see also Mann 2014). While tertiary education and employment in the public sector enabled a relatively stable financial standing in the first post-independence decades, post-1980s neoliberal economic restructuring has altered these conditions of possibility (Behrens and Lentz 2012: 155). In the age of flexible capitalism and jobless growth (Ferguson and Li 2018), when capital generates rents for elites rather than "decent jobs" (Barchiesi 2011a; Comaroff and Comaroff 2012; Standing 2016), those who manage to secure salaried jobs are subject to intense expectations. However, professionals are also subject to downsizing, inconsistent salary structures, ineffective labor laws, and abrupt changes in company ownership. The result is that even at the apex of the formally employed, there is guilt and frustration about their failure to live up to social expectations of the kind of adulthood that others could depend on (see Honwana 2012: 30–59).

In this chapter I argue that Frankie and his peers navigate these changed conditions by cultivating an ethical vision of work and career premised upon vocational excellence. By tracing how the ideal of vocational excellence is enacted through both reflective stances to the moral economies of work that underpin their career trajectories, and concrete performances and "talk" about work, the chapter complements contributions to the Africanist anthropology of work that explore waged work, and particularly its absence (Barchiesi 2011b; Honwana 2012; Mains 2012) in relation to dependencies and social obligation (e.g., Comaroff and Comaroff 1987; Ferguson 2013; Bolt 2015). Taking inspiration from regional sources that explore work as a technique of self-realization (Guyer 1993: 253–56; Barber 2006; Zoogah and Bolaji 2014; Gaibazzi 2015) and pursuit of professional aspiration (Lentz 2014; Hull 2017, 2020), I argue that work among young professionals in Accra's private media is a mode of becoming a particular kind of ethical subject—a skilled professional who asserts authorship of his work outputs (see also Jones, this volume). From late-night sessions in the media office perfecting one's craft of film-editing, to endless hours learning how to make better PowerPoint slides and hushed discussions on whether to report one's immediate boss for routinely accepting bribes, being "serious" about work is a satisfying, but also an ambiguous endeavor prone to dispute. Doing ethnographic justice to these observations calls for an analytic that considers work as an object of concerted performance, "rhythm," and reflection. This complements what Spittler (2008: 12–13) describes as "externalizing" accounts of work that consider it in relation to social obligation, relations of production, national duty (or, one could add, religious piety and the disenchanted pursuit of material wealth: see Rudnyckyj 2014). While some Ghanaians explicitly equate the pursuit of career excellence with divine calling and God's will (Kauppinen 2020), in this chapter I probe young media professionals' largely profane preoccupation with the "quality" of their work as a puzzle that animates negotiations on career aspirations.

Despite the loud echo of quality and excellence as catchwords of neoliberal audit regimes (see Stein 2018), in this chapter "excellence" as a metric of worth matters for very specific reasons. To foreground why this matters, I first discuss the post-independence struggles that ensued from the Ghanaian state seeking to redefine work as a national duty, which collided with the local value of work autonomy. I then describe the young professionals' negotiations of the value of work in their families and workplaces, a conjuncture where new ideas of work as a pursuit of professional excellence emerge. My subsequent focus on authorship and shared pursuits of quality work contrasts with a structuralist account that would likely view these preoccupations as a response to neoliberal labor precarity, which calls for evermore spectacular displays of personal professional virtue. It also departs from conceptualizing work as an individualized mode of self-realization along the lines of neoliberal governmentality, because "quality work" is pursued together, in the close company of fellow peers. Throughout this chapter, I show that a host of factors in the interstices of structures of labor precarity animate shared efforts to flesh out work as a realm that transcends civic duty, family obligations, and what the young professionals experience as their seniors' ideology of work as wealth accumulation towards a "big man" status (cf. Bayart 1993; Nugent 1995). While these efforts cut across young professional men and women, here I focus on young men and how work also articulates with gendered expectations of successful male adulthood. Ultimately, I argue that their pursuit of vocational excellence, which I identify in efforts to assert authorship of their work outputs, fleshes out not only an alternative ethical vision of work, but in so doing negotiates the desirability of Ghanaian hegemonic ideals of masculinity (see Miescher 2005).

In presenting an ethnographic theory of vocational excellence within a political economy contextually defined, but not subjectively determined by neoliberal economic restructuring, this chapter contemplates the possibility of a positive freedom (Berlin [1958] 2002) inherent in work as a category of experience. Positive freedom does not emerge from "lack," or doing away with external obstacles to freedom, but from reflective pursuits of actions and objectives esteemed valuable. Work as "shared self-realization" thus provides an important perspective to the comparative anthropology of work among the "emerging" middle classes (Lentz 2015: 29), whose perceptions of work provide clues towards broader questions of what constitutes social worth beyond formal metrics of accrediting expertise.

Emancipatory Work, Autonomy, and the Post-colonial State

> Moral inducements to work arise in addition to material incentives. Owing to this, labor is becoming evermore meaningful, gradually turning from a mere means of existence into a matter of honor.[5]
>
> —Okore, *Labour in a Socialist Society*

The emergence of vocational excellence as the goal of young professionals in Accra implies a peculiar moral dimension, given the Ghanaian genealogy of articulating work as *primarily* a contribution to a collective good, external to the worker himself. Ghana's history of state socialism illustrates the moral difficulties that viewing work as a contribution to the nation state has generated. Controlling the narrative of work was a key mechanism of nation-building when the country obtained its independence in 1957. The state's first president, Kwame Nkrumah, framed work as a tool of emancipation from the colonial empire (Ahlman 2017: 115–16): a good worker was the kind of person who foregoes capitalist, bourgeois instincts of personal accumulation and understands work in terms of honor and sacrifice, voluntarily performed for the advancement of the nation's political and economic freedom. The socialist worker was committed to working harder in order to produce more goods. Nkrumah thought Soviet-style socialism could outperform Western capitalism. Work was thus a collectively performed act against Western imperialism and white supremacy—not only a matter of material production, but a means for achieving "economic self-determination," a term Nkrumah often used at public rallies, and in speeches and books (ibid.: 42–43). Work had the potential to overcome the legacies of colonial extraction and punitive taxation, which had been resisted by Ghanaian labor unions (Atuguba 2006: 8). Simply put, political freedom was not sufficient—Nkrumah and the ruling Convention People's Party (CPP) viewed hard work as the means through which Ghana could attain economic freedom. Work was thus a deeply moral act performed to serve the nation.

While highly influential in African-American and Pan-African intellectual circuits, these narratives fitted uneasily alongside older traditions in which the moral dimension of work was an exercise of autonomy (Ahlman 2017: 138). When he equated personal accumulation and self-interest with colonial bourgeois mentality, Nkrumah overlooked popular ideologies of work as a contribution to one's family lineage (Goody 1977: 32–33). In the precolonial Asante kingdom, work to accumulate wealth was a personal virtue as well as the basis of social order, while public display of wealth communicated the responsibility to protect and nurture the people lower in the social hierarchy (McCaskie 1983: 27). This logic extended to women who historically occupied visible public roles as priestesses and traders, and whose display of wealth indicated their social status and capacity to nurture dependents (see Clark 1994; Akyeampong 2000). Autonomy has generally been highly valued in Africanist genealogies of work shaped by histories of domestic and transatlantic slavery (Roitman 2005: 61). Among migrant cocoa farmers that Polly Hill (2012: 1–7) studied in the 1950s, the ideal of work autonomy translated into explicit resistance against the "bureaucrats" of the state. Postcolonial state agents have struggled to reconcile this valuation of autonomy with rallying the public behind a moral economy of work as a contribution to the nation. The upshot is that state-driven narratives of moralizing work have, since colonial times, generated alienation rather than identification (Ahlman 2017: 116).

State-led discourses elevating work in terms of civic virtue continue to this day: Ghanaian officials have recently started to declare that young people should "stop chasing white-collar jobs."[6] "There is a crisis in the world of work, there are no jobs!" as Mrs Sackey, the CEO of a Ghanaian human resource company, exclaimed during an interview on the employment prospects of young people. Young people are increasingly encouraged to become entrepreneurs and to choose vocational training in place of university education. Training programs on entrepreneurship are organized nationwide. However, young Ghanaians resist these neoliberal discourses (Ghana Labor Market Profile 2020). They continue to apply for universities and other certificate courses that promise access to the world of professionals, even though the rate of graduate unemployment continues to rise. Similar to peers elsewhere in Africa (Mann 2014; Hull 2017: 10), the aspirations of young Ghanaians remain focused on professional careers, the appeal of which extends way beyond financial factors and towards ideals of respectability and social status (cf. Spronk 2020: 471). At the same time, they have become increasingly vocal about the responsibility of the state to create "decent jobs."[7]

To situate the persistence of professional aspiration in Ghana, I return to Frankie and his group of male colleagues at TV Central. I first describe how they encountered visions of work as a means to generate material prosperity in their families and workplaces, which they recognized as an important goal, and yet also as inadequate as the primary endpoint of their career trajectory. I maintain that reflective engagement with the "quality" of one's work is under-theorized in social science literatures, which oscillate between work as a source of alienation versus work as a means of participating in local moral economies of cooperation, exchange, and reciprocity (see Harris 2007). Yet, these local moral economies crucially underpinned these reflective stances.

Professional Sons: Work, Money, and Making the Middle Class

Frankie and the group of male colleagues who I call Kodjo, Dr. Mandu, Timothy, and Kumaru became friends at their workplace, TV Central, where they spent most of their waking hours and sometimes even slept under the humming air conditioners. This "young adult phase" in their late twenties and early thirties before marriage, when work occupied them from morning till night, implicated their families as observers who hardly saw their sons at home or in family meetings, leading to the kind of confusion I described earlier between Frankie and his mother. This illustrates the moral economy of work that underpins relations between "professional sons" and their family members, who had numerous reasons to expect household contributions as the main worth of their work.

Firstly, in many cases these families, including extended families that incorporated uncles, aunts, and cousins, had invested major resources for their sons' education up to university level. Frankie and his peers had obtained specialist tertiary-level education thanks to this investment. Frankie had a Bachelor's degree in Media Production from the University of Ghana. Dr. Mandu had completed various certificate courses in IT alongside learning to code and hack on his own. He had earned his nickname "Dr." Mandu due to his "big English," using expressions such as "cosmological universes" and "psychological dispositions". Kodjo and Timothy were editors and filmmakers who had completed Bachelor's degrees at the National Film Institute. Kumaru had studied marketing and business administration at a polytechnic. Typical of young professionals elsewhere, these studies were paid for through a combination of resources from their immediate families as well as extended families, and in some cases, family friends.

Funding these degrees had required major investments, financial and otherwise, from the families in question.[8] These families were far from being "comfortable middle class," with resources to fund their children's professional ambitions without having to strategize or "choose" the most deserving child—such were the families of doctors, lawyers, politicians, bankers, as well as the elite "intelligentsia" marked by prestigious surnames that indexed a pedigree of professionalism dating back to the colonial era (Nugent 1995). The families of the group of young men at TV Central could best be described as "modest middle class" (Sassen 2013), who do not go hungry but who experience daily financial hardship and are vulnerable to shifts in the national economy. They build their houses brick by brick over the course of ten or twenty years due to a lack of access to affordable financing, while exhibiting strong aspirations to educate their children and strive towards a better life. In most cases, their parents had migrated to Accra from Ghana's other regions with these aspirations in mind. Mothers typically worked in trading or retail, while fathers held civil service jobs that paid a low pension. Or, as in the case of Mandu and Timothy, they were raised by single mothers and grandmothers who were traders, or who, like Mandu's mother, held lower-ranking administrative jobs.

Rachel Spronk (2020) has called this stratum in Ghana "the middle class in the making," emphasizing the processual nature of the term as against its fixation to a predefined level of income. Investing in children's education is one element of making the middle class, which often involves the work of transforming signs and cultural properties that index "middle-classness," not as the "final destination" (ibid.: 484) but as an object of innovation.[9] Most recently, occupational desires have become part of this work of transformation. Frankie and his peers, for instance, had studied fields that oriented them towards jobs in the private sector, rather than the public sector, which appeared to them to be both more "closed" (open only to those with political contacts) as well as a "less ambitious" realm in which to pursue their careers. This was typical of the kind of new Ghanaian middle classes coming from outside the established intelligentsia (ibid.: 485), for whom the private sector had more promise.[10]

It was thus logical that the families in question expected these "professional sons" pursuing careers in the private sector to pay their dues and contribute to household finances. But apart from their precarious employment in the private media industry, which I return to later, these young men desired to spend their salaries outside the household, such as saving towards renting their own flat or buying a car. A car was not only a status symbol, but a means of production, facilitating their movement around the city to various "meetings" and outside the city to pursue their own film productions. But extending their material desires beyond the household resulted in family conflicts. While women in West Africa played active roles as contributors to the household (Akyeampong 2000), the role of the male child as the protector and provider remained a strong expectation (Miescher 2005: 11). Veritable secrecy thus surrounded their salaries, families rarely knowing the exact amount of income their sons earned. The sons, for their part, were frustrated by the requests for money that they were not able to respond to, as Kumaru once described: "Yesterday, I came home late. I had been working the whole day, going here and there, trying to get money. My mum and sister were just nagging. Why haven't you bought this, why haven't you bought that?"

While they spent a diminishing amount of time with their natal kin and resisted requests for money, the young men were highly aware that their access to the world of professionals was financially underpinned by investment from their family members. Applying Meillassoux's classic model of the link between capital and social reproduction (1975), these families subsidized the labor costs of the Ghanaian private sector by enabling their sons' transition from unpaid interns into waged workers. They provided free accommodation, food, and electricity to charge their mobile phones. Even after they had become waged workers, these young men often remained dependent on their families for shelter. This continued into married life, when wives typically moved into their husband's family house before the young couple had enough money to rent a place of their own. While expressing frustration, these young men also felt guilty for not being able to respond to demands for money, and perhaps also for not spending enough on their natal household. They envisioned a future when they were financially stable and capable of improving their family's living conditions, and could honor their parents with "big celebrations." Timothy, for instance, was constantly on the lookout for a better house for his single mother, who lived as a tenant in a shared compound house in a low-income neighborhood. Planning for this future when they would be more capable of helping their families was thus firmly on the horizon, but not as the primary purpose or endpoint of their careers.

For their families, work was first and foremost a source of monetary contributions to household, which could not make up for the prestige of working in an office and being a producer at a well-known television station.[11] These children did bring status prestige; but if money was missing, the status was not enough. To illustrate, one Saturday morning I was spending time in Kumaru's family house. We were sitting in the living room, watching the repeat of a TV-show that he was producing. When the end credits started rolling and his name appeared on the screen as the "director," I exclaimed, "Look, Mama Eunice, there is your son's name!" Mama Eunice looked at me, smiled wryly, and said, "And what is he earning? *Eeeh?* Show me the money!" For Mama Eunice, her son's name on the television screen was not impressive; the "fame" failed to materialize in tangible household contributions. She also implied that the money was being hidden somewhere, betraying her uncertainty about her son's actual earnings.

Such discordances are a window into the moral economies of work in which young professionals in Accra were embedded in their day-to-day lives. While they aspired to be able to support their families, the main source of their frustration derived from their experience of the household as a realm that was interested in one specific aspect of their career: their capacity to contribute materially. To use an investment idiom, these professional sons were like "stocks" that had failed to yield "interest," which generated controversy, mutual disappointment, and frustrating uncertainty about whether one was truly an adult or still a dependent child. Living through such controversies foregrounds professional men and women as part of a specific class of young people who are innovating new thought paradigms to challenge dominant regimes that seek to own the codes of, say, respectable sexuality (Spronk 2012), or what constitutes the worth of work (see also Awal, this volume). The media professionals' language of work illustrates these shifting notions. The Twi-term for work, *adwuma*, refers to physically strenuous agricultural or manual work, which subsequently came to stand as a generic term for work (Mierscher 2005: 221fn13).

Perhaps due to the lasting connotation of *adwuma* as physical work, they hardly ever said "*Me ko adwuma*" (I go to work). They would say "*Me ko office*," emphasizing the distinctive workspace and the kind of work being performed, and evoking imageries of work as a distinct space separate from household, and perhaps also its associated regimes of valuing work's worth. This was certainly how work appeared at TV Central, where I turn to next.

"Big Men," Private Media, and Wealth Accumulation

TV Central stood on a large compound in a prime spot in Accra, close to a major traffic hub. The walls that circled the various buildings displayed colorful signboards of their most popular television shows and telenovelas. Minibuses dropped workers right at its company gates, where an occasional visitor signed a large booklet before getting a name tag and entering the front compound filled with big 4x4 cars that belonged to the CEOs and other "big men," and a few "big women." TV Central was part of the first wave of new TV and radio stations that emerged in the immediate aftermath of mid-1990s' liberalization of Ghana's airwaves (De Witte 2008). Over the years, the station had changed ownership several times between foreign-owned media conglomerates and Ghanaian private investors. The station had become one of the most popular private free-to-air channels. Its airwaves were filled with locally scripted drama series, program concepts imported from the global reality-TV scene, and telenovelas from Latin America. The station followed the global business model of private media premised upon profits derived from "sponsors"; in Ghana this especially meant multinational telecoms giants such as Vodafone and MTN, which bought airtime for advertisements (Thalén 2011). What the ostensibly privatized, colorful appearance of the premises concealed was that TV Central used to be a state-owned media company. The station was thus a mix of constantly changing shareholders and CEOs, long-standing employees who had shifted from being public sector civil servants into being private sector "executives," and young, enthusiastic, university-educated men and women such as Frankie and his peers, who brought their distinctive ambitions and conceptions of work to the company.

While the salaries in Ghanaian media were infamously low (Hasty 2005: 17), thus plausibly many professionals formally earned less than a taxi driver, the industry was replete with "off the books" informal money-making opportunities. Big and small money moved in private media through official accounts but also via informal routes, exchanging hands and pockets in bars and car parks, and even during church services, weddings, and funerals. But before one could get access to such circuits of opportunity, which was largely regulated by male networks of friendship, one first learned the trade from employees higher up in the organizational hierarchy, most commonly male middle managers.[12] The ultimate, highly gendered objective was to become a "big man," sometimes even called "the media mafia." These big men drove big cars, had extensive networks to Ghanaian high society, from politicians to famous pastors, from entrepreneurs to CEOs of multinational corporations. They accumulated wealth by acting as brokers managing access to the liberalized airwaves, which was a precious currency in a privatizing economy where new products and services were seeking to capture consumer attention.

When I first came to TV Central in 2010, Frankie, Timothy, Dr. Mandu, and Kumaru had recently finished their internships and been granted temporary contracts working for designated managers. Kodjo joined them a couple of years later as a producer, thanks to his prior work experience as a media producer for a family business. At the beginning of their careers at TV Central, they observed such monetary circuits and big men from a distance, focusing on their work as production assistants to prove that they were worthy of a permanent employment contract. This meant long working hours and great sacrifices. As Timothy put it years after, "I wanted them to feel my absence. I didn't take any holidays for years. When I finally took my first holiday, when my daughter was born, my bosses were like, 'Where is Tim, where is Tim?' Soon after, they picked me."[13] They came to work as early as 6 a.m., and left back to their family houses as late as 10 p.m. The long days were given rhythm by a constant flow of tasks from their managers, from production assistance to running personal errands. The bosses could call them at any moment, especially evenings and weekends, when the station broadcast live shows. They hoped that once they had proved themselves reliable they would be given more responsibility, such as taking charge of the production of an entire program. They aspired to perform each task to the highest standard, knowing that remaining in the organization and becoming a permanent employee was dependent on their protection and recommendation.

These managers and employees higher up in the company hierarchy eventually also facilitated access to informal circuits of making money. This was the point when relations between the employees got explicitly gendered. While they had dutifully worked for female managers and shared offices and productions with numerous female colleagues, the closest friendships between colleagues were predominantly male. From early on, Frankie cultivated a close friendship with Richard, who was not a manager, but a permanent producer. "Richard is my money," he would say, and leave the office to follow him to various meetings where informal deals were struck. These deals typically involved approaching musicians, filmmakers, entrepreneurs, pastors, and others who had a product to market or who could be framed as experts on a given topic. The producer would offer them a slot in a current affairs segment or an entertainment program that gave them visibility. Typically, they paid what was called "service money." "Everybody does that," Frankie would say, giving a chronicle of producers up to the executive level who brought in unaccounted guests to their shows. This implied that within the ostensibly stringent bureaucratic hierarchy a certain degree of autonomy was allowed after proving oneself reliable and accessing the company's inner circle. Richard, who was a charismatic man with extensive networks to Ghana's top musicians and movie stars, taught Frankie how to use the media station for personal benefit. However, business was often slow, and months could pass without these opportunities; at those times it was back to relying on the salary.

Timothy, Kodjo, Kumaru, and especially Dr. Mandu were not always impressed by Frankie's exploits. At times they did participate in these meetings, but as the years passed the pattern started to feel repetitive. "We are supposed to be professionals. And here we are, chasing other people's pockets!" Dr. Mandu exclaimed one evening in September 2013, by which time they had all secured permanent contracts (although Mandu at another TV station), and Kodjo had joined their core group. Mandu's comment struck a chord; silence fell around the table, betraying that he had raised an important issue. That evening we found ourselves, once again, spending a Friday night waiting for some "big people" to pay service money for the already executed informal deals. Dr. Mandu was keen among his peers to remind them that they were not in the industry "just for the money"—they were in the industry in order to be and act as "professionals." For Dr. Mandu, service money was something akin to bribery, which he did not condemn on moral grounds (like vocal Charismatic Pentecostal Christians, who describe bribery as a sin), but which he described as "useless" regarding their professional development. He told his colleagues to focus on cultivating their craft of filming, editing, and production, and developing new program concepts that they could eventually start selling as independent producers and establish their own production house. While everyone was under pressure to make more money, both for their natal kin and especially to secure the prospect of marriage, Dr. Mandu tried to steer them away from the idea of wealth accumulation as the ultimate goal of their career trajectory. At the same time, he viewed the pursuit of vocational excellence as a precondition for achieving future work autonomy as independent company owners who would not need to play according to the rules of a "media mafia."

There was a further element to the figure of the wealth-accumulating "big man," which Richard embodied, that even Frankie found almost terrifying: political affiliations. Some of their senior managers had openly proclaimed their support for one of Ghana's two dominant political factions, the NDC (National Democratic Congress) and the NPP (New Patriotic Party). They quickly learned that such proclamations could cost them their job. Whenever the company was in foreign ownership, these declarations did not seem to matter. But in the early 2010s, when the TV station changed ownership to a Ghanaian group of companies known for its support of the ruling party at that time, those managers known for their support for the opposition party were either downsized or removed from positions of influence. Assumptions of party support were drawn from the employee's ethnic background, given the high polarization of voting patterns in Ghana according to ethnicity. Frankie, whose surname clearly indicated his ethnic background, was disturbed when he was directly approached by one of the CEOs for a "discussion" that he felt should have gone through his immediate superior. Although this might have presented an opportunity for career advancement, Frankie disclosed the incident to his immediate boss, who told him to "play the game." Frankie was astonished by his response. He was wary of any high-level political maneuver that connected the present capital owners with the ruling party. This was due to the dangers that according to many young professionals were inherent in political involvement; such affiliations could cost one's job, or even one's life. Rumors circulated of high-level media professionals who had suddenly died from a curse or poisoning from the opposition party when they had transitioned to positions of political influence.

These instances showcase how the young men contested, and in some cases rejected, the figure of a politically affiliated, mafia-like "big man" whose work is primarily a means of wealth accumulation and/or political influence. This was a hegemonic ideal of masculinity that prevailed in various industries and circles, from media to politics, banking, and the upper echelons of the "informal sector," where entrepreneurs could earn and accumulate way more than formally employed "career persons." This figure, in some sense, embodies the value of work autonomy reminiscent of the wealth accumulating big men and big women in the precolonial Asante kingdom at the apex of social hierarchy (McCaskie 1983), when colonial administrators and Nkrumahist state officials had struggled to rally behind a bureaucratic mode of governance (Ahlman 2017: 154). As Dr. Mandu's example made clear, the young men in question desired other forms of work autonomy.

Work, Excellence, and Asserting Authorship

Decades ago, Jane Guyer studied workers at a Cameroonian iron smelt, where "one man spontaneously demonstrated the rhythmic movements of the bellows work he had done as a youth. Percussive sounds, dance movements, and athleticism were combined in a way that expressed beyond the capacity of words the pride a young man might feel from exhibiting strength, stamina, and musical talent. At the smelt 'there was joy. And we sang. We sang well.'" While this description is redolent of early ethnographic studies of work dating back to the nineteenth century, Guyer went on to argue that there might be a "potential for self-valuation, for partial authorship, in the competitive validation of the work contributions" (Guyer 1993: 254). With her notion of partial authorship, she suggested that work opens up a space, even if limited within structures of capitalist extraction, for realizing an aspect of one's self that might otherwise remain hidden. Guyer's insight on "partial authorship" is a useful starting point to unpack the acts and discourses of vocational excellence that emerged among the young men at the center of this chapter. The explicitness of vocational excellence as an ethical vision of work is the crucial observation. While voicing critical stances towards surrounding discourses of work in their families and workplaces, vocational excellence attested as a conscious pursuit expressed through distinctions drawn between "us" and "them," time and attention dedicated to the performance of work, and attempts to "formalize" their performance of work, even in spaces that appeared ostensibly "informal."

Becoming permanent employees and gaining more autonomy of the work process made the young producers critical of their managers. As described earlier, Frankie, although he was highly involved in informal money-making circuits, experienced the workplace as dominated by line managers who were "mediocre." They were not interested in the quality of his work outputs, such as recognizing the amount of time he had put in to ensuring that any feature he produced was of top quality. Access to equipment was hard, as producers often fought for slots to use the best cameras that ensured good quality footage.[14] Kodjo, who joined the TV station in 2013, quickly found a comrade in him because, similarly to Dr. Mandu (who by that time had joined another TV station), he was highly ambitious about the quality of his work. On many occasions when I visited Kodjo and his wife Fafali in their small rented flat on Sundays, Kodjo would be sitting on the couch absorbed by his laptop. While seemingly performing the hegemonic masculine ideal of a husband working while the wife does housework, less hegemonic elements were present in this scene, as Fafali was a financially independent woman with her own income working as a nurse, and refusing to cook or clean when she thought Kodjo had "misbehaved." He was writing new scripts for television dramas, watching films while taking notes of good shots, writing new concept notes, and finding out information about international award schemes. As Fafali said, her husband was "always working." Kodjo, on his part, would present his ideas to Frankie, Timothy, and Kumaru, with whom he often roamed the city looking for good locations to shoot their own productions.

Instead of adhering to what they perceived as the middle management's satisfaction with "mediocrity," their objective was to produce "serious programs." Whenever they were given the responsibility to produce entire segments or feature-length documentaries, they approached these projects with a highly ambitious mind-set. The quality of even the shortest clips mattered to them—they wanted to use the best cameras for shooting, and spent hours editing to unearth this elusive quality called "seriousness." As a source of inspiration and self-training, they used the company's broadband to download movies and shows from a variety of international television channels, from the BBC to Al Jazeera. I often participated in watching these shows, learning and taking notes. We would try to imagine how the shooting situation had been orchestrated, and where exactly the cameraman and director had been standing. Most of them had graduated in broadcast media, journalism, or performance arts, but few had fine-grained film editing or shooting expertise—these skills were learned on the job, in the company of others. They finally set up their own YouTube channels, where they uploaded these features and short films in the hope of reaching global audiences.

Their own productions were "shadow," informal activities executed outside formal accounting books. Producers often solicited help from editors, cameramen, and others, but behind the backs of the middle management. They mobilized the labor of other employees by suggesting that these unofficial projects came with the potential for reputation—for instance, if the program were to be noticed by the BBC, CNN, or Al Jazeera through YouTube. Shadow productions required movement at night and careful orchestration to bypass official auditing. While occurring in spaces of informality, various techniques sought to formalize the mode of work itself. Oftentimes when they gathered in a bar to discuss new program concepts, Dr. Mandu would be careful to direct the discussion to focus on "ideas," and not just gossiping. "Let's make a list. Let's note everything down. Let's not waste this," he would say. They maintained an archive of what they had discussed and committed to. In these instances, work could also become a realm of competition and conflict if certain colleagues were thought not to be "helping" enough but were pursuing their own selfish goals. The pursuit of excellence thus had its own moral economy of exchange of favors across official and unofficial realms; it was thus not an individual entrepreneurial pursuit, but a shared endeavor that emerged from concentrated work performed together till the late hours. Some projects became conflictual, as favors were not always reciprocated. Friendships could be broken. The pursuit of excellence as the moral dimension of work was thus collectively enabled and policed.

Self-realization was exemplified in the mode of asserting authorship, which also took the form of a shared discursive experience, such as recalling particular "quality works" they had done in the past. This act of remembering in the midst of daily work could be joyful, and enjoyable in itself (cf. Miller and Angé, this volume). Video clips, features, live productions, and other artefacts were not simply alienable commodities produced to generate profit for the private corporation (cf. Bear 2018). These artifacts became part of their makers' professional life cycle and were thus memorable. Producers, as they conversed, could recall in detail particular features and video clips that they had produced at different stages of their career. Some were represented as instances of "learning," while other productions had exceeded their expectations and fed into fond memories. External recognition was crucial to the feeling and memory of having produced excellent work. This recognition, or "feedback" in global HR terms, was solicited from various sources, including senior management, foreign visitors (including anthropologists), and other collaborators. Natal kin rarely featured as the source of this type of recognition, while recognition from wives and romantic partners, such as Fafali, indicated that they "understood the job" beyond material production.

The sense of authorship and memorable fruits of labor underpin work as a mode of shared self-realization among the young men described here. Of course, there are other ways of framing work as a mode of self-realization. While asserting authorship of creative outputs might be particularly typical of private media, newer Africanist ethnography of work demonstrates that these social dynamics are more widespread. For instance, Lentz's (2014) Ghanaian public sector interlocutors cultivate a strong discourse of adhering to "professional ethics" as the key constituent of their definition of excellence, expressed through the idiom, "I take an oath to the state, not to the government." In rural Gambia, young unemployed men cultivate a discourse of "luck" as active engagement with "the indeterminacy of life," which underpins an idealized vision of work as gradual, highly contingent movement towards fulfilling one's God-given destiny (Gaibazzi 2015). In rural South African hospitals, nurses reflect on new audit regimes that police their work outputs, while they frame professional aspiration as key to performing ideals of respectable citizenship (Hull 2017). What unites these findings is the emergence of "work itself" as an object of knowledge and ethical reflection, which earlier Africanist accounts treated primarily in relation to social obligations and relations of production (cf. Spittler 2008). These emerging ethical visions of work are clearly highly variable. Given their bypassing of formal auditing mechanisms when doing "serious productions," the young men described here would not have satisfied Lentz's (2014) public sector interlocutors' ethical standards. Yet they too strive to become a particular kind of ethical subject: a skilled professional reflexively exploring what counts as "quality work" in his branch.

The fact that these discourses and acts were explicitly focused on being and becoming perceived as a "serious person," in the sense that the producers in question wanted to "make a point," implies that vocational excellence was not simply a neoliberal trope of fashioning individual entrepreneurial career subjectivities. Nor was it an ascetic mode of work reminiscent of Max Weber's *Protestant Ethic*. Rather, I suggest that this pursuit emerged from reflectively interrogating what, ultimately, constitutes the worth of their work as young professional men in Ghana in the twenty-first century. These negotiations of the worth of work reached towards new visions of masculinity and full adulthood, which in Ghana have historically been mediated through work as the expression of man's productive capacity (Miescher 2005). Besides material production, and becoming the epicenter of extensive networks of dependents and collaborators, these expressions increasingly incorporated vocational excellence as an index of a person who was recognized as indispensable, reliable, and most importantly "serious."

Conclusion

One of the defining characteristics of the emergence of the "global middle classes" lies in their changing notions of work, which urgently calls for new research from a broad comparative perspective (Lentz 2015: 21–22). This chapter has explored some of the ways in which work can be conceptualized as a mode of self-realization among aspirant, but not quite secure, middle-class men who lack the legacy of professional achievement in their family history. Among the Ghanaian youth coming from these aspirant classes, work and career is purposefully refashioned as more than an instrument towards a livelihood and meeting social obligations. Work can be a source of frustration, a financially precarious existence, and it can cause conflicts in the family. Equally, it can be a realm of bitter competition, causing breakdown of friendships, envy, and greed. But despite all these dramas, which characterize work lives quite universally, young professionals in Accra also experience work as a realm of self-knowledge, self-realization, and self-transformation: being "capable," producing quality, and becoming part of a world that appears different to where they come from. These feelings are significant in their own right, and provide a fuller analytic towards work beyond alienation and social obligation.

At the same time, I have drawn attention to the gendered notions of adulthood that characterize the process of discovering this new "freedom" at work, suggesting that new ethical visions of work necessarily articulate with local moral economies of evaluating work's worth. The reason young professional men at TV Central were preoccupied with "excellence," dubbed "seriousness," did not emerge in a vacuum from these situated concerns. While the Ghanaian economy has undoubtedly been profoundly transformed as a result of the post-1980s currents of neoliberal restructuring, I have suggested that the actual discourses, acts, and relationships that emerged to cultivate vocational excellence defied neoliberal regimes of cultivating entrepreneurial selves detached from the social.

Although careers may be in free fall in the face of neoliberal rentier capitalism, pandemics, and climate change, not to mention automation and artificial intelligence, which are already transforming the valuation of professional skills (Benanav 2019), the allure of pursuing a life course that involves a "career" remains firmly in young people's sights. Future anthropology of professionals and professional work, which thus far has tended to focus on professionals' roles as "experts" rather than as citizens (cf. Hull 2017: 10), family members, partners or friends, will benefit from more attention to how acts and discourses of expertise articulate with more situated concerns of evaluating work's worth.

Acknowledgments

This chapter emerged from doctoral fieldwork funded by the London School of Economics PhD Scholarship (2012–2015) and writing supported by the Max Planck–Cambridge Centre for Ethics, Economy and Social Change. I am grateful to my friends and family in Ghana who constantly challenge my preconceptions of work. This chapter came into being thanks to vibrant conversations in Halle in December 2019, and insightful comments from Chris Hann, Chris Gregory, and Rachel E. Smith along the way; thanks also to an anonymous reviewer.

Anna-Riikka Kauppinen is a research associate at the Max Planck–Cambridge Centre for Ethics, Economy and Social Change.

Notes

1. All the names of organizations and individuals are pseudonyms. The material for this chapter was collected over the course of ten years (2010–19) of ethnographic engagement with young professionals who worked in private sector companies in Accra. Some of them became my close colleagues when I worked in these companies as an intern. Some were friends of colleagues, whom I met through evening gatherings in bars and other public spaces, as well as at life-cycle rituals such as weddings and funerals. Some became lifelong friends, some adopted me into their families, and others remained more distant. The key locale of this chapter, which I call TV Central, was one among a number of field-sites during my doctoral fieldwork in 2013–14; I had previously interned at this company in 2010. The language of fieldwork was Ghanaian pidgin and English (which were both mixed in offices), while conversations with families and outside the office incorporated many languages from Ewe to Asante Twi, English, pidgin, and specific slang expressions.
2. While the English term "professional" was used at times between colleagues, the more common term was a "career person," which families and people outside professional circles used to indicate a person who usually worked in an office and had had higher education.
3. A "dash" is a gift of money that does not have to be paid back; however, it is not a "free" gift due to the reciprocal relationship that ensues. Oftentimes, when the month was coming to an end, many employees in private media had run out of money. That is when most requests for "dashes" were made, both toward one's seniors and peers.
4. Ghana Labour Market Profile 2020. https://www.ulandssekretariatet.dk/wp-content/uploads/2020/02/Ghana_lmp_2020.pdf (last accessed 20 March 2020).
5. Anoma Okore, *Labour in a Socialist Society*, 1963; Cit. in Ahlman 2017: 115.
6. https://www.graphic.com.gh/news/general-news/stop-chasing-white-collar-jobs.html (last accessed 15 May 2020).
7. https://www.pulse.com.gh/news/local/nana-addo-has-disappointed-us-unemployed-graduates-cry/lvhj4gk (last accessed 15 May 2020).
8. In many instances, funding the university education of one "chosen" child meant that other siblings needed to sacrifice their educational ambitions, or seek help from outside the family. While here I focus on young men as the objects of this investment, girls could also emerge as legitimate recipients. However, patrilineal families in particular conceived of sons as the most likely source of future household contributions, as daughters would eventually be married outside the family whereas sons were destined to inherit the family house.
9. See Lentz (2015) for similar discussion on the "boundary work" of making the middle class.
10. See Appel (2017) on the broader structures of feeling that surround "the private sector" in Africa as a solution to unlocking economic growth, perceptions of greater "access," and greater productivity.
11. Media in Ghana is only recently, following the post-1990s liberalization of the public sphere, becoming perceived as a field that can promise career advancement. Especially during the years of Jerry Rawlings' military dictatorship in the 1980s

and early 1990s, journalists lacked the respectability that they currently enjoy as 'watchdogs' of democracy (Hasty 2005: 60). Entertainment and film production have also become more valued, given the potential of global audiences in the era of digital channels of distribution.

12. Recently, high-profile women in the Ghanaian media industry have voiced dissatisfaction with the overtly masculine constitution of the sector, where men act as gatekeepers and informal income-generating activities are distributed in male networks of solidarity. While men and women share offices and work together in productions, during my fieldwork in 2010–14 women found it harder to access the more lucrative positions and business opportunities. While gender relations go beyond the scope of this chapter, it is worth noting that the industry shows signs of change, with increasing numbers of women starting their own production houses. These conversations are obviously not unique to the Ghanaian media and entertainment industry, as "#Metoo" has revealed.
13. "Pick me" in this instance refers to being granted a permanent employment contract.
14. Nowadays, iPhones and good quality mobile phone cameras have democratized access to independent digital production, which in 2013–14, when the majority of fieldwork took place, were not widely available.

References

Ahlman, Jeffrey S. 2017. *Living with Nkrumahism: Nation, State, and Pan-Africanism in Ghana*. Athens: Ohio University Press.

Akyeampong, Emmanuel. 2000. "Wo pe tam won pe ba" ("You Like Cloth But You Don't Like Children"): Urbanization, Individualism and Gender Relations in Colonial Ghana c. 1900–39." In *Africa's Urban Past*, ed. David Anderson and Richard Rathbone, 222–34. Oxford: James Currey.

Appel, Hannah. 2017. "Toward an Ethnography of the National Economy." *Cultural Anthropology* 32(2): 294–322.

Atuguba, Raymond. 2006. "The Tax Culture of Ghana: A Research Report Prepared for the Revenue Mobilisation Support (RMS)." Accra: German Development Cooperation (GTZ).

Barber, Karin. 2006. *Africa's Hidden Histories: Everyday Literacy and Making the Self.* Bloomington: Indiana University Press.

Barchiesi, Franco. 2011a. "Against Job Creation: Precarious Work as a Challenge to Employment-Centered Normativity in Postcolonial Africa." Global Labour University conference at Wits University (Johannesburg). https://www.global-labour-university.org/fileadmin/GLU_conference_2011/papers/Franco_Barchiesi.pdf (last accessed 25 April 2020).

———. 2011b. *Precarious Liberation: Workers, the State, and Contested Social Citizenship in Postapartheid South Africa*. Albany, NY: SUNY Press.

Bayart, Jean-Francois. 1993. *The State in Africa: The Politics of the Belly*. London: Longman.

Bear, Laura. 2018. "The Vitality of Labour and Its Ghosts." *Terrain: Anthropologie & sciences humaines* 69. https://journals.openedition.org/terrain/16728 (last accessed 20 May 2020).
Behrends, Andrea, and Carola Lentz. 2012. "Education, Careers, and Home Ties: The Ethnography of an Emerging Middle Class from Northern Ghana." *Zeitschrift für Ethnologie* 137(2): 139–64.
Benanav, Aaron. 2019. "Automation and the Future of Work, Part I." *New Left Review* 119: 5–38.
Berlin, Isaiah. (1958) 2002. "Two Concepts of Liberty." In *Liberty*, ed. Henry Hardy, 167–217. Oxford: Oxford University Press.
Bolt, Maxim. 2015. *Zimbabwe's Migrants and South Africa's Border Farms: The Roots of Impermanence*. New York: Cambridge University Press.
Clark, Gracia. 1994. *Onions Are My Husband: Survival and Accumulation by West African Market Women*. Chicago: University of Chicago Press.
Comaroff, Jean, and John Comaroff. 1987. "The Madman and the Migrant: Work and Labor in the Historical Consciousness of a South African People." *American Ethnologist* 14(2): 191–209.
———. 2012. "Theory from the South: Or, How Euro-America is Evolving toward Africa." *Anthropological Forum* 22(2): 113–31.
De Witte, Marleen. 2008. "Accra's Sounds and Sacred Spaces." *International Journal of Urban and Regional Research* 32(3): 690–709.
Ferguson, James. 2013. "Declarations of Dependence: Labour, Personhood, and Welfare in Southern Africa." *Journal of the Royal Anthropological Institute* 19(2): 223–42.
Ferguson, James, and Tania M. Li. 2018. "Beyond the 'Proper Job': Political-Economic Analysis after the Century of Labouring Man." *Working Paper* 51, Institute for Poverty, Land and Agrarian Studies (PLAAS). https://tspace.library.utoronto.ca/bitstream/1807/89444/1/Beyond%20the%20%E2%80%9CProper_TSpace.pdf 9 (last accessed 1 April 2020).
Gaibazzi, Paolo. 2015. "The Quest for Luck: Fate, Fortune, Work and the Unexpected among Gambian Soninke Hustlers." *Critical African Studies* 7(3): 227–42.
Ghana Labour Market Profile 2020. https://www.ulandssekretariatet.dk/wp-content/uploads/2020/02/Ghana_lmp_2020.pdf (last accessed 20 March 2020).
Goody, Jack. 1977. *Production and Reproduction: A Comparative Study of the Domestic Domain* (No. 17). Cambridge: Cambridge University Press.
Guyer, Jane I. 1993. "Wealth in People and Self-Realization in Equatorial Africa." *Man* 28(2): 243–65.
Harris, Olivia. 2007. "What Makes People Work?" In *Question of Anthropology*, ed. Rita Astuti et al., 137–67. Oxford: Berg.
Hasty, Jennifer. 2005. *The Press and Political Culture in Ghana*. Bloomington: Indiana University Press.
Hill, Polly. (1986) 2012. *Development Economics on Trial*. Cambridge: Cambridge University Press.
Honwana, Alcinda. 2012. *The Time of Youth: Work, Social Change, and Politics in Africa*. Sterling, VA: Kumarian Press.

Hull, Elizabeth. 2017. *Contingent Citizens: Professional Aspiration in a South African Hospital*. London: Bloomsbury Publishing.
———. 2020. "Going Up or Getting Out? Professional Insecurity and Austerity in the South African Health Sector." *Africa: The Journal of the International African Institute* 90(3): 548–67.
Kauppinen, Anna-Riikka. 2020. "Citizens for Ghana and the Kingdom: Christian Personal Development in Accra." In *Spirituality, Organization, and Neoliberalism: Understanding Lived Experiences*, ed. Emma Bell et al., 126–48. Cheltenham: Edward Elgar.
Lentz, Carola. 1995: "'Unity for Development': Youth Associations in North-Western Ghana." *Africa* 65(3): 395–429.
———. 2014. "'I Take an Oath to the State, Not the Government': Career Trajectories and Professional Ethics of Ghanaian Public Servants." In *States at Work*, ed. Thomas Bierschenk and Olivier de Sardan, 175–204. Leiden: Brill.
———. 2015. "Elites or Middle Classes? Lessons from Transnational Research for the Study of Social Stratification in Africa." Working paper no. 161 of the Department of Anthropology and African Studies. https://openscience.ub.uni-mainz.de/bitstream/20.500.12030/92/1/4119.pdf (last accessed 20 March 2021).
Mains, Daniel. 2012. *Hope is Cut: Youth, Unemployment, and the Future in Urban Ethiopia*. Philadelphia, PA: Temple University Press.
Mann, Laura. 2014. "Wasta! The Long-Term Implications of Education Expansion and Economic Liberalisation on Politics in Sudan." *Review of African Political Economy* 41: 561–78.
McCaskie, Tom. 1983. "Accumulation, Wealth and Belief in Asante History: I. To the Close of the Nineteenth Century." *Africa* 53(1): 23–43.
Meillassoux, Claude. 1975. *Maidens, Meal and Money: Capitalism and the Domestic Community*. New York: Cambridge University Press.
Miescher, Stephan F. 2005. *Making Men in Ghana*. Bloomington: Indiana University Press.
Nugent, Paul. 1995. *Big Men, Small Boys and Politics in Ghana: Power, Ideology and the Burden of History, 1982–1994*. London: Pinter.
Roitman, Janet. 2005. *Fiscal Disobedience: An Anthropology of Economic Regulation in Central Africa*. Princeton, NJ: Princeton University Press.
Rudnyckyj, Daromir. 2014. "Regimes of Self-Improvement: Globalization and the Will to Work." *Social Text* 32(3): 109–27.
Sassen, Saskia. 2013. "The Middle Classes: An Historic Actor in Today's Global World." *Juncture* 20(2): 125–28.
Skinner, Kate. 2009. "'It Brought Some Kind of Neatness to Mankind': Mass Literacy, Community Development and Democracy in 1950s Asante." *Africa* 79(4): 479–99.
Spittler, Gerd. 2008. *Founders of the Anthropology of Work: German Social Scientists of the 19th and early 20th Centuries and the First Ethnographers* (Vol. 14). Münster: LIT.
Spronk, Rachel. 2012. *Ambiguous Pleasures: Sexuality and Middle-Class Self-Perceptions in Nairobi*. New York: Berghahn Books.

———. 2020. "Structures, Feelings and Savoir Faire: Ghana's Middle Classes in the Making." *Africa* 90(3): 470–88.

Standing, Guy. 2016. *The Corruption of Capitalism: Why Rentiers Thrive and Work Does Not Pay*. London: Biteback Publishing.

Stein, Felix. 2018. "Anthropology's 'Impact': A Comment on Audit and the Unmeasurable Nature of Critique." *Journal of the Royal Anthropological Institute* 24(1): 10–29.

Thalén, Oliver. 2011. "Ghanaian Entertainment Brokers: Urban Change, and Afro-Cosmopolitanism, with Neo-Liberal Reform." *Journal of African Media Studies* 3(2): 227–40.

Zoogah, David B., and Mohammed H. A. Bolaji. 2014. "Work, Self-Expansion and Self-Protection in Ghanaian Culture." In *Global Leadership Practices: A Cross-Cultural Management Perspective*, ed. Bettina Gehrke and Marie-Thérèse Claes, 238–52. Basingstoke: Palgrave Macmillan.

6

Capitalism, Overwork, and Polanyi's Dialectics of Freedom

Emerging Visions of Work–Life Balance in Contemporary Urban China

Gonçalo Santos, Yichen Rao, Jack L. Xing, and Jun Zhang

In March 2019, a public debate blew up in China on what came to be known as "the 996 schedule" (9 to 9, six days a week). The controversy started when a group of IT developers based in the booming southern city of Shenzhen, adjacent to Hong Kong, created an online GitHub project called *996.ICU* to share their personal experiences of 996 schedules. The designation *996.ICU* came from cases in which IT developers worked so hard under 996 that they had to go to an intensive care unit (ICU) for burnout treatment. Blog entries portrayed the grim life of IT workers, with long working hours that had highly negative impacts on their lives. In a matter of days, these blog entries became a national social media sensation, triggering debates on the fragilities and the legality of the 996 overtime work culture. Of course, not everyone in China is critical of 996. Jack Ma, the founder of tech giant Alibaba, responded to the 996 controversy by declaring 996 schedules to be "a blessing for employees who love their job and who strive to obtain the success that 'ordinary people' do not have" (Ma 2019). Ma's views are shared by many tech company managers, as well as by other employers and employees in China, revealing significant tensions in society surrounding the desirability of 996 schedules.

The 996 controversy offers a good entry-point into larger moral conversations in urban China regarding working hours and notions of work–life balance. China's shift to a market economy from the 1980s onwards has generated a culture of long working hours that mixed pre-existing values of entrepreneurship and industriousness with new neoliberal ideologies of work, success and the striving individual. The Labor Law introduced in 1995 was intended to curb the trend towards long work hours by stipulating a standard working week of forty hours (and no more than eight hours daily). This did not prevent a high incidence of overtime in many occupational communities, from factory workers (Pun 2005, 2016) to professionals such as lawyers, doctors, accountants, and IT workers (Nie, Otterbach, and Sousa-Poza 2015; Peng 2020).[1] By the early 2010s, this culture of overtime work was increasingly perceived as a social problem leading to a growing number of cases of *guolaosi* (from the Japanese term *karoshi*) or "overwork deaths" (*China News* 2013; Monet 2014).[2]

These Chinese debates reflect global uncertainties regarding work–life balance under neoliberal policies of labor management and digital capitalism. In the United States, Silicon Valley has promoted long hours and rebranded "workaholism" as the ethos of the tech sector (Lyons 2017). But here too the new "religion of workism" is frequently contested (Thompson 2019). In Europe, the trend towards reducing work hours is well established (Spiegelaere and Piasna 2017), but here too the emergence of a generation of "workaholic" professionals is a source of concern (Mihala 2018). Global uncertainties about work–life balance are not just about work hours. The stability of jobs is equally important. Neoliberal economic restructuring and the rise of the platform economy have fostered flexibilization and the precarity of labor (Sennet 1998; Wajcman 2015; Hann and Parry 2018). In East Asian countries such as Japan, neoliberal reforms have challenged traditional forms of employment (Gagne 2018). More flexible work arrangements, though undoubtedly welcomed by some, are often associated with longer working hours, closer interpenetration of work and life, and reduced job security (Streeck 2014; Wajcman 2015; Rosenblat and Stark 2016; Scholz 2017; Rosenblat 2018).[3]

The emergence of the 996 controversy in China in 2019 spoke directly to this climate of global uncertainties. Its main trigger was the economic slowdown, which by the late 2010s had impacted on most sectors of the economy, including the booming tech sector, leading to decreasing income levels and shrinking career prospects. This was the context in which Chinese workers started engaging in a public debate on the hardships of 996 work schedules. They asked: what is the point of working overtime and sacrificing oneself when pay is declining and promotion prospects are limited? Questions about changing ethical aspirations were also posed: is it morally desirable to work from 9 a.m. to 9 p.m., 6 days a week? What are the emotional and the health costs of this 996 schedule? How is it possible to reconcile such employment with family life? The larger question in the background concerned the very nature of work: is it about personal achievement or is it about securing social relationships and fulfilling moral responsibilities?

This chapter addresses these moral conversations by juxtaposing the perspective of IT programmers with that of a very different occupational community in the city: licensed taxi drivers. We chose to compare IT programmers with taxi drivers because these two groups are associated with very different urban social strata (the IT programmers with the middle class, and the taxi drivers with rural migrants and laid-off workers). Our aim is to show that contemporary concerns with work–life balance transcend the class boundaries that affect most occupational communities in urban China. The diverging views of both IT programmers and taxi drivers are shaped by an underlying moral tension between two contrasting conceptualizations of work: work as the pursuit of personal achievement and work as the pursuit of meaningful social relationships. Both conceptualizations of work are important, but they have very different implications in terms of the perceptions of IT programmers and taxi drivers of their empowerment and self-realization through work. Here we argue that these implications can be productively explored in light of a conceptual distinction—partly inspired by the work of Karl Polanyi ([1927] 2018)—between two different kinds of freedom: "personal freedom" or the freedom to detach oneself from others, and "social freedom" or the freedom to live a life connected to others "through duty and responsibility."

Polanyi occupies a rather unique position in early twentieth-century theorizations of work, ethics, and freedom (Cangiani 2017; Brie and Thomasberger 2018; see also Hann and Hart 2009: Introduction). With the growth of capitalist laissez-faire ideologies in the nineteenth century, there was an increasing trend to approach work and freedom in individualistic terms, and to look at the free market economy as the guardian of individual freedom. Working as a journalist in the Red Vienna of the 1920s, Polanyi was skeptical of this development, and he started questioning the growing methodological individualism of the economic sciences and the use of abstract models that lost sight of the organic, interrelated reality of economic processes. In a famous essay entitled "On Freedom" (Polanyi [1927] 2018), he criticizes the liberal emphasis on the notion of "personal freedom," arguing that it was a "bourgeois ideology" that gives little space to the question of social responsibility. Freedom, he argued, is not just about freeing oneself from the burden of external ties and constraints; it is also about acknowledging interdependencies and taking responsibility for our share in mutual human relationships. Polanyi maintained that the rise of market capitalism encouraged the development of a number of social institutions that promoted the selfishness of individuals and blocked the flourishing of a more socially responsible vision of freedom. For Polanyi, the only way to fight this narrowing down of the scope of human freedom was to challenge the dominance of market fundamentalism and to promote the development of new forms of associational socialism (see also Polanyi [1944] 2001: Ch. 24; and Brie and Thomasberger 2018).

The twenty-first century is a very different world from that in which Polanyi developed his critique of the market economy a century ago (Hann and Hart 2009; Graeber 2011; Streeck 2014). Yet, the neoliberal revival of market capitalism has led to renewed social science interest in the contributions of Polanyi. We would like to contribute to this neo-Polanyian resurgence, with one small caveat. Polanyi's 1927 critique of the ideology of personal freedom is timely in light of the dominance in contemporary societies of neoliberal ideologies of individual choice and personal freedom, but we distance ourselves from Polanyi's implicit model of unilinear evolution: from capitalism to socialism, and from personal freedom to social freedom. Socialism, however defined, is not the only moral and political philosophy or the only politico-economic formation that encourages the flourishing of a notion of freedom based on social responsibility, and it is possible to imagine capitalist societies that promote the growth of personal freedom along with the cultivation of social freedom. Hence, we argue that Polanyi's contrast between a more egotistic and a more socially responsible notion of freedom is useful not as a binary scheme of unilinear evolution but as a theorization of a continuum between two ideal types of human freedom that can be studied ethnographically in different social and cultural contexts, in modern and non-modern economies, and in socialist and capitalist societies.

Although we continue to use Polanyi's terminology to refer to a continuum between two ideal types of human freedom, our conceptualization is not part of a political project of associational socialism but amounts to a new anthropological vision of the relation between work and freedom. Instead of imagining that there can be societies dominated by one type of freedom or the other, we argue that the experience of work in all human societies is shaped by an important tension between the pursuit of personal freedom and the pursuit of social freedom. This tension can take many different forms (because what counts as personal freedom and social freedom varies from context to context), but the relation between these two forms of freedom always takes a dialectical form. Rather than being conceived as an antithesis or as a fatal flaw of some kind, the tension between personal and social freedom is what is necessary to produce workable versions of freedom in any given context. Polanyi's 1927 essay already points in the direction of such a dialectical conceptualization, but here we develop this dialectic conceptualization in a more explicit manner.

We use this dialectical approach to make sense of contemporary Chinese moral debates on 996 work schedules as seen through the lens of two different occupational communities. We are not claiming that our idealized contrast between personal and social freedom is an emic conceptualization. It is an etic conceptualization that helps us understand the moral claims of our interlocutors regarding the meanings of work. This last point has implications for the kind of anthropology of work, ethics, and freedom that we are putting forward in this chapter. The term "freedom" figures prominently in recent work in the new anthropology of ethics, where it is often invoked to question conventional assumptions of "unfreedom" in classic anthropological studies of morality (Laidlaw 2002, 2013; Mahmood 2005; Robbins 2007, 2012). James Laidlaw in particular has argued against this Durkheimian legacy of "ethical unfreedom," noting that moral action typically involves a process of reflection that entails some degree of freedom and choice. This freedom is not that of modern ideologies of individual choice and autonomy. Rather it is "constructed out of the role given to choice in various cultures, and in various domains within specific cultures" (Laidlaw 2002: 323). We find this Foucauldian conceptualization of freedom a useful provocation, but we agree with Webb Keane (2016) that reducing freedom to a question of choice is very limiting, and ends up narrowing the analysis to the study of first-person perspectives (individual and/or collective). There is much to be learned from an approach that focuses on the construction of first-person perspectives in specific social-material contexts. This is Laidlaw's science of freedom. But here we propose an approach that also takes seriously the importance of third-person perspectives and their capacity to reveal the larger structural constraints that shape the making of first-person subjectivities (Ortner 2016).

Our account analyzes the ideals of work–life balance of two different occupational communities in urban China, associated with different social strata, proposing a comparative ethnographic approach to the construction of differentiated spaces of freedom in relation to work. The notion of freedom must be expanded to include questions of social freedom or the capacity to live a life connected to others through social and moral responsibilities. This expanded conceptualization of human freedom resonates with a conceptual dualism that runs through much of modern Chinese political and philosophical thinking about freedom: freedom as a matter of personal liberty, and freedom as a matter of social responsibility (Fung 2006). While the dominant trend in Chinese thinking about freedom is to emphasize the moral superiority of social freedom, one must be wary of Orientalist depictions of China (past and present) as a collectivist society. The Chinese tradition considers both personal freedom and social freedom important, and conceptualizes the relation between the two in dialectical rather than antithetical terms. The form of this dialectics varies according to occupational community.

IT Developers

What are the ideals of work–life balance of IT developers in China's "Silicon Valley," Shenzhen, the starting point of the 996 controversy? One of us, Yichen Rao, did online and offline fieldwork with IT workers in Shenzhen in 2019 and 2020 in light of recent 996 debates.

Mr. Chen works as a senior project manager for Tencent, the Chinese IT giant that is renowned for its online games and its social media platforms QQ and WeChat. Mr. Chen started out his career at Tencent in 2011 with a monthly salary lower than the present-day average for a university graduate (i.e., RMB 15,000–20,000 or c. USD 2,100–2,800), but his salary has since increased substantially following his upward-career progression and the boom of the IT industry. Between 2011 and 2019, Mr. Chen saw his annual salary double and then triple to reach a record RMB 900,000 (c. USD 130,000), including RMB 200,000 (c. USD 28,000) of stock shares, which was more than fourteen times higher than the average annual income in Shenzhen in 2019. Mr. Chen married Ms. Li in 2018. Ms. Li works as a data analyst for ByteDance, an IT company that has seen huge success in recent years for several machine learning-enabled content platforms like Tou Tiao (Headlines) and Dou Yin (Tik Tok). Mr. Chen's salary is higher than that of Ms. Li. They live in an apartment in the affluent Nanshan District where many IT companies are based, paying a mortgage of over RMB 18,000 (approximately USD 2,500) per month.

Ms. Li has a 996 work schedule, while Mr. Chen's work schedule is more like 10-11-6. Even when Mr. Chen is off work (as when Rao interviewed the couple in Bao'an District on a Sunday), he continues to respond to WeChat messages from his director on work-related issues. During the interview, the couple disagreed about 996. Mr. Chen said: "If I was still working as a frontline programmer,[4] I would probably not welcome 996. But if I think like a project leader, then I would embrace 996. I am saying this objectively: I think 996 is not a moral issue. It is an economic issue. One does not accept 996 simply because one is not paid enough . . . Like it or not, it is sometimes necessary to have 996. The product manager working in our team is always thinking about traveling and sightseeing. How can such a person make good products?" Ms. Li immediately disagreed: "You programmers are so easily brainwashed. Why can't a product manager who likes traveling and sightseeing be a good product manager? 996 is very unhealthy and unsustainable. It is a moral issue and it is exploitation. It can and should be changed on moral grounds by means of policy interventions!"

Ms. Li expressed particularly strong concerns about the incompatibility between 996 and the moral duties of family life. She told the story of a colleague—a married man in his forties—who worked so hard at their company that his wife threatened to leave him for leaving all the family burdens to her. After Ms. Li mentioned this case to Mr. Chen, he stepped back and rephrased his views on 996. He said that 996 is not always good for the family but he recognizes that his long working hours at Tencent gave him a good income and a "sense of achievement" (*chengjiugan*), especially because he comes from a relatively modest family in a small city. Towards the end of the interview, Ms. Li summed up her hopes by saying: "Aiya, I hope that one day we will be able to put an end to 996?" Mr. Chen replied, "Maybe when we reach forty?" Ms. Li shouted, "Forty?!? I will be too old then. . . ." Mr. Chen said, "I read a book that said that forty is the prime age for women." Ms. Li was annoyed, "Who told you that? Could we still have a child?"

The debate between Mr. Chen and Ms. Li points to two very different conceptualizations of the goals and the meanings of work: work as *the pursuit of a sense of achievement*—something that is clearly aligned with the construction of what we call personal freedom; and work as *the pursuit of social and moral responsibilities*—something that is clearly aligned with the construction of what we call social freedom. These two pursuits are closely connected, as we show below, but they can be distinguished analytically. Despite being married to each other, Ms. Li is more concerned with questions of social and moral responsibility, whereas Mr. Chen is more concerned with questions of personal achievement. Men and women often have different moral conceptions of work and work–life balance, and these different moral orientations are shaped by enduring gendered divisions of labor in the family that give middle-class working women like Ms. Li a much larger share of labor when it comes to handling the social and moral responsibilities of family life (Santos and Harrell 2017; Zhang 2017; Zhong 2019). But these contrasting moral orientations are not just about gendered divisions within the family but reflect larger moral divisions within the IT sector and in Chinese society generally.

From the interviews undertaken by Rao, we get a fuller picture of what kinds of IT workers look at 996 schedules as an opportunity to further their sense of success and personal achievement. IT workers with this moral orientation often come from a relatively humble family background (usually a family based in a rural area or in a small city). These workers hope to prove themselves in the job in order to rise in the workplace hierarchy and earn a high salary. For them, having a 996 schedule is primarily a question of personal achievement and economic ambition. Such aspirations are not unusual in other occupational communities, especially amongst young unmarried workers, but the tech sector is particularly affected by this ethos of personal achievement and economic ambition because it is strongly driven by a philosophy of striving for success and a culture of overtime work. This culture of overtime work has both moral and economic dimensions, and its emergence was shaped by a larger technocratic engineering culture in which labor is treated as "human capital"—a "fictitious commodity" in the sense of Karl Polanyi ([1944] 2011), to be bought and sold in the interests of profit maximization.

Mr. Chen told Rao that firing people at Tencent is often likened to a necessary "system optimization," and the vision of internal career progression is based on a clear-cut "chain of disdain" (*bishilian*). At Tencent, the lowest levels of the job hierarchy are P1–P3 employees (usually low-level assistants and customer service staff), followed by P4 employees (junior specialists) and P5 employees (senior specialists). Most college graduates land a position at the P5 level or above, depending on their educational qualifications. The move from P6 to P7 is an important threshold in terms of economic success and sense of achievement. P7 employees become team leaders and they start to be rewarded with stock shares. The salary of a P8 employee is double that of a P7. Mr. Chen is a P7 and leads a team of ten to twenty IT developers. His career is a story of success according to the moral logic of Tencent's "chain of disdain" and the way it evaluates personal achievement, but there are far more cases of failure than of success. Employees who "fail" to reach P8 by the age of forty are viewed within Tencent as "systemic errors" that need to be cleared. As Mr. Chen commented, the system cannot afford to attend to individual needs. Hence the system has to make clear-cut differentiations between winners and losers. People like Mr. Chen view themselves as winners insofar as they were able to prove themselves and reach P7 by the age of thirty. This sense of achievement gives Mr. Chen a "sense of ownership" (*yongyougan*) over his life and career.

The expression "having a sense of ownership" is useful to unpack the moral dimensions of what counts as success in the IT industry. The term was used by Ms. Li to explain the difference between the work of young academic researchers and the work of young IT developers. Both work very long hours but have a very different sense of "ownership" of work. Young academic researchers work hard for a project but they usually get some kind of recognition as co-authors of papers or as acknowledged names in a publication. However, in China's IT industry, a young programmer's devotion to a project as a "coding peasant" (*manong*) will never be credited to his/her name because the project was made by a large team and is owned by the company. The only person who will be remembered is the team leader, and very few ground-level programmers will ever manage to climb up the ladder and reach a leadership position. Most will leave their companies with no recognition other than the money they earned, and for Ms. Li this is the reason why IT developers get so upset if they work long hours but are not paid enough.

This sense of resentment has become more intense with the economic slowdown of the 2010s. In the early years of the IT industry, as recalled by both Mr. Chen and Ms. Li, the pay was not as high as it is today but there was a sense that hard work would be rewarded with a rapid salary increase. Today, there is no longer a clear-cut connection between working hard and getting economic rewards for one's hard work. There are just too many aspiring IT workers out there, and if one is not willing to work hard and have a 996 schedule, someone else will. The slowdown of the IT sector has also helped turn 996 into a more regimented institution, as team leaders started to feel empowered to send WeChat warnings to employees, with admonishments like: "Why did you leave the office so early? Do you think you have learned enough?" Ms. Li said that these WeChat warnings are often well intended but they are not very effective, because frontline staff no longer see a clear-cut connection between working harder and having a salary increase. Ms. Li added that this management philosophy is very mechanical in a "Chinese" style: "It is just like our school days; when we did not perform well in exams, teachers and parents would give us a warning: 'You need to work harder by reciting and copying the text, doing as much homework as you can, and learning until midnight.'"

Frontline programmers in today's China are becoming increasingly aware not just that their hard work might never turn into a salary increase but also that their hard work might never turn into something they own, in the sense explained above. Frontline programmers do not own anything; they are coding peasants. Owning projects is what makes the CV of a programmer look good; it is also what makes a programmer develop a sense of achievement and security in the industry. But very few manage to develop this sense of ownership and achievement. Mr. Chen and Ms. Li have seen many disillusioned colleagues leave the industry with nothing but a less-than-average salary after many years under 996 work schedules. Some left because they could not take it anymore, others because their skills were outdated or were no longer appreciated. After leaving the industry, these colleagues started doing things like opening a restaurant, or becoming an insurance agent, and many say that it was only after leaving the industry that they were able to look for things that they could own.

Reclaiming a Sense of Ownership over One's Work and Life

Mr. Hua is one of the disillusioned IT developers who left Shenzhen after nine years of hard work in order to reclaim a sense of ownership over his work and life. He had joined tech giant Tencent in Shenzhen in 2010, and in the process his monthly salary had more than double to 6,800 RMB (c. 950 USD). Because this was a very high salary for someone with a college degree, Hua thought that he would be able to save enough money to purchase a home after a few years. His company in Shenzhen did help him transfer his household registration (*hukou*) to Shenzhen so he could enjoy all the benefits of a full resident, including access to various welfare services. But his career in Shenzhen was not as fruitful as he had initially envisioned. Although, after nine years of hard work with the same company his annual income had reached 400K RMB, which was more than most of his friends were making in other industries, he still found himself stuck at the P7 position and could not move further as he lacked the skills to manage a team project and make it scalable. In 2019, his line manager refused to grant him the usual year-end bonus of 200K RMB on the grounds that his performance was "below expectations." This was a severe blow to Hua's home ownership aspirations. After almost ten years of working hard in Shenzhen, Hua had still not managed to purchase a home in the Nanshan District, and with property prices constantly increasing, it was unlikely that he would ever be able to make enough money for the down payment.

After a discussion with his wife, Hua decided to quit his job and they moved to a smaller city where he started to work as an IT programmer for a local medical beauty company. Hua is now able to leave his office daily no later than 5 or 6 p.m., so he has more time for himself. His salary is not as high as it was in Shenzhen, but he has additional part-time jobs that he likes. This new work arrangement has brought more flexibility and stability to his life, and he has a stronger sense of achievement at work, meaning that he can engage in projects that are more meaningful and that give him more recognition. Hua also feels that he has a stronger sense of achievement in life because he has managed to purchase a home at an affordable price. Hua said: "I left Shenzhen simply because I could neither develop a sense of family stability (*anjia*) nor develop a sense of professional stability (*liye*). But here I am able to do both. I feel a closer connection between me as a person and the things I create [through work]."

Popular idioms like *anjia liye* or *chengjia liye* point to the capacity to have both a "stable family and an established profession," and highlight the close connection between family life and work life in the "traditional" Chinese value system. Even today, the capacity to have both a successful career and a family life remain key criteria to evaluate someone's maturity and their achievements in life. This means that in the Chinese context the conceptualization of work as the pursuit of personal achievement cannot really be separate from the conceptualization of work as the pursuit of meaningful social relationships, including various kinds of family and social responsibilities. These intersections are crucial in discussions of the Chinese work ethic. Stevan Harrell (1985) has argued that the best way to make sense of the well-documented phenomenon of Chinese industriousness is to pay attention to the kind of goals to which hard work is directed. In most instances, Harrell argues, people are willing to work hard because they think that this will allow them to contribute to the long-term benefit of the family, including in some cases the larger patrilineal joint family, or even a whole village or personal network. If Harrell is right, when an IT worker says that they work hard because they are driven by the pursuit of success and personal achievement, one must bear in mind that this philosophy of striving is often an attempt to fulfill social and moral responsibilities toward their family and personal networks. The case of Hua seems to confirm this entanglement. After working hard for many years under 996 schedules in Shenzhen, Hua decided to quit his job and move with his family to a smaller city. The reason for the move was not just related to his perception of a lack of success and personal achievement in the workplace; there was also the fact that he was not making enough money to take proper care of his family and to realize the middle-class dream of home ownership. These are all important moral responsibilities in the lives of ordinary frontline developers like Hua, and these responsibilities are a key component of a form of "social freedom" that is built primarily around the moral idiom of the family and its multiple circles of relations, duties, and obligations.

Hua's pursuit of social freedom is somewhat incompatible with the more egotistic philosophy of work, success, and personal achievement celebrated by the IT industry in Shenzhen, but not all IT developers are willing to leave Shenzhen like Hua did in the pursuit of a better work–life balance. Many frontline programmers are supportive of 996 work schedules because they are caught in commitments such as mortgage payments that depend on the extra income from overtime work.[5] But there are also many frontline programmers who are no longer willing to work so hard because they think that they will never be able to get themselves on track to have a "stable family and established profession." These young programmers are pessimistic about their prospects in terms of career progression because they have seen older programmers being made redundant or quitting out of frustration or exhaustion, and they fear that something similar will happen to them in the future. They are especially concerned about housing. We have already seen that the high cost of housing in Shenzhen was an important factor behind Mr. Hua's decision to quit his job and move to a smaller city, but there are other examples. Mr. Zhang, a 24-year-old programmer who has been working in a medium-size IT company since 2017, told Rao that his project team leader had decided to leave his job at the age of thirty-four to open a hot-pot restaurant in Chengdu because he was resentful of the fact that the high costs of living (especially of rented accommodation) in Shenzhen did not allow him to save much money out of his relatively high annual income of about 700,000 RMB (or 100,000 USD) pre-tax. This episode made Zhang worry about his future because his parents were not rich enough to help him to purchase real estate. Zhang still felt "welcomed" at his company as a new graduate, a single person, and relatively cheap labor, but he knew that this welcoming attitude would change once he reached the "mid-level" bottleneck and started to become more concerned with family responsibilities. Even if he managed to make enough money for a down-payment on a small apartment in Shenzhen's suburbs, he would still have to spend the rest of his life working 996 schedules to be able to afford his monthly mortgage payments.

At his farewell party, the project team leader advised Zhang to spend more time on taking care of his own health and personal enrichment, because these are the most precious forms of capital one could "own." Zhang has taken this advice seriously, and has started planning his future: "I already gave up the idea of owning a home in Shenzhen. I am now learning financial knowledge and looking at investment channels to turn my savings into capital to help me get something I could own." Rao asked: "What kind of things do you envision?" "I am not sure," Zhang said; "I always hoped to see the outside world by earning a graduate degree in the US or in Europe, but I did not have enough capital. So I may try to use my money to get a graduate degree overseas and experience a different trajectory of life."

Ms. Xiao, a newly graduated trainee working at ByteDance, described her experience so far as a liminal process of "gold-plating" (*dujin*). "I never thought of staying here for long," she said, "I am just here to learn stuff. The dream in Shenzhen is just too hard to sustain, even for someone like me who was born here." Ms. Xiao came from a solid middle-class family in Shenzhen so she was less anxious about home ownership; she was also less enthusiastic about the local culture of success and the striving individual. But she still appreciated the business knowledge one could learn through working in a big IT company, which she believed could be useful in her future career plans. For her, the imagination of success and ownership is different from the older generation of Shenzhen migrants who aspired to acquire the means to have a prosperous life with home ownership. Ms. Xiao has more resources at her disposal to strategize her life trajectory and avoid being absorbed into the alienating machinery of the IT industry. When asked about her career plans in the future, Xiao told Rao that she would like to become an independent game designer working for the international market. She believes that she has learned a number of skills at ByteDance that will help her start her own business in the future.

Most IT programmers continue to aspire to have a sense of ownership and personal achievement, but this is difficult to sustain in the context of an increasingly vulnerable economy with high costs of living, especially housing. However, there are still many IT programmers who are strong supporters of 996 schedules and the philosophy of the striving individual. Some of these 996 supporters, including Mr. Chen, managed to move up the ladder of success within a few years. They are now earning a high salary, and this experience of upward mobility only reinforces their conviction that the pursuit of moral responsibility is closely related to the pursuit of personal achievement. But not everyone agrees with this vision of success. Unlike Mr. Chen, the biggest dream of Ms. Li is not to move up the career ladder and expand her sense of ownership of work; although she likes to work hard, she also wants to have a baby while she is still youthful and she feels that 996 does not allow her to realize this dream. For Mr. Chen, the IT industry is bound to be stressful and it necessitates long working hours, but Ms. Li disagrees. She is envious of her sister, who leads a more balanced family life in Germany. She said, "Look at the workers in Germany, they earn a respectable income without 996. They get off work on time." Mr. Chen has a counterargument: "Europe is already lagging behind in the IT sector. People are becoming lazy. We should look towards Silicon Valley, where they have an overtime working culture. And China is just catching up with them and will be leading the future. As Chinese, we still have a lot to do, so we need to work hard."

Taxi Drivers

Our second case study focuses on licensed taxi drivers, an occupational community with a much lower educational and income level than IT developers. This section draws on materials gathered by one of us, Jack Xing, through fieldwork in the second-tier city of Xi'an, Shaanxi province, Central China, in 2017–18.[6] Xing noticed during fieldwork that many employed taxi drivers were refusing to become e-hailing drivers for companies like Didi Chuxing (China's Uber, hereafter "Didi") despite the promise of a higher income and a more flexible working practice, and one of the main factors behind this refusal was considerations of work–life balance and resistance to 996 ideologies of workism and algorithmic flexibility (Xing 2019).

Employed taxi drivers in Xi'an are predominantly male and middle-aged (thirty to fifty) and most are either state-owned enterprise (SOE) laid-off workers or rural migrants without urban housing.[7] Most come from Xi'an itself or else from neighboring parts of Shaanxi province. Two-thirds of Xing's informants had been in the business for between five and twenty years. Employed drivers make about RMB 4,000–5,000 per month, but usually need to support one or more dependents. The drivers' monthly disposable personal income is less than the average monthly disposable personal income in Xi'an (Xi'an Statistics Bureau 2019), and their monthly salary is two to three times less than the average monthly salary of frontline IT developers in Shenzhen.[8] Such a monthly income falls within the parameters of what sociologist David Goodman (2014) has called urban China's "mid-to-low income group" (Notar 2012; Zhang 2016). About 58 percent of all taxi drivers in Xi'an finished high school, but a significant percentage (about 36 percent) did not make it past middle school or primary school. These low levels of education highlight the low social position of taxi drivers in urban society. This low social status helps explain why their reflections on work reveal strong concerns with basic questions of survival and employment stability. This is not to say that drivers do not have ambitions in terms of career progression, but their career prospects are structurally limited. Drivers who are committed to the profession dream about becoming cab bosses or owners of their own licensed cab, but they know that this is largely unachievable because of the high price of licensed cabs and the restrictive regulatory frameworks guiding the taxi business industry.[9]

The taxi business in Xi'an is run according to a government-controlled franchise model managed by the municipal Taxi Administration Office (hereafter TAO). In the early to mid-1990s, the city government allowed the operation of taxicabs on the basis of a sole proprietorship model, but, in 1998, after a number of reforms, all taxicabs had to be registered and managed by taxi companies except for a few who acquired their licenses in the sole proprietorship era. The way these reforms were implemented in Xi'an has some local specificities, but it also illustrates some general trends and patterns. Whenever the city government auctions new cab licenses, taxi companies are invited to make bids for these licenses through official procedures. If granted a number of new licenses, taxi companies will have to buy a corresponding number of cabs at a standard TAO-regulated price, and the operational rights of these licensed cabs can then be sold to cab bosses who can then resell these rights to other cab bosses, and so on, at prices ranging from RMB 200,000 to 700,000, depending on the type of licensed cab. The purchase of these operational rights does not entail full proprietorship because the cab remains officially registered under the name of a taxi company, and cab bosses are always required to pay a monthly administrative and management fee to the taxi company. The size of this monthly fee varies from RMB 1,000 to 9,000, again depending on the type of licensed cab.

Largely unable to afford the high costs of purchasing and running their own licensed cab, employed taxi drivers are structurally located at the bottom of the pecking order of the licensed cab business. Cab bosses have to rely on employed drivers to operate their taxi business, just as taxi companies have to rely on cab bosses to operate licensed taxicabs. Most cab bosses drive ten-hour shifts and employ a licensed driver to do the other ten-hour shift of the day, but there are also a few cab bosses who fully delegate the work of taxi driving to two or more employed drivers. Employed drivers tend to get at least four days off monthly, and it is the responsibility of cab bosses to arrange replacement drivers. To become a licensed driver, one needs to have at least three years driving experience and pass a set of examinations to get a professional license. Employed taxi drivers do not get a fixed salary from cab bosses; they are given the usage of the taxicabs to earn income against the payment a daily "rental" fee. At the end of each shift, drivers are expected to pay cab bosses a fixed amount of money that is known as *fenziqian*—literally, "one's share of the money." Unlike cab bosses, the income of drivers depends only on their labor and they must make enough money every day to pay their *fenziqian*. The rest of their daily revenue, apart from fuel costs, corresponds to their margin of profit. The amount of *fenziqian* is usually set for a relatively long period (usually one or two years), but there are frequent price adjustments to reflect changing business conditions. In 2018, the standard amount of *fenziqian* in Xi'an was RMB 160 per day per shift. In theory, this daily payment is mandatory, but there is some margin for negotiation, such as when drivers request a day-off to their cab boss. This margin for negotiation can be bigger or smaller depending on the quality of the relationship between the driver and the cab boss.

Taxi drivers have to work hard daily to be able to pay the *fenziqian* and have some revenue, but despite this pressure, most experienced drivers favor a model of work that is not based on 996 work schedules. For these drivers, the pursuit of economic benefits is important, but even more important is to have a model of work that maintains a stable and balanced life. Having a fixed schedule is a key part of this vision of work–life balance. Contrary to public perception, conventional taxi drivers usually have a very stable work schedule, which follows certain patterns that are shaped by key spatial and temporal constraints. All drivers follow rigid ten-hour shifts. A driver's time to start and stop work is strictly fixed, and the time they have to refuel cabs is both fixed and limited. Many drivers like to stick to a regular circulatory driving pattern in the city. This element of fixity goes hand in hand with a high degree of personal autonomy and flexibility when it comes to daily operational procedures, and drivers talk very positively about this aspect of their work. Most taxi drivers, especially experienced ones, are satisfied with this balance between fixed work schedules and flexible operational procedures. Drivers like to have a certain degree of personal freedom at work, but they are averse to last-minute arrangements, and they avoid any work responsibilities other than driving and transporting passengers. Many drivers told Xing that they do not want to worry (*caoxin*) too much about work matters. For them, driving is a job rather than the meaning of their lives. They favor a model of work that combines fixed schedules with flexibility in daily operational procedures, because this work arrangement allows them to have time to attend family matters and to engage in social interactions with colleagues, thereby building a sense of community and stability.

Most drivers are very keen on having regular exchanges and gatherings with other drivers after work. They call or send WeChat messages to one another, agree a meeting time, choose a familiar restaurant near the taxi depot, and head in that direction by picking up passengers going to nearby destinations. During these after-work gatherings, drivers talk about their work experiences, share news, and tell one another scandalous stories or dirty jokes. This is a good way to meet old friends, including drivers who went through training and certification in the same year, and drivers who regularly offer support during daily work activities. Other participants in these after-work gatherings include friends of friends, and these new acquaintances further expand the network of support for drivers. Through these gatherings and other related social outings, an occupational community network is constantly being formed and reconstructed.

Building this sense of community is only possible because there is some degree of stability within the profession. Being an employed taxi driver is not an easy job (not everyone is able to endure driving ten-hour shifts daily) and the career prospects are limited (few drivers will ever be able to own their own licensed cab), but a significant percentage of drivers end up staying in the profession for more than just a few years. More than half of all employed drivers interviewed by Xing had worked in the taxi business for more than five years, and many were strongly committed to defending the interests of their occupational community in the face of new threats posed by e-hailing business companies like Didi. In the last few years, a significant number of taxi drivers in Xi'an have been actively involved in strikes and protests to defend the interests of professional drivers against e-hailing and the trend towards algorithmic automation. This resistance to e-hailing was shaped by many factors, but here we only have space to discuss the issue of work hours and work schedules. Employed drivers in Xi'an do not want to become e-hailing drivers, because although the new platform economy offers the promise of more income and more work flexibility, it goes hand in hand with the enforcement of a regime of labor based on 996 work schedules that is incompatible with their conceptualization of work as the pursuit of social and moral responsibilities.

Resistance to Algorithmic Driving and the Pursuit of a Stable Life

The work patterns of conventional taxi drivers are very different from those of e-hailing drivers working for Didi platforms. Xing learned a lot about these differences when he started to interview taxi drivers who had decided to shift to e-hailing because of the prospect of earning more money and having a more flexible working arrangement. Many of these drivers decided to switch back to conventional taxi driving after a few months, and their main reason was that they did not identify with e-hailing values of work organization and work–life balance.

Consider the case of Mr. Wang, a former state-owned enterprise textile mechanic who had worked as a taxi driver for twelve years and who decided to buy a private car and become a Didi driver in 2015, at the height of the rise of Didi in China. Xing spent one day in the summer of 2018 with Mr. Wang to learn about the routine of e-hailing drivers. Their day started soon after 8 a.m., and they had a quick pause for lunch at around noon, in between Didi algorithmic instructions and requests. Time passed very quickly and at 5 p.m., after seven hours of work, Mr. Wang told Xing that it is easy to lose track of time as an e-hailing driver: "You see how time flies? You don't feel it. When driving a taxi, you have a clock in your mind: 4p.m., time to go home. Now the algorithm doesn't make you feel it: orders come one after another, and because you want to make a little more money, you end up accepting it and continue." While some might appreciate this flexibility, Mr. Wang does not like it: "You seem to be pushed by an invisible hand to work longer. Last week, I had three days on which I came home later than 9 p.m. I was worn out, and my wife was angry. She reproached me for working too long and ruining my health to make money." The truth is that it is difficult to stop: "This is your full-time job, and it's easy to work longer if there's no fixed schedule and no issue outside work demands your attention. But your body feels it. My lower back problem [a common problem among taxi drivers] has worsened quite significantly in these past few years [working for Didi], and it's ridiculous that I thought it would get better after I switched to Didi!"

That afternoon, Mr. Wang continued responding to Didi's algorithmic instructions for a few more hours until he realized—at 8p.m.—that he had completed a twelve-hour shift and that it was time to return home. He looked at his smartphone and started doing some accounting: "Let me see . . . a total of twenty-four tips today. I get a RMB 60 prize from Didi. This is not very much. Back in 2015, when I started, it was RMB 150." Xing nodded and asked: "How much did you make today?" Mr. Wang browsed his screen and said: "RMB 320 in total. After deducting the expenses for meals and gas costs, it's around RMB 250. That's okay. This is why I bought a car with a one-time payment. If I leased it or paid it in installments, I'd need to give around RMB 100 to the companies." But when Xing asked about Didi's rates, Mr. Wang hesitated: "I'm not sure. I didn't check [the rates] recently. Many Didi drivers don't check. You know that Didi won't tell you the rate explicitly. There's a surge in pricing during peak hours, and they only show your share without telling you how much is their split. I guess it should be around RMB 1.2–1.4 per km. Before, it was higher, but now Didi is increasingly exploitative and it is becoming more difficult to make money as a full-time driver."

Xing's exchange with Mr. Wang explains some of the distinctive features of the work of Didi drivers. Unlike conventional taxi drivers, most Didi drivers have a flexible schedule that allows them to choose when to start work, how much to earn, and when to end the work. For most part-time Didi drivers, who usually have other jobs or responsibilities, this flexibility is what allows drivers to make some extra money. However, full-time Didi drivers like Mr. Wang do not experience this flexibility.[10] These drivers need to have a rigid work schedule because the only way for them to earn enough is to regularly work long hours, with only a few days off. Furthermore, the absence of outside time constraints, with the algorithmic orders randomly and uncontrollably crowding in, makes it easier for full-time Didi drivers to work longer than they had expected. Hence it is not uncommon for them to have daily work shifts of twelve or thirteen hours, an arrangement that is comparable to the 996 work schedules of frontline IT programmers in Shenzhen. Additionally, full-time Didi drivers need to follow the algorithmic instructions of the Didi app closely, even with regard to where and when they refuel and rest. This does not allow drivers to develop a spatial–temporal working plan to boost their income and match their preferred work habits.

The work arrangements shaping the practice of Didi driving have several shortcomings from the perspective of the value system of conventional taxi drivers. The first is the (potential) loss of a sense of stability and security. On the one hand, it is difficult to maintain a stable work schedule. The boundary between work and leisure time is blurred, and the responsibilities towards work and family are often in tension, as shown by Mr. Wang's complaint about the driving aggravating his lower back problem, and his wife's complaint about his long work hours. On the other hand, because drivers now have to follow algorithmic instructions that they cannot control, they are confronted with new uncertainties. The system's algorithmic instructions do not always suit the drivers' personal needs, and they often lead to traffic jams, difficult passengers, unprofitable drives, and dangerous areas, which could have been avoided if drivers were allowed to have more control. There is also the question of the loss of a sense of community at work. E-hailing drivers do not meet their colleagues for lunch or at after-work gatherings. This makes it difficult to build and maintain social relationships with colleagues. This leads many taxi drivers like Mr. Wang to feel unhappy about e-hailing.

The shift to Didi was meant to increase their sense of ownership over their work, but this did not happen, and many drivers like Mr. Wang end up shifting back to conventional taxi driving. These drivers struggle to find meaning in the flexibility of algorithmic driving because they favor having a fixed work schedule that allows them to develop a sense of community and work–life stability. In contrast, the Didi approach to work is based on 996 schedules and the ideology of the striving individual. Didi work arrangements are dominated by flexible work schedules and algorithmic control of the drivers' spatial–temporal working arrangements. This approach to work leads drivers like Mr. Wang to work longer and have less control over daily operational procedures, and this results in aggravated health problems, limited leisure time, and a lack of a sense of family and community.

Does this mean that professional taxi drivers favor work arrangements that allow the pursuit of social freedom or the freedom to fulfill social and moral responsibilities? It is true that taxi drivers who are critical of e-hailing favor having stable work arrangements because this allows them to have more time to fulfill their responsibilities to their families, community, and collectivities, thus pursuing social freedom. But there are also drivers who are positive about the switch to e-hailing, feeling that it has allowed them to make more money and achieve financial freedom (*caiwu ziyou*). These drivers describe the work of algorithmic driving not as a disruption of work–life balance and social responsibilities but as an opportunity to maximize economic benefits. This vision of work is closer to personal freedom than to social freedom. Hence what we have here is a moral tension between two different conceptualizations of work: work as personal freedom—in this case, financial freedom—and work as social freedom and social responsibility. Taxi drivers, like IT programmers, are divided in the way they approach work, but as we have seen in our discussion of the IT sector, there is an ongoing dialectic between these different approaches to work. This means that something that may seem to be connected to the pursuit of personal freedom from one perspective can also be a way to fulfill moral obligations of social freedom from another perspective.

This last point can be illustrated by looking in more detail at the views of young taxi drivers in their twenties who are critical of the work arrangements of the conventional taxi industry. For this younger generation, maximizing the accumulation of economic benefits is a prerequisite to control the future, and the fixed work schedules of the taxi industry are an obstacle to achieving this sense of control. For example, Mr. Xiao Zhang, who has since switched to e-hailing, told Xing: "The taxi industry is doomed. . . . With this rigid ten-hour work schedule, who can set up a family or launch a career? We young people have great health to fight for our lives, and we want to make as much money as possible to be able to get a house. Without a house and some money, who will marry us, and how will we be able to set up a family? Making money is definitely the top priority for me. Without money, how can I control my future and achieve the things I am yearning for?" For young drivers like Mr. Zhang, the key to success is to work hard to make money. These drivers are not very interested in building community ties with other taxi drivers, and they are not very concerned with questions of work–life balance because they do not have a family and they feel that they do not have time to take family responsibilities. For them, the primary purpose of work is to achieve "financial freedom" in order to have more control over the future.

There is no doubt that this concern with financial freedom is closely connected to the pursuit of a higher degree of personal freedom, but one should be wary not to read the notion of financial freedom in too individualistic terms. In their descriptions of what they do, young taxi drivers repeatedly connect the pursuit of financial freedom to the larger moral obligation of "establishing a family and starting a career" (*chengjia liye*). By presenting this larger moral obligation as the ultimate goal of financial freedom, these young drivers are echoing the views of the more experienced taxi drivers and their emphasis on an approach to work that allows drivers to fulfill key social responsibilities to family and community, and thus participate in the construction of spaces of social freedom.

Work–Life Balance and the Dialectics of Personal / Social Freedom

We have looked at two different case studies of urban occupational communities and their ideals of work–life balance against the background of larger public debates on China's overtime work culture. Both case studies point to the prevalence of ambiguous moral attitudes towards 996 working regimes. For taxi drivers in second-tier cities like Xi'an, the experience of 996 is closely linked to the threat of e-hailing. For IT programmers in China's "Silicon Valley," the experience of 996 is closely linked to a climate of shrinking salaries, reduced career prospects, and rising costs of living. Taxi drivers are more critical of 996 than IT programmers, but both occupational groups include voices that are supportive of 996 and others that are critical of it. Some taxi drivers, especially older married ones, are very critical of 996 because they are used to having fixed ten-hour shifts that allow them to fulfill key social responsibilities to family and community. But there are also taxi drivers, especially young unmarried ones, who are positive about 996 and are willing to become e-hailing drivers and work longer hours in order to earn more income and thus pursue financial freedom. Most IT programmers start out their careers favorable to 996, but many of them end up disillusioned with this regime of overtime work not just because they find it unrewarding economically but also because it does not give them any social recognition.

The moral attitudes of both groups of urban professionals to 996 work schedules are shaped by an important moral tension between two different ways of conceptualizing work: work as the pursuit of personal achievements and rewards—or "personal freedom"; and work as the pursuit of social and moral responsibilities—or "social freedom." Many IT programmers, such as Mr. Chen, are strong supporters of 996 work schedules and the ideology of the striving individual; but others, such as his wife—also in the IT sector, are critical of this model of work because it lacks work–life balance. Most IT programmers tend to be optimistic about 996 in the early stages of their careers because they need the money and because they dream about becoming project team leaders and "owning" their own projects. But this optimism starts to become less salient after a few years working as "coding peasants." Experienced IT programmers like Mr. Hua, who have decided to get out of the 996-burnout routine in Shenzhen, say that the relentless pursuit of personal achievements and rewards is too unbalanced and is getting in the way of the fulfillment of key moral responsibilities towards normative collectives such as the family.

Most experienced taxi drivers would sympathize with Mr. Hua. They approach work less as a form of pursuing personal achievements and rewards, and more as a form of fulfilling social and moral responsibilities. These taxi drivers are skeptical of 996 ideologies. Having a fixed working schedule provides a stable organizational structure to the lives of taxi drivers, and this stability allows them to expand the scope of their community-building activities, including the fulfillment of moral responsibilities towards family members and other colleagues. But there are also taxi drivers—especially younger ones—who approach work as an opportunity to achieve financial freedom and get some degree of social recognition. These drivers want to make money not just because they want to find ways to detach themselves from others and pursue personal freedom but also because they want to achieve basic social and moral responsibilities of "establishing a family and launching a career." IT programmers like Ms. Li would endorse this view of work as social and moral responsibility, but her husband, Mr. Chen, does not agree with her criticism of China's overtime work culture. He thinks that the future of China's IT sector lies not in European models of reduced working hours and work–life balance but in the ethos of workism and individual success in places such as Silicon Valley.

We thus return to our idealized distinction between personal freedom and social freedom. In this chapter, we have been interested in freedom not as an indicator of ethical agency and choice but as an important value and aspiration in the struggles of workers and the politics of labor around the world. Inspired by Karl Polanyi, we explored visions of work–life balance in two very different urban occupational communities in China through the lens of a tension between alternative notions of freedom in connection to work: freedom as personal freedom and freedom as social responsibility. Conceptualizing this tension as a dialectical relationship is useful in making sense of workers' experiences of 996 work schedules. The pursuit of freedom through work is not just about earning the capacity to detach oneself from others; it is also about earning the capacity to live a life connected to others "through duty and responsibility." This dialectical conceptualization of freedom is crucial to the future of work in China and in the whole world. Karl Polanyi was convinced that the machines of industrial capitalism would promote the bourgeois ideology of personal freedom, and that this would then inhibit social freedom. This chapter has refined Polanyi's conceptualization of human freedom to show how the global neoliberal economy is producing new tensions between more individualistic and more social aspirations of freedom.

Acknowledgments

We would like to thank Jiazhi Fengjiang, Stephen Gudeman, Chris Hann, Patrice Ladwig, Wolfgang Streeck, Peter van der Veer, and the anonymous reviewers for their comments and suggestions. This work was partly supported by grants from the Research Grants Council of the Hong Kong Special Administrative Region, China (Project No. 17636016 and Project No. 17612719).

Gonçalo Santos is an assistant professor of Social-Cultural Anthropology in the Department of Life Sciences, University of Coimbra, and is a full member of the Research Centre for Anthropology and Health (CIAS), University of Coimbra. He has previously held positions at the London School of Economics, the Max Planck Institute for Social Anthropology, and the University of Hong Kong. He is the author of *Chinese Village Life*

Today (2021) and the co-editor of *Transforming Patriarchy* (2017). He is the director of the Sci-Tech Asia Research Network.

Yichen Rao is a PhD candidate in Anthropology / Science and Technology Studies at the University of Hong Kong. He was an Ernst Mach global fellow at the University of Vienna. He is a member of the Sci-Tech Asia Research Network.

Jack L. Xing is a PhD candidate in Science and Technology Studies at the Georgia Institute of Technology. He is a member of the Sci-Tech Asia Research Network.

Jun Zhang is an assistant professor of Anthropology at the Department of Asian and International Studies at the City University of Hong Kong. She is the author of *Driving Toward Modernity. Cars and the Lives of the Middle Class in Contemporary China* (2019). She is a member of the Sci-Tech Asia Research Network.

Notes

1. Independent observations made by two of us—Jun Zhang and Gonçalo Santos—in the city of Guangzhou from the 1990s onwards confirm the consolidation of this pattern of long working hours and normalized overtime work amongst white-collar professionals. The tech sector has become the major symbol of this working regime in the twenty-first century. Employees of tech giant Huawei are rumored to keep foldable beds underneath their desks to facilitate overtime.
2. All Chinese words cited in this chapter are in Standard Chinese and are transcribed using the official pinyin system.
3. Some of these developments intensified in 2020 during the Covid-19 pandemic.
4. A frontline programmer is an entry-level position in the IT industry. Frontline programmers are poorly paid and have long working hours without having any claims over the results of their work output.
5. One of Rao's informants told him in June 2020 that when ByteDance tried to implement a five-day work schedule to fit international standards, this initiative met with significant resistance from frontline developers, saying that they depended on overtime work to pay their monthly mortgage payments.
6. Chinese cities are officially classified in different hierarchical layers reflecting differences in population size, consumer behavior, income level, consumer sophistication, infrastructure, talent pool, and business opportunity. The four undisputable "first-tier cities" in China are Beijing, Shanghai, Shenzhen and Guangzhou. Xi'an is in the group of cities immediately below. This group of "second-tier cities" is now differentiated in two subgroups: "new first-tier cities" and "second-tier cities."

7. Some SOE laid-off drivers have houses inherited from their parents who were former SOE staff.
8. Some scholars have argued that taxi drivers in major cities are guaranteed various kinds of job-related forms of social security (Chen 2018), but this claim should not be overstated. In Xi'an, neither cab owners nor employed drivers have mandatory pensions, unemployment insurance, or medical insurance regulated by the Social Insurance Law. Taxi drivers have access to a number of affordable nationwide social welfare schemes, such as the New Rural Social Pension Scheme and the Unified Urban and Rural Basic Social Pension Scheme, but these schemes are voluntary and offer limited protection.
9. According to a quantitative survey undertaken by Xing in Xi'an in 2019, only a relatively small percentage of employed drivers (about 5 to 10 percent) have managed to make the leap from employed driver to cab boss in the last fifteen years.
10. These findings echo Rosenblat's analysis of Uber drivers (Rosenblat 2018).

References

Brie, Michael, and Claus Thomasberger, eds. 2018. *Karl Polanyi's Vision of a Socialist Transformation*. Montreal: Black Rose Books.

Cangiani, Michele. 2017. "'Social Freedom' in the Twenty-First Century: Rereading Polanyi." *Journal of Economic Issues* 51(4): 915–38.

Chen, Julie Yujie. 2018. "Thrown under the Bus and Outrunning It! The Logic of Didi and Taxi Drivers' Labor and Activism in the On-demand Economy." *New Media & Society* 20(8): 2691–2711.

China News. 2013. "每年60万" 过劳死" 不靠谱？ 专家称人数难以统" [Mei nian 60 wan 'guo lao si' bu kao pu? zhuan jia cheng ren shu nanyi tong / 600,000 "overwork deaths" a year? Experts say the number is difficult to calculate], October 2013. http://www.chinanews.com/gn/2013/10-14/5373713.shtml (last accessed May 2020).

Fung, Edward. 2006. "The Idea of Freedom in Modern China Revisited: Plural Conceptions and Dual Responsibilities." *Modern China* 32(4): 453–82.

Gagne, Nana Okura. 2018. "'Correcting Capitalism': Changing Metrics and Meanings of Work among Japanese Employees." *Journal of Contemporary Asia* 48(1): 67–87.

Goodman, David. 2014. *Class in Contemporary China*. Hoboken: John Wiley & Sons.

Graeber, David. 2011. *Debt: The First 5000 Years*. Brooklyn, NY: Melville House.

Hann, Chris, and Keith Hart, eds. 2009. *Market and Society: The Great Transformation Today*. Cambridge: Cambridge University Press.

Hann, Chris, and Jonathan P. Parry, eds. 2018. *Industrial Labor on the Margins of Capitalism: Precarity, Class, and the Neoliberal Subject*. New York: Berghahn Books.

Harrell, Stevan. 1985. "Why Do the Chinese Work So Hard? Reflections on an Entrepreneurial Ethic." *Modern China* 11(2): 203–26.

Keane, Webb. 2016. *Ethical Life: Its Natural and Social Histories*. Princeton, NJ: Princeton University Press.

Laidlaw, James. 2002. "For an Anthropology of Ethics and Freedom." *Journal of the Royal Anthropological Institute* 8(2): 311–32.

———. 2013. *The Subject of Virtue*. Cambridge: Cambridge University Press.

Lyons, Dan. 2017. "In Silicon Valley, Working from 9 to 5 Is for Losers," *The New York Times*, 1 September. https://www.nytimes.com/2017/08/31/opinion/sunday/silicon-valley-work-life-balance-.html (last accessed November 2019).

Ma, Jack. 2019. "马云谈996：能够996是修来的福报，很多人想做没机会." [Ma Yun tan 996: néng gòu 996 shi xiu lái de fu bao, hen duo ren xiang zuo mei ji hui / Jack Ma debates 996: Being able to 996 is a blessing, many people want to do it but do not have the chance], April 2019. https://www.thepaper.cn/newsDetail_forward_3291793 (last accessed November 2019).

Mahmood, Saba. 2005. *The Politics of Piety: The Islamic Revival and the Feminist Subject*. Princeton, NJ: Princeton University Press.

Mihala, Lorelei. 2018. "Could You Be a Workaholic, Addicted to Your Job?" *BBC News*, 4 April 2018. https://www.bbc.com/news/business-43485981 (last accessed 5 May 2020).

Monet, Charmika. 2014. "Working to Death in China: A Look at the Nation with the Highest Instance of Death from Overwork in the World." http://thediplomat.com/2014/03/working-to-death-in-china/ (last accessed 6 May 2020).

Nie, Peng, Steffen Otterbach, and Alfonso Sousa-Poza. 2015. "Long Work Hours and Health in China." *IZA Discussion Paper* No. 8911, Bonn.

Notar, Beth E. 2012. "'Coming Out' to 'Hit the Road': Temporal, Spatial and Affective Mobilities of Taxi Drivers and Day Trippers in Kunming, China." *City & Society* 24(3): 281–301.

Ortner, Sherry B. 2016. "Dark Anthropology and its Others: Theory since the Eighties." *HAU: Journal of Ethnographic Theory* 6(1): 47–73.

Peng, Xinyan. 2020. "The 6pm Struggle: The Changing Meaning of Work, a Culture of Overtime Work, and Corporate Governmentality in Urban China." *Asian Anthropology* 19(1): 39–52.

Polanyi, Karl. (1944) 2001. *The Great Transformation: The Political and Economic Origins of Our Time*. Boston, MA: Beacon Press.

———. (1927) 2018. "On Freedom." In *Economy and Society: Selected Writings*, ed. Claus Thomasberger and Michele Cangiani. Cambridge: Polity Press.

Pun, Ngai. 2005. *Made in China: Women Factory Workers in a Global Workplace*. Durham, NC: Duke University Press.

———. 2016. *Migrant Labor in China: Post-Socialist Transformations*. Malden, MA: Polity Press.

Robbins, Joel. 2007. "Between Reproduction and Freedom: Morality, Value, and Radical Cultural Change." *Ethnos* 72(3): 293–314.

———. 2012. "On Becoming Ethical Subjects: Freedom, Constraint, and the Anthropology of Morality." *Anthropology of This Century* 5.

Rosenblat, Alex. 2018. *Uberland: How Algorithms are Rewriting the Rules of Work*. Berkeley: University of California Press.

Rosenblat, Alex, and Luke Stark. 2016. "Algorithmic Labor and Information Asymmetries: A Case Study of Uber's Drivers." *International Journal of Communication* 10: 3758–84.

Santos, Gonçalo, and Stevan Harrell, eds. 2017. *Transforming Patriarchy: Chinese Families in the Twenty-First Century*. Seattle: University of Washington Press.

Scholz, Trebor. 2017. *Uberworked and Underpaid: How Workers Are Disrupting the Digital Economy*. Cambridge: Polity Press.

Sennet, Richard. 1998. *The Corrosion of Character: The Personal Consequences of Work in the New Capitalism*. New York: W.W. Norton.

Spiegelaere, Stan de, and Agnieska Piasna. 2017. *The Why and How of Working Time Reduction*. European Trade Union Institute, https://www.etui.org/sites/default/files/2020-07/The%20why%20and%20how%20of%20working%20time%20reduction-2017-WEB-2.pdf (last accessed 20 March 2021).

Streeck, Wolfgang. 2014. *Buying Time: The Delayed Crisis of Democratic Capitalism*. London: Verso.Thompson, Derek. 2019. "Workism is Making Americans Miserable." *The Atlantic*, 24 February. https://www.theatlantic.com/ideas/archive/2019/02/religion-workism-making-americans-miserable/583441/ (last accessed 20 March 2021).

Wajcman, Judy. 2015. *Pressed for Time: The Acceleration of Life in Digital Capitalism*. Chicago: University of Chicago Press.

Xi'an Statistics Bureau. 2019. "Xi'an Shi 2018 nian guomin jingji he shehui fazhan tongji gongbao" [The statistics report of domestic economic and social development of Xi'an city, 2018], http://www.tjcn.org/tjgb/27sx/35830.html (last accessed 20 March 2021).

Xing, Jack. 2019. "Technological Choices of Chinese Taxi Drivers under E-hailing: Conventional Occupation Groups under the Impact of Digital Automation and Post-Fordism." MPhil thesis, University of Hong Kong.

Zhang, Jun. 2016. "Taxis, Traffic, and Thoroughfares: The Politics of Transportation Infrastructure in China's Rapid Urbanization in the Reform Era." *City & Society* 28(3): 411–36.

———. 2017. "(Extended) Family Car, Filial Consumer-Citizens: Becoming Properly Middle Class in Post-Socialist South China." *Modern China* 43(1): 36–65.

Zhong, Yishan. 2019. "Mothering with Mobile Communication Technologies in Urban China." MPhil dissertation, University of Hong Kong.

7

From Freedom to Loaf to Freedom to Work

The Late Socialist Countermovement and Liberalization from Below in Yugoslavia

Ivan Rajković

This chapter traces the changing relations between labor, freedom, and "the social" from the origins of Yugoslav socialism to its collapse in the 1980s. For most parts of the Eurasian and Euro-Atlantic world, employment in the twentieth century included some form of social protection. Neither Fordism nor central planning were as obsessed with productivity as the proponents of basic income schemes would nowadays have us believe. From the first victories of English trade unions, through the October Revolution, the New Deal, and the Keynesian welfare states consolidated after World War II, increasingly comprehensive mechanisms were put in place by states to make wage labor more than a purely contractual relationship between employer and employee. Collective agreements, social and health-care insurance, pensions and annual leave, not to mention the eight-hour working day and expanded concepts of leisure—all these developments undermined the "hegemony of work." Workers accepted drudgery and alienation in exchange for inclusion in the social body and the new opportunities that wage labor opened up. Twentieth-century employment thus functioned as both subordination and relative emancipation from previous forms of exploitation and vulnerability. Labor was more than a factor of economic production. It became the focus of juridical obligations regulating distribution and lifeworlds: what Robert Castel has called "wage for security" (Castel 1996: 618).

In the 1970s, however, the work–welfare nexus in the West came under attack. It was alleged by conservative and liberal critics that the "nanny state" was depressing productivity and inhibiting innovation. At the same time, for a variety of voices in the East, socialist regulation was detaching income from skill and achievement. In Yugoslavia, with its distinctive institutions of self-management, labor autonomy came to be seen as precluding meritocratic recruitment and promoting undemocratic redistribution by a dominant class of cadres (Djilas 1966; Pešić 1988). Flexible contracts, private businesses, and individualized careers were attractive to all those who felt disadvantaged by state paternalism. What earlier generations had perceived as a threat—pure forms of wage labor—now seemed empowering in comparison to the unfairness of protection. This was a move back from status to contract.

An Uber driver in Manchester brought this point home to me a few years ago. He had previously worked for a taxi company that offered a better hourly rate of pay, with social insurance included in the package. But there were not enough customers for all the drivers, and the telephone operators allocated rides to kin and friends. Lacking such networks, this driver could not support his family and so switched to Uber instead. The rate was lower, insurance and vehicle maintenance were his responsibility, and he needed to work longer hours (at least seventy per week), but at least he could support his family without being enmeshed in personal networks. To this driver, collective labor protection was a cynical invitation to unfairness in a situation where labor was de facto individualized.

To understand the allure of neoliberalism it is helpful to go back to Karl Polanyi's (1944) notion of the "double movement": pursuit of self-regulatory markets brings reactions in the form of social re-embedding. In the wake of the Industrial Revolution, the spread of the free market (movement) induced efforts to reinstitutionalize the economy in social relations (countermovement). Through trade unions and interventionist states, whether social democratic, socialist, or fascist, society sought to protecting itself from the forces that threatened to rip it apart. The form of the countermovement depends on the historical context and the precise nature of the dominant movement. When the hegemonic force appears as an undemocratic and unfair variant of embeddedness, I argue, it is only natural to imagine freedom as an escape from the clutches of this protection. It is as true today as it was in the era of the Speenhamland provisions analyzed by Polanyi: one cannot live from protection alone if wage work is still present. When uneven embeddedness and the commodification of work combine, a yearning inevitably arises: release the commodification.

Karl Polanyi (1944) and Michel Foucault (1997, 2008) both penetrated the myth of laissez-faire deregulation: (neo)liberal capitalism could only emerge as a planned state project (loathed by the one, and cheered by the other). For both, freedom meant not just freedom "from," but freedom "to" accomplish something—a form of responsibility. Both grasped the necessary entwinement of responsibility towards others and responsibility towards oneself—an ethical quandary that each resolved as best he could, given the historical ambiguities of the times in which he lived.

Karl Polanyi discerned "personal freedom" as the ability to detach oneself from others, while "social freedom" was the ability to fulfill duties to others (Polanyi 2018; cf. Santos et al., this volume). Locating the first in Kant's categorical imperative and the bourgeois dream of becoming "a master in one's house," he equated the second with democratic socialism. This social freedom, he argued, does not contradict but in fact boosts personal freedom. Only someone who "has paid for everything that he has enjoyed at the cost of others"—social debts, Polanyi thought, are being incurred through hidden labors in the bourgeois world—can say "I am responsible to no one in this world" (Polanyi 2018: 22). By repaying their dues to the world, socially responsible individuals become truly free from that world. Furthermore, Polanyi understood "proletarian ethics" as the "continuation of ethics beyond its bourgeois possibilities." If the bourgeois citizen invoked personal responsibility to reject the collective mores of God and King, he soon came up against "the market" as the new domain of necessity. The modern "social" emerged in an individualist liberal cage: "the ethical preconditions of a new social order develop in the womb of the old society" (ibid.: 20).

We find a comparable attentiveness to the evolving character of liberation in the work of Foucault. On the one hand, he saw ethics not as a realm of norms but as a "practice of freedom"—the ability to shape oneself into a particular virtuous project (Foucault 1997; Laidlaw 2014). His privileging of "care for oneself" rather than "care for others" has led many to perceive him as an apologist for neoliberalism. But such a classification conceals the fact that Foucault saw liberalism not as a single ideology, but as a "tool for criticism of reality: criticism of a previous governmentality from which one is trying to get free; of a present governmentality that one is trying to reform and rationalize by scaling it down; or of a governmentality to which one is opposed and whose abuses one wants to limit" (Foucault 2008: 320). Liberalism is both a regulatory face of the state and the utopia of its most radical opponents. The constant scrutiny of governmentality means that wholesale rejections of social orders are rare: rather, policies are selectively redeployed and reconfigured, bridging the old and the new. (Neo) liberalism does not cancel out the social, argues Foucault, but calls for its reconfiguration (Collier 2011). He reminds us that the Physiocrats called for laissez-faire in order to save sovereign rule, not to overturn it. In the same way, East European social movements called for economic liberalization to fulfill the promises of socialism, not to erase them (Bockman 2011). Liberalism is thus a two-headed beast: a reprogramming of reality in terms interior to it.

What Polanyi's concept of "double movement" and Foucault's "neoliberal reason" have in common, therefore, is their framing of liberation as a historically situated practice. Its contents are not positively fixed but emerge dialectically in a given context, with all its oppressions and opportunities: "in the womb of the old society." To consider emancipation as both a transcending and a constraining practice, reflecting the manner in which "the ethical requirements of an outlived social order also point beyond its own limits" (Polanyi 2018: 20), is a fruitful direction for historical anthropologists. Rather than study freedom in abstract, timeless ideations—what Sopranzetti (2017) calls "Freedom with the big F"—we can study how freedom emerges as "a relational and contextual practice that takes shape in opposition to whatever is locally and ideologically conceived as un-freedom" (Brown 1995: 5). The counterhegemony responds to real problems and contradictions, drawing together processes from above and processes from below (Hall 1988: 43; Gramsci 1997). From such a perspective, popular calls for liberation that went under drastically different ideological banners—anti-imperial socialist uprisings, the rise of Margaret Thatcher, Eastern Europe's market revolutions of 1989—can be compared as varieties of countermovement that all combine the ideas and plans of elites with mass experiences on the ground. All countermovements are reactive to the old order and proactive towards the new. All reconfigure the normative relation between personal and social freedom into a new common sense. In this chapter, I study liberation both "from" and "for" work as a dialectically evolving and moving target.

From Freedom to Loaf to Freedom to Work

Across most of Eurasia, the institutionalization of employment in the twentieth century came about not through market capitalism but through the socialist modernization of hitherto "backward" areas through the vanguard role of the state. The Socialist Federal Republic of Yugoslavia (SFRY) was both an example and a highly exceptional case. Its Communist Party was, from its foundation in 1919, a member of the Communist International, and highly dependent on the USSR. Following a clash with Stalin and expulsion from the Cominform, from 1948 the Yugoslav leadership launched a critique of Soviet socialism as a bureaucratic perversion. Instead, denationalization and self-management were declared to be true socialist tools to promote the "withering away of the state." Rather than central planning, governance was devolved to a plethora of decentralized bodies, including workers' councils that exercised considerable power at the level of the enterprise. Western powers were complicit with financial support

(Woodward 1995). Yugoslav "market socialism" and President Josip Broz Tito's role in the Non-Aligned Movement were unique products of the balancing act between Cold War superpowers.

The result was an ethical minefield in the field of economy. Workers' councils had to negotiate a path between waves of state pressure and market forces, often from abroad (Comisso 1979). The socialist promise of liberation from the market was subverted by the rent-seeking behavior of the new class, and by de facto market pressures—the latter becoming very visible in the IMF debt crisis of the 1980s. As a result, the Yugoslav economy was unable to reconcile the tensions of production and distribution.

Central to this failure was the institution of employment, which functioned in a particular way. The *radno mesto* (workplace) was not conceived as a place of exchange but a means of positioning citizens into systems of distribution and affiliation in a holistic process. The socialist social calculus meant that political, national, and social questions were of higher order than profit accumulation—even if profit *was* critically present. Redistribution mechanisms (accommodation, health care, child care, holidays, transportation hobby groups) were built into the workplace and financed by the factory, not provided as welfare mechanisms outside of it. Work was the point where political identities, economic interests, and social rights intersected: "one's place of work was the center of one's social universe" (Woodward 2003: 76). In Polanyian terms, this was an attempt to shift the "dialectics of market and redistribution" (Hann 2015, 2019) to a decentralized level that had no precedent elsewhere, in West or East.

In contrast to this institutionalized embedding of employment, however, late Yugoslav socialism began to commodify labor. By commodification I mean the capture of human creativity into an object that can be measured and transacted to promote the extraction of surplus value, both in capitalist economies and in "really existing socialisms." In addition to enabling class exploitation and profit extraction, commodification nourishes a quasi-objective form of social domination, one that elevates work into a hyper-moralized organizer of worth and social life. Karl Marx did not so much critique capital from the standpoint of labor as critique labor as such (Postone 1995).

Capitalist relations are insidious because they instill a particular form of work. As Martha Lampland put it: "In capitalism, labor is the touchstone of social life: it is a material property of human actors, bearing physical, nearly tangible qualities. It is also the touchstone, the foundation, of subjectivity and morality. Labor does not occupy such a position outside capitalism" (Lampland 1996: 11). As in socialist Hungary, the object of Lampland's study, commodification on Yugoslav shop floors, emerged gradually as a way to make sense of and critique the official remuneration mechanisms.

Because employment was governed by a mix of contributivist logic (to each according to their labor) and the logic of redistribution (to each according to their needs), the productivist impulse intensified in the 1980s as both an outcome of the increasing integration in global capital and an internal reaction to widening social inequalities (see also Konrad and Szelenyi 1979). For both managers and shop floor workers, labor aristocracies and *Gastarbeiter* migrants, work became the hegemonic framework for voicing the resentments. The Yugoslav countermovement thus resembled workers actions in Poland and elsewhere in late socialist Central and Eastern Europe, where pro-privatization sentiments developed as a way of reclaiming the factory from what seemed as state nomenklatura's capture of industry (Kalb 2009: 211).

At the same time, productivism had particular moral qualities in late Yugoslavia. It happened at a time when everything looked like a loss of virtue, a poor imitation of the shock-work zeal of the pioneers of socialism (Dimitrijević 2017). While their grandfathers had made sacrifices for the common good, new workers appeared as individuals motivated only by their paychecks. The debt crisis of the 1980s was thus quickly attributed to socialist "non-work." In contrast to both the sacrifices of the partisans and the work discipline of the West, late Yugoslav employment was perceived as an imitation of real productivity, what I have termed elsewhere "mock-labor" (Rajković 2018). The crisis of socialist underproductivity thus masked a progressive decoupling of matters of productivity and reciprocity. The failed syndicalist-socialist attempt to abolish the liberal binary between economy and social life became the catalyst of a movement against the social. Whereas postwar work could be plausibly represented in terms of collective freedom from poverty and a declaration of sovereignty, late socialist employment called for individual freedom from bureaucratic ties and their uneven protections. What appeared as a righteous critique of state nomenklatura from the point of labor—exploitation of the working class—simultaneously heralded new forms of work.[1]

The Socialist "Liberation of Work"

Before World War II, wage labor in the Kingdom of Yugoslavia was confined to a few industrial centers. Only a quarter of the population lived in towns. With the exception of a few militant trade unions—Serbian armament workers, Montenegrin printers, Macedonian tobacco laborers—the stronghold of the Communist Party was outside industry, primarily in the ranks of the administrative salariat (Woodward 1995: 42). Production geared to foreign capital created pockets of urban unemployment and homelessness, while some peasants commuted daily to factory jobs, without abandoning agriculture as the main source of income. These worker-peasants were pejoratively referred to as "halfies" (*polutani*) (Kostić 1955).

It was the war, not endogenous processes related to work, that instigated a mass mobilization. A guerrilla movement guided by the Communist Party gained legitimacy across social strata, combining antifascist struggle, class war and interethnic solidarity. After the liberation, partisan mobilization spilled into reconstruction efforts, which were marked by Soviet policies of shock-work (Matošević 2015; Senjković 2016).

For Marshall Tito and the party leaders, such work actions (*radne akcije*) epitomized the liberation of labor (*oslobođenje rada*). In comparison to the capitalist past and the Axis occupation, they claimed, new types of work were neither forced nor wage labor, but a free giving of the entire self for the betterment of the country. This was more than an ideological interpellation, however. Shock-workers responded to the party's "gift of freedom" by returning the only thing they had: their own work power (*radna snaga*) (Matošević 2015). Work actions were thus practiced as a direct continuation of the partisan struggle, a determination of the "people" to free themselves from historical oppression and create a better future (Supek 1963). "There can be a heroism in labor equal to that in war," the young E. P. Thompson, himself a volunteer in building the Šamac–Sarajevo railway, noticed in 1947. "It springs from the pride in ownership by the ordinary man of his own country, its sources of wealth and its means of production" (Thompson 1948: 2). Liberated work was meant to embody a liberation of territory, peoples, and individuals by connecting processes from "above" and "below."

Shortly after this, the leadership launched large-scale urban industrialization based on social ownership. This meant more than job security: the aim was "to reorganize economic activity and social relations fundamentally in order to make unemployment economically unnecessary and to deprive it of its political role" (Woodward 1995: 5). Socialist employment was imagined as a radical break, transcending both the need to sell one's *radna snaga* (the word for "wages/salary" was replaced by "income") and dependence on the redistribution policies of the state. Workers were to associate their work with others and to share profits.

For the values of worker self-management to work, they needed to be translated into local idioms of need. In state media, comfort, hospitality, and grace were inscribed into new jobs. Consider for example the following excerpt from an Istrian coalmine newspaper, published in 1949:

> The very first day Đuro got a comfortable flat and food, and he could not believe that living was so nicely ordered here. White sheets on a bed, a matress and warm blan-

> kets. A desk in the room, wardrobes and chairs—all of it gave the impression that he would live nicely and comfortably there. Food in the canteen, with red wine and even cookies every day; in short, a better life than at home . . . Cinema, various events, a Culture House where he can always play chess with . . . He finds time for everything after eight hours of work.[2]

Đuro's comfortable habituation to the mine ("better than at home") reminds us that socialism was a substantive economy that aimed to meet all the human needs of workers, a variety of biopolitics (Collier 2011). In postwar Yugoslavia, the social question was initially a "peasant question," namely how to include large numbers of the "underproductive" while avoiding the financial consequence of overemployment. Industrialization was to absorb large swaths of rural labor surplus, while simultaneously respecting the imperative of economic growth. Peasants were initially reluctant to move to towns, and the first migrants were the landless. But in less than a decade urbanization was valued for its own sake, trumping earlier narratives of economic necessity. The peasant urbanites whom Bette Denich studied in the 1960s perceived city jobs as offering more stable rewards for their work. Comparing the regular flow of wages, pensions, access to health care and social housing to the vagaries of labor-intensive agriculture, vulnerable to hail and drought, urban newcomers saw industrial jobs as providing comfortable livelihoods while requiring less drudgery than jobs in the village. "You work less and live better in the city," claimed her interlocutors, one of whom declared that she would rather hang herself than return to her village (Denich 1973: 554). Industrial employment appealed because it offered freedom from the exhausting precarity of subsistence-oriented agriculture. Wage work may have instilled a new clock-time discipline, but it also gave opportunities for mobility through education, higher living standards, and a chance to experience the thrills of urban life. By the 1970s, the state ideology of urbanization was entrenched. It included an entitlement to employment, which, when unfulfilled, became a source of discontent.

This double bind of industrial employment—as both factory discipline and freedom from other forms of drudgery, both productivity and social protection, work and non-work—requires a revaluation of Yugoslav socialism. As a number of authors have pointed out (Duda 2005, 2010; Mihelj 2011; Patterson 2011), consumerism, tourism, and leisure were not mere side effects but key expectations fostered by the Yugoslav state. Having based its legitimacy upon them, it foundered when it was not able to meet them. For many years, Yugoslavia's non-aligned position, its "Third Way" policies and openness to Western markets, created more spaces for citizens to flourish than any other form of socialism. Realizing the maxim that liberated labor required liberated leisure, the Yugoslav dream was lived—albeit unevenly—as "a reliable provision of experiential wealth" (Patterson 2010: 367). Notwithstanding these visions of leisure, vernacular visions of welfare remained rooted in the workplace. The worlds of leisure and work were not antithetical—the place of work continued to function as the key social node, "a second home" (Bonfiglioli 2019).

The holistic repositioning of the workplace between the logics of production and redistribution can be theorized with the concept of "emplacing." A translation of Serbo-Croat *sm(j)eštanje*, with connotations of both locating and hosting, emplacing refers both to the objective social place one occupies through employment and the comparative experiential (dis) comfort of being in that place. This requires seeing the workplace not simply as an empty space in which labor is exchanged, but, in line with the emic perspective, as a "station" in an overall landscape of provision, with its own properties geared to need fulfillment. It was of decisive importance whether one was employed in a large, multiunit factory system or in a small workshop; in a city like Belgrade or Zagreb or in more "passive," underdeveloped regions such as Sandžak or Kosovo. Work was differentially rewarded according to position, and even within the same position income varied significantly according to educational qualifications. Enterprises differed in the benefits and perks they could offer, and also in terms of prospects for social mobility. Some allowed greater windows of opportunity for rule-bending: the materials that one could appropriate informally; the professional skills such as those of a car mechanic or an accountant that one could exploit outside the factory; the lax treatment of absenteeism that would allow one to take seasonal work in the fields. All these made up what the inhabitants of Kragujevac call *vajda* and *vajdica* (literally "little gain"): the forms of need fulfillment that one could realize through a job, beyond the paycheck.

While informal perks are very widespread in industrial employment, the Yugoslav workplace and its resulting inequalities were unique. The dominant understanding of social status and (dis)grace was not articulated in terms of one's line of work, education, or class. Rather, the ability to enjoy a "good life" was connected to one's niche in the wider architecture of opportunity and care of work emplacement. The ubiquitous question Yugoslavs asked when meeting a stranger—*Gde radite?* (Where do you work?)—was meant to elicit the interlocutor's place and comfort in the Yugoslav work-welfare system. There was a lot of tacit knowledge concerning what it was like to be a member of a certain work collective, the opportunities and social security it offered, and also its drawbacks. Work emplacement made the enterprise an encompassing haven, a source of life as well as of stress, "a mother and a stepmother," as many spoke of their enterprises. To understand this better, let me now make the analysis concrete with reference to Crvena Zastava Automobili, a car-producing plant that was part of the wider Crvena Zastava industrial complex in the central Serbian town of Kragujevac.

Zastava's Social

Founded in 1953 to mark the centenary of an important armaments plant in the town, Zastava quickly became one of the biggest employers in the country, producing cars for the home market and for export. In was enmeshed in finance from the start; the credit it received from FIAT and the Italian government in 1959, amounting to 55 million dollars, was the first foreign investment in postwar Yugoslavia. Two key trends crystallized in this enterprise: budding liberalization and reliance on debt.

Although Kragujevac never became a monotown, the sheer size of the Zastava complex—employing over fifty thousand people in its heyday—gave it overwhelming gravitas. Many other local institutions and factories dating back to the nineteenth century adapted to its needs. Kragujevac resembled Soviet "enterprise-centric towns" that linked industrial development, population growth, and social welfare in a substantive planning bundle (Kotkin 1992; Collier 2011).

The company built a heating system for its own production process, which expanded to heat much of the town. It constructed new housing estates, operated its own transport system, an independent health-care center, and two kindergartens. It ran two vocational high schools, employed teachers to staff it, and awarded Zastava grants to pupils. It collaborated with the Faculty of Engineering and Faculty of Economics of the city's university, where more than 70 percent of students were from working-class families, offering them factory scholarships and guaranteeing jobs after graduation. Zastava's activities extended to recreation, hobbies, and art, in line with Yugoslav conceptions of new socialist (wo)man transcending distinctions between manual and intellectual labor. It supported clubs in poetry, painting, sculpture, folk dancing, and drama; hotels for its employees in Dalmatia and Macedonia; half a dozen sport associations, both amateur and professional; a factory media team and a scientific library.

At first, the number of vehicles produced expanded in line with the number of employees and the urban population. However, tensions between "the economic" and "the social" gradually increased. Branislav Čukić, an organizational psychologist and head of the company's HR department, have repeatedly argued that the root cause was "unproductive employment" (Čukić 1985, 2013). As the biggest employer in the town, he noted, Zastava was pressured by the municipal committee of the League of

Communists to find jobs for certain groups, regardless of the enterprise's actual needs. Managers tended to enlarge their teams to increase their influence. While this was common throughout the socialist world (Kornai 1992; Verdery 1996), in Yugoslavia managers had to worry about saving face vis-à-vis the workers' council, and it was easier to hire additional employees than to sack those underperforming. Whereas such findings seemed to echo a widespread sentiment that self-management was economically irrational, as workers were able to distribute the entire surplus on their own incomes—a stance going back to Ward's (1958) "Illyrian" model—Čukić's implication was exactly the opposite. Self-management paradoxically gave a huge advantage to bureaucracy, especially after the constitution of 1974 which broke the factories into smaller and overstaffed units, creating an excess of white-collar workers and a shortage of production workers. By 1964, the latter numbered less than half of all employees in Zastava factories.

Income distribution was riddled with paradoxes. Use of the word for "income" (*dohodak*) rather than the one for "wages/salary" (*plata*) was meant to underline that employees were not selling their commodified labor, but rather "associating" their labor with that of others in their self-managed enterprise, from which they received a share of the total revenues. In practice, however, remuneration followed a complex points-based system that quantified the kind of work one did and one's success in doing it, together with revenue from sales. The parameters oscillated in relation to external variables, including shifting prices, changes in federal trade and credit policies, and problems with supply. The result was a highly obscure and volatile oscillation in monthly incomes. By 1973, an official anniversary publication stated that the motto of "distribution according to work" was not being achieved, as it was "hard to discern whether the revenues are the result of work or of changed business circumstances" (Milojković 1973: 98).

Zastava management tried to balance the situation in informal ways. Toleration of mass seasonal absenteeism, for example, made sense in a situation where, due to periodic shortages of car parts, shop-floor workers oscillated between being supernumerary (when production was low) and too few (in days of storming). In such context, as Čukić concluded in his internal HR research, the granting of sick leave en masse represented a tacit agreement between managers and workers, enabling the latter to finish agricultural work and the former to impose overtime in other periods, while alleviating the need for redundancies (Čukić 1985; Schult 2014, 2017). And yet, the conflicts between the economic and the social cumulatively corroded the ethos of collective reciprocity that had connected the workers and the factory in its infancy. Grievances were fully expressed in an antisocialist countermovement in the 1980s.

Non-Work: A Productivist Ethos and the Joys of Embeddedness

Informal solutions at Zastava remind us that all state socialisms underwent internal deterritorializations: accommodations that were neither ideologically prescribed nor performed as resistance, but which belonged to ordinary actors' practical strategies. Such deterritorializations simultaneously enabled socialist states to function, and changed them from within (Deleuze and Guattari 1988; Yurchak 2006). Socialist economies were exposed to the multiplicity and protean nature of human desires, which bent and decentered them to a variety of ends. This was particularly salient in employment. Taking a nap in a newly produced truck, celebrating a birthday by drinking on the shop floor, or having sex in the company's cellars – such practices were relatively common at Zastava. The workplace was a relaxed hosting station which (quite literally) allowed room for pleasure beyond the official aims of work. To the extent that such transgressions were routinized, being employed acquired the connotations of joyous embeddedness, often expressed with allusions to warmth, coziness, sweetness, and sex. Whereas the first anti-productivist expressions of joy, "non-work" (*nerad*) and idleness emerged in the dissident art of the 1960s (Kolanović 2011), by the 1980s they were normalized across a wide range of popular media and everyday discourse. Jokes such as "*Radio, ne radio, svira ti radio*" (Whether you work or not, your radio is playing), "*Al' je lep ovaj režim, lova kaplje a ja ležim*" (This regime is so sweet, money's pouring while I sleep), and "*Ne mogu oni mene toliko malo da plate, koliko ja mogu malo da radim*" (They can't pay me as little as I can work) came to mock the ideology of work, simultaneously voicing one's pleasure in the system and criticizing the uneven distribution of such joys.

Parallel to this celebration of (non-)working, the 1980s witnessed increasing critiques of idleness, and grassroots calls to return to the work ethic that the system had supposedly abandoned. This happened against the background of an evolving public debt crisis, which obliged the state to negotiate a refinancing loan of 3 billion dollars accompanied by a host of structural adjustment measures. Unemployment soared beyond 20 percent, and inflation beyond 50 percent. In this context, social stratification was increasingly understood in socialist productivist terms—that is, as a gap between the productive members of the society (the "working people") and those seen as rent-seeking groups parasitic upon them.

For example, while entire work collectives continued to contribute to housing funds from salary contributions, the waiting time for an apartment for low-skilled employees grew ever longer. It is no wonder they started to see this form of housing as "paid for by the workers, occupied by the bureaucrats" (Le Normand 2012; Archer 2016). Finding a job became dependent on white-collar social capital. With income distribution less and less transparent, social scientists declared the state celebration of productivist logic to be an ideological fetish, since "it matters more where one works—in which sector, group, line of work—than how much and how well" (Vušković 1976; Berković 1986a, 1986b; cf. Pešić 1988). The entire ideology of self-management and "distribution according to work" came to be seen as a facade to conceal rent-seeking behavior by managers and the contingencies of market shocks.

In this context, something extraordinary happened: popular demands to eliminate the anti-productive forces of "bureaucracy" and, in the same vein, to decouple income distribution altogether from the social question. While primarily targeting the superior access to resources and privileges of managerial elites, critique was tacitly extended to the entire system of emplacement. The difference between rent-seeking and social aid became blurred, as both required appropriation of the fruits of other people's work.

Svetlost, the town's weekly newspaper, followed the antagonisms of the 1980s closely. Under the title "Needy on multiple floors," it reported a conflict between the residents of Jovanovac, a village on the outskirts of Kragujevac, and migrants from Kosovo who had moved there in the 1970s. Both groups were ethnic Serbs. After they had sold their houses in the southern province and built new lavish ones in Jovanovac, the newcomers were alleged not to have reported their new property in order to enjoy employment priority and qualify for state benefits. This led eventually to fisticuffs between the two communities, as the original inhabitants resented that "in the summer, when the peasant has most of his work, you can see them [the newcomers] loafing in the shade."[3]

Under titles such as "Social aid from the armchairs" and "Rent as a springboard," journalists revealed that local directors were abusing housing lists and utility subsidies for the poor.[4] Such transgressions were pervasively mediatized as federal government attempted to curb the emergence of charismatic managers who flouted the norms for their personal advantage. During the strikes of the "anti-bureaucratic revolution" in 1988, the large *fotelja* (armchair) of the manager became a symbol of protest that was carried aloft by demonstrating workers.

How should we understand this sudden enthusiasm for productivity and the demonization of idleness and privileged comfort? Labor rationalization was promised when the Yugoslav state approached the IMF for credits to deal with its public debt. This strategy eventually created "an entire society organized around labor rationalization" (Woodward 2003: 78). Individual citizens had little choice but to compete for scarce jobs in the social sector, along with the protection they offered. In this atomized fight of all against all, "the rhetoric of 'exploitation' [was] transferred from its Marxist origins to economic relations between nations in the federal system, and began to be used by individuals to explain their declining fortunes" (Woodward 2003, 82; cf. Unkovski-Korica 2015). While much post-Yugoslav scholarship has sought to explain how such productivism fueled a conflict between "deserving" and "slacking" nations, here I build upon the work of social historians who describe how fragmentation worked within the working class itself.

The key register in which late Yugoslavs expressed their social grievances was "exploitation of work by non-work" (Archer and Musić 2020; see also Schult 2014; Musić 2015; Grdešić 2016, 2017). *Nerad*—a word that translates as non-work, idleness—was invoked frequently to juxtapose those who produced value and those who did not, and were hence parasitic. This often entailed a blue-collar vision of manual work as the basic source of value, and scorn towards managers as *režija*—a "direction" living off industrial labor. But for the managers, blue-collar workers were the bloated unproductive group in need of market discipline. Each group was certain that the other was idle. Far from being a single ideological stance, the new language of productivity became a "common material and meaningful framework"—a hegemonic modality for performing contestation (Roseberry 1994: 361).

Zastava accrued more debts when the sales of its Yugo America models declined in the 1980s. Credits taken up to import foreign technology and boost competitiveness abroad did not pay off. Nevertheless, the company came under pressure to continue to export to the US markets for a lower price than the production cost, because of the federal government's desperate search for hard currency (see Palairet 1993; Vuic 2010). Management reacted by trying to reform its business models and rationalize production. Labor surplus was now specified as a key problem, and mass redundancies were touted.

In this situation, the factory newspaper became a forum where various categories of employee could comment on the crisis, and represent their own contribution to the factory in comparison with that of others. Regular features included "Man and a shop line" (usually an interview with a highly dedicated shop-floor worker), "Rationalizations" or "Innovations" (articles outlining new techniques introduced to cut losses in production), and "Pensioners" (life histories of retired workers). While meant to boost identification with the factory, these rubrics provided space for blue-collar workers to make accusations of blame, in shifting alliances (cf. Schult 2014). Female blue-collar workers, for example, who in one context would criticize their male colleagues over income inequality, would join them to complain about the devaluation of shop-floor labor in general. Pensioners echoed the journal's editors in alleging that young workers were responsible for the waning of the work ethic, but their retrospectives also pointed to declining living standards and management's inability to reform the company. Innovators attacked bureaucrats for delays in patenting innovations, and the labor aristocracy disparaged both management and unskilled blue-collar labor alike. In complex cross-cutting alliances, all these groups evoked productivity as the common discursive framework.

A Town Red with Shame

That workers objectified their work in conditions of crisis should neither be seen as a spasmodic reflex of socialist morality, nor as unconditional support for market-oriented reforms. Workers wanted to save their companies and their jobs in an increasingly unstable economic climate. In this struggle, they mixed the old Yugoslav socialist promises of workerism with liberal narratives of market objectivity (cf. Archer and Musić 2020). However, by articulating a critique of the inequalities of the socialist system from the standpoint of labor, workers inadvertently endorsed the capitalist abstraction of labor and its separation from social concerns. Asking for the delivery of the unfulfilled goal of distribution according to labor as well as need, they helped to shape a system in which distribution was granted according to labor only.

The initial push came from reformists who used the term "buying social peace" (*kupovina socijalnog mira*) to disparage what they saw as populist abuses of employment. Postulating some supposedly natural, common sense logic according to which the social peace should not be bought but earned, these economists and politicians started to disentangle employment from the sphere of redistribution, in effect reducing it to an ideal type of wage labor—what Polanyi (1944) referred to as a "fictitious commodity." A new labor law and collective labor agreements replaced *dohodak*, referring to a share in the revenues of the enterprise, with *plata* (wage/salary), referring to renumeration for work done according to specified rates and education level (and nominally taking account of living costs). The impulse for commodification acquired its full moral force when the workers received something they appeared *not* to have earned.

On the evening of 31 December 1989, a group of four hundred Zastava workers, mostly blue collar, protested in front of the factory's headquarters. The trigger was the austerity measure of the Yugoslav Central Executive Committee, at the behest of the IMF, to freeze all wages from the following day, despite inflation. Having heard that the managers of some Slovenian and Croatian companies were protecting their employees by raising wages on the eve of the freeze, the protesters accused senior management of being unpatriotic, of not caring for "Serbian workers." They emphasized the managers' higher wages and comfortable emplacement: "Just what air conditioning, heating, lace curtains they [the managers] have, while we, production workers, don't even have winter awnings," one speaker exclaimed. One slogan proclaimed: "We want bread."[5] The demands included a thirteenth monthly paycheck and the ousting of key managers. The protestors, lubricated with alcohol, threw snowballs at the office windows, marched to the town center, and finally gained entry to the town hall. Although the demand for the additional paycheck was quickly conceded, the *Crvena Zastava* newspaper commented critically: "When it became clear that arguments don't work, but only obnoxiousness, violence and physical solutions, it was decided that another salary would be paid."[6] New Year's Eve concluded with the drunken crowd trashing a nearby tavern.

When the New Year holidays came to an end, the editor of this weekly devoted an entire issue to the event. Translating the requests for social justice into the demand for an additional monthly wage, he aggressively dismissed them as illegitimate, illegal, and forced upon the management. Under the title "Market—the main arbiter," Zoran Prokić announced that in future "there will be only that much money that we ourselves make, through the sales of our products and services."[7]

If this demonization was to be expected from an editor close to the enraged management, the critiques of the normally pro-labor journalists of the town's weekly *Svetlost* were just as intense. Margita Cvetković and Ankica Vesić claimed that a small minority of the workers had perpetrated a political protest to oust the management and continue a holiday shopping spree. In a context in which republic elites were sidelining federal policies by mobilizing workers through nationalist rhetoric, the journalists were worried about governance. They portrayed the protesters as rude, violent, blue-collar drunkards. Of course, similar middle-class critiques of working people developed in other countries of Central and Eastern Europe (Buchowski 2006; Kideckel 2008). But the moral crux of the *Svetlost* journalists' critique revolved around emotions of shame and demoralization that the extra paycheck supposedly induced among the very employees. To receive more money for no additional work meant that "Kragujevac was indeed red as never before—but red because of shame," argued Margita Cvetković.[8] The lumpen protesters who extorted an extra wage packet, she claimed, surely did not have as fathers and grandfathers those valiant shock-workers who founded Zastava with their dedicated work and salary contributions. The behavior of the protesters had rendered the entire town morally corrupt in the pursuit of unearned, undeserved benefits. At the Self-Managers' House a week after the protest, a meeting was held between representatives from other local industries, whose employees were asking for the same treatment that Zastava workers had received. The journalist Ankica Vesić commented:

> The snowball was thrown, even literally, by Zastava workers, but then an avalanche ensued: almost all employees in Kragujevac got another November wage. Most of them are aware that what is being given is unearned and that the law is being broken, but they grab it according to the logic: if they can do it, why can't we?[9]

This protest solidified a structure of feeling that was prevalent in late socialism, one revolving around the dissipation of virtue. As Cvetković and Vesić described them, the protesters had lost the revolutionary substance of Zastava pioneers who had selflessly contributed their work. Rather, the New Year's Eve protesters were opportunistic idlers, foraging to raise their paychecks. A photo commentary in the Zastava bulletin displayed a worker asleep on the shop floor over the caption: "Heroes are tired." The rhetoric of "buying social peace" thus gave rise to an understanding that concessions to workers were a matter of gifts or charity, when what was really needed was a wage that had been earned.

Freedom's Twists

It has become somewhat of a truism to understand late socialism as a shift from "production for production's sake" to "production for employment's sake" (Kotkin 1992: 17; Collier 2011: 114). Fixated on their gigantic infrastructures, planning structures, and work ethics, East European industries supposedly had trouble moving on. But while capturing aspects of the postindustrial afterlife of many plants, this interpretation obscures the change of optics that occurred in late socialism. The rise of productivism as a countermovement to parasitism in Yugoslavia was not a remnant of some rigid socialist ethos. Rather, while repeating the form of socialist values and their undelivered promises, shop-floor contestations created a new understanding of productivity. One was to clearly know the length of their shift and the hourly price of their work, in order to stop free riders from extracting the fruits of their labor. Contesting redistribution, workers supported the commodification of their work.

Between the first apotheosis of productivity in the 1940s and the calls for reform in the 1980s, the moral valences of work changed drastically. If shock-work was seen as a break from wage work, and if factory jobs were experienced as a mixture of production and emplacement, comfort and toil, in the 1980s calls for a radical separation of the problematic of labor and the problematic of social assistance grew louder. What was initially intended as a move to abolish the liberal binary between economy and social life—socialist work—became the starting point for a movement against the social. In short, this was a shift from "freedom to loaf" to "freedom to work."

I have focused on these two moments—liberation *from* and *for* work—to show how countermovements cannot be reduced to institutionalized calls from above. Rather, they align processes of different scales, connecting elite and popular idioms of liberation, and capitalizing on possibilities inherent in the old order. The socialist ideologues of the 1940s could never have succeeded if the peasants had not come to see a personal emancipation in their policies. The messages of liberal economists resonated with moonlighters, *Gastarbeiter* and the downtrodden of the socialist working class in a similar way in the 1980s. Both were formative moments, aligning different class interests and life projects in a new common sense. Like today's Mancunian Uber drivers, Thailand's motorcyclists (Sopranzetti 2017), and Brazil's waste pickers (Millar 2014), neoliberal work deregulation was partially backed from below because it articulated the resentments of precarious subjects, already exposed to commodification of their work.

Of course, pro-market sentiments were not evenly spread. As in the Poland of *Solidarność*, they developed with the backdrop of internal frictions between workers, separating "those who stood to gain from capitalism and were . . . hoping to finally get a fair price for their labor, and those who were seen as going to fail the test of the new value regime" (Kalb 2019: 212; cf. Archer and Musić 2020). Labor aristocracy, skilled and flexible young workers became the first to support new regulations, echoing what Kasmir and Carbonella (2008) have described as capitalism's production of difference among the dispossessed. But again, in the epic debt crisis and prelude to war in late Yugoslavia, productivism had a salvatory zeal that resonated across the fault lines. At the ceremonial start of the Yugo America line in 1985—set to coincide with anniversary of the People's Liberation Struggle in World War II—we see the metalworker M. M. doing the first operation with a shout "Get away, people, let us work" (Antonijević 1986: 42). Five years later, we hear a technician's cry to the management to find new export deals: "We are tired of politicization; let us work, let us get out of the crisis, let us earn a living."[10] Between former socialist ethos and new capitalist zeal, it was work that was the common link.

Indeed, such productivist morality prevailed even when the state sought to ease the social dislocations emerging from new market relations. In the 1990s, Zastava plunged into a major crisis as the result of mounting debt and the loss of suppliers, formerly scattered across the federation. Unlike Poland, Yugoslavia's international debt was not written off. For the first time, the state intervened to support Zastava wages in a major deal that included thousands of funded redundancies. However, such state redistribution was inherently delegitimizing, as the "buying of social peace" constantly implied that welfare was unearned. In the absence of work, state welfare became a form of economic and moral indebting of citizenry, which paved the way for actual state appropriation and, later, the privatization of industry (Rajković, n.d.; cf. Yoltar 2020). When Milošević's government was ousted and Zastava was subjected to market reforms in 2001, a layoff of fifteen thousand workers was justified by the claim that most of them were not working anyhow. By the time I did my fieldwork in Kragujevac in 2011–13, precarious workers on the dole discussed whose position was more deserving. The infamous protest for the thirteenth wage packet was widely remembered as the beginning of Zastava's demise—a time when the proletarian opted for income rather than investment, a time when "workers turned factories into social institutions" and "ate their own machines." And when the car plant was finally handed to Fiat in 2011, this had a large measure of support from those who yearned for "proper" labor and "proper" capitalism to be a clear arbiter of social worth and economic legitimacy. The Italians were expected to separate the workers from the then idlers, "wheat from the chaff," in a situation in which it was no longer clear whether wages were being earned or merely received.

In sum, in post-Yugoslav factories freedom has re-emerged as a dialectical negation of protected employment, in the same way that industrial employment was once praised as liberation from poverty, imperialism, and agricultural toil. This is the broader irony we see today: calls for "pure labor" bring the Marxist idea of distribution according to work to its dark culmination. Neoliberal deregulation both repeats and inverts the socialist dream of "liberation of work." In the longue durée, countermovements change sides: freedom is a slippery word.

Acknowledgments

I am grateful to Chris Hann, Goran Musić, Rory Archer, and Ulrike Schult for their generous comments on previous versions, as well as to Gordana Vučković, the archivist of Home Library of Kragujevac, for her support in the research for this chapter. Archival research was funded by a CEELBAS grant of the School of Slavonic and East European Studies, University College London.

Ivan Rajković studied psychology in Belgrade and received his PhD in social anthropology from the University of Manchester in 2015. He has held postdoctoral fellowships in London and Halle/Saale, and is currently a postdoctoral researcher based at the University of Vienna, investigating green capitalism, river-grabbing, and eco-populist mobilization in the Balkans.

Notes

1. The empirical sections that follow, though based mainly on archival data, are related to my ethnographic research in Kragujevac since 2011 (mostly focusing on its car industry). The changing forms of work membership are at the center of my book manuscript, "The Gift of Work: Indebting the Social in a Post-Yugoslav Factory" (Rajković, n.d.).
2. Raški rudar 1949 11/3, cited in Matošević (2015: 33).
3. "Socijala na više spratova," *Svetlost*, 12 January 1989, p. 7.
4. "Socijala iz fotelja," *Svetlost*, 26 January 1989, p. 10; "Stanarina odskočna daska," *Svetlost*, 2 February 1989, p. 10.
5. "Ruženje radnika," *Svetlost*, 11 January 1990, p. 4.
6. "Najduži dan," *Crvena Zastava*, 17 January 1990, p. 1.
7. "Tržište glavni sudija," *Crvena Zastava*, 17 January 1990, p. 1.
8. "Ruženje radnika," *Svetlost*, 11 January 1990, p. 4.
9. "Račun bez krčmara," *Svetlost*, 11 January 1990, p. 1, 5.
10. *Crvena Zastava*, 24 October 1990, p. 7.

References

Published Sources

Antonijević, Dragana. 1986. "Ritual puštanja montažne trake u pogon u proizvodnji 'Juga 55V.'" *Etnološke sveske* 40(VII): 39–47.

Archer, Rory. 2016. "'Paid for by the Workers, Occupied by the Bureaucrats': Housing Inequalities in 1980s Belgrade." In *Social Inequalities and Discontent in Yugoslav Socialism*, ed. R. Archer, I. Duda, and P. Stubbs, 70–88. Abingdon: Routledge.

Archer, Rory, and Goran Musić. 2020. "When Workers' Self-Management Met Neoliberalism: Positive Perceptions of Market Reforms among Blue-Collar Workers in Late Yugoslav Socialism." In *Labor in State Socialist Europe after 1945*. Budapest: CEU Press.

Berković, Eva. 1986a. "Praksa, međutim, pokazuje." *Glas Omladine*, 1986, November edition.

———. 1986b. *Socijalne nejednakosti u Jugoslaviji*. Ekonomika.

Bockman, Johanna. 2011. *Markets in the Name of Socialism: The Left-Wing Origins of Neoliberalism*. Stanford, CA: Stanford University Press.

Bonfiglioli, Chiara. 2019. *Women and Industry in the Balkans: The Rise and Fall of the Yugoslav Textile Sector*. London: I.B. Tauris.

Brown, Wendy. 1995. *States of Injury: Power and Freedom in Late Modernity*. Princeton, NJ: Princeton University Press.

Buchowski, Michal. 2006. "Social Thought and Commentary: The Specter of Orientalism in Europe: From Exotic Other to Stigmatized Brother." *Anthropological Quarterly* 79(3): 463–82.

Castel, Robert. 1996. "Work and Usefulness to the World." *International Labour Review* 135(6): 615–22.

Collier, Stephen. 2011. *Post-Soviet Social: Neoliberalism, Social Modernity, Biopolitics*. Princeton, NJ: Princeton University Press.

Comisso, Ellen. 1979. *Workers' Control under Plan and Market: Implications of Yugoslav Self-Management*. New Haven, CT: Yale University Press.

Čukić, Branislav. 1985. *Apsentizam u radu i samoupravljanju: istraživanje u Zavodima Crvena Zastava*. Svetlost.

———. 2013. "Produktivna i neproduktivna zaposlenost." In *'Zastava' u drugoj polovini 20. veka*, ed. Rodoljub Micić, Kamenko Sretenović, and Predrag Galović, 343–46. Kragujevac: Udruženje 'Kragujevac – naš grad'.

Deleuze, Gilles, and Félix Guattari. 1988. *A Thousand Plateaus: Capitalism and Schizophrenia*. London: Athlone Press.

Denich, Bette S. 1973. "Why Do Peasants Urbanize? A Yugoslavian Case Study." *Annals of the New York Academy of Sciences* 220(6): 546–59.

Dimitrijević, Branislav. 2017. "In-between Utopia and Nostalgia: Or How the Worker Became Invisible on the Path from Shock-Worker to Consumer." In *Nostalgia on the Move*, ed. Mirjana Slavković and Marija Đorgović, 30–41. Belgrade: Muzej Jugoslavije.

Djilas, Milovan. 1966. *The New Class*. London: Unwin Books.

Duda, Igor. 2005. *U potrazi za blagostanjem: o povijesti dokolice i potrošačkog društva u Hrvatskoj 1950-Ih i 1960-Ih*. Zagreb: Srednja Europa.

———. 2010. *Pronađeno blagostanje: svakodnevni život i potrošačka kultura u Hrvatskoj 1970-Ih i 1980-Ih*. Srednja Europa.

Foucault, Michel. 1997. "The Ethics of the Concern of the Self as a Practice of Freedom." In *Essential Works of Michel Foucault, Vol. 1: Ethics: Subjectivity and Truth*, ed. Paul Rabinow, 281–301. London: Allen Lane.

———. 2008. *The Birth of Biopolitics: Lectures at the Collège de France, 1978–1979*. Translated by Graham Burchell. New York: Palgrave Macmillan.

Gramsci, Antonio. 1997. *Selections from the Prison Notebooks*. Translated by Q. Smith Hoare. New York: International Publishers.

Grdešić, Marko. 2016. "Serbia's Anti-bureaucratic Revolution as Manipulation? A Cultural Alternative to the Elite-Centric Approach." *Comparative Studies in Society and History* 58(3): 774–803.

———. 2017. "Images of Populism and Producerism: Political Cartoons from Serbia's 'Anti-Bureaucratic Revolution.'" *Europe–Asia Studies* 69(3): 483–507.

Hall, Stuart. 1988. *The Hard Road to Renewal: Thatcherism and the Crisis of the Left*. London: Verso.

Hann, Chris. 2015. "Goody, Polanyi and Eurasia: An Unfinished Project in Comparative Historical Economic Anthropology." *History and Anthropology* 26(3): 308–20.

———. 2019. *Repatriating Polanyi: Market Society in the Visegrád States*. Budapest: Central European University Press.

Kalb, Don. 2009. "Conversations with a Polish Populist: Tracing Hidden Histories of Globalization, Class, and Dispossession in Postsocialism (and Beyond)." *American Ethnologist* 36(2): 207–23.

———. 2019. "Post-Socialist Contradictions: The Social Question in Central and Eastern Europe and the Making of the Illiberal Right." In *The Social Question in the 21st*

Century: A Global View, ed. Jan Breman et al. Oakland: University of California Press.

Kasmir, Sharryn, and August Carbonella. 2008. "Dispossession and the Anthropology of Labor." *Critique of Anthropology* 28(1): 5–25.

Kideckel, David. 2008. *Getting by in Postsocialist Romania: Labor, the Body, and Working-Class Culture*. Bloomington: Indiana University Press.

Kolanović, Maša. 2011. "Jedan roman i omladina na putu bratstva: poetika osporavanja romana Čangi Alojza Miletića." In *Desničini Susreti 2010: Zbornik Radova*, 137–59. Zagreb: Faculty of Philosophy.

Konrad, George, and Ivan Szelenyi. 1979. *The Intellectuals on the Road to Class Power*. New York: Harcourt Brace Jovanovich.

Kornai, Janos. 1992. *The Socialist System: The Political Economy of Communism*. Oxford: Oxford University Press.

Kostić, Cvetko. 1955. *Seljaci industriski radnici*. Belgrade: Rad.

Kotkin, Stephen. 1992. *Steeltown, USSR: Soviet Society in the Gorbachev Era*. Los Angeles: University of California Press.

Laidlaw, James. 2014. *The Subject of Virtue: An Anthropology of Ethics and Freedom*. New York: Cambridge University Press.

Lampland, Martha. 1996. *The Object of Labour: Commodification in Socialist Hungary*. Chicago: Chicago University Press.

Le Normand, Brigitte. 2012. "The House That Socialism Built: Reform, Consumption, and Inequality in Postwar Yugoslavia." In *Communism Unwrapped: Consumption in Cold War Eastern Europe*, ed. P. Bren and M. Neuburger, 351–73. Oxford: Oxford University Press.

Matošević, Andrea. 2015. *Socijalizam s udarničkim licem: etnografija radnog pregalaštva*. Institut za etnologiju i folkloristiku.

Mihelj, Sabina. 2011. "Negotiating Cold War Culture at the Crossroads of East and West: Uplifting the Working People, Entertaining the Masses, Cultivating the Nation." *Comparative Studies in Society and History* 53(3): 509–39.

Millar, Kathleen. 2014. "The Precarious Present: Wageless Labor and Disrupted Life in Rio de Janeiro, Brazil." *Cultural Anthropology* 29(1): 32–53.

Milojković, Mirko, ed. 1973. *1853–1973: Od topa do automobila*. Kragujevac: Zavodi Crvena Zastava.

Musić, Goran. 2015. "'They Came as Workers and Left as Serbs': The Role of Rakovica's Blue-Collar Workers in Serbian Social Mobilizations of the Late 1980s." In *Social Inequalities and Discontent in Yugoslav Socialism*, ed. R. Archer, I. Duda, and P. Stubbs, 132–54. Abingdon: Routledge.

Palairet, Michael. 1993. "Mismanaging Innovation: The Yugo Car Enterprise (1962–1992)." *Technovation* 13(3): 117–32.

Patterson, Patrick Hyder. 2010. "Yugoslavia As It Once Was: What Tourism and Leisure Meant for the History of the Socialist Federation." In *Yugoslavia's Sunny Side: A History of Tourism in Socialism, 1950s–1980s*, ed. H. Grandits and K. Taylor, 367–402. Budapest: Central European University Press.

———. 2011. *Bought and Sold: Living and Losing the Good Life in Socialist Yugoslavia*. Ithaca, NY: Cornell University Press.

Pešić, Vesna. 1988. *Kratki kurs o jednakosti: koncepcija jednakosti u zvaničnoj ideologiji jugoslovenskog društva*. Sociološko društvo Srbije.

Polanyi, Karl. 1944. *The Great Transformation: The Political and Economic Origins of Our Time*. New York: Farrar & Rinehart.

———. 2018. "On Freedom." In *Economy and Society: Selected Writings*, 15–41. Cambridge: John Wiley & Sons.

Postone, Moishe. 1995. *Time, Labor, and Social Domination: A Reinterpretation of Marx's Critical Theory*. Cambridge: Cambridge University Press.

Rajković, Ivan. 2018. "For an Anthropology of the Demoralized: State Pay, Mock-Labour, and Unfreedom in a Serbian Firm." *Journal of the Royal Anthropological Institute* 24(1): 47–70.

———. n.d. "The Gift of Work: Indebting the Social in a Post-Yugoslav Factory." Book manuscript.

Roseberry, William. 1994. "Hegemony and the Language of Contention." In *Everyday Forms of State Formation: Revolution and the Negotiation of Rule in Modern Mexico*, ed. Gilbert Michael Joseph and Daniel Nugent, 355–66. Durham, NC: Duke University Press.

Schult, Ulrike. 2014. "Social Fragmentation of Industrial Workforces: Yugoslav Motor Vehicle Industry during Self-Managed Socialism." *Südost-Forschungen* 73: 351–73.

———. 2017. *Zwischen Stechuhr und Selbstverwaltung: Eine Mikrogeschichte Sozialer Konflikte in der Jugoslawischen Fahrzeugindustrie, 1965–1985*. Vol. 15. Münster: LIT.

Senjković, Reana. 2016. *Svaki dan pobjeda: kultura omladinskih radnih akcija*. Zagreb: Institut za etnologiju i folkloristiku.

Sopranzetti, Claudio. 2017. "Framed by Freedom: Emancipation and Oppression in Post-Fordist Thailand." *Cultural Anthropology* 32(1): 68–92.

Supek, Rudi. 1963. *Omladina na putu bratstva: psiho-sociologija radne akcije*. Beograd: Mladost.

Thompson, Edward Palmer. 1948. "Omladinska Pruga." In *The Railway: An Adventure in Construction*, ed. Edward Palmer Thompson, 1–33. London: British-Yugoslav Association.

Unkovski-Korica, Vladimir. 2015. "Self-Management, Development and Debt: The Rise and Fall of the 'Yugoslav Experiment.'" In *Welcome to the Desert of Postsocialism: Radical Politics after Yugoslavia*, ed. Srećko Štiks Horvat, 21–43. New York: Verso.

Verdery, Katherine. 1996. *What Was Socialism, and What Comes Next?* Princeton, NJ: Princeton University Press.

Vuic, Jason. 2010. *The Yugo: The Rise and Fall of the Worst Car in History*. New York: Hill & Wang.

Vušković, Boris. 1976. "Social Inequality in Yugoslavia." *New Left Review* 95(1): 26–44.

Ward, Benjamin. 1958. "The Firm in Illyria: Market Syndicalism." *The American Economic Review* 48(4): 566–89.

Woodward, Susan. 1995. *Socialist Unemployment: The Political Economy of Yugoslavia, 1945–1990*. Princeton, NJ: Princeton University Press.

———. 2003. "The Political Economy of Ethno-nationalism in Yugoslavia." *Socialist Register*: 73–92.

Yoltar, Çağrı. 2020. "Making the Indebted Citizen: An Inquiry into State Benevolence in Turkey." *PoLAR: Political and Legal Anthropology Review* 43(1): 153–71.
Yurchak, Alexei. 2006. *Everything Was Forever, Until It Was No More: The Last Soviet Generation*. Princeton, NJ: Princeton University Press.

Archival Sources

Crvena Zastava
Svetlost
Nezavisna svetlost

8

Max Weber's Heirs?

Work and Ethics among Small Business Owners in East Germany

Sylvia Terpe

Introduction

Freedom in the sense of being able to make choices and control one's actions is a necessary condition for moral responsibility and hence for any kind of ethic. People who feel that their lives are determined by entities or processes over which they have no control, such as the forces of "the market" in the "iron cage" of developed capitalism, are not free to take responsibility for themselves or for others. After outlining my argument theoretically with reference to Max Weber and Karl Polanyi in the first section of the chapter, the second section brings them together and proposes variations on classical themes. I show that householding can be conceptualized as an "economic ethic" in Weber's sense. Following Wolfgang Streeck, I show that open-ended desires drive capitalism with the same efficacity that a Protestant work ethic did in the past. The third section explores how work ethic, economic ethic, and social ethic are manifested in the East German context. I show that a strong work ethic may go hand in hand with an orientation to householding, and that a weakened work ethic is fully compatible with a strong profit-orientation. The two cases I examine in depth both exhibit an idea of individualism that Polanyi, like Weber, associated with capitalism; but they fall short of the social ethic implied by Polanyi's notion of true freedom and responsibility. I conclude by highlighting the importance of an idea of "social debt" for this social ethic: if it is missing, social responsibility becomes an empty shell.

Work Ethic, Economic Ethic, and Freedom

One of Max Weber's central arguments in *The Protestant Ethic and the Spirit of Capitalism* (Weber [1920] 2011a) engaged with Martin Luther's use of the term *Beruf* in his translation of the Bible into German. The idea that "the fulfillment of duty in vocational callings" was "the highest expression that moral activity could assume" was a radical innovation (ibid.: 100). For Weber, it was "truly beyond doubt" that "this moral legitimation of vocational life was one of the Reformation's most influential achievements, and in particular the achievement of Luther" (ibid.: 101).

Weber's concept of vocational ethic refers to work (Swedberg 2005: 294). To have an *Arbeitsethik* means to appreciate work "as virtuous in itself" (ibid.: 310). It comprises initiative, self-discipline, perseverance, "competence and proficiency" (Weber 2011a: 81) in one's this-worldly professional activities. These attitudes are expressions of good moral character. Another central argument of Weber is that the new Protestant work ethic was the powerful driver of modern capitalism:

> In fact, this peculiar idea of a duty to have a vocational calling . . . is the idea that is characteristic of the "social ethic" of modern capitalist culture. In a certain sense, it is even of constitutive significance for it. It implies a notion of duty that individuals ought to experience, and do, vis-à-vis the content of their "vocational" activity. (Ibid.)

Weber regarded this back then unprecedented work ethic as "constitutive" of capitalism because it entailed "[t]he 'capitalist' orientation of profit-making activity" (Weber 1978: 164). Put simply, profit making or "acquisition" (Weber 2019: 179) is about "money making" (Swedberg 2005: 211). It means an orientation "to opportunities for seeking new powers of control over goods" (Weber 1978: 90). This in itself was not new, but when combined with the Protestant work ethic (*Arbeitsethik*), profit making could develop into a new economic ethic (*Wirtschaftsethik*). Weber describes this as "the spirit of capitalism's comprehension of the acquisition of money as a 'calling'—as an end in itself that persons were obligated to pursue" (Weber 2011a: 94). As an ethic, profit making is no longer a means to other ends such as (luxurious) consumption. Instead,

> the acquisition of money, and more and more money, takes place here simultaneously with the strictest avoidance of all spontaneous enjoyment of it. The pursuit of riches is fully stripped of all pleasurable (*eudämonistischen*), and surely all hedonistic, aspects. Accordingly, this striving becomes understood completely as an end in itself . . . Here, people are oriented to acquisition as the purpose of life; acquisition is no longer viewed as a means to the end of satisfying the substantive needs of life. (Ibid.: 80)

In short, devoting one's life to work gave rise to an economic ethic dedicated to profit making for its own sake. The Protestant ethic thereby denied that economic activity was a means to satisfy other ends. Weber distinguishes two kinds of economic action.[1] *Haushalten* (literally, to keep house, to economize) is best translated as "householding." It denotes the management of a budget, or the "allocation of resources in providing for a given set of needs" on the part of a household (Parsons, in Weber 1978: 207). The household might be a "family," but it might equally be any other collective unit that pools and shares resources (ibid.: 340). In householding, people "resort to economic action only so far as . . . it [is] necessary" for "the satisfaction of . . . wants" (ibid.: 340, 339). Householding is associated with "consumption" (ibid.: 87). It corresponds to "what is generally known in English as a 'subsistence economy'" oriented to maintenance rather than profitability (Tribe, in Weber 2019: 462, 466, 469f). Wolfgang Streeck links this disposition with "minimization of effort" (Streeck 2011: 141, 149). The motivation to work does not stem from a work ethic that values work as such, but from other sources such as the desire to secure a "good life." Householding is thereby subject to the law of "marginal utility" (Weber 1978: 92; Weber 2019: 181); work and other economic activities such as commerce are means to satisfy other ends, and one engages in them only so far as is necessary. Streeck calls this traditionalism, and declares that it is "profoundly incompatible with the spirit of maximization that is at the heart of the capitalist mode of production and is idealized in its ethos" (Streeck 2011: 152).

The pendant of *Haushalten* is *Erwerben* (literally, to acquire), best translated as "acquisition" (by Tribe, in Weber 2019: 181). This is not regulated by marginal utility but by profitability (Weber 2019: 181). The "devotion to a 'calling' of money making" (Weber 2011a: 93) was not to be confused with a pursuit of wealth. Profit making, in the sense of an ethos, aims to maximize capital for reinvestment rather than wealth available for the purposes of consumption. As Weber exemplified: "A pensioner's purchase of securities to enjoy the monetary proceeds is not an investment in 'capital,' but in wealth" (Weber 2019: 189). Hence aiming for "rent" is no different from work under *Haushalten* (Swedberg 2005: 26, 211). In householding, income from work or rent "is used to make life more pleasant" (ibid.: 26). Only the Protestant work ethic, with its moral devaluation of (luxurious) consumption could spur the steady flow of investments that defines capitalism. In *The Protestant Ethic*, Weber offered vivid descriptions of the restlessness of business owners (*Unternehmer*) whose thoughts always circled around their work and the expansion of profits, and for whom leisure was a waste (Weber 2011a: 77ff, 398f).

The orientations to work and acquisition as ends in themselves qualify them as moral and ethical (Schwinn 1998: 305).[2] However, in a well-known passage at the end of *The Protestant Ethic* in which Weber reflects on the capitalism of his own age, he notes that "The Puritan *wanted* to be a person with a vocational calling; we *must* be" (Weber 2011a: 177; emphasis in original). Developed capitalism presented itself as an "iron cage" (Weber 1992: 123)—or "steel-hard casing" in the most recent, more precise translation by Kalberg (Weber 2011a: 177):

> The capitalist economic order of today is a vast cosmos into which a person is born. It simply exists, to each person, as a factually unalterable casing (*unabänderliches Gehäuse*) in which he or she must live. To the extent that people are interwoven into the context of capitalism's market forces, the norms of its economic action are forced onto them. Every factory owner who operates in the long term against these norms will inevitably be eliminated from the economy. With the same degree of inevitability, every worker who cannot or will not adapt to the norms of the marketplace will become unemployed. (Ibid.: 81)

In the "mighty cosmos of the modern economic order" (ibid.: 177), participation in economic (market) activities appears as a necessity, an external force. This is far from the "inner compulsion to work" (Swedberg 2005: 310) experienced by the early Protestants.

Weber here adopts the stance that freedom is a prerequisite for morality. Where only force, determinacy, and inevitability prevail, freedom and responsibility for one's actions are absent (Wuthnow 1987: 74, 355). But responsibility is necessary if action is to be judged morally. Weber's formulation of the Protestant who "wanted to work in a calling" implies that he had the freedom to do so and hence to act morally and ethically, whereas his contemporaries were caught in the "factually unalterable casing" of mature capitalism. From the individual's perspective, such a capitalism seems to "have an objective existence" in the sense that "the individual confronts [. . . it] as given, as existing independently of his own action" (Brubaker 1984: 72). The economic realm adopts the quality of natural laws or of a "life order" (Terpe 2016, 2020). Weber speculated that modern capitalism rests "on a mechanical foundation" and no longer needed a particular work ethic (Weber 2011a: 177). This mechanical foundation precluded the freedom that was necessary for any kind of morality or ethics.

But the picture of modern capitalism can be drawn differently. Mary Douglas highlights that the boundary between the inevitable and the intentional (the space for potential responsibility) is not objective or fixed: "The line between natural [or quasi-natural] and man-made causes . . . is a wavy, unsteady line, always in debate and reflecting cultural bias" (Douglas 1985: 26f). Weber was careful not to assert that capitalism *is* a "factually unalterable casing," merely that it is experienced in this way. Other perspectives could highlight its man-made character and thereby uncover spaces for potential freedoms and responsibilities. Following Marx and Engels, Karl Polanyi did exactly this. Analytically, he too proceeded from the assumption that freedom is only possible where necessity does not reign, where human beings are "masters of themselves" and thereby able to "choose" how to act (Polanyi 2018: 302, 304). The price for this freedom is responsibility for one's actions (ibid.: 306), but the reward is the possibility of a "moral existence" (ibid.: 305). From a Weberian perspective, Polanyi's vision of a "true concept of freedom" belongs in the realm of value judgements, but it may nonetheless generate questions that can be investigated empirically.

Like Weber, Polanyi starts with the observation that in the capitalism of his day "[c]apitalists and workers alike, human beings in general, appear as mere players on the economic stage" (Polanyi 2018: 299). Economy and state have become "reifications," governed by "pseudo-natural laws" (ibid.: 299ff). Yet this world is characterized by a particular idea of freedom and responsibility that has its historical roots in Calvinism (ibid.: 302f) and was adopted by the bourgeois society. The individuals of this society believe in personal responsibility and freedom, but because they have "no inner participation in the objective social powers," they feel themselves to be "isolated foreign element[s] within a corporative [capitalist and bourgeois] society" (ibid.: 303). While valuing personal responsibility and freedom, they deny the responsibility they have by creating exactly those forces they perceive as external. They do not recognize their own participation in the reproduction of existing economic and political conditions. For Polanyi, this limitation of responsibility, and thereby freedom, is arbitrary and distorted. One could speak of a bourgeois or capitalistically bisected responsibility and freedom.[3]

In contrast to individualized responsibility and personal freedom, Polanyi outlines a concept of responsibility and freedom that "include[s] the social dimension" (Polanyi 2018: 304). This "social freedom" (see also Rajković and Santos et al., this volume) is based on

> the twofold insight that there is, on the one hand, no human behavior that is completely without social consequences, and that, on the other hand, there is no existing entity, no power, no structure and no law in society, nor can there be, that is not in some way based on the behavior of individual human beings. (Polanyi 2018: 304)

In Polanyi's vision of a socialist society, human beings realize that the world they live in is constantly re-created by themselves. They recognize that there is no external power, no state, market, or any other "authority" to "blame for human troubles, mutual dependency, the limitation of needs or common misfortune" (Polanyi 2018: 306). People become aware that these reifications are made by themselves, that they have "built the cage" that renders them "helpless" (ibid.: 306). This awareness permits true freedom, and Polanyi emphasizes the possibility to choose; but this freedom incurs the cost of assuming responsibility "for all social effects of our existence" as we go about satisfying our wants (ibid.: 307, 309). This is a distinctive *social* ethic that implies moral responsibility in the shaping of social relations between strangers in all spheres of life (economy, politics, etc.). Polanyi adds that this society would need "clear and transparent" social relations in order to be able to "directly track the repercussions of our life impulses on the lives of all the others" (ibid.: 306). In other words, social relations must allow for clear attributions of responsibility so that the effects of actions "no longer evaporate into the twilight of the indefinite boundaries of the allegedly infinite mass of people and goods" (ibid.: 308).

Whether or not one shares Polanyi's vision of freedom and responsibility, or believes in the practicability of such a "transparent" society, these ideas can be combined with those of Weber to generate fruitful empirical questions.

Combining Weber with Polanyi (and Streeck)

If one is interested in whether small business owners in Halle, a city in East Germany that brands itself as a "cradle of the Reformation" (*Wiege der Reformation*),[4] still show any signs of the work and economic ethic described by Weber, one does well to begin by investigating their attitudes toward work. Why and how they work depend on the freedoms and constraints they perceive. Seen from this perspective, it is possible to distinguish more clearly between a work ethic and an economic ethic. While Weber connected the Protestant work ethic to the capitalist ethic of acquisition, we may question this causality. It is possible that people feel partly free (and thereby potentially morally responsible) in what they do (or do not do) for a living, but nevertheless constrained by larger "economic forces" that supply them with justifications and strategies of moral neutralization. Hence one should ask in which particular actions and spheres of life people feel free to choose, and when they do not see any possibility of choice or room for maneuver. If they feel free, is this accompanied by a sense of moral responsibility? And if so, is this individual or social in character?

The supposedly uncontrollable forces must also be differentiated (Terpe 2009: 96–109; Terpe 2016: 12ff). This becomes obvious when one looks more closely at Polanyi's argumentation. He is close to Weber when he portrays humans as "mere players on the economic stage" (Polanyi 2018: 299). If people attribute the conditions of the current world to powers that they perceive as impersonal, such as "globalization" or "climate change," they absolve themselves of moral responsibility. These forces can be held responsible in a causal sense. Although they can be praised for their effects (such as the social benefits seen to be generated by an "invisible hand of the market"), it is difficult to blame them in a moral sense. But the picture changes when Polanyi speaks of reifications like the "state" or "authority" (ibid.: 306). These entities or processes may also appear overwhelming, but people are usually more aware of their man-made character, and associate them with concrete actors (e.g., politicians). Although the effect overlaps with that of the more anonymous forces (absolution from one's own moral responsibility), it is different because from these more concrete actors some remedial action may be expected. Hence moral indignation and anger may be evoked when no measures are taken.

A focus on the question of freedom allows one to conceptualize householding more clearly as an economic ethic. This requires more careful attention to what Weber called *Bedürfnisse,* variously translated as "needs" and "wants." Keith Tribe favors the former, because householding "'meets agents' immediate needs, but no more" (Tribe, in Weber 2019: 462). However, even "immediate needs" are not fixed but depend on societal definitions. Food, shelter, and clothing are usually seen as basic material needs. In Germany (and many other contemporary societies), access to drinking water, sanitation, means of transportation, health facilities, and educational institutions are also regarded as basic needs.[5] These formulations are open to interpretation. Many people sense a distinction between "basic needs" and other "wants," whose fulfillment is not absolutely necessary for subsistence. But sometimes these wants also appear as necessary if one is to live a good or happy life. Wolfgang Streeck emphasizes "the evolution of consumer 'needs,' or better: desires," as an important factor in the dynamic of capitalism (Streeck 2012: 10). Just as acquisition is directed towards maximization, so is the development of these "open-ended" desires (Streeck 2011: 149). Capitalism flourishes not by meeting established needs but by creating new ones. Yet this is at the same time a potential flaw: "It is only if consumers, almost all of whom live far above the level of material subsistence, can be convinced to discover new needs, and thereby render themselves 'psychologically' poor, that the economy of rich capitalist societies can continue to grow" (Streeck 2012: 10f). In this context, to decide against the fulfillment of "consumer needs" and opt instead for a life closer to "subsistence level" may adopt a moral quality: a renewal of the ethic of householding. At the same time, Streeck's reflections on contemporary capitalism suggest that people's "desires" and the "dreams, promises, and imagined satisfaction[s]" associated with them (ibid.: 10) may be just as efficacious in motivating work as the original Protestant work ethic. Whether such desires can be the basis of an economic ethic is an open question, theoretically and empirically.

Work, Economic, and Social Ethics of Small Business Owners in Halle

Against the theoretical background developed so far, I will now focus on two business owners who were in their late forties and early fifties in 2016–17. Both had had their vocational training in the German Democratic Republic (GDR) of the late 1980s and became business owners at about the time of the *Wende*, when the socialist state disintegrated. Each ran a successful small firm created by his own "hard work." The importance of work in their lives was indicated in the answers they gave in a questionnaire, and later confirmed in qualitative interviews and informal talks. In the questionnaire they stated that work was "a duty towards society," that "hard work usually brings a better life," that to "develop your talents, you need to have a job," and that "people who don't work turn lazy."[6] Assent to these normative statements may be interpreted as evidence of a work ethic in the Protestant tradition. However, like most inhabitants of contemporary Halle, religion hardly plays any role in the lives of these business owners. Neither belongs to a religious denomination or regards himself as a believer.[7] The two men differed in important respects: while one (whom I shall call Andreas) agreed with the statement that "work should always come first, even if it means less spare time," the other (Karsten) disagreed. Karsten considers himself a socially committed person—a possible indicator for a social ethic in Polanyi's sense. Let us analyze them more closely.

"We Are Moving on, on and on, on and on": Andreas

Andreas appears to exemplify the Protestant work ethic—except that religion is a topic that does not matter to him at all. It was difficult to make an appointment with him, because "it is always busy around here." His firm specialized in a particular timber construction and had seven employees, including his wife, his brother, his son, his daughter, and his son-in-law. His narration of the firm's history bristles with examples of the obstacles he had to overcome. He applied to register his family business in the last years of the GDR, and recalls his experience with the municipal council as "running the gauntlet." He was successful only after "long, long struggles," receiving his authorization shortly before the *Wende*. It then needed "strenuous efforts" to find a location and to organize machines and wood. In spring 1990 he started the business on his own. After a couple of months, he hired his father as his first "journeyman" (*Geselle*) and "things really took off. We expanded quickly, [. . ., hired more employees], needed a larger workshop

. . . which we got after many, many laborious talks and threats . . . There was an enormous amount of work . . . and a huge demand."

The demand for the firm's products and services increased in the following years. When I met Andreas for the first time, he told me that they were in the middle of "modernizing" the firm by buying new technology, building a new and larger shop floor, and reconstructing the firm's showroom. All this might suggest an economic ethic of acquisition. Andreas told me proudly that, thanks to this renewal, they would be able to meet customers' wishes even better, while maintaining high quality. "We have a reasonably modern firm, not like these 'museums' with old machines . . . you still often see in joineries today." He emphasized that they had "always tried in recent years to acquire new machines" and that it was important to invest in a firm, because otherwise one could never sell it. However, selling is not an issue for Andreas, because it is planned that his son will take over the firm. The continuous process of modernization is for the son, who should not have to (and would not want to) take over a "pile of scrap" (*Schrotthaufen*).

The continuous acquisition of new machines "costs a lot of money." Andreas had managed to borrow the necessary funds from a bank, and was hoping to receive a building permit soon. He had even applied for the first time for public funds from the federal state—a step motivated by his anger that "usually the only firms that receive funds are big ones that close after a couple of years and move on [to another place] to cash in again." Although the application process was a struggle due to all the bureaucracy, Andreas "struggled through"—this time, to his own surprise, with the help "of a woman [at a counselling center financed by the federal state] who really tried hard . . . so that we managed to fill out what felt like five hundred forms." He assumed that he had received this assistance, because "they" (the federal state government) had finally understood that it was also necessary to support smaller firms.

Like the restless Protestants described by Weber, Andreas's life revolves around his firm and work. If he talks about himself, he uses the term "self-employed" (*Selbständig*), which is the opposite of being employed and is used for the owners of small businesses, irrespective of whether they have employees. Andreas likes to quote the saying that "self-employed means being on your own, constantly" (*Selbständig sein heißt selbst und ständig*). In other words, one must care for oneself in every respect, incessantly. This is exemplified by the fact that for more than twenty years Andreas and his wife took no holidays. Even now, they take only a few days off per year. But he does not experience this as a burden. It is something that comes from "inside" and makes up his character:

> If you are self-employed—and you just have to have it in you—then you always say: "We are moving on, on and on, on and on." . . . And as long as there is work, this is also some kind of fun (*Spaß*). I cannot imagine a condition without work. I have never experienced it. But you have to be here, all the time, always. . . . And this is also the motivation you have. You always have to be there. It is up to you, that you keep on generating the work.

This approximates the ideal Protestant's inner compulsion and commitment to work. Andreas likes what he regards as his real work: taking care of orders and liaising with customers; not to mention the skilled and arduous woodwork, not all of which can be mechanized. He is particularly satisfied (*freuen*) when his firm helps in the conservation of historic buildings. This is the kind of hard work he considers fun. But he finds other kinds of work annoying, because he perceives them as getting in the way of his real work: tasks like getting permits and complying with various regulations. However, in Andreas's narration these obstacles can be overcome; they do not have the character of anonymous forces he cannot control. Rather, he identifies concrete actors who need to be laboriously convinced, influenced, or circumvented.

While Andreas comes close to Weber's notion of a work ethic, there is a fundamental difference to Weber's account of the economic ethic of money making. While the Weberian ideal type features open-ended expansion and maximization, Andreas has come to reject this. By the mid-2000s the firm had expanded to fourteen employees, but at this point he realized, "I had to take orders that I didn't really want—just to pay the people." The market segment of standardized products in which he had to seek commissions was characterized by an "enormous price fight" driven by people he derogatively called "cronies" (*Spezis*). In order to hold on to his workforce, he had been compelled to lower the price of his products. At the same time, he was discontented with the attitude of many of his workers, mostly former apprentices whose training had cost him time and money. Some of them had "little interest in the profession" (*kein Interesse am Beruf*) and "only came to us to have work" (*nur um Arbeit zu haben*)—implying that they worked out of necessity but lacked the professional ethos that Andreas expected. Eventually Andreas decided that "we don't want so many employees anymore." He refocused the firm's activities, reduced standardized production, laid off personnel, stopped training apprentices and acquired new machines so as not to be "dependent on other people." The only two non-family employees he retained "care for the firm as if it were their own"—by which he meant that they had a work ethic similar to his own.

Andreas's narrative suggests that he switched his orientation from profit making to something closer to householding, but which still allows him—by focusing on a specialized core business—to live according to his own ideals of a work ethic. Of course, the standard of living of his family is well above that of basic subsistence. Andreas is satisfied with the profit level he continues to enjoy through his hard work. This was crucial because he needed to carry on providing for himself, his family, and those employees he perceived as deserving. From his perspective, the reorientation of his business activities was a free decision. He was able to dismiss employees whose work ethic did not match his own, and to withdraw from a market dominated by mass production and competition that squeezed profit margins. Andreas rejects these trends from both a moral and an economic point of view: price competition was an obstacle to making any profit at all, which would in turn prevent the self-employed from providing work for those who deserve it. It therefore seemed rational and morally justified to change the course of his business: Why bother to take responsibility for those who do not act responsibly themselves?

Andreas thus believes in and acts upon an idea of individualized responsibility and freedom that both Weber and Polanyi associated with capitalism. With Weber and Polanyi, one might also expect this to be accompanied by consciousness of uncontrollable forces, and indeed, these appear in two forms in Andreas's narrative. First, he takes it as given that a market segment is dominated by agents who drive prices down. He cannot change this; all he can do is opt out of this segment. But it is important to note an implicit distinction that Andreas makes between a market logic and concrete agents. His derogatory description of these agents suggests that he sees them as greedy and stupid, because in the long run a business that drives prices and quality down is bound to fail and vanish from the market. This derives from the anonymous logic of the market. Andreas agreed strongly with the statement in the questionnaire that "competition is good," because it "stimulates people to work hard and develop new ideas." In his perception, in the long run, market logic breeds healthy competition for the best ideas but punishes extreme price reductions. This mechanism is not controlled by any particular human beings, but operates magically (cf. Moeran and de Waal Malefyt 2018). Reasonable firm owners can adjust to it.

Politics is another zone that Andreas perceives to be out of his control, but where blame can be apportioned. German educational policy has neglected vocational training in recent years, and therefore politicians are responsible for the lack of enthusiasm and skill among apprentices and employees.[8] Andreas complains that nowadays kids are told in school that "without an *Abitur* (high-school diploma) you're not a real human being and you will never make it." His firm had had "forty to forty-five applications for each apprenticeship place in the 1990s . . . without our even advertising it," but the supply had dried up, he suspects, due to politicians' privileging of higher education. In the 1990s it was very difficult for school-leavers in East Germany to get an apprenticeship, or if one did, to move into appropriate employment afterwards (Lutz et al. 2004). Andreas overlooks this. He attributes the privileging of higher education to the fact that "we craftsmen have . . . no real representation. No one represents our interests. . . . No party, no chamber of commerce, and no guild (*Innung*)—which I quit years ago."[9] Although Andreas votes in elections—because it is "better than back then [in the GDR]" when election results were known in advance—he does not see that this has any influence on politics; on the contrary, he perceives politicians to act against his interests. When he had raised issues in his guild, it turned out to be a waste of time. The only solution was to transform the profile of his business, by reducing personnel and specializing.

But his modernization measures were not motivated solely by a shortage of qualified labor. Andreas remarks that the younger generation, including his son and designated successor, "wants to live a bit more" (*mehr leben*). For his son, it is important to have leisure time and free weekends. Andreas's investment was heavily influenced by this attitude. He suspected that the business could only maintain profits and allow the leisure time stipulated by his son if the production process were to be further digitalized. This turned out to be correct: nowadays everyone in the firm has no choice but to "do nothing from Friday afternoon to Sunday evening." Andreas concedes that this development has brought "a bit of life quality" (*Lebensqualität*), but he still has trouble adjusting. For example, he cannot help looking into the books at the weekend. But digitalization has enabled him to motivate his son to join the firm in a more committed way. His son likes "anything with computers," and so this was a way to draw him into the firm. In his son's dealing with computers, Andreas recognizes an aspect of the work ethic he appreciates: his son was "never satisfied with standard," but was always on the lookout for ways to "improve" the digitally run processes.

Does Andreas's sense of personal responsibility add up to a social ethic in the sense of Polanyi? I would say no. His work ethic emphasizes individual responsibility, and he agreed with the statement in the questionnaire that "hard work usually brings a better life." Andreas feels responsible only for those who deserve it because they prove their work ethic in his firm. He cares for them by providing them with well-paid work and thereby a livelihood that is clearly above the subsistence level. In return he expects them to show commitment to the firm. He feels no responsibility for anyone outside this small circle. Andreas regards the amount of tax he pays as too high. If "hard work usually brings a better life," then everybody can and should be responsible for himself or herself. He does not wish to extend state support to citizens who fail to deserve it due to their own lack of effort (*Mühe, Anstrengung*). This is a "capitalistically bisected responsibility," and not the true freedom or social ethic advocated by Polanyi.

"I Really Like to Make Money!": Karsten

My first appointment with Karsten was delayed for two months. Although initially agreeing to take part in my study, he was unavailable. When we finally met, he talked enthusiastically about the long foreign holidays he had enjoyed in the interim. When I asked how he managed to reconcile such an extended absence with his work, he proudly explained that he had already arranged his succession, and that his successor was able to take care of everything. The firm supplies technical office equipment "individually adapted to customer needs," and has eleven employees. Karsten was "only marginally involved in the daily business," which anyway was not really his "strength" (*nicht meine Stärke*). He described his own contribution in terms of strategies, visions, and "realizing ideas" (*Ideen realisieren*). For him it was important "always to have a desire for new projects and new customers," and if things were not fun (*Spaß*), then he would lose interest. He handled relatively few customers himself ("maybe ten or twenty"), with whom he had established several new firms. These were managed by staff of his main firm, and were all profitable.

By founding new firms, Karsten was able to solve a problem that, in this form, Andreas never faced. Andreas had expanded his firm because it had seemed the obvious thing to do as long as demand for his products was strong. By contrast, Karsten wanted to expand his main firm in order to make more profits. But, similar to Andreas, he had trouble in doing so due to a shortage of suitably qualified workers: "We do not want to grow, not seriously. Because it's limited by [the scarcity of] staff. . . . If the market does not provide enough personnel, growth is fatal. Then you punish yourself with growth because profit shrinks and you have to do everything yourself. I don't want that." In this passage, again similar to Andreas, Karsten posits the market as the impersonal background for his own actions: "the market does not provide enough personnel." When asked if he might offer apprenticeship positions himself, he answered negatively because he needed "people who have experience, five to ten years." Furthermore, as all his employees were "specialists," he "could not afford" to use them to train apprentices. Hence, for Karsten, "an apprentice in the firm is the most expensive employee" because he brings hardly any performance as he is still training, and he takes up the "precious" time of his specialists. Like Andreas, Karsten has circumvented the particular problem "the market" presents to him by changing his business strategy. But unlike Andreas, he did not consider the economic ethic of "householding." Instead, he expanded profits by founding new firms. He does not style himself as self-employed (*Selbständig*), but as an *Unternehmer*, which may be translated as "businessman" or "entrepreneur." For Karsten, *Unternehmer* are people who continuously have creative visions about how to increase profits. This gives him a feeling of agency and reinforces his impression of being a self-made man. Yet this strong orientation towards profit making is very different from Weber's notion of the economic ethic of capitalism. The latter avoids "all pleasurable . . ., and surely all hedonistic, aspects" (Weber 2011a: 80). Karsten does not display his wealth ostentatiously but he does enjoy the possibilities his money allows him, notably travelling.

Enjoyment and excitement were also important when it came to work itself. Karsten attributed his economic success to "hard work," but in recent years his work has rather had the character of a hobby, where he meets the customers he gets along with, some of whom are business partners with whom he would like to socialize anyway. In short, he works not for the sake of work itself—as in the ideal type of the Protestant work ethic—but because work means pleasurable sociality and opens up social contacts. This enables him to frame large parts of his life outside his office as "work": whenever and wherever he meets his customer and partner friends, they discuss their businesses.

Having said that, Karsten never tires of stressing that his work is also a "responsibility towards employees." He declared in our first interview that "we business owners want (*wollen*) to earn money," but then added immediately that "we need (*müssen*) to make money to pay our people." From his perspective, his own work and the early appointment of his successor had "secured" the jobs of his employees. He emphasized the benefits his workforce enjoyed: good pay, regular hours, no antisocial overtime: "They should have planning security and the certainty that they can shape their [family] life." His employees were able to choose the firm car they wanted—"fast car or family car, I don't care about that." These measures, he conceded, were introduced in order to attract and retain highly qualified staff. Although he boasted that the "satisfaction of my employees in the company is the greatest asset I have," he would probably be less generous if labor market conditions were more favorable to him.

Karsten seemed to view "regular working hours" as his gift to the workforce, rather than something regulated in German labor law. He views the latter as an annoying anachronism. It might have been necessary "twenty years ago in call centers where staff were exploited," but in his firm it was superfluous as "we cannot exploit because we need the employees." According to Karsten, "everyone has his chance. If he does not use it, he has to start from scratch somewhere else." The labor law was "far too protective of employees" and therefore "morally wrong." He is indignant and responds to this external (but clearly man-made) constraint by trying to avoid having anything to do with it: "My time is simply too precious to deal with such nonsense." Karsten's rejection of the specification of social rights in state law throws revealing light on his idea of responsibility: although he claims to be socially responsible, he thinks it should be up to him alone to determine the kind and extent of that responsibility. He casts the benefits he grants in almost philanthropical terms, when in fact the scarcity of qualified labor leaves him with no choice. He presents the fact that his firm is located in Halle as an expression of his desire "to do something for the city and area where I live." In his self-representation, entrepreneurs act in socially responsible ways through their very existence. The idea of social responsibility thus degenerates into mere rhetoric.

That Karsten's idea of social responsibility is ultimately based on a notion of individualized responsibility can be shown in his social commitment (*soziales Engagement*) for an independently operated local school (*Schule in freier Trägerschaft*). This commitment leads him to disagree with the statement that "work should always come first." Like his work, this commitment is exciting and generates "fun." It is one of those things "that come easy to me," and over the years it grew into a "hobby." Karsten first became involved because he was discontented with the state schools attended by his children, where teachers routinely reacted to problems by saying: "That's none of my business." As state education has the same characteristics for him as the state's labor law—man-made, yet uncontrollable by the individual—he joined an initiative to support a private school that was still in its infancy at the time. The possibility to choose between a public and a private school is exactly the kind of choice he appreciates from his perspective of individualized responsibility.

In the private school, Karsten could bring in his own social philosophy and shape the educational experience. Just as he emphasizes teachers' "utmost commitment" (*höchstes Engagement*), children have to show "performance" (*Leistung*) and "a willingness to achieve" (*Leistungsbereitschaft*), because this is the only way to raise successful entrepreneurs and committed employees. Although the school also admits children with learning disabilities, it is important to him that the "high-performance" (*leistungsstarke*) pupils are not held back. He makes an analogy with what he regards as the solution for all social problems: "We have to force the poor to do more, and we have to force the rich to cede a bit." While the first part of this statement makes it clear that in his eyes the poor are responsible for the fact that they are poor, in the second part he implies that it is up to people like him to help them to change. But he regards helping as a moral imperative only as long as others try hard and show the kind of individual responsibility to which he attributes his success as an entrepreneur. Against the background of this expectation, he complains repeatedly that "young people, . . . in particular in East Germany," are "simply sluggish" (*träge*). In contrast to "the poor" they "have it too easy" (*zu gut gehen*) and hence lack the "energy" and "willingness to do anything beyond the basics" (*Grundmaß*) and "standard." They do not want "more" as he does, but seek only to "earn as much as possible for as much leisure time as possible." This comes close to householding, which he despises.

As with Andreas, Karsten's belief in an ethic of hard work has promoted an idea of individualized responsibility. Although Karsten feels responsible for a broader social circle than Andreas, his social philosophy merely feigns social responsibility, and in fact only generates what Polanyi would have called a distorted or arbitrarily impoverished social ethic. His social commitment actively promotes this distorted social ethic; he does not feel responsible for its negative consequences, as he himself appreciates living in a world in which ultimately everybody is responsible for themselves. The abbreviated social ethic of Karsten is also expressed in his attitude towards politics. Although he regards himself as "very interested politically" and sees voting as an obligatory "must" (*ein Muss*), he distances himself from the sphere of politics and politicians whose horizons are restricted to a "legislative period." Like Andreas, he does not see his interests represented, nor does he believe this will ever happen. Voting functions as a way to "complain" (*beschweren*). But because one cannot change anything through politics, it is even more important to be socially committed by enacting and promoting individual responsibility in other parts of life.

Conclusion

The combination of Weber's notions of a Protestant work ethic and a capitalist economic ethic with both Polanyi's idea of freedom, responsibility, and social ethic and Streeck's observation about the role of desires in developed capitalism turned out to be fruitful for the analysis of the two cases of business owners in East Germany. First, it revealed contemporary variations on Weber's themes. While one business owner shows a persistent work ethic within an orientation to householding—admittedly well above the level of mere subsistence —the other displays a persistent economic ethic of profit making combined with a weakened work ethic, which, however, still praises hard work as the key to economic success. Second, the analysis revealed that the work ethic of both these business owners has affinities with notions of individualized responsibility, which attribute (economic) success and failure solely to one's own endeavors and hard work. Effort, new ideas, and work are the decisive factors in a market whose anonymous logic rewards those who display them and are competent in adapting to its conditions. Hence the social consequences of this logic appear to be morally justified, because it is up to each individual to create her or his own life.

At the same time, the world of these business owners is inhabited by annoying, man-made forces that, in the form of politics, labor law, and education system, are forever putting obstacles in the way of personal endeavors and work. Andreas and Karsten have "no inner participation" in these powers, and feel as "isolated foreign element[s]" in their presence (Polanyi 2018: 303). Although they both participate in the political system by voting, this does not give them any impression of agency beyond exercising a right to complain. They see themselves as only able to enact their idea of making a difference through individual responsibility in other spheres of life, mainly in work-related activities. Social responsibilities connected to the workplace could be interpreted as emerging from "acknowledging interdependencies" (see Santos et al., this volume). Andreas and Karsten are certainly aware that they could not run their businesses successfully without employees. But this awareness does not suffice to generate the kind of social responsibility Polanyi imagined, nor the impression that they enjoy something at someone else's expense (Polanyi 2018: 307). They do not feel they owe anything to others (i.e., they have no "social debts"—see Rajković, this volume), because they can apparently accomplish everything on their own. Social debt seems to be crucial for the social ethic implied by Polanyi's notion of true freedom and responsibility. Without a sense of social debt, acts of "social responsibility" turn into mere "gifts," granted by generous benefactors on the basis of a sacred individual freedom.

Acknowledgments

I thank Chris Hann for his helpful comments on an earlier version of this chapter. This work was supported by the European Research Council under the European Union's Seventh Framework Programme (FP7/2007-2013)/ ERC Grant Agreement No. 340854 (REALEURASIA).

Sylvia Terpe is a sociologist at the Martin Luther University, Halle-Wittenberg. She was a research fellow at the Max Planck Institute for Social Anthropology in Halle (Saale), where she worked as a member of the research group REALEURASIA.

Notes

1. Weber explored the differences between *Haushalten* and *Erwerben* in various passages of *Economy and Society* (Weber 1978: 87, 90ff, 94, 98f, 339f). The most precise overview can be found in his introduction to the *General Economic History* (Weber 1995). This was the first work of Weber to be translated into English, in 1927. Unfortunately, the translator thought, wrongly, that "[t]he highly technical introduction . . . [had been] prepared by the German editors" rather than Weber himself (Winckelmann 1958, cited in Weber 2011b: 9; own translation), and it was therefore left out of the English edition.
2. I use the terms ethos/ethic/ethical and morality/moral interchangeably. However, German philosophy distinguishes between *Moral* (referring to what is regarded as good or bad, right or wrong, in lived experiences) and *Ethik* (reflections on or explicit prescriptions—e.g., in organizational codes of conduct—about what *should* be regarded as good or bad, right or wrong).
3. This coinage is inspired by Habermas's formulation of a "positivistically bisected rationalism" (*positivistisch halbierter Rationalismus*), which he used in the positivism dispute (*Positivismusstreit*) to criticize the methodology of Karl Popper and Hans Albert.
4. https://www.halle.de/de/Kultur/Stadtgeschichte/Beruehmte-Personen/Martin-Luther/Reformationsjubilaeum/Jubilaeumsjahr/index.aspx | https://www.luther2017.de/de/erleben/staedte/halle-saale/index.html (last accessed 10 July 2020).
5. This is based on a dictionary specification of minimal conditions for "subsistence level" (*Existenzminimum*). See https://www.bpb.de/nachschlagen/lexika/lexikon-der-wirtschaft/19557/grundbeduerfnisse (last accessed 13 July 2020).
6. This questionnaire was used in the larger project group "RealEurasia: Moral Economy and Civilization in the 21st century." The business owners in my sample in Halle filled out the questionnaire on their own, and some of their answers will be found in the analysis above. However, the bulk of my data comes from the interviews and informal conversations I had with them in 2016 and 2017.
7. According to the last census in 2011, more than 80 percent of Halle's inhabitants are not affiliated to any religious denomination. Roughly 11 percent belong to the Evangelical Church, and 4 percent to the Catholic Church. https://ergebnisse.zensus2011.de/#StaticContent:150020000000,BEG_4_2_6,m,table (last accessed 14 July 2020).
8. There is some truth to this observation, because the proportion of young people with an *Abitur* and who then proceed to college has increased continuously over the last decades.
9. In fact, the proportion of representatives in the German Bundestag with an academic degree constantly increased over the years, and reached around 90 percent in 2009. Of the 709 representatives in the current Bundestag, only 9 have vocational training in the skilled crafts, while 115 have a background in law. https://www.mpifg.de/forschung/forschung/themen/schaefer_akademikerrepublik.asp | https://www.sueddeutsche.de/politik/neuer-bundestag-das-sind-deutschlands-volksvertreter-1.3720219 (last accessed 5 June 2020).

References

Brubaker, Rogers. 1984. *The Limits of Rationality*. London: Routledge.

Douglas, Mary. 1985. *Risk Acceptability According to the Social Sciences*. New York: Russell Sage Foundation.

Lutz, Burkhart, et al. 2004. *Jugend—Ausbildung—Arbeit: Bildung und Beschäftigung in Ostdeutschland Band 2*. Berlin: Berliner Debatte Wissenschaftsverlag.

Moeran, Brian, and Timothy de Waal Malefyt. 2018. *Magical Capitalism: Enchantment, Spells, and Occult Practices in Contemporary Economies*. Cham: Palgrave Macmillan.

Polanyi, Karl. 2018. "On Freedom." In *Karl Polanyi's Vision of a Socialist Transformation*, ed. Michael Brie and Claus Thomasberger, 298–319. Montreal: Black Rose Books.

Schwinn, Thomas. 1998. "Wertsphären, Lebensordnungen und Lebensführungen." In *Verantwortliches Handeln in gesellschaftlichen Ordnungen*, ed. Agathe Bienfait and Gerhard Wagner, 270–319. Frankfurt/Main: Suhrkamp.

Streeck, Wolfgang. 2011. "Taking Capitalism Seriously: Towards an Institutionalist Approach to Contemporary Political Economy." *Socio-Economic Review* 9(1): 137–67.

———. 2012. "How to Study Contemporary Capitalism?" *European Journal of Sociology/ Archives Européennes de Sociologie* 53(1): 1–28.

Swedberg, Richard. 2005. *The Max Weber Dictionary: Key Words and Central Concepts*. Stanford, CA: Stanford University Press.

Terpe, Sylvia. 2009. *Ungerechtigkeit und Duldung: Die Deutung sozialer Ungleichheit und das Ausbleiben von Protest*. Konstanz: Universitätsverlag.

———. 2016. "Max Weber's 'Spheres of Life': A Tool for Micro-sociological Analysis." *Working Papers* 179. Halle (Saale): Max Planck Institute for Social Anthropology.

———. 2016. "Working with Max Weber's 'Spheres of Life': An Actor-Centred Approach." *Journal of Classical Sociology* 20(1): 22–42.

Weber, Max. 1978. *Economy and Society*. Trans. Talcott Parsons. Berkeley: University of California Press.

———. 1992. *The Protestant Ethic and the Spirit of Capitalism*. Trans. Talcott Parsons. London: Routledge.

———. 1995. *General Economic History*. Trans. Frank H. Knight. New Brunswick, NJ: Transaction Books.

———. 2011a. *The Protestant Ethic and the Spirit of Capitalism*. The Revised 1920 Edition. Trans. and introduced by Stephen Kalberg. Oxford: Oxford University Press.

———. 2011b. *Wirtschaftsgeschichte: Abriß der universalen Sozial- und Wirtschaftsgeschichte*. Berlin: Duncker & Humblot.

———. 2019. *Economy and Society. A New Translation*. Ed. and trans. by Keith Tribe. Cambridge, MA: Harvard University Press.

Wuthnow, Robert. 1987. *Meaning and Moral Order: Explorations in Cultural Analysis*. Berkeley: University of California Press.

9

Click for Work

Rethinking Freedom through Online Work Distribution Platforms

ILANA GERSHON AND MELISSA CEFKIN

Introduction

Work distribution platforms such as Uber or Amazon's Mechanical Turk change how work is distributed, and thus encourage people to examine anew how work is defined and allocated. These platforms allow work to be distributed by "open calls" rather than by assignment or predefined job role requirements and commonly involve crowdwork and open-source principles. They provide structures that significantly alter how work is organized, significantly enough to require that users re-examine what forms of social organization can and should accompany work. Many view these platforms as harnessing new imaginaries of collaborative engagement. They allow participants to operate as if they do not have to subject themselves to a job position whose commitments and activities they may not wish to perform. That is, they offer a neoliberal take on an age-old question at the heart of work and organization studies: Why would workers agree to subordinate themselves to others? (Boltanski and Chiapello 2005; cf. Burawoy 1979; Weeks 2011). These platforms offer workers the chance to imagine themselves as autonomous entrepreneurial selves, and thus reply to this age-old question: "I don't have to."

Inspired by observations of several work platforms, in this chapter we indicate how online work platforms operate in contexts where neoliberal logics prevail. We explore what happens to work that is performed through these mechanisms. While there is great diversity in platform structures, the chapter provides a conceptual framework for analyzing the broad commonalities. These platforms do not merely extend existing work processes through piecework. They transform how tasks are classified, made distinct, and performed.

In what follows, we first problematize work distribution platforms as exposing a contradiction at the heart of neoliberalism—that between the entrepreneurial self and the structure of the firm. We then provide a framework for seeing the commonalities that underlie the platform economy. This framework is constituted by crowdwork and open-work experiments and efforts that take place wholly inside the confines of a large corporation. These platforms are not exclusively geared towards externalizing labor. Drawing on observations of these experiments, we specify three ways in which work is being reshaped through use of these mechanisms: (1) the design of work; (2) the dissemination of and access to work; and (3) the control, management, and authority over work. While online work distribution platforms change the organization of work, these work practices are informed, as we will discuss in the conclusion, by participants' own neoliberal perspective on work, which projects a tension between autonomy and firm efficiencies.

Problematizing Work

One of the hallmarks of neoliberalism, according to its critics, is that the self is an entrepreneurial self (Rose 1998; Foucault 2004; Gershon 2011). Yet that claim, that the neoliberal self is an entrepreneurial self or is to be treated as an investment, is a bit vague. The term does not explain which parts of being a business translate into being a human from a neoliberal perspective. We need a more rigorous definition of the neoliberal self as a bundle of skills, assets, experiences, qualities, and alliances—a bundle that should be continually managed and improved (Gershon 2011, 2017). When this self is in a relationship with others, the relationship is a contractual one in which the work that this metaphorical contract supposedly accomplishes is to ensure that risk and responsibility are equitably distributed. In practice, the question of what precisely is equitable is often contested.

By enabling participants to imagine themselves as entrepreneurial selves, work distribution platforms create a peculiarly neoliberal contradiction between the entrepreneurial self, as described by Foucault, and the benefits of the firm, as imagined by influential economists such as Ronald Coase (1937).[1] Accepting the general neoliberal assumption that markets are the ideal form of social order, Coase asked: As corporations do not operate internally according to market principles, why do firms exist in the first place? He concluded that firms can lower "transaction costs" through the managerial organization of production, thus making them economically superior to the market for certain purposes (Coase 1937; see also Benkler 2002). In short, there is a tension between the strong appeal of not having a boss, and the efficiencies of the firm. This tension becomes visible when we analyze how the platform economy reorganizes work.

While open-call work distribution is not a new phenomenon (for historical examples, see Nelson 1990; Scholliers and Schwarz 2003), online platforms validate Benkler's prescient insight that the digital can transform the firm/market distinctions drawn by Coase (Benkler 2002). The appeal of work distribution platforms is grounded in neoliberal sensibilities that encourage workers to view themselves as businesses in their own right. While these platforms align themselves well with contemporary ideological shifts in concepts of work, they undercut many of the solutions evolved by firms to resolve the practical dilemmas of working with others. As we show, these platforms encapsulate a contradiction that is internal to neoliberalism, counterposing the ideal of autonomy with Coase's rationale for a firm's existence. Thus, these systems force all participants to revisit questions of coordination, cooperation, and collaboration with others.

Work Distribution Platforms

The expansion of the platform economy since the turn of the century enables tasks of tremendously varied scope to be tendered. Work distribution platforms allow both work requesters and work seekers to opt in to soliciting and selecting work assignments. Work assignments are made available broadly, rather than being assigned due to an organizational position. They use a range of market mechanisms as contractual forms, from fixed-price bids to auctions to contests, and may include traditional hourly or salaried pay or outcome-based work (pay for results). We focus on open-call systems that rely on internet-based mechanisms to function. Depending on the platform, participants respond by claiming tasks, applying to be selected to perform work, or submitting results to a simple request or a contest. Some systems, such as Mechanical Turk and Topcoder, only support digital work. But not all the work performed is digital. For instance, through Task Rabbit people can find others nearby to perform chores—helping cook for a party, or assembling furniture. Participatory systems common to citizen science efforts enable volunteers to use telescopes or other instruments to gather data on the skies, waters, or soils. In some systems the work is performed as a crowd, involving degrees of coordinated action. In others, any given effort can be performed singularly. Nonetheless, even when offline work occurs, the work distribution, contracting, and communication about tasks take place online. The platform economy promises workers the freedom to work when, where, and on what they like.

These platforms vary widely in the nature of the task being distributed (Doan, Ramakrishnan, and Halevy 2011). Online marketplaces such as Upwork and Freelancer.com act as intermediaries to match work projects requiring certain skills with specific producers, such as getting legal work performed or software code written. Mechanical Turk is known for its decomponentization of work into tiny bits, or microtasks such as translating ten words. Microtasks can be disseminated, claimed, and performed by people worldwide within minutes. At the other end of the spectrum, InnoCentive and Kaggle provide platforms through which other enterprises seek to solve large, complex challenges by soliciting submissions to contests. Even crowdfunding plays into these dynamics. People can identify work they would like to see undertaken, such as producing an artwork, and at the same time solicit investment in the form of others' time and money to get it done.

Work distribution platforms change how the workplace functions as a forum for facilitating connective action. Platform-driven work acts to transcend and even displace traditional occupational communities and forms of workplace sociality engendered by organizations—forms that affect workers' experiences both positively and negatively. Participation in intra-organizational crowdwork and open-call work initiatives has prompted participants to reflect on their identity at work (Cefkin, Obinna, and Moore 2014). It also puts into relief for workers their relative commonality with, or distance from, fellow workers. To a significant degree, online work platforms provide an infrastructure to create the type of workplace communities that some of the intellectual founders of neoliberalism looked to the market to fashion on a larger scale. Friedrich Hayek, among others, believed the market could create shifting and impermanent allegiances based on momentary needs (Hayek 1939). Neoliberals dreamed of a global market, one without borders or tariffs, in order to undermine historical commitments to a region and a people. Hayek was deeply concerned that nationalism, and even emotional commitments to neighbors, had created the political problems of his day, notably fascism. In describing the negative consequences of nationalism, he wrote:

> Such economic frontiers create communities of interest on a regional basis and of a most intimate character: they bring it about that all conflicts of interests tend to become conflicts between the same groups of people, instead of conflicts between groups of constantly varying composition, and that there will in consequence be perpetual conflicts between the inhabitants of a state as such instead of between the various individuals finding themselves arrayed, sometimes with one group of people

against another, and at other times on another issue with the second group against the first. (Hayek 1939: 132)

A global market in its ideal form would make it as likely that an agent would feel a strong tie (albeit an economic one) to someone halfway around the world as to a neighbor. He acknowledged that it was inevitable that communities would form through events, but he believed that a global market could shift the ways in which people commit to their neighbors by promoting cross-cutting ties across different locales. Neoliberalism is supposed to create alliances based on market advantage, and because of the way that the market works to order the world, these alliances will inevitably be temporary. The platform economy introduces this vision of temporary and economically grounded connections into the firm itself.

Yet these platforms do not inherently undermine firms' boundaries. They can also be used internally among full-time employees. Open-call work distribution is not synonymous with freelancing per se. These platforms can, but do not inevitably, lead to shedding jobs from companies and a freelancer market. Our cases in the following section are drawn from inside IBM. Yet even when firm boundaries remain in place, the platforms potentially undermine the "transactions costs" argument of Coase by introducing market mechanisms for distributing work.

A Framework for Analyzing Work in Online Distribution Platforms

In this section we outline the features of work on these platforms, focusing on three general components: (1) work design; (2) dissemination and access to work; and (3) authority and control. Before we elaborate on these three components, we briefly introduce the ethnographic material that informs our analysis.

Ethnographic Inspirations

The framework that we propose in this chapter has been informed by studies that Cefkin conducted with colleagues at IBM. They participated in several projects that experimented with intra-organizational crowdwork. Three projects in particular inform our narrative. One was a crowd-funding initiative run in a corporate research lab. Lab members were granted a (virtual) sum of money that they could use individually to invest in projects proposed by their peers in a custom-designed platform that supported similar actions to the Kickstarter platform. Cefkin and her colleagues studied how the project unfolded, including participants' experiences as both proposers and investors.

The second project was a crowdwork system primarily for executing technical work such as software development. The system was designed to support work components expected to take between half a day and seven days of effort. Participants responded to open requests with bids on how they would accomplish the work and naming a "price." Workers throughout the company could participate, along with vetted external contract workers. Internal workers were encouraged to see this as a chance to further develop their skills or to fill unused time (such as during a code-freeze in a development team). External workers were paid real dollars.

The third project was a "marketplace" designed for peer-to-peer work exchange. Any participant could post a request and others could offer to perform the work. The system was deployed among a select community of workers in the company—those trained in organizational change management methods. Cefkin and her colleagues designed and helped support the pilot of the system using user-centered design approaches.

Cefkin and her colleagues conducted over fifty interviews with individual participants (by phone, or in person where possible). They also observed meetings in which initiative leaders discussed plans and statuses, reviewed documentation, and followed informal exchanges about the efforts when possible. Fieldnotes and/or meeting and interview transcripts were kept by researchers and analyzed in the context of the applied research projects. In addition to sharing the numerous conference presentations and publications that resulted from these efforts inside IBM with Gershon, Cefkin re-examined these data, observations and analyses in conversation with Gershon, and the present chapter is the result of our collaboration.

Shifting How Work Is Designed

We see work requesters—people who turn to these platforms to have work performed—as themselves essential workers in the system. They must fashion a vision of the work that allows it to be accomplished through the system's mechanisms. This means considering how tasks are made into distinct units, as well as how they are to be segmented and how the resulting products will travel and be recombined. The platforms give rise to new ways of designing work, either by componentizing it, or, alternatively, by shifting to more holistically assembled larger parts—an aspect often overlooked by critics (Anya 2015). Contest mechanisms enable requesters to specify desired results, freeing themselves up from identifying the parts of the work, or even knowing what the parts are. The requesters leave it up to those who will perform the work to assemble or disassemble as they see fit. In engaging with this necessity to divide up tasks in new ways, workers could be understood as seeing the workplace more and more from the vantage point of an optimizing business.

When studying a crowdwork system for software development, Cefkin and her colleagues found that figuring out how to get quality work done was complicated by dilemmas emerging from the intricacies of segmenting work. This is part of the invisible work of making crowdwork happen, and the downside of introducing market mechanisms into the firm (Cefkin et al. 2014; Anya 2015). There is effort involved in specifying a request for unknown workers, especially when the work has to be performed in a specific way, such as some software development where strict standards and security protocols must be adhered to. Requesters cannot assume shared understandings about what terms mean or what the typical processes should be (Suchman 1995). As one work requester succinctly explained: "To a retained team member I can simply say, 'scramble an egg,' whereas to a [crowdwork system] player, I have to say, 'open the refrigerator,' 'remove the egg carton,' 'open the egg carton,' 'remove one egg,' and so on.

System users felt that every possible aspect of performing the tasks needed to be elaborated to get satisfactory results, forcing the worker requesting the task to perform work that he or she would not previously have been required to perform.

Work at a distance (whether geographically, temporally, or conceptually) often surprises participants with areas of knowledge and perception that turn out to have locally specific meanings in moments when universal understandings had been expected (Bailey, Leonardi and Barley 2012; Guesling 2013; Moore et al. 2014). For example, the seemingly straightforward task of extracting addresses from a set of data could reveal tacit assumptions. One work requester needed data for integration into a mass emailing, but because she failed to make clear its purpose or the preferred form of delivery in the work specs, the results she got back were not properly formatted for her email system. They had to be significantly reworked, nearly negating any financial benefit from outsourcing the task. Members of her local team would have known why she wanted this information and anticipated the best way of providing the desired results. This example illustrates that scrambled eggs are never just scrambled eggs. Scrambled eggs could be for breakfast or for mixing into an emulsifier. They can be prepared hard or soft, plain or salted. Work activities are always already embedded in systems of meaning. Introducing work distribution platforms within existing systems of work disrupts those meanings. People have to conceptualize and design work in new ways when unknown workers, with their own worlds of experience and knowledge, are involved.

Segmenting tasks in new ways also has some upsides. In their study of the peer-to-peer work exchange for organizational change management tasks, for example, Cefkin and her colleagues found that many participants viewed their chance to do work through the system as an opportunity to learn something new, venturing outside their regular tasks as fixed by their workplaces' hierarchical and role-based division of work. This resonates with neoliberal corporate discourses advocating that workers should always be on the lookout for opportunities to enhance their skills. Yet the platforms often thwart the users' hopes by not providing transportable evidence that the user has acquired a skill and is thus better qualified to be hired outside the platform. One needs to be able to document that one has learned these skills in an appropriate and circulatable form (see Gershon 2017).

Workers could at times creatively combine their existing knowledge and experience—in many instances, knowledge and experience that requesters were unaware they possessed—with the work that was requested. For example, one participant recognized that the task she signed up to complete, surveying the adoption of a new program, would not be complete without a communication plan, something she felt especially excited to work on.[2] In consultation with the requester, she expanded her scope to include that. During the crowdfunding effort, a scientist who was also a hobby fruit grower attempted to bolster a proposed project to create an employee garden by suggesting technologies and practices for soil improvement and watering.

Segmenting work in new ways potentially creates new roles in the workplace. Media scholars have long observed that new technologies give rise to new professions—telephone operators in the case of telephones (Fischer 1992) or stenographers in the case of institutional shorthand machines (Kittler 1990; Inoue 2011). Work platforms are no exception. Depending on how the platform is organized, these platforms can be accompanied by people specializing in digital dispute resolution or evaluation, although they are not always recognized or remunerated (Gillespie 2010). When tasks are distributed in new ways, roles often emerge to assist participants in coordinating these new tasks, and addressing problems that spring up throughout the process.

As these examples suggest, platforms encourage their users to engage with work as a conscious arrangement of tasks, which can be segmented and recombined in various ways. Determining just where a task starts and ends is work that both requesters and those performing the work have to face—should the task include removing the eggs from the carton or should that be a separate task for another worker? Might an adoption plan include a plan for communications too, or is that work that does not need to be done at all? When focusing on how tasks are segmented, requesters also have to anticipate future uses of the results—some results will travel differently or combine in more limited ways than others. They have to develop new strategies for planning work and for envisioning the directions through which the work will circulate (Bailey et al. 2012). New forms of segmented tasks can also lead to unexpected consequences—previously unidentified talents might come to the fore and new work roles emerge (Mikolajewska-Zajac 2016). In practice, work platforms do not simply connect work requesters and work performers in new ways: they challenge all involved to think anew about how tasks are segmented and combined in ways that transform all elements of how work is conceptualized and performed. They engage participants, in other words, as if they themselves were a business and in control of planning work. This brings the experience of operating as if oneself were a business into the performance of even mundane tasks, and redefines the efficiencies a firm offers.

Transforming the Dissemination of and Access to Work

One of the defining features of work distribution platforms is the open-call approach—announcing tasks broadly for people to select and apply for. This mechanism overtly changes how work is disseminated and who can access it. Airbnb allows homeowners to become hoteliers. Uber allows non-professional drivers to work as drivers using their own cars. People are encouraged to imagine themselves as bundles of assets that they can bring to the marketplace—including people whose work opportunities have been highly constrained. Thus, Samasource directs work from Mechanical Turk to poor women, youths, and residents in refugee camps who are less likely to find work, and who may even be barred from local work opportunities (Fish and Srinivasan 2011).

Even within organizations, these mechanisms provide access to work that people might not otherwise have the opportunity to do. Cefkin participated in designing and testing a system for exchanging work among dispersed and loosely affiliated employees interested in organizational change management, a human resource allied practice that uses principles and theories from the behavioral and social sciences to guide people in organizations through transitions. Although it is an increasingly professionalizing field, few dedicated positions for change management specialists exist. The work exchange platform was designed to extend opportunities for performing change management related tasks. Participation was voluntary, and often motivated by the chance to do uncommon work. A participant in China explained that change management had barely taken hold in China and the work exchange was providing her with a chance to work on tasks directed to other parts of the world. She saw it as a chance to advance her knowledge and experience, while using her time in a way that would be viewed as productive.[3] However, as a part of the company consulting division responsible for billable hours, she ran up against the limits of the platform, which did not allow her to be compensated on a par with her billable client work. When this member stopped participating, she acted from the same anxiety many consultants feel when too much "unbilled" time makes them liable to be laid off. This illustrates how bringing market logic into the firm undercuts the benefits of the Coasian firm, not encouraging companies or workers to develop knowledge for addressing sporadic problems.

From the perspective of those disseminating the work, work distribution platforms enable work to be performed that requestors would not know how to perform, or would not have the capacity to do so. More kinds of work are carried out by "strangers," people with whom we have little or no knowledge or contact. At some level this is nothing new—few people know who drove the trucks that delivered the food they buy at a supermarket. But these mechanisms transform the relationship to that "stranger." Anyone using a crowdwork system can commission a complete stranger to build a website, or arrange a travel itinerary. They may be known only by an online alias, if specified at all. This puts into sharp relief questions of qualification and the adequacy of training. Can you trust your Uber driver? Will the worker you are hiring understand exactly what "scramble the eggs" means?

Despite being premised on stranger-interactions, sustained connections do develop over time, both among workers (Martin et al. 2014; Salehi et al. 2015; Gray et al. 2016) and between workers and requesters. Cefkin observed a particularly interesting discussion among work requesters in the crowdwork platform she studied, who met weekly to discuss successes and challenges in using the system. Workers in the system used account names rather than real names.[4] In one discussion, a manager raised an issue: the results she received from a crowdworker were incomplete. Based on prior experience with this worker (known by his screen name), she felt certain that this was a simple error; the worker had uploaded the wrong document. When she shared his account name, others agreed based on their own prior positive interactions with this worker. All became concerned as she indicated that repeated messages to him through the system were going unanswered. Might something have happened to him? Might he have meanwhile gotten a full-time job and "left" the platform? Might he be sick? Was there anyone who could find out who he (really) was and where he lived, and check on him? Platform users quickly began to imagine a wider set of obligations, because someone had begun to act in ways perceived as deviating from their previous platform-mediated interactions. They were quickly stymied in their efforts to act on these obligations because the ways that the platform offered information made off-platform interaction difficult, if not altogether impossible.[5]

For many, the promise of these platforms is that the distribution of work will be less biased. As a speaker in a panel discussion on work distribution platforms expressed hopefully: "It's about the work, it's not about whose ass I kiss around the water cooler." But this introduces uncertainty. One participant in the change management work exchange said: "I don't know their background. They don't know mine . . . So it was kind of a leap of faith." Later she added: "It's very rare for me to work with someone who has no idea of who I am. That's very brave of them." This participant was reflecting on how much courage she felt it took to work with someone without having met them directly, with only the briefest of communication, and without having been specifically selected into, and vetted by, the manager's organization—precisely the actions that can lead to systematic biases in hiring and work distribution.

The reality is complicated by system design elements and practices in using the systems, which can function to create new biases.[6] Timing, for instance, can create imbalances in terms of who gets preferred access to work opportunities. In systems with global participation, it is not uncommon for new work requests to be opened during working hours. To the extent that a large portion of requests originate from the United States, this is more advantageous to those working in the US time zones, because there is often a bias towards the first to respond. Workers in other time zones may adjust their work schedules in the hope of accessing preferred gigs by working nights, thus creating disjuncture with their local settings.[7] This can be addressed by changing the system's design: but if some jobs are released at other times, a reverse bias might be created. As Graham and Anwar (2018) explain: "Clients located primarily in high-income countries can force workers from around the world (in rich and poor countries) to compete with one another in a giant labor market."

Participation is heavily guided, in most cases, through profiles and reputation systems. This too can introduce imbalances into who secures preferred participation. For instance, frequent and longer-serving performers benefit from prior experience in the system, which produces greater measurable traces of activity. It can be a challenge for newcomers to gain entry, while those with less frequently called-on skills and experience may be made less visible. Algorithms guide the selection of where and how to place inputs to the system. They determine, for example, which edits to prioritize in the event of changes to an entry in a crowdsourced resource such as Wikipedia, or which item to rank at the top of a list. Numerous factors may be used in the design of the algorithms, but most include an element of frequency or density of prior activity.

The platform economy is reputed to transform who has access to opportunities to work. Supposedly the platforms create a form of equality—anyone willing and able to work can earn money through these platforms, and anyone willing to pay has access to work. Because connections are made virtually (and thus there is little information available about the offline identities), biases based on gender, age, race, or religion are that much harder to enact. It is not only that strangers are contracting with strangers, but little is known about these strangers other than their willingness to work or their willingness to pay for work.

The fantasy is that this will be a marketplace operating without the social ways in which people fashion identity. Ethnographic research reveals how complicated enacting this ideal can be (Lampinen et al. 2015; Schor et al. 2015). Interactions between strangers can change rapidly as people develop relationships through working together, relationships that the platform's structure can end up thwarting. While platforms can provide new paths towards connecting work requestors and work providers, the work still needs to be performed and evaluated as work that was done well or not. Here the objective promise of a metric reputation can be at odds with how workers interact with each other to build up a history through common, intersubjective experiences. As platforms encourage evaluations to accrue, added barriers to newcomers emerge. Some workers begin to feel tied to the platform, anchored because they have accrued a metric reputation that does not transfer easily to other platforms, a contrast with résumés that enable workers to transfer to another job. Stranger interactions come with their own social conundrums, and the solutions to these conundrums may have complicated and unpredictable social consequences. While neoliberal ideals of a relatively unconstrained free market of business-to-business relations dominate, undercutting the advantages of a firm makes trying to operate through purely transactional norms of business hard to realize and even harder to sustain.

Reorganizing Control, Management, and Authority

Open-call work platforms potentially enable a wider range of participants to engage in tasks than traditional forms of hierarchical control allow. These platforms have spawned a range of contractual terms, thereby changing how work is controlled and managed.

In many ways, work requesters maintain strong control over what the work is and how it is performed. This is supported by a number of mechanisms designed into the systems. The platforms may enable requestors to specify procedures that workers are required to follow closely. Typically, the smaller the task, the more constrained the means of performing it. They may include built-in tracking systems for monitoring time-on-tasks, as UpWork does. Indeed, comments in the discussion forums that commonly accompany these platforms have frequently referred to its big-brotherly presence. Another means of retaining control is allowing requestors to determine the terms on which final results are accepted. One risk to workers in contest and micro-task work sites is that people will perform the work, but then experience its rejection, often with little or no explanation. Dispute settlement is often problematic (Irani and Silberman 2013). Some systems, such as the technical crowdwork platform that Cefkin and her colleagues studied, are designed to encourage transparent acceptance and rejection policies, and provide processes for appeal. While potentially increasing fairness, these elements also significantly increase the effort required of work requesters to manage work through the system. They demand that requesters specify all potential aspects of the work that could affect acceptance ("whoops, I failed to indicate that the egg needed to be removed from the carton before scrambling . . .") and the criteria for evaluation, exceeding the taken-for-granted understanding workers develop in face-to-face relations.

These risks are also present outside the platform economy. Entrepreneurs have always had to deal with breaches of contract, chase clients for payment, and listen to inadequate explanations as to why work was rejected. The short duration and/or limited scope of work in the platform economy may be appreciated by some participants because the opportunities and risks are widely spread. This ability to select and assemble a range of opportunities is considered one of the upsides to these systems. Workers claim a sense of control over how their work is evaluated by avoiding an excessive "lock" into any specific client.

When workers are able to select their work, managerial regimes of authority can be threatened. Management is a system for commanding resources, including employees' time and efforts. Systems that invite employees to choose freely what work they want to spend time on destabilize the old hierarchies. There were a number of questions sparked by these changes that Cefkin and her colleagues faced in helping design the work marketplace for change management professionals. Should managers participate in their staff members' selections, and if so how? Should a manager be asked to give explicit approval per work task, and if so, should the system be designed not to move a bid forward without manager approval? Should a manager be notified of an employee's participation, but be left without any means to voice support or disapproval of the employee's effort within the system? Or should the manager not be notified at all?[8]

Reputation mechanisms are one of the most direct forms of control built into these platforms. They are used to identify participants, and to measure their activity. Objective measures and subjective assessments of performances may not be similarly represented. A senior HR partner in the division sponsoring the work at IBM acknowledged that people's own assessments of their performance mattered. And yet, the metrics used in most systems were designed toward objective measures, such as task completion rate and accuracy. A large number of reputation mechanisms are used across the platforms, from subjective evaluations of approval, such as the styles of ratings or "liking" on sites such as Yelp, to measured participation rates. For workers, these ratings can signal the number of tasks applied for, selected for, completed, on-time work, and so on. Echoing what Cefkin and her team found in the crowdwork system for technical work, Martin et al. argue that reputation mechanisms often create hidden work for those completing tasks on Amazon Mechanical Turk: "Reputation management tactics are often defensive, and the Turker shoulders the potential cost of the practice. These practices include ensuring they can do the work before accepting it, specializing in known tasks for specific requesters, getting training on tasks from co-workers, ensuring the completion code would load, and so on" (Martin et al. 2014: 10).

Currently, workers bear the brunt of negotiating that reputation mechanisms work smoothly. When interviewing participants of the work marketplace, for instance, Cefkin and colleagues at times encountered participants who were anxious about their reputation measures, and hoped that her team could intercede to ensure that faulty measures could be rectified. One participant in India, who had taken on a task for a US-based interest, shared that a task had been "miss-characterized" by the work requester. In fact, the work performed by the worker met the need, even though the system marked it as a "miss." He claimed that the work requester was aware of the problem and agreed that the work was satisfactory, but the system trailed in showing an accurate measure, thus making it appear that his overall performance was below standard. He worried this meant he would be passed over in his pursuit of additional tasks until the problem was rectified. This is not, however, a necessary feature of these platforms, that the burden of reputation management falls almost entirely on the requestor. On a number of platforms, it is also possible for work requesters to be rated according to their responsiveness, effectiveness in specifying work, and other criteria.[9]

Reputation mechanisms are the most blatant of several ways in which work distribution platforms use market demand and competition to discipline workers (Rosenblat and Stark 2016). Workers are still being controlled and disciplined, but because this occurs through technological platforms that reallocate and often obfuscate where the source of control might be located, workers have trouble determining who is responsible for what, and thus need to develop strategies to locate responsibility to change working conditions and/or the payment system of the platform economy (Irani and Silberman 2013; Irani 2015; Crawford 2016). The autonomy these platforms seem to promise becomes elusive in the process. These shifts in how work is controlled, and how it is harnessed through the shape and design of the work distribution systems, raise concerns about fairness as well as freedom. They can reinvigorate debates on the relationship of workers to their work, to their co-workers, and to their bosses.

Conclusion

Open-call platforms, almost by definition, remove certain hierarchical relationships found in most workplaces. The supervisor no longer assigns jobs; instead, workers select for themselves the tasks they want to do. They may even make requests of others to do work for them. Champions of these platforms view this as providing more autonomy to workers and allowing them to enter into more equitable relationships with each other. In this perspective, a temporally bound contract stands in for equity (Malone 2004; Kittur et al. 2013). That workers are continuously choosing the work they do, and may even in turn "outsource" tasks to others, is seen as evidence that they are working as equals among individuals also able to select tasks and structure their time on their own terms.

Here the classic liberal fantasy of the freedom of the contract underlies the hope that open-call platforms displace hierarchy. Social scientists have long understood that neither the temporary contract (however short) nor any technological infrastructure (such as the ones that support open calls) can in themselves be harbingers of autonomy or equity. These can only arise from the beliefs and routinized practices shaping the use of technologies and the implementation of contracts. A platform's structure is too underdetermined to produce freedom or equity on its own—understandings of work, obligation, and freedom inform how participants will interact with these platforms, and thus with each other.

Open-call work distribution platforms have entered the scene at a moment in which neoliberal logics dominate how many people understand ideal work relationships. The developers typically promise that these platforms will encourage work relationships based on the autonomy and equity that one supposedly has when the employment contract is viewed as a business-to-business contract. Some platforms, such as Uber and Lyft, make this central to their legal defense when workers sue them for misclassification. They argue that they are not a firm providing transportation services, but rather a technology company enabling small business owners, their drivers, to connect to customers (Tomasetti 2016). These neoliberal takes on autonomy and equity are not inherent to the platforms. Rather, the platform economy is underdetermined enough that many different practices coexist. Yet these possibilities are often limited by organizational infrastructures already in place, and by neoliberal understandings of how cooperation and work distribution should occur. This results in a tension between the promise of workers' autonomy and the efficiencies that a firm promises. This tension then shapes how these platforms are integrated into established work processes, influenced by users and companies' beliefs, organizational routines, and material infrastructures surrounding appropriate work relationships.

The neoliberal framing can obfuscate the multiple ways in which these platforms reorganize work, both within and outside of firms. The platform economy leads users back to perennial questions about authority, control, and the nature of tasks. As these platforms reshape the social organization of work, they bring the market into the firm in ways that undercut what neoliberal theorists themselves have previously understood to be the benefits of managerial controlled production. This creates social dilemmas for participants that must be resolved—how should one best segment or recombine a set of tasks; and how does one evaluate the work or the worker? Many of the solutions that have emerged to address these dilemmas end up reinscribing older problems that people have had with work, in new packages (Suchman and Bishop 2000: 331). Our data show how discipline, surveillance, and competition continue to shape how workers are controlled in these systems, albeit now enabled through marketplace interactions that frame competition as a means to discipline and define workers.

As new ways of distributing work become possible, people have to develop new skills for coordinating with strangers, and new techniques for circulating information and arranging tasks to accommodate a greater fluidity in who participates in particular work projects. This often involves erasing the benefits that Coase (1937) believed firms offered. As getting work done shifts away from a work contract that revolves around command and obedience, people still have to address the problems of coordination that are omnipresent in any project: planning the work, disseminating the work, and then controlling the work process. Since this is a fundamentally social task, when the principal conceptual resources people have for thinking about these processes are variants of a neoliberal logic, the solutions developed often encourage a belief that all engaged in this work process should be treated as businesses in their own right.

Acknowledgments

We would like to thank Chris Hann and Ekaterina Chertkovskaya for their thoughtful editorial suggestions, and *Ephemera* for publishing an earlier version of this argument. We also wish to thank Hamid Ekbia, Lilly Irani, and Julia Tomasetti for all their input. We owe a special debt of gratitude to Obinna Anya, Robert Moore, and all of Melissa Cefkin's former colleagues, as well as the participants in these early work distribution platforms.

Ilana Gershon is the Ruth N. Hall professor of anthropology at Indiana University. She studies how people use new media to accomplish complicated social tasks, such as breaking up or hiring. She has written three monographs: *The Breakup 2.0: Disconnecting over New Media* (Cornell, 2010); *No Family Is an Island: Cultural Expertise among Samoans in Diaspora* (Cornell, 2012); and *Down and Out in the New Economy: How People Find (or Don't Find) Work Today* (Chicago, 2017). She also has edited *A World of Work: Imagined Manuals for Real Jobs* (Cornell, 2015), and co-edited with Natalie Porter the volume *Living with Animals: Bonds across Species* (Cornell, 2018).

Melissa Cefkin is a principal scientist and manager at the Alliance Innovation Lab Silicon Valley, where her work focuses on potential futures with highly automated and connected vehicles as interactive agents in the world. A Fulbright award grantee, and the author of numerous publications including *Ethnography and the Corporate Encounter* (Berghahn Books, 2009), Dr. Cefkin remains active in professional service, serving in a variety of professional leadership roles for the National Academies of Science and the EPIC (Ethnographic Praxis in Industry Conference) organization, among others.

Notes

1. By engaging with Coase, we depart from much of the Foucauldian scholarship on the entrepreneurial self by asking how this self operates in relation to a corporation (for other exceptions, see Swan and Fox 2009).
2. This was only possible because of the platform's affordances; not all platforms allow this.
3. Other participants, too, referenced the resume-building skills gained by participating in the system.

4. A number of work distribution platforms use the approach of screen names. One reason is the wish to avoid identifiers that could lead to bias. Another is to ensure that all activity has to happen through the system itself. Interactions brokered by the system but that move outside the system can no longer be monitored for their acquiescence to the terms of engagement. Salehi et al. (2015) describes having to address the implied risk by designing in additional layers of anonymity to their Dynamo system, a community system developed to facilitate collective action by Turkers to protect any other Turker.
5. See Lampinen, Hotari, and Cheshire (2015) for another example of how anonymity on a platform affected offline interactions, and how people used the platform.
6. See Schor et al. (2015) for a discussion of class bias in these systems.
7. See Aneesh (2006) for a discussion of the lived consequences of the "temporal dissonance" created by efforts to create temporal integration across time zones.
8. Cefkin and her team, together with their stakeholders, recommended the second option, notification, on the assumption that this would lead to improved direct communication between employees and management.
9. Arvidsson (2014) explores the potential of such reputation mechanisms to signal not only workers' competence at tasks, but their proclivities to act ethically.

References

Aneesh, A. 2006. *Virtual Migration: The Programming of Globalization*. Durham, NC: Duke University Press.

Anya, O. 2015. "Bridge the Gap! What Can Work Design in Crowdwork Learn from Work Design Theories?" Paper presented at CSCW 2015: Proceedings of the 18th ACM Conference on Computer Supported Cooperative Work (CSCW) & Social Computing, Vancouver, BC, Canada, March 14–18.

Arvidsson, A. 2014. "Public Brands and the Entrepreneurial Ethics." *Ephemera* 14(1): 119–24.

Bailey, D., P. Leonardi and S. Barley. 2012. "The Lure of the Virtual." *Organizational Science* 23(5): 1485–1504.

Benkler, Y. 2002. "Coase's Penguin, or Linux and *The Nature of the Firm*." *The Yale Law Journal* 112(3): 369–446.

Boltanski, L., and E. Chiapello. 2005. *The New Spirit of Capitalism*. Trans. Gregory Elliott. London: Verso Books.

Burawoy, M. 1979. *Manufacturing Consent: Changes in the Labor Process under Monopoly Capitalism*. Chicago: University of Chicago Press.

Cefkin, M., A. Obinna, and R. Moore. 2014 "A Perfect Storm? Reimagining Work in the Era of the End of the Job." *EPIC: Ethnographic Praxis in Industry Conference Proceedings*: 3–19.

Coase, R. 1937. "The Nature of the Firm." *Economica* 4(16): 386–405.

Crawford, K. 2016. "Can an Algorithm Be Agonistic? Ten Scenes from Life in Calculated Publics." *Science, Technology & Human Values* 41(1): 77–92.

Doan, A., R. Ramakrishnan, and A. Halevy. 2011. "Crowdsourcing Systems on the Worldwide Web." *Communications of the ACM* 54(4): 86–96.

Fischer, C. 1992. *America Calling: A Social History of the Telephone to 1940.* Berkeley: University of California Press.

Fish, A., and R. Srinivasan. 2011. "Digital Labor is the New Killer App." *New Media and Society* 14(1): 137–52.

Foucault, M. 2004. *Birth of Biopolitics.* New York: Palgrave Macmillan.

Gershon, I. 2011. "Neoliberal Agency." *Current Anthropology* 52(4): 537–55.

———. 2017. *Down and Out in the New Economy.* Chicago: University of Chicago Press.

Gillespie, T. 2010. "The Politics of 'Platforms.'" *New Media & Society* 12(3): 347–64.

Graham, M., and M. A. Anwar. 2018. "Labour." In *Digital Geographies,* ed. J. Ash, R. Kitchin, and A. Leszczynski, 177–187. London: Sage.

Gray, M., S. Shoaib, S. Suri, and D. Kulkarni. 2016. "The Crowd is a Collaborative Network." Paper presented at CSCW '16. Proceedings of the 19th ACM Conference on Computer Supported Cooperative Work and Social Computing, San Francisco, 27 February – 2 March.

Guesling, J. 2013. "Being There: The Power of Conventional Ethnographic Methods." In *Advancing Ethnography in Corporate Environments: Challenges and Emerging Opportunities,* ed. B. Jordan, 23–37. Walnut Creek, CA: Left Coast Press.

Hayek, F. 1939. "The Economic Conditions of Interstate Federalism." *New Commonwealth Quarterly* V(2): 131–49.

Inoue, M. 2011. "Stenography and Ventriloquism in Late Nineteenth-Century Japan." *Language & Communication* 31(3): 181–90.

Irani, L. 2015. "Difference and Dependence among Digital Workers: The Case of Amazon Mechanical Turk." *South Atlantic Quarterly* 114(1): 225–34.

Irani, L., and M. Silberman. 2013. "Turkopticon: Interrupting Worker Invisibility in Amazon Mechanical Turk." Paper presented at CHI '13: Proceedings of the SIGCHI Conference on Human Factors in Computing Systems, Paris, 27 April – 2 May.

Kittler, F. 1990. *Discourse Networks 1800/1900.* Stanford, CA: Stanford University Press.

Kittur, A., J. Nickerson, M. Bernstein, E. Gerber, A. Shaw, J. Zimmerman, M. Lease, and J. J. Horton. 2013. "The Future of Crowd Work." Paper presented at CSCW '13: Proceedings of the 16th ACM Conference on Computer Supported Cooperative Work and Social Computing, Paris, 27 April – 2 May.

Lampinen, A., K. Hotari, and C. Cheshire. 2015. "Challenges to Participation in the Sharing Economy: The Case of Local Online Peer-to-Peer Exchange in a Single Parents' Network." *Interaction Design & Architecture(s) Journal* 24: 16–32.

Malone, T. 2004. *The Future of Work: How the New Order of Business Will Shape Your Organization, Your Management Style, and Your Life.* Cambridge, MA: Harvard Business School Press.

Martin, D. B., V. Hanrahan, J. O'Neill, and N. Gupta. 2014. "Being a Turker." Paper presented at CSCW '14. Proceedings of the 17th ACM Conference on Computer Supported Cooperative Work and Social Computing, Baltimore, MD, 15–19 February.

Mikolajewska-Zajac, K. 2016. "Sharing as Labour and as Gift: Couchsurfing as an 'Affective Enterprise.'" *Ephemera* 16(4): 209–22.

Moore, R. J., M. Cefkin, O. Anya, and S. Stucky. 2014. "Sharing Local Knowledge in Task-Based Sourcing." Paper presented at CSCW '14. Proceedings of the 17th ACM Conference on Computer Supported Cooperative Work and Social Computing, Baltimore, MD, 15–19 February.

Nelson, B. 1990. *Workers on the Waterfront*. Urbana-Champagne: University of Illinois Press.

Rose, N. 1998. *Inventing Our Selves: Psychology, Power and Personhood*. Cambridge: Cambridge University Press.

Rosenblat, A., and L. Stark. 2016. "Algorithmic Labor and Information Asymmetries: A Case Study of Uber's Drivers." *International Journal of Communication* 10: 3758–84.

Salehi, N., L. Irani, M. Bernsteing, A. Alkhatib, E. Ogbe, K. Miland, and Clickhappier. 2015. "We Are Dynamo: Overcoming Stalling and Friction in Collective Action for Crowd Workers." Paper presented at CHI Proceedings: Proceedings of the 33rd Annual ACM Conference on Human Factor Systems. Seoul, Republic of Korea, 18–23 April.

Scholliers, P., and L. Schwarz. 2003. *Experiencing Wages: Social and Cultural Aspects of Wage Forms in Europe Since 1500*. New York: Berghahn Books.

Schor, J., C. Fitzmaurice, L. Carfagna, and W. Attwood-Charles. 2015. "Paradoxes of Openness and Distinction in the Sharing Economy." *Poetics* 54: 66–81.

Suchman, L. 1995. "Making Work Visible." *Communications of the ACM* 38(9): 56–64.

Suchman, L., and L. Bishop. 2000. "Problematizing 'Innovation' as Critical Project." *Technology Analysis & Strategic Management* 12(3): 327–33.

Swan, E., and S. Fox. 2009. "Becoming Flexible: Self-flexibility and Its Pedagogies." *British Journal of Management* 20(s1): S149–S159.

Tomasetti, J. 2016. "Does Uber Redefine the Firm? The Postindustrial Corporation and Advanced Information Technology." *Hofstra Labor & Employment Law Journal* 34(1): Article 3.

Weeks, K. 2011. *The Problem with Work: Feminism, Marxism, Antiwork Politics, and Postwork Imaginaries*. Durham, NC: Duke University Press.

10

Unicorn-Makers Working for Freedom (and Monopolies)

The Work of Venture Capital Investors

JOHANNES LENHARD

When I started interviewing investors in venture capital funds, it was not obvious to me what work really meant for them. During two years of fieldwork, I encountered them mostly at conferences and chatting over coffee. When I turned up at their offices, I often found them empty, regardless of whether or not I had an appointment. I began to wonder: how do these people really spend their days?

Early-stage venture capitalists (VCs) give money to young and unproven companies, often before they have a fully formed product and have started to generate revenue. In recent decades, support for start-ups has been a driving factor in the emergence of the digital economy (Nicholas 2019; see also O'Mara 2019). Many of the most highly valued and most talked about (consumer-facing) companies today—from Amazon, Microsoft, and Google, to Facebook, Airbnb, and Uber—were originally funded by VCs. These tech giants are part of what has been called platform capitalism (Srnicek 2016), surveillance capitalism (Zuboff 2018), or the age of "the code" (O'Mara 2019). The structure whereby VC general partners (GPs) raise money from limited partners (LPs) such as pension funds, university endowments, high net worth individuals, and familial trusts, only took shape following World War II.[1] According to this GP–LP structure, VCs have a fiduciary duty to pay back their LPs within approximately 8–12 years, depending on the lifetime of the fund. To understand how these investors work, how they conceptualize what they do, and what motivates them to finance one kind of activity rather than another, is important, because the work VCs do today will shape our social and economic world of tomorrow.

In the present era of financialization, anthropologists and other social scientists have investigated institutions such as banks (Ho 2009; Appadurai 2015; Leins 2018) and central banks (Holmes 2013), and also intermediaries such as asset managers (Tuckett 2011; Arjaliès et al. 2017), traders (Zaloom 2006), and consultants (Stein 2017; Chong 2018). My aim in this chapter is to apply a similar approach to VCs, paying particular attention to their day-to-day work, their ethics, and their values. After reviewing the most pertinent recent studies of gig work and financial services more broadly, I proceed in three steps. First, I lay out the incentive structure for VCs, their striving to generate above-average returns—or, as they often put it themselves, "to work towards the bottom line." Second, I demonstrate that narratives of freedom, and of enhanced access, choice, and power for consumers and workers, are crucial determinants of their investment decisions. Finally, I analyze how the return ("the bottom line") is generated operationally in the currently dominant environment of digitally enabled consumer-facing products.[2] The goal is to invest in companies that become quasi-monopolist "unicorns" dominating their markets. In conclusion, I ask how VCs manage in their everyday work to reconcile the "ethical tension" between narratives of freedom and aspirations to monopoly power. It turns out, economically speaking, that this is all built into the system—with the well-documented consequences.

Fieldwork with Venture Capital Investors

Since late 2017, I have been conducting fieldwork and interviews with venture capital investors. Following on from a professional engagement (as a part-time investor for a small VC fund), I started my work speaking to investors and attending industry conferences, as well as continuing in different advisory roles. My pre-existing connections enabled me to overcome the access burden many other anthropologists encounter when "studying up" (Souleles 2019). Over the last few years, I have extended my network and field experiences widely to include dozens of conferences, demo days, and meet-ups between Berlin, London, San Francisco, and New York. Altogether, I have conducted over 250 one-on-one interviews with almost 200 investors, spread more or less equally between the above places. These were mostly based on warm introductions and do not follow a specific sampling technique. The interviews were predominantly with venture capital general partners (or GPs), but at times I also engaged with more junior staff in VC funds as well as angel investors and limited partners. All of the names and institutions mentioned in this chapter are anonymized to protect the identity of my informants.

While venture capital investing—and the start-up ecosystem more generally—is often associated with California and Silicon Valley, I was keen on including a range of different actors in a variety of related but possibly distinct ecosystems. In future analyses, I will work further at teasing out some of these differences, but what I am focusing on here is a "way of venture investing" that is not geographically specific. Flows of people and capital between my different field-sites in fact connect them in an intimate way, producing what I will describe as a set of observable practices (Sassen 2001). Many of the investors I interacted with would, for instance, invest in both the United States and Europe; at times, funds would have offices in different geographical locations that would coordinate activities. Investors would often travel between the different places and be engaged in a very connected ecosystem, enabled and facilitated by international conferences and accelerator events, but also by (often sector-focused) WhatsApp groups, newsletters, Twitter, and LinkedIn. In this chapter I will similarly abstract from the differences that might stem from the diversity of investors themselves along such lines as gender, race, and educational background.[3] The question I want to ask is: what is at the core of the work venture capital investors do? I will first take cues to contextualize this question by engaging with recent anthropological work on both "new work" and investors more broadly.

Ethnographies of New (Gig) Work and Investors

Talking about venture capital investors means two things: it means talking about the digital economy and the rapidly changing forms of work it promotes, and it means talking about financial professionals. Recent accounts trying to understand the contemporary forms of work involved in these two sectors focused on three observations which are also helpful in understanding the work of VCs: the ethical tensions involved in the work, the use of narratives, and the important role of emotion and affect in decision-making processes.

To date, studies of working conditions in the platform economy have been carried out mostly by sociologists focusing on the USA. Research so far has been on companies such as the ride-hailing company Uber (Rosenblat 2019) and gig-economy and sharing platforms such as TaskRabbit or Airbnb more generally (Ravenelle 2019) that enable what used to be called "blue-collar" workers to find (temporary) employment (see also Prassl 2018).[4] While the kind of work described in these texts is hence very different from the work mostly elite venture investors do, there is a crucial link: most of these gig-economy companies have been funded by venture capital money, at least in their early phases, and we will go into this more below. The values underpinning these platforms—entrepreneurialism, self-reliance—and exemplified by the platform founders, is embraced directly by venture capital investors. Many VCs are supporting this idea of work, and promote it with their investments.

However, the above volumes analyzing the gig economy pinpoint at tensions at the core of the work the platforms enable: workers might be promised flexible working hours, high pay, and entrepreneurial sensibilities, but the reality of daily work is often governed by surveillance (e.g., driver tracking enabled by GPS), restricting "incentives" (e.g., minimum acceptance rates for Uber drivers), and false expectations (e.g., around "surge" pricing), not to mention the lack of worker protection. In terms of security and overall conditions, many gig workers are "returning . . . to the workplace of the early industrial age" (Ravenelle 2019: 111). The work itself and the income it generates are highly unstable, governed by algorithms, changing commission rules, non-transparent gigs and rides, and a culture of competition and hustling without solidarity (Gershon 2017: 249; Rosenblat 2019: 84, 91). I will argue below that this tension observable for the workers in the gig economy is also something that venture capital investors are caught in with their own work—tension between promoting freedom, access, and entrepreneurialism, but ultimately being dependent on (quasi-)monopolies to achieve the necessary returns. Let me first, however, contextualize the VCs' work from a perspective of ethnographies of finance.

VCs have a unique position in the chain of finance, the "sequence of intermediaries" (Arjaliès et al. 2017: 4) that manage financial flows from savers (companies, charities, individuals) to "the market" (of stocks, bonds, and other financial or non-financial assets). Along the chain, different intermediaries cause "leakages" in the form of fees and expenses (ibid.: 14) in exchange for investing money profitably. VCs allocate limited partners' (LPs) money as an investment partnership of general partners (GPs) into nascent companies. They act as asset managers with a specific expertise in the field of start-up investment to make investment decisions on behalf of pension funds, endowments, foundations, family offices, and "high net worth" individuals that have contributed money to the venture capital fund. The VCs are (mostly) not investing their own capital and are hence working towards a simple goal: paying back their LPs, their investors, a multiple of the money they invested in the VC fund to begin with. In this working towards returns, narratives play a key role—something that several commentators in the anthropology of finance have observed.

Leins, in his analysis of Swiss investment banking analysts, goes as far as to put the investment narrative or story at the core of what financial analysts do (see also Arjaliès et al. 2017: 43): "While the less experienced analysts fill in the numbers and do the calculations, the more experienced analysts interpret the figures and construct a persuasive story. They translate the strategies that are based on calculation, affect, and normative assumptions into narratives that can be communicated to investors" (Leins 2018: 105). The goal is to produce a manageable version of the future (of a specific financial asset) that enables asset managers, in our case the VCs, to make decisions about where to invest money.[5]

A second finding in the recent anthropology of finance that speaks to my own analysis of investors in start-ups is the role that emotions and affect play in triggering investment decisions. Already in Zaloom's (2006) trading pit ethnography, the embodied beliefs of traders, and the choreographed gestures and language of conquest and control, play a key role in how the market was made—at least before algorithms took over much of the execution. Tuckett (2011) re-embeds this role of emotions, hunches and "group feel" when making investment decisions (he interviewed investment managers in multibillion-dollar funds) into the medium of the narrative. In his analysis of fund managers, investment decisions are justified by stories and bringing together both more modelled data and "emotions, intuition, and gut feeling" (ibid.: 57; see also Souleles 2019). Excitement, anxiety, and group think help to identify "phantastic objects" in the form of start-up companies, and the ideas and people behind them—models, abstractions, and quantifications are never enough.

Ethical tensions, and how they are managed, are also further analyzed in this branch of the literature. Where Tuckett (2011: 85) sees the influence of what he calls "divided masters" situating the financial investment decision between, for instance, anxiety about short-term returns and long-term strategies, Rudnyckyj (2018), in his studies in Kuala Lumpur, Malaysia, lifts the analysis onto a higher plane of ethics. He found that the different parties involved in practicing Islamic finance—financial practitioners, Islamic economists, regulators, and shariah scholars—were all balancing the "competing demands of religious and financial logic" (ibid.: 123). Taking the financial professional as the closest of the four to a venture capital investor, this is the concrete challenge they face (ibid.: 57): "On the one hand they must fulfil the expectations of those who expect the appellation 'Islamic' to yield a morally superior means of facilitating commerce . . . on the other hand, they must survive amid intense competition with both Islamic and conventional financial institutions." This resembles the ethical tension identified in the gig-work literature, and it applies to VC investors too. Market powers to generate a financial return—what I describe in "Step 1" below as the "bottom line" for VCs—are met with objectives and narrative involving freedom, autonomy, and improved choice, particularly in the "Step 2" process of connecting with the start-up founders (and their companies) that they wish to invest in. Let me now walk literally step by step into the work that venture capital investors do, and show how the bottom line and freedom are narratively in tension but concretely connected.

The Bottom Line—The VCs' Ethical Obligation to Achieve Outsized Returns

Venture capital funds as they exist in their current structure are a recent phenomenon. Their ethos can be traced back to whaling expeditions of the late 1800s, but their modern form of the LP–GP relationship was initiated by Draper, Gaither & Anderson (DGA) in California's Silicon Valley in 1959 (Nicholas 2019: 145). Greylock Partners followed in 1965, and Venrock in 1969. The fact that VCs do not invest their own money but act as investment managers for LPs creates a specific incentive structure.[6] When I asked Nick, a senior partner at one of Europe's best-known venture capital funds operating a global portfolio out of Switzerland, what he was trying to do, his reply was simple:

> Looking at it from the LP [limited partner, the VC's investors] perspective, they want returns. They want a two-digit IRR [internal rate of return], they need to make up the risk of the equity class they are in. The GP [general partner, VCs themselves] wants to—they want to get over the hurdle rate and then get a carry [part of the profit].

Nick described how the VCs themselves earn money in two ways during the initial investment and exit process. They charge an annual management fee—usually 2 percent of the fund size—for expenses such as salaries, travel costs, and office space. But the big payout comes in the form of a share of the profit accrued when a successful investment is "exited." While the majority of that—conventionally 80 percent—goes to the LPs, VCs keep the rest (what is called "carried interest" or "carry"). Given the risky nature of the VCs investment activities—only a small fraction of the start-ups they back will make a profit for them within the lifetime of the fund (Gompers 2006)—they depend on what they call "outsized returns." Based on an average of eight to twelve investments during a fund cycle and the low success quota, they in practice depend on paying back all of their investors with the profits earned on just a very few investments. As Dennis, a partner in a big German fund, put it to me early in my research:

> The decisive factor at the end of the day is whether you are a profitable fund; do you have a clear position, do you have a team, and are you slightly different from all the

> others. . . . They [the LPs] don't really want to have any kind of influence. At the end of the day, it is a question of money.

Dennis points at how important generating outsized returns compared to other venture funds is for the future of one's own. In order to survive as a firm and raise more money from limited partners, VCs need to generate high returns.[7] The core work, the bottom line, the main goal for any VC, is a multiplication of the investment capital during the fund's lifetime with highly risky bets on supposed unicorns that "disrupt and innovate industries." How do VCs do this concretely? What does their "work" look like?

Step 1: Using Data to Identify and Analyze Opportunities

The above description of the underlying business model for VCs describes the overarching ethical directionality that VCs are working towards, and the obligation they are trying to fulfill: namely, to achieve above-average returns for their limited partners. In a first step, VCs like other investors use spreadsheets and datasets to approach this goal (cf. the private equity investors Souleles 2019 describes): they analyze market and industry growth data to identify target markets; they look at revenue and sales numbers to identify possible investment targets on the company level; and they refer to user engagement and cohort analysis of customers to scrutinize start-ups. But unlike their peers in investment banking or private equity, the early-stage investors I engaged with do not use data or spreadsheets to make conclusive decisions. Tom, a VC partner in a prominent and very well-established fund in London, whom I interviewed several times, explained the usage of this kind of data to me:

> The excels, the excel spreadsheets and the roadmaps, and the PDFs and all that stuff—those are all just tools or implements with which to prod a conversation. So, you know, you look at the sales pipeline, you stare at it, not because you are trying to actually calculate . . . [it] gives you insight into how they look at sales, and whether they look at sales, and how involved they are. . . . [T]he data's there to be able to stimulate the conversation rather than to actually decide.

For Tom, numerical data, specifically data about the company itself, was a way of starting a conversation, of understanding the underlying thought processes of the founders, but not of making a final investment decision. In fact, most early-stage investors were not able to calculate expected returns using, for instance, the widespread banking tool of discounted cash flow analysis, because the necessary data was simply unavailable. Many of the businesses they were looking at barely had a product in the market, and were often only generating small amounts of revenue; the expectation was that these companies would grow exponentially. Numerical data was only one factor in the investment process, often limited to the identification of "good investments," but it did not enable a conclusive decision to be reached. The decisive factor in ultimately making an investment was based on value judgments about the team.

Karl, an investor in a German fund based out of Munich, made this point very clear to me, mirroring many other investors' opinions.[8] He highlighted several soft and emotional factors his VCs focused on when it came to the team:

> The chemistry with the team has to be right . . . Experience in the area helps us to judge people but it is not always based on facts but on empathy . . . [W]e have to be happy on both sides; we always try to have dinner with the team. [We ask ourselves] Can we stand each other's smell? (*Kann man sich riechen?*)

Data can be used to identify good (economic) opportunities but in order to take a decision, the vetting of the team is crucial. An emotional attunement is necessary, a process that as Karl also makes explicit can easily turn into a mutual endeavor. This takes us to what I argue is at the core of the VCs' work towards the bottom line of outsized returns: the mutual vetting in which founders need to be attracted and convinced by narratives and performances of freedom.

Step 2: Increasing Freedom—What VCs Say and Perform to Attract Founders

> We help entrepreneurs invent new industries and disrupt existing ones. (Hoxton)
> We help pioneers change the world. (Octopus)
> Limits are just a state of mind. (eVentures)
> Backing those who dare. (Holtzbrinck)
> We invest in founders with transforming ideas that decentralize markets, empower users, and liberate data (BlueYard)

These are the mission statements of just five of the over 150 different venture capital funds I spoke with. From Silicon Valley to Germany to London, they are bold claims about what the investors aim at with their investment activities. An obvious starting point is their focus on newness, on innovation. VCs are in the business of understanding what the future looks like; which new industries—and, more broadly, new ways of doing things—will become important. Current limits and frontiers to economic activities are to be overcome by driving change and "disruption."

Bob, a long-term venture capital partner in Cambridge, whom I met early in my fieldwork in 2018, explained to me what kind disruption and change he and his fund were interested in with a simple example:

> Another example might be . . . there's been an insertion of a layer but it's definitely disruptive, is something like personal transportation apps like Uber or even MyTaxi, where they are about providing a single place to give access to services on a very geographically dispersed basis, and it's a marketplace, really. . . . You know, it's just that you get access to them without [telephoning] anymore—you get access through the app.

Bob talked at length about the kinds of disruptive businesses his fund is interested in, and they were often about building new layers, new intermediaries making a service or product easier, cheaper, or faster to access. Bob here hits the core attribute of the kind of business that VCs are looking for: they are keen on extending access, liberating users, increasing democracy, and decentralizing (incumbents') power. In short, many VCs are driven by values of freedom, of liberation, of choice, of distribution.

This kind of freedom is comparable to what Laidlaw calls "soaring" Freedom (Laidlaw 2014b: 96, 102; following Flathman 2003), one that is about the absence of constraint. In the words of many VCs (see, for instance, Thiel and Masters 2014), the association is libertarian, often understood as a freedom from the state. Greene (2018) traces the origins of this idea in Silicon Valley back to an early ideological battle between the idea of the free internet (exemplified by Barlow's *Declaration of the Independence of Cyberspace* from 1996) and the internet's incorporation into capitalism. Instead of reliance on a variety of communities and institutions, including the regulatory framework of the state, today's libertarian entrepreneurs and investors, such as Peter Thiel and the so-called "Paypal Mafia" around him, aspire to the absence of constraint *tout court*. They believe that start-ups, and the disruption they necessarily cause as they prove themselves through market mechanisms, offer a superior "route to solving the world's challenges" (Greene 2018: 31).

So far, I have only described this libertarian freedom in the VCs' narratives and mission statements, in the VCs' marketing speeches. This is what VCs "say" they do and want. But these mission statements play a specific role in the mutual exchange of information that is at the core of VCs' work: they are one of the tools to attract founders. One of the most important parts of the mission statements is about the kind of founders that VCs want to invest in: they call them pioneers, "those who dare," disruptors, inventors, change-makers, and again, liberators. Being aligned with the vision of the start-up founders that VCs want to invest in is crucial. So, while to a certain extent the mission statements can be hollow, a marketing hoax, they have to be concretely performed on a day-to-day basis in order to attract start-up founders and convince them to let the VC "close the deal" (i.e., make an investment).

This is further driven by the recent market environment of low interest rates and abundant capital intensifying competition between VCs, and creating a world that puts the sought-after start-up founder in a position of power. In this context, VCs' day-to-day work is not about generously handing out checks but revolves around advertising, bidding for and convincing founders.[9] Many investors described to me how founders were choosers in this environment. Bridget, a VC whom I saw regularly over several weeks of fieldwork in San Francisco, grumbled: "We only lead rounds so we have to win deals [i.e., to be the only institutional investor]. There are so many investors out there competing for the good founders—we have to win. How do you do that?" I observed her struggle with a specific potential company in which she wanted to invest. She met the founders, one of whom was an acquaintance of hers, several times, both socially and in their office. She knew about the competition—two other funds that were at the time interested in the specific company, and had more expertise in their field—and put a lot of effort into selling her fund as the best partner for this start-up. Nick, the partner in the Swiss fund I spoke about above, mirrored this struggle for "being let in" succinctly:

> I have Accel and Sequoia [two big American VC funds] as my competitors—the top companies always have several term sheets [investment offers] on the table, so we had to fight for that. For me, a first conversation with a founder is really not about traction or KPIs [key performance indicators] but about the basic values that people have, and why they want to become a founder.

The mission statements and the values associated with them—access, choice, freedom—hence play more than merely a theoretical role. They condition the emotional interaction between VCs and founders. VCs had to talk about them and indeed perform them with the start-up founders they wanted to invest in. Ian, a VC who worked in Germany, was particularly vocal about the importance of forging personal connections in the competitive investment context:

> It's a people game. It is really about finding good people, understanding them, working with them . . . You have to get along and [you] have to have the same idea about the vision . . . [about] what you want to do in the world . . . you have to both understand each other.

I observed Ian in numerous interactions with founders in which he performed "emotional work" (Zaloom 2006) to ascertain and promote the alignment he needed in order to be let in. Once he had decided that he wanted to invest in an idea and market, a phase of what was called "due diligence" followed. Ian was, like most of my interlocutors, an early-stage investor, which meant that many of the businesses he looked at were without a fixed business model and often without revenue. The decision to invest was hence often based largely on a vetting of the team and the founders' characters and values. Ian was always keen to ask as many "why" questions as possible. He would start the questioning with: Why do you want to be an entrepreneur? Why this market? Why with these co-founders? Why will you be good at it? The character of the founder was important to Ian, especially because of the long-term nature of the relationship ("If everything goes well, we have to work together for ten years. I have to like that guy"). Most importantly, certain values had to align, just as Nick described above.

Ian, too, was a strong libertarian, keen on promoting private actors and wrestling power away from the state and the incumbent multinational companies. "We are agnostic in terms of geography but we want to invest in start-ups that take on big, old industry and use technology to make it quicker, cheaper, more accessible, digital." His social philosophy translated into a specific kind of founder he wanted to back. Taking on an established industry and breaking it open would involve flouting conventions, rules, sometimes even laws; Ian was fine with that. "These big companies have not been challenged for a long time; they are still sending orders by fax. This is bad for everyone, particularly the customers." He imagined entrepreneurs as freedom fighters, liberating customers from the grip of big industry. And as an investor, he himself was able to support this fight for increased freedom. In his eyes, that is what his work was ultimately about on a day-to-day basis.

When he was in the process of investing in a real estate start-up from the United States, which had just come out of a famous start-up accelerator, Ian engaged intensively with the three founders by telephone and email. Mark was a co-founder and the COO of the company, and was leading the fundraising and interactions with investors. The motivation behind Mark's 6-month-old start-up was to increase home ownership in the US through the simple "trick" of helping its customers to make cash offers on properties (apparently, a cash offer was ten times more likely to be accepted by a seller compared to a mortgage offer). He and his partners wanted to circumvent big mortgage lenders and thereby help more people to become homeowners.

Ian had already been convinced about the potential of the industry before meeting Mark and his company. Growth in the real-estate market was still massive at the time, and there were lots of opportunities for doing something differently, for increasing freedom by taking a piece of the pie away from the big developers and agencies. And his mind was quickly made up about Mark after the first phone conversations: he wanted to invest. However, given the easy availability of funds for start-ups like Mark's that came with the right credentials, the co-founders had the last word in deciding which investor would be "let into the deal." The dynamic switched from Ian questioning the founders to them quizzing him. A track record in the sector and a network of potential customers or follow-on investors would play a role in these conversations. But they were not a unique selling point, as most VCs would be able to help with that. One major focus was hence on the aligned vision, this time from the perspective of the founder.

When Ian started talking to Mark and his co-founders, their round was already full—several big VCs had already wired the money—but they were still open to having Ian on board. Mark liked Ian and his fund because they were also entrepreneurs driven by the same motivation: to be self-made, self-governed, and to focus on doing something in the world. He also liked Ian because the earlier investments he had made focused on a very similar vision: increasing access for consumers, for instance, in the travel booking space. It was certainly because Mark was keen on learning from Ian, but it was also to counteract a regular fear of founders: intervention from the investors.[10] Mark did not want an investor on board who would interfere in the founders' decisions. It was important for him to make sure that they had the same values, the same vision for his start-up. Ian fitted that bill, given his prior track record. In the end, Mark decided to let Ian into the round, mainly, I argue, because they were affectively attuned and focused on the same values.

The narrative and performance of freedom—the entrepreneurial self, with a strong motivation to provide "free" services and to enhance autonomy and access for the end user—was a core part of VCs' daily work. VCs not only had to find, identify, and analyze a start-up before they invested; part of their work was vetting the founders' character and values, and making sure they aligned before, in a second step, they had to be successful in convincing the founders to take their investment offer. I observed how this crucial process of mutual vetting was driven by a desire for increased freedom—not only talking about it but also performing freedom. Making money—reaching the bottom line—was dependent on getting access to competitive deals and hence on being (affectively) aligned on this vision of freedom. Before turning to the third step in the process of a VC's work, and describing how money was ultimately made, I want to theorize the kind of freedom at stake here in an anthropological context.

The soaring freedom that both founders and investors narrate, perform, and work towards is based on a rejection of old institutions—incumbent companies and the state alike. Caroline Humphrey observed a similar kind of freedom in the Soviet context as *volya*, a "boundless release, something that one experienced away from society or any kind of limitation" (Humphrey 2007: 6).[11] Similar to the libertarian freedom my VC informants sought, *volya* is strongly focused on the individual will and its rights, and indeed can point at an absence of the state in unrestricted, new, and alternative ways. The VCs in turn follow a path of Schumpeterian creative destruction towards solutions that are, as Humphrey describes, outside of former structures in a mode of "everything-is-permitted-ness" (ibid.).

I follow Laidlaw's skepticism, however, in that this kind of unbounded freedom is mostly unobtainable, both in Humphrey's description of the Russian *volya* and in the actions of VCs and the start-ups they back. Laidlaw argues that "the power relations that constrain and enable, and weaken and empower, some in relation to others, are emphatically not mere appearance in contrast with a reality of freedom. They give such freedoms as people are ever able to exercise, both their shape and their scope" (Laidlaw 2014a: 500). Freedoms of different kinds are in this sense embedded in power relations. In fact, this chapter started with, and will now return to, the original power relation constraining the investor's freedom: the bottom line of working towards outsized returns that investors are fundamentally constrained by. In the last section of this chapter ("Step 3"), I return to VCs' work on the bottom line—and how that work is on the one hand seemingly in (ethical) tension with the narrative of libertarian freedom, but in practice goes hand in hand with it.

Step 3: Monopolistic Returns—What VCs Really Want to Accomplish

> We are looking for market leaders, companies that dominate a whole industry. . . . It is a number's game—if the market is $xbn big and they get 10 percent of that market, they are going to be a fund returner.

This is Ian again offering a more economic perspective on work, both his own and that of the start-ups in which he invests. In addition to the emotional-ideological fit around libertarian freedom, the start-up ultimately had to return a profit: ideally, it would become a market leader or dominator to contribute to his bottom line.

Dan, a London venture capitalist working on his first fund, explained the logic behind the "fund returner" in slightly more detail:

> So, three to five exits is sort of the top I can expect from the fund. We expect 20 percent of the companies to return the entire thing, and it requires each of the winners—each of the 20 percent [of the 3–5 exits]—to be fairly sizable in valuation at exit . . . to generate that return.

When you assume, for instance, a fund of £50m that has to triple the return to LP investors, then in this case each of the three to five exits has to make £30–50m. Dan's fund will own 10–20 percent of each of these companies, meaning that the companies' valuation by the time of the exit event will need to be somewhere between £300m and £500m. This is only possible when picking market winners. As VC investor and industry commentator Nicolas Colin has pointed out, successful companies "take the vast majority of the market at (almost) any cost . . . based on superior increasing returns to scale" (Colin 2018: 125). These highly successful companies would often grow to become unicorns, companies valued at over $1bn. Investing in one of these is highly improbable, as there are fewer than fifty unicorn companies in France, Germany, and the UK together, for instance. The new wave of these are chased by several hundred funds.

Investing in a quasi-monopolistic unicorn is the ultimate gold rush. As entrepreneur-turned-investor Peter Thiel argues,

> if you want to create and capture lasting value, you should look to build a monopoly. . . . Google has an 88 percent market share in online searches . . . Amazon has a 70 percent market share in electronic book sales . . . Facebook has a 77 percent market share in mobile social media monopolies. (Taplin 2018: 21)

Most importantly, however, investing in a fund-returner, often a unicorn, is not just the ideal outcome for a VC fund but the outcome that is needed to reach the bottom line. Achieving outsized fund returns was a prerequisite in order to be able to raise a new fund and stay alive in the industry, as I described earlier. I asked another investor about the kind of company they were searching for, the ones that would be "returning the fund": "Facebook didn't just become a market leader, it created a market . . . Google the same . . . they are the market really; they are almost monopolies . . . even Uber . . . that is the company we are all chasing to survive."

Conclusion: Schumpeter Revisited

We have now come full circle. I identified a bottom line and the three steps that venture capital investors employ towards the goal of reaching it. The VCs' general bottom line is set by their obligation to return a profit, both for their investors, the limited partners, and for themselves. In Step

1, the question of how (numerical) data is used to identify possible investment targets was addressed, arguing that data's analysis is not a necessary condition for taking a decision. Step 2 then focused on the mutual vetting process around deploying and performing narratives of (libertarian) freedom, choice, autonomy, and access. In order to "win rounds" competing against other investors, the visions of the founders and the VCs had to align emotionally. In Step 3, it was shown that the bottom line of "returning the fund" depended upon the start-ups becoming (quasi-)monopolists, creating and dominating their markets.

At first glance, the goals I described as part of the narratives of freedom and the eventual realization of monopoly power contradict each other ideologically and legally. Monopolies or duopolies (Lynn 2011)—total market domination—and increased (consumer) autonomy, freedom, and choice are diametrically opposed ideologically, and also legally speaking.[12] But at another level, in the world of VCs, they are indispensable together. The promise of freedom, access, democracy, and autonomy goes hand in hand with the creation of monopolistic "network effects" based on user data in the case of many recently successful VC-backed companies (e.g., Facebook).[13]

Similar to the tensions that the gig economy literature points out between their narratives of entrepreneurship and the actual AI-driven surveillance systems, the tension at the core of the VC work I have described above is systemically inherent. I want to contrast the work VC investors do in this regard with what Rudnyckyj (2018) observed for Islamic financial professionals in Malaysia. While his informants are balancing competing demands between religious (Islamic) and financial (market, competition) logics, VCs manage a tension between an affective narrative of expanding freedom and a reality of striving to create monopoly companies. Both have to be in place, however, in order to satisfy the bottom line.

But the tension was anticipated by Joseph Schumpeter in 1950 in his *Capitalism, Socialism and Democracy*. In fact, as Joseph Stiglitz explains in his introduction to the latest edition of Schumpeter's magnus opus, economics can easily bring together the opposing poles I see at the core of the work of VCs: "To Schumpeter, the heart of capitalism was innovation, and innovation required some degree of monopoly power . . . innovation leads one monopolist to be replaced by another" (Stiglitz 2016: ix, xi). In other words, Schumpeter, who coined the concept "creative destruction," which is so widely aspired to in the start-up world, did not see a tension at all between (freedom-seeking) innovation and monopoly power. So economically speaking, we are all fine here.

As Stiglitz in his commentary goes on to point out, however, Schumpeter missed something that was important historically: the development of corporatist welfare, "where the power of the state is used to protect the rich and powerful, rather than the poor and society more generally" (Stiglitz 2016: x). The venture capital model I have described above can produce companies such as Microsoft, Google, and Amazon that end up "devot[ing] considerable resources to the creation of socially unproductive entry barriers" (ibid.: xi). They generate unsustainable growth and increase social inequality. This is what the next step in the analysis of the work of venture capital investors could turn to—to the effects, the possibly unintended consequences, that their work can have. Where does the VCs work, narratively focused on freedom, really lead?

Acknowledgments

My fieldwork was funded by the Max Planck–Cambridge Centre for Ethics, Economy and Social Change. For comments on earlier drafts of this chapter, I thank Caroline Humphrey, Bill Janeway, James Laidlaw, and an anonymous reviewer.

Johannes Lenhard holds a doctorate in social anthropology from the University of Cambridge. He is an ethnographer of homelessness and venture capital, and currently coordinates the Max Planck–Cambridge Centre for Ethics, Economy and Social Change.

Notes

1. Contrary to general belief, this structure is standard in the venture capital industry. Most of the capital invested by VC general partners is not their own, but LP capital. The GPs manage the LPs capital and are paid a management fee for these services (usually 2 percent of the overall fund per annum); at the end of the fund's life (usually after 8–12 years) profits are split between themselves (20 percent) and the LPs (80 percent). It follows that, while GPs have a stable annual income, their "big payouts" very much depend on individual fund-level achievement (and sometimes individual partner-level achievement). I will describe these mechanisms further.
2. Most of the VCs I spoke and interacted with were indeed focused on financing digital technology products, mostly with a consumer-facing (B2C) part to them. In contrast, so-called deep-tech investors (comparable to the original VCs pushing the semi-conductor revolution in the second half of the twentieth century) and also biotech investors operate differently in their values and conflicts. Building (blitzscaled) "unicorns" is specific to this currently dominant group of venture

capital investors. (A unicorn is a privately held start-up that is valued at more than $1bn. The term was coined by American VC Aileen Lee in 2016.)

3. In fact, my overall group of interviewees, comprising about 80 percent men, is more (gender) diverse than statistics for both the US and the UK would indicate, where only about 12 percent of VC decision makers/partners are female (NVCA 2019; Diversity VC 2019).
4. Gershon (2017) focused more directly on "white-collar" (college-educated) workers, but her ethnography is mainly concerned with hiring and finding employment—something that is only tangentially comparable to the work of the VCs.
5. Souleles (2019) makes a similar argument concerning the "value story" constructed by private equity investors, who often invest in the same companies as the VCs, but later on in the start-up's life cycle.
6. Some GPs have small allocations in their own funds, thus doubling as LPs, but the majority of the venture capital fund is money from big asset managers—pension funds, endowments, family offices, and (specifically in Europe) government vehicles.
7. This average is usually measured against the performance of a dominant index, for instance the S&P500, during the same time period. So, if the average return of the S&P500 per year was 7 percent, a VC fund would be expected to generate significantly more (otherwise the high risk would not be warranted). This business model and the accompanying measurement shows very little variation across Western Europe and the USA.
8. The decision has attracted much attention in economics, too, and is often designated as a choice between the horse (business/business model) or the jockey (team) (see Kaplan, Sensoy, and Omberg 2009; Mitteness, Baucus, and Sudek 2012).
9. This abundance has been driven by low interest rates for other investment opportunities (bonds, stocks). Venture capital and private equity profited from this trend throughout the 2010s by achieving increased capital allocation from LPs searching for outsized returns for their portfolio.
10. Bill Gurley had Travis Kalanick thrown out as Uber CEO after ongoing conflicts about, among other things, not treating employees well and breaking regulations in different jurisdictions. Arguably, here, the visions of the main investor(s) and founders were not aligned, leading to prolonged conflict (Isaac 2019).
11. Related words include *vol'nyi rynok* (free market) and *vol'naya prodazha* (unrestricted sale).
12. These laws have not been applied against the tech giants because they do not disadvantage consumers monetarily (as they do not charge fees for many of their services).
13. Mazzucato (2017: 215) makes this case very strongly. While on the one hand these companies provide some services for free, promising more freedom, access, or user-autonomy (what I call the narrative of freedom), they are creating quasi-monopolist networks. As Mazzucato (ibid.: 218) states succinctly: "[These] network effects are increasingly centralizing the Internet, thereby placing an enormous concentration of market power in the hands of a few firms."

References

Appadurai, Arjun. 2015. *Banking on Words: The Failure of Language in the Age of Derivative Finance*. Chicago: University of Chicago Press.
Arjaliès, Diane-Laure, Philip Grant, Iain Hardie, Donald MacKenzie, and Ekaterina Svetlova. 2017. *Chains of Finance: How Investment Management Is Shaped*. Oxford: Oxford University Press.
Chong, Kimberly. 2018. *Best Practice: Management Consulting and the Ethics of Financialization in China*. Durham, NC: Duke University Press.
Colin, Nicolas. 2018. *Hedge—A Greater Safety Net for the Entrepreneurial Age*. London: The Family.
Diversity VC. 2019. "Diversity in UK Venture Capital 2019." http://www.diversity.vc/wp-content/uploads/2019/07/DiversityInVC_Report_10.07.2019_for_Web.pdf (last accessed 10 March 2021).
Flathman, Richard E. 2003. *Freedom and Its Conditions: Discipline, Autonomy, and Resistance*. London: Routledge.
Gershon, Ilana. 2017. *Down and Out in the New Economy: How People Find (or Don't Find) Work Today*. Chicago: University of Chicago Press.
Gompers, Paul. 2006. *The Venture Capital Cycle*. Boston, MA: MIT Press.
Greene, Lucie. 2018. *Silicon States: The Power and Politics of Big Tech and What It Means for Our Future*. Berkeley, CA: Counterpoint.
Ho, Karen Zouwen. 2009. *Liquidated: An Ethnography of Wall Street*. Durham, NC: Duke University Press.
Holmes, Douglas R. 2013. *Economy of Words: Communicative Imperatives in Central Banks*. Chicago: University of Chicago Press.
Humphrey, Caroline. 2007. "Alternative Freedoms." *Proceedings of the American Philosophical Society* 151(1): 1–10.
Isaac, Mike. 2019. *Super Pumped: The Battle for Uber*. New York: Norton and Company.
Kaplan, Steven N., Berk A. Sensoy, and P. Omberg. 2009. "Should Investors Bet on the Jockey or the Horse ? Evidence from the Evolution of Firms from Early." *Journal of Finance* LXIV (4): 75–115.
Laidlaw, James. 2014a. "Significant Differences." *HAU* 4(1): 497–506.
———. 2014b. *The Subject of Virtue: An Anthropology of Ethics and Freedom*. Cambridge: Cambridge University Press.
Leins, Stefan. 2018. *Stories of Capitalism: Inside the Role of Financial Analysts*. Chicago: Chicago University Press.
Lynn, Barry. 2011. *Cornered: The New Monopoly Capitalism and the Economics of Destruction*. London: Wiley.
Mazzucato, Marina. 2017. *The Value of Everything: Making and Taking in the Global Economy*. London: Allen Lane.
Mitteness, Cheryl R., Melissa S. Baucus, and Richard Sudek. 2012. "Horse vs. Jockey? How Stage of Funding Process and Industry Experience Affect the Evaluations of Angel Investors." *Venture Capital* 14(4): 241–67. https://doi.org/10.1080/13691066.2012.689474.
Nicholas, Tom. 2019. *VC: An American History*. Boston, MA: Harvard University Press.

NVCA. 2019. "NVCA-Deloitte Human Capital Survey Report." https://nvca.org/research/nvca-deloitte-human-capital-survey/ (last accessed 10 March 2021).

O'Mara, Margaret. 2019. *The Code: Silicon Valley and the Remaking of America*. New York: Penguin Random House.

Prassl, Jeremias. 2018. *Humans as a Service: The Promise and Perils of Work in the Gig Economy*. Oxford: Oxford University Press.

Ravenelle, Alexandrea J. 2019. *Hustle and Gig: Struggling and Surviving in the Sharing Economy*. Oakland: University of California Press.

Rosenblat, Alex. 2019. *Uberland: How Algorithms Are Rewriting the Rules of Work*. Oakland: University of California Press.

Rudnyckyj, Daromir. 2018. *Beyond Debt: Islamic Experiments in Global Finance*. Chicago: University of Chicago Press.

Sassen, Saskia. 2001. *The Global City: New York, London, Tokyo*. Princeton, NJ: Princeton University Press.

Souleles, Daniel. 2019. "How to Study People Who Do Not Want to Be Studied: Practical Reflections on Studying Up." *Polar* 41 (September): 51–68. https://doi.org/10.1111/plar.12253.Page.

Srnicek, Nick. 2016. *Platform Capitalism*. Cambridge: Polity.

Stein, Felix. 2017. *Work, Sleep, Repeat: The Abstract Labour of German Management Consultants*. London: Bloomsbury Academic.

Stiglitz, Joseph E. 2016. "Introduction." In *Capitalism, Socialism and Democracy*, ix–xiv. London: Routledge.

Taplin, Jonathan. 2017. *Move Fast and Break Things: How Facebook, Google, and Amazon Have Cornered Culture and What It Means for All of Us*. London: Macmillan.

Thiel, Peter, and Blake Masters. 2014. *Zero to One: Notes on Start Ups, or How to Build the Future*. New York: Virgin Books.

Tuckett, David. 2011. *Minding the Markets: An Emotional Finance View of Financial Instability*. London: Palgrave Macmillan.

Zaloom, Caitlin. 2006. *Out of the Pits: Traders and Technology from Chicago to London*. Chicago: University of Chicago Press.

Zuboff, Shoshana. 2018. *The Age of Surveillance Capitalism: The Fight for a Human Future at the New Frontier of Power*. New York: Profile Books.

11

Individuality, Teamwork, and Work Processes in a Financial Services Center in Germany

MAGDALENA DĄBKOWSKA

Introduction

The financial crisis, which started in the United States in 2007 and subsequently affected the rest of the world, prompted questions about risk management and the efficiency of banking regulations. In response, banks enhanced their risk management functions to promote financial certainty and sector stability (Tombs 2017). One way of achieving this aim was to develop nearshore financial services centers, to which risk management functions were transferred from financial hubs. The nature of work in these centers demonstrates a contradiction at the heart of neoliberalism—that between the entrepreneurial self and the structure of the workplace (cf. Gershon and Cefkin, this volume).

In this chapter I show that the process of establishing a nearshore financial services center symbolizes the entrepreneurial freedom of neoliberal market actors, which in the context of the financial crisis was dictated by new rules and structures imposed by regulators. These structures were subsequently recreated in the design of work processes that allow little room for deviation, in order to guarantee effective risk management strategies. Employees negotiate their individuality within the work processes through acquiring technical and soft skills that enable them to build professional relationships and thus demonstrate determination, dedication, and creativity that enhance their individual profiles. Structures and clearly defined processes give rise to entrepreneurial selves, but employees need to switch between individuality and teamwork if this is to happen.

Freedom and Regulation: The Rise of Nearshore Financial Services

The financial crisis and its aftermath provoked criticism of abstract financial instruments (Gudeman 2016) and faulty risk management processes (Admati and Hellwig 2014). To reduce financial uncertainty in the future, as part of regulatory reforms enshrined in the Basel III framework,[1] banks were obliged to improve their risk management strategies. For example, calculation of risk assigned to assets owned by banks was to be unified to make it easier to compare institutions' exposure. In addition to these requirements, financial institutions have been "reassessing and adjusting their business strategies and models, . . . scope of activities and geographic presence . . . to reorient their business away from trading and more complex activities, [and] towards less capital-intensive activities" (Basel Committee on Banking Supervision 2017). More complex and riskier activities were separated from standardized reporting tasks. For the world's biggest investment banks, this meant that complex activities would continue to be performed in the hubs—that is, the global financial centers—while anything that could be standardized was transferred to cheaper geographic locations.

Neoliberal globalization since the late 1970s is a process whereby companies focus on products that bring the highest return, and outsource low-returning divisions to other countries (Gudeman 2016: 161). Offshoring has been used by companies to cut costs mainly in manufacturing, but it has subsequently spread into technology and services sectors (Davis-Blake and Broschak 2009). Tasks can be outsourced to an external service provider, or reallocated within the same company to another location. The benefit of the latter is that all locations report to the same global management, theoretically assuring that tasks will be performed in strict accordance with the rules and standards of the firm. Problems such as unqualified personnel, lack of adequate oversight, or incompatible or outdated computer systems are eliminated. The rationale is marked by the theory "that human well-being can best be advanced by liberating individual entrepreneurial freedom" (Harvey 2007: 2). In similar fashion, financial services have been experiencing an internal split between hubs and support centers in nearshore locations. This grew more profound after the financial crisis. Nearshore locations that took over risk management functions are located, for example, in Berlin, Kraków, Jacksonville, Raleigh and Nashville in the United States, and Bournemouth in the United Kingdom. These cities are sufficiently close to Frankfurt, New York, or London to be easily reachable by management when necessary. Additionally, these locations fall within the scope of European Union or US laws and banking regulations, which minimizes exposure to regulatory risk. Banks are thus exemplary neoliberal organizations that "make no attempt to hide the celebration of their global reach and integration, their technological innovations, and the triumph of late capitalism" (Ho 2005: 70–73). However, the entrepreneurial freedom to set up financial services operations in new geographic locations can be contrasted with the very structured ways in which work is organized in these locations.

In 2011, in response to the financial crisis, a German global investment bank set up risk management operations in Berlin to facilitate early warning systems to protect itself from negative economic events. The unit is sometimes referred to internally as a "center of excellence," to underline the specificity of the tasks performed. It is an integral part of the investment bank, so the employees say that they work for the bank. The outsourcing of financial services affects the host city, which is being reshaped and reimagined by finance capitalism (Gupta 2019). This is most visible in the construction of new office buildings used by corporate services that appropriate urban areas (Sassen 2001). Finance capital as the most abstract form of capitalism conquers physical space (Chong 2018). The transfer of operations to another location became more feasible when trading shifted to electronic platforms, and communication was by telephone or e-mail. Digitalization enables financial services work to be "carved out" from a financial institution's core operations, and its relocation elsewhere enables executives to present themselves as profit-maximizing neoliberal agents (Ofstehage 2018).

Due to Berlin's complicated post-World War II history, after German Reunification in 1990 the city suffered similar problems to the whole of East Germany, but most notably unemployment, which still remains relatively high compared to major cities in the former West Germany.[2] In 2005, Germany adopted the labor law reforms known as Agenda 2010, which cut social benefits and led to a significant decrease in unemployment.[3] Statistics show that the post-financial crisis wave of unemployment had less impact on Germany than on most other countries.[4] In particular, unemployment and precarity in Southern Europe have created an underclass of young people, sometimes referred to collectively as "the 500 euro generation," many of whom decided to leave their homelands to pursue careers elsewhere (Matos 2012: 218).[5]

The decision to transfer risk management operations to Berlin coincided with the spike in unemployment across Europe, which helps explain the international working environment of the nearshore center I investigated. The center employed citizens of many countries, and work could be performed in many languages: English, Italian, and Dutch, as well as German. This was an attractive opportunity to launch a professional career, unavailable in other companies in Berlin. Within a few years, the center had recruited some five hundred employees, the majority of them non-German, who initially came from countries most affected by the unemployment crisis: Spain, Italy, and Greece, as well as former international students who studied in Germany and stayed in the country to pursue a professional career. Given that the idea behind the center was to address risks inherent in investment banking, which by itself is heavily focused on international finance, the teams mostly supported banking activities outside Germany, and for this reason were also very multicultural.

Team composition in terms of nationalities also varies across departments because the center is in a state of constant flux due to permanent restructuring aimed at cost optimization. Restructuring is also the result of management changes, so that with every new resignation and appointment at the top, which occurs fairly frequently, reporting lines may change too. This means that teams may be allocated to a different manager in the hub, or decommissioned altogether. Accordingly, lower-level employees may want to change jobs and move to a different team, or leave the company, which results in significant staff rotation. Over time, the restructuring has also created new teams covering Germany, and employing mostly Germans, although they remain a small fraction of the total operations.

Initially team management responsibilities remained located mostly in the hubs. A senior bank employee would manage a team in Berlin remotely via telephone and e-mail communication, with occasional on-site visits. Subsequently, as the nearshore employees gained experience in their work, an opportunity arose to become a team head in Berlin. This role would normally go to the most senior person within a team, or someone who possessed the required language skills. Team heads were in effect trained on the job because initially it was not possible to recruit skilled talent in Berlin, which lacked experienced candidates. This could explain why I did not find evidence of cronyism in recruitment. However, one can certainly notice some form of cronyism in appointments to team head roles, which depend on support from more senior colleagues. There is a referral bonus awarded to any employee who suggests an external candidate for a role and who then successfully passes the probation period. The bonus reflects the time and effort saved by the human resources department or an external head-hunting agency in looking for a new candidate. However, externally referred candidates are extremely rare, and most candidates actively apply for vacancies.

Employees promoted to team head roles take on extra responsibilities, including managerial tasks, and report to the manager in the hub. All teams in the nearshore center ultimately report to someone in one of the hubs. The option to be promoted to a team head role diminished with time, as it was easier to recruit experienced employees in Berlin. An increase in experienced external candidates could be observed after the UK voted to leave the European Union in 2016. At present, almost all team head roles are recruited externally. The fact that external candidates are preferred over internal who already possessed pertinent skills and knowledge is reflected in the low job satisfaction levels expressed by team members, who complain about lack of meaningful career development. As in most international corporations the work environment is arranged around vertical hierarchies that must be observed, especially concerning career development and salary negotiation topics. These conversations take place with one's direct manager located in the nearshore center, although it does sometimes happen that employees who have been repeatedly refused promotion by their direct manager challenge the hierarchy by reaching out to the responsible manager in the hub to complain about slow career progression or a long overdue raise. But this is rare, as it risks damaging the relationship with the direct manager or the whole team.

What all teams and departments have in common is that the average age of the employees is relatively young, and some have very young children. Gender composition is split equally between men and women. In some teams, women were more numerous, apparently in the belief that employing more women in risk management can help to curb excesses.

My fieldwork started in 2013, when Berlin had been experiencing an influx of foreigners unable to find jobs in their home countries for at least a couple of years.[6] Jane was born in Argentina but educated in Austria. She speaks fluent Spanish, English, German, and Hebrew. After completing her degree in finance in Vienna she moved to Berlin to work for a small German company. The bank was more attractive:

> The bank offered an opportunity for professionals to work in English in the banking sector in Berlin. I haven't come across too many other employers with this characteristic. Berlin attracts young professionals, and having this type of work benefits both the city and the employer. I was previously working for a German company. At the time, the offer I received [from the bank] was better financially and with a permanent contract, which my former employer wasn't able to provide.

Cosmopolitan work environments were a novelty in the Berlin job market for young professionals. The nearshore center made this its strongest selling point, boasting in a recruitment invitation that "Specialists from 58 different countries and entirely different backgrounds work together to develop and implement risk management tools and processes for the future."

Manifesting Freedom in the World of Standards and Processes

Individual freedom in the Berlin nearshore center can only be nurtured within the constraints of "process-driven" tasks, that is tasks that can be broken down to a checklist, which must be completed in a prescribed sequence. No process exists in isolation. The tasks of a global workflow are performed by employees who work in teams in different nearshore or off-shore locations, before reaching a climax in hubs where final decisions are taken (and data made available to regulators, as appropriate).

Each task performed by an individual can be broken down into steps that are specified in Key Operating Procedures. Describing tasks in this way is essential, so that the banking regulator can see how exactly they are performed. The procedures are described to the regulator during audits, after which recommendations are issued to correct inadequacies or mistakes. Of course, standardization also helps when a task is allocated to a new employee, or when a sick colleague has to be replaced at short notice. The data that is passed from one employee or team to another is automatically checked for errors by whoever is currently processing the data. Some tasks are so complex that they must be divided into several parts. Process-driven work requires cooperation and coordination between employees. Data and information are requested, obtained, analyzed, modified, or used to produce a completely new set of data or information, which is subsequently requested by another employee, who processes it according to her or his responsibilities—and the cycle continues. The data might take the form of a legal document template, a software-generated Excel file from the loan operations department, or a confidential intelligence report on a high-risk client. Depending on the task, the chain of employees involved in the process can consist of few or many individuals, or whole teams.

Process-driven work is repetitive and quite unlike the more creative and project-oriented work that takes place in the hubs. This was a big issue for Miriam, who was born and grew up in Germany, but used to work in a financial hub for a British investment bank before she decided to move back to her hometown, Berlin. The decision to leave her well-paid job was motivated by an unsatisfactory work–life balance, but she admitted she was disappointment with her new responsibilities:

> My job was very repetitive. Same reports to be delivered every day, week or month. There were rarely tasks out of the ordinary . . . I didn't really have responsibilities. Work had deadlines, however if they were not met it wasn't the end of the world. The job took me two steps back in my career. I delivered the best service, as that is my work attitude and ethic. However, I didn't feel that was necessary. I was not kept motivated even after asking several times to join in on extra projects to network with

> other teams and gather more experience. I was told I would be informed if a project were to come up, but that didn't happen during my stay.

Although Miriam had been prepared for the fact that her new job in Berlin would not be as interesting as her previous job, the lack of challenges eventually forced her to start looking for a new job. She did not want to go back to working in a hub, because she preferred the relaxed pace of life that Berlin offers. For this reason, she decided to look for a job internally at another office in the city which employs relationship managers who have direct contact with corporate clients, and is geographically focused on the German-speaking market. The office does not have a multicultural work environment as it almost exclusively employs Germans who are much older than their counterparts at the nearshore location. Miriam had past experience working directly with clients in a hub, which is why she instantly felt as if she was the right candidate for the job. Her job interview went smoothly as it transpired that she was indeed highly qualified for the position, and her fluent English gave her an advantage over other candidates: "Now having moved internally to a new role, I feel more valued in what I do, and there is a lot more structure. I do not work in the back office anymore; I have my own client portfolio and client contact, which means that my job is more diverse and interesting."

The division of work into fragmented processes devalues skills. In this respect, young professionals are no different from other workers (Braverman 1974). Deskilling impacts on employees' motivation and satisfaction levels. Much work in financial services is based on standardized documents provided by a professional body to establish good practice. Legal documents such as the International Swaps and Derivatives Association's Master Agreement (an industry standard document that sets out provisions governing over-the-counter derivative transactions) are usually negotiated in nearshore or offshore locations. Although the document itself can be very complex, each institution can decide the "risk appetite" within which it is negotiated. The process is standardized by creating templates that specify which clauses can be deviated from and which cannot. As Ellen Hertz commented to Annelise Riles, financial markets are not hard to understand, and stressing the complexity of financial documentation serves only to exoticize finance lawyers (Riles 2010: 808).

Miriam described differences between nearshore workers in Berlin and hub workers that are especially visible to those who can compare the experiences: "Tasks in Berlin are purely operational, fully process-driven. In the long run you lose contact with the outside world, and realize your tasks cannot be performed outside the organization. It is clear that the main rationale for this state of affairs is cost-cutting." The biggest differences relate to the nature of tasks, salary, availability of external training, and opportunities to travel for business. Nearshore employees are confined to stationary work, while their mental labor is transported to its destination virtually: their work migrates elsewhere, but their bodies do not (Chong 2018). To travel for work is seen by some as a privilege, hence they aspire to be promoted to roles where it is required. Although technology has contributed to the emergence of horizontal networks that connect offices in different locations, this has done little to undermine the traditional corporate culture or vertical hierarchies, which impact more profoundly on nearshore workers. These hierarchies determine career goals and motivate employees to achieve the freedom of the entrepreneurial self to achieve them. This can be done by demonstrating skills: technical knowledge, which employees obtain as part of their education or as on-the-job training, and also soft skills, including communication, the management of expectations, conflict resolution, and knowing when to comply with instructions and when to ask questions or request help. In its recruiting brochures, the Berlin center emphasized both teamwork and independent skills:

> Strong team skills and the ability to work independently . . . service-oriented, strong work ethic, pursuit of excellence and a proven ability to work effectively with minimal supervision, proactive attitude and initiative.
>
> Self-confident and involved appearance in dealing with clients . . . High level of discretion and trustworthiness . . . Self-motivated and comfortable managing your own career as a team player . . . Team spirit and the ability to work in an international and diverse environment. The individual will need to demonstrate that she/he is self-motivated and innovative, and be able to work independently and effectively under pressure.
>
> [T]he candidate will have . . . confidence, drive and enthusiasm, coupled with a positive attitude and a delivery focus . . . Excellent team-working capabilities and the ability to build strong business and team relationships . . . The ability to work with minimal supervision on multi-task assignments, to set priorities and ensure consistent delivery of high-quality services.

The phrase "self-motivated and comfortable managing your own career as a team player" suggests that it is possible to develop one's individual career while working together with other people, and that the assessment of an employee's individual performance will include teamworking skills.

The interplay between freedom and teamwork creates opposing subjectivities that young professionals sometimes struggle to balance. Lorna studied musicology. Originally from London, she moved to Berlin in 2008 after graduation, tempted by lower costs of living and a lack of job prospects at home. Although her academic background was unusual, she was recruited in 2011 and was still working in the same team at the time of my research in 2016. Although she is now fluent in German, Lorna was hired to work in English, and continues to do so to this day. Her job was to support credit officers by making sure that their databases were updated with the latest credit ratings and regulatory requirements. She also processed large datasets and analyzed the underlying data. The work had to be carried out according to defined procedures on a daily, weekly, monthly, and quarterly base. After a few years of this work, Lorna decided that her educational background was placing her at a disadvantage when it came to promotion chances. She therefore enrolled on a two-year master's course in finance at a local Hochschule. Her boss supported her by allowing her to reduce her working hours for the duration of the studies, and to take educational leave when writing her thesis. Lorna was grateful. She ended up being promoted as a team head. Her tasks did not change dramatically, but they began to involve managerial responsibilities and human resources tasks. She never complained about alienating work processes but, by studying, she clearly impressed her managers by creating a new set of responsibilities for herself. Neoliberal subjectivity has been strongly inculcated, including the readiness to learn new skills. However, skill acquisition can be exclusionary, and while certain people can master skills that will help them in their careers, others may not be able to do so due to gender, social status, or power dynamics (Carswell and De Neve 2018). To study for a master's degree and continue working may not be an option for an employee with children, especially if they are a single parent. Lorna lives with her German boyfriend (who helps her with her written German when the need arises) and has no children.

Lorna's case shows that to manifest an entrepreneurial self against process-driven work is ultimately the freedom to choose a way of showing individualism that fits one's character and circumstances. This can take many forms. While Lorna was proactive, Jane opted for a slightly different strategy. Her job was an integral part of financial products approval, which was crucial to the authorization of trades. Inadequate performance would translate into lost revenue for the bank. Jane recalls:

> I was doing the same job for over four years without changing teams. It wasn't a difficult job, I just had to know what to click and when. I know some colleagues were thinking that I didn't have ambitions, or that I wasn't smart enough to change teams internally and progress. But I had a plan. I wanted to learn as much as I could, get to know the systems I was using inside out, so that if someone from the hub had a problem, they would always come to me. In this way I was working on my brand within the team, and the department. And it paid off. People were asking me for help, not the team head. At one point, when my team in Berlin was threatened with cuts, I was offered a job by the people I used to support [from the hub], who knew me well and knew that I had the knowledge and experience required for the position.

Jane was promoted to work in the same area of expertise in one of the hubs. She invested time in becoming excellent in her position as a nearshore employee, thereby advertising her skills and knowledge to superiors, who scouted her once an opportunity arose. It was her individual decision to continue working in one position for a long period of time, even though there were earlier opportunities to move internally. She preferred to perfect the same role because she felt that this was the best way to raise her profile as a dedicated employee in the eyes of the senior managers at the hub, who relied on her input.

Not everyone, however, stays so committed to their job and professional network. Rachel was a young graduate who moved to Berlin from New Zealand to be with her German boyfriend. She came from a traditional Indian family, and moving to Europe with her boyfriend was a bold move toward self-realization, as it established boundaries with her parents. She admitted it was very difficult to settle at first, especially because of the language barrier. But Rachel had a degree in finance and, even though the nearshore center was only her second job, she knew what she wanted in terms of career goals. Soon after arriving in Berlin, she noted that the relatively low renumeration would not suffice for the long-term career planning:

> The salary is small but it's ok. It's ok because it's enough to have a comfortable life in Berlin, but it's nowhere near what you could earn in London for example. I do love the team and the work atmosphere though. I like that it's so international and that there are people from different cultures. You can get inspired by it, and I find it very motivating to do something outside of work. I get motivated by people who do things in their free time, and I want to do the same. I was thinking of maybe becoming a dog trainer in my free time, or to volunteer with a sustainability-focused NGO.

Apart from the low salary, Rachel grumbled about the repetitive nature of the tasks she had to perform. After two years she left the job to join another company in Berlin, because she was unable to negotiate better financial conditions and her tasks never changed, which translated into low motivation to continue performing her responsibilities. Rachel's tenure of two years is typical for those who are not satisfied with their tasks and who do not believe that an internal promotion would make their work more interesting. Instead of investing time and effort in establishing closer relationships with her superiors, or with colleagues in other teams, who might have been able to advise her where the best chances were for quick career progression, she decided to try her luck elsewhere. Her desire to dedicate more time to her personal growth set her apart from other employees, who were content to remain in the comfort zone of the company.

Given that financial services jobs in Berlin as scare, whoever succeeds at finding another position at another company is seen by former colleagues as someone who has progressed in their careers, because finding a financial job in the city is challenging. I have often heard expressions describing such people as ambitious, motivated, or not easily satisfied—or statements such as: "They had had enough," and "It was too boring for them." In fact, leaving the company is sometimes regarded higher than switching teams internally. Due to internal rules, a successful candidate upon an internal transfer to a new team is not offered a pay rise, even if the new role is more senior. In such a situation, one is given a development plan that outlines the required steps to progress to a more senior role and within what timeframe. Only upon meeting these conditions can an employee be promoted. This process, however, is highly arbitrary and non-transparent, as some employees were given a promotion a month after joining a new team, but some had to wait a year. This system cannot be challenged other than by leaving the company, which explains why doing so is regarded as a bold move that shows initiative and control over one's own career progression. This system was the main reason why Rachel was discouraged from applying for an internal position and decided to leave. Like Jane, she was driven and independent in the way she steered her career, which led her to leave the nearshore center, thus taking more control of when and on what conditions she would be promoted.

Foreigners such as Rachel and Jane worked in teams where responsibilities are performed in English to support the bank's English-language operations. Few of their colleagues were German. Exclusively German teams work in their native language. Employees in these teams are generally older, with most born and raised in Berlin. Franziska studied law and worked for a German law firm, but failed to qualify as a lawyer. Her situation was similar to that of unqualified lawyers working in the back office of a top-tier Tokyo bank, who assist traders by negotiating derivative documentation (Riles 2010):

> I was working as a legal assistant for a German law firm. I had a lot of serious responsibilities. I had to prepare court documents and make sure that all the deadlines were met. We were working with real people on complicated cases that directly impacted on their lives, yet the money was so little that I had to look for another employer. And this is how I ended up working here. At first, I started working in an English-speaking team, and this was a big challenge, because I had never worked in English before. I didn't fully understand the terminology in the contracts and other documents. It made me always so stressed that I was making even more mistakes because of this. I switched to a German-speaking team later and I then felt more confident in my job.

Franziska struggled with contract negotiation, mostly because it required fluency in English, which she did not possess. She therefore changed jobs internally several times, always to a German-speaking team. She has been employed at the bank for five years now, but has only once received a pay raise. Despite her dedication (she works long, often irregular hours), Franziska has not accomplished a consistent professional development, at least not in the form of regular promotions. Although she considers herself competent, she admits that she finds it hard to "promote herself" and "advertise" her work. When her team head from one of the hubs visited the Berlin office, she thought about requesting a private meeting with this key player in the bank, aware that a personal conversation would give her a better opportunity to highlight her hard work. But Franziska was timid and aware of her shortcomings as a communicator. She discussed whether or not to pursue this opportunity with her colleagues, but even when one of them encouraged her to propose a short meeting, she hesitated to do so. On another occasion, when I asked what made a good team, Franziska replied:

> For me, the most important thing is that there is someone helpful in the team, someone who is kind enough to explain things to me. I had different experiences with people here at the bank; some were very helpful and never said no to me when I asked for clarification, but others made me feel so stupid when I approached them. So the best teammate would be someone who can support others, and these are people I feel most comfortable working with. I also help whenever I can—I enjoy that, and I also expect that from others.

Franziska's outlook on work is focused on support and cooperation, rather than self-realization by taking on new challenges. Technical skills and knowledge are a prerequisite for the efficient deployment of soft skills to promote the entrepreneurial self. Franziska admits that she lacks confidence in speaking English and that she needs to ask a lot of questions before she understands a task in that language. Her relationships in the workplace differ from those of more ambitious colleagues because they are "not opportunistic," as she puts it. Rather, they are based on her past experiences of mutual support.

The first thing that new employees are told during their induction process is to "take ownership of work." This means assuming responsibility, dedicating time and effort to the delivery of high-quality work. To take ownership of one's work implies a proactive strategy that minimizes the likelihood that the work will be challenged due to mistakes, or lack of punctuality. In a process-driven work environment, employees have several ways in which to take ownership. Franziska emphasizes that she takes her responsibilities at the bank very seriously, as she had done in the past when working as a legal assistant. She always makes sure that the tasks are completed on time, working late to meet deadlines when necessary. This is a key aspect of "shareholder mentality" (Cushen 2013). Neoliberal subjectivity is based on trust in the employer to provide an environment conducive to individual self-realization. The tacit bargain juxtaposes the worker's entrepreneurial self with the comforting structure of being inside an organization.

The entrepreneurial self, associated with initiative, creativity, and determination, can also be a fabrication. Employees who work long hours to create the impression of a heavy workload may be observed taking lengthy coffee breaks during the day. Miriam considered the nearshore center an undesirable place to work, because the salaries were not commensurate with employees' excellent qualifications. Jan, a native German who had previously worked in the banking sector in Luxembourg, commented on why some colleagues might feel uncomfortable sharing their experiences with me:

> Whoever tells you that they like this job is lying. They are fake and double-faced, but this is their way of surviving and being promoted. They are just playing games and they pretend to have your best interest in mind—but in reality, they will leave you alone and protect only themselves. They don't tolerate honesty or openness about the things you don't like about your job. You can't trust anyone.

Jan's statement confirms that "the level of general fear, stress, and paranoia appears to be much greater in banks than in most of the other enterprises . . . Employees are under enormous pressure not to ask too many questions" (Graeber 2018: 168). According to Graeber, bankers are afraid to question their responsibilities because to do so would almost certainly lead to redundancy. It would also undermine professional relationships, hinder realization of the entrepreneurial self, and jeopardize professional development.

Jan's situation is somewhat similar to that of Rachel. Immediately after joining the bank in 2013, he signed up for a sabbatical scheme that would allow him at some point in the future to request extended leave. After five years of full-time work, he left Berlin to teach German in Albania. Always very positive, with a constant smile on his face, he was confident that this would be a great career move that would show his individuality. When he returned, he found that this initiative had in fact set him back. He was allocated to a new team, as his previous job had been decommissioned. This did not bother him and he was happy to have plenty of time to find another role within the Berlin office, preferably one that would allow him to build on his teaching experience. Two months later, after several unsuccessful interviews, Jan concluded that his sabbatical work experience was being seen as an abnormality:

> I think that the people who interviewed me don't like what I did. I always tell them what I did in Albania because I am so proud of it. This motivated me to apply for new

> jobs in which I thought I would be able to show the new skills that I learned, and that because of my additional skills I would be the perfect candidate. I talked a lot about my experiences in Albania during the interviews, but I don't think it helped me—I think it actually did the opposite. I think that if you decide to leave the company to do something else, it is perceived that you are not committed to the bank. For me it was about showing my independence, problem-solving, and creativity. But I think that for the hiring managers it showed a lack of dedication to the bank and to work, because a dedicated employee would not have gone on sabbatical in the first place.

Jan's example shows that an adventurous interpretation of freedom at work can hinder career progression. Jan was not the only one who took a sabbatical, but he expressly stated that his motivation was to acquire new professional skills as a teacher, and not mere travel.

Jan's entrepreneurial approach to self-realization can be contrasted with that of Javier, who joined the nearshore center in 2014 to work on contract negotiation. Originally from Spain, he was a qualified lawyer who worked alongside other lawyers on minimizing risk within derivative documentation. Although these responsibilities were in line with his education, Javier changed jobs internally to work as a credit analyst, motivated by enhanced prospects for promotion in this new role. However, he soon found his new tasks to be just as alienating and repetitive as the old ones, and so in his free time he started working on his own business idea. Having learned how to analyze balance sheets and financial statements, he had the skills to draft his own business plan:

> I realized at some point that I can't expect much from the roles here and that I need to do something else. I started working in the evenings from home with my wife on our small business. I didn't know anything about registering a company in Germany, or tax issues, so I spent evenings at home after work reading and trying to understand how it works in this country. I would sleep three or four hours per night sometimes, after which I was coming to the office really tired and had to work full time. But I wanted to do it.

While launching his own retail business, Javier continued working at the nearshore center, before finding a better-paid position as a lawyer in another Berlin company. He continued in this secure post after opening his private shop and hiring staff; 25 percent of every item sold in his shop is donated to a charity, and Javier says that any profit he makes is secondary to helping those in need. He uses social media to advertise his business and offers the space for private hire, thereby showcasing the entrepreneurial skills that made him a popular speaker at public events in the city. He appears to be juggling his professional responsibilities with ease, and never loses a cheerful grin on his face, despite being a young father who is no stranger to sleepless nights. Although his nearshore experience resembles that of other colleagues, he never dwells on the negative aspects of work. Javier's strong work ethic is visible in his attitude towards setting his own goals, which he strives to achieve by remaining a contracted employee, even after opening his own shop. He says that his office job has helped him in the process of setting up his own business, especially with tax and accounting, and he never thought of reducing his hours or going part time. This is, however, an exceptional case.

Other employees of the nearshore center found time for small-scale entrepreneurial initiatives, such as the young professional who sewed attractive cotton bags and purses, which she sold to colleagues. Employees negotiate their own understanding of freedom, and they can exercise freedom precisely because they have the safety net of a stable income that comes with their employment contracts. The few who engage in after-work activities, no matter how complex or time consuming, do so not out of disillusionment with their daily work, but because they are in a situation that allows them the luxury of experimentation and improvisation with new tasks. The benefits of such flexibility became apparent with the onset of the COVID-19 pandemic in 2020, during which employees continued receiving salaries, even though their private ventures were suffering losses.

The individualism demonstrated by employees who are also professionally active outside work can be contrasted with "Intrapreneur" initiatives organized by the bank for all its employees, including the Berlin center. These programs focus on developing innovative products or services to increase revenue, usually by attracting new clients. The rationale is as follows:

> The importance of innovation cannot be overstated . . . Staying ahead of the competition is no longer simply a matter of competing on price or reach; clients now expect the companies . . . to understand their individual needs and to tailor the ways they provide their services. . . . We launched the Intrapreneur initiative, which enables our employees to develop and execute business ideas like entrepreneurs . . . [to] unleash potential in our bank.

Applicants are encouraged to propose innovations at the level of the institution globally, or at lower levels. Short-listed candidates are invited to a series of interviews to test their business acumen and assess their motivation. The successful ones are divided into groups of five, each of which works on a new business idea for two weeks before pitching it to the board of directors at the bank's headquarters. During the program, the daily responsibilities of the intrapreneurs are reassigned to other employees. Those selected must get clearance from their managers, but as participation is seen as a prestigious opportunity that can raise the profile of the intrapreneur's team, consent is normally a formality. The board decides which idea will receive funding, and the winning team then has three months to implement it.

The intrapreneur initiative is an opportunity to engage in new tasks with new people. It allows employees to demonstrate their knowledge of the company and to suggest how they would improve it. The skills required for successful completion of the task are, however, directed inwards, as the aim is to increase the company's revenue. The Berlin employees who have taken part in the initiative are mostly senior staff members, but the majority of participants come from the hubs, where employees are in a better position to identify clients' needs. In any event, the company-wide intrapreneur initiative underlines the causality between freedom to be creative and innovative, and the structure of the company that grants opportunities for independence, but only within prescribed rules, and subject to the criteria of growth and profitability.

Conclusion

This chapter has investigated the juxtaposition of individuality and teamwork in the context of standardized work processes in a nearshore financial services center. Manifestations of the entrepreneurial self can lead some employees to seek new employment opportunities elsewhere, but others stay. Individuality is expressed via technical and soft skills that show dedication to the workplace. Only initiatives that show this dedication are accepted and recognized. Freedom in the nearshore center is heavily constrained, because it has to reinforce the ultimate business objectives of the company and shareholder mentality. Rules and processes promote a freedom that is directed inwards to maintain the structure, and ultimately to increase revenue. The freedom that is defined by structures is effectively invalidated by a control mechanism that promotes order and discipline within the organization.

Acknowledgments

My thanks to the organizers and participants of the "Work, Ethics, Freedom" workshop in Halle, and also to my co-workers in the nearshore offices in Berlin, who through their openness allowed me to learn and grow.

Magdalena Dąbkowska has a background in international law as well as social anthropology. She is a faculty member at the Berlin School of Economics and Law, where she teaches business finance, while simultaneously working on her doctoral thesis at the Humboldt University.

Notes

1. The Basel Committee on Banking Supervision is an international organization composed of financial regulators and central banks from twenty-eight jurisdictions. Its decisions are not binding, and there are no penalties for non-compliance. To become legally binding, the committee's recommendations must be implemented as law by national governments. The initial phase of Basel III reforms was published in 2010. The text was finalized in December 2017, and is supposed to be fully implemented by 2022.
2. Unemployment was 7.8 percent in Berlin in September 2019 compared to 2.2 percent in Munich, and 4.8 percent in Frankfurt: https://statistik.arbeitsagentur.de/Navigation/Statistik/Statistik-nach-Regionen/Politische-Gebietsstruktur/Hessen/Frankfurt-am-Main-Stadt-Nav.html (last accessed 30 April 2020).
3. The extent to which the drop in unemployment was directly caused by the reforms is debated. According to research by the Friedrich Ebert Foundation (Fink, Hennicke, and Tiemann 2019), Agenda 2010 contributed to growing economic inequality.
4. https://statistik.arbeitsagentur.de/Navigation/Statistik/Statistik-nach-Regionen/Politische-Gebietsstruktur/Hessen/Frankfurt-am-Main-Stadt-Nav.html (last accessed 30 April 2020).
5. In 2013 it reached 27.5 percent in Greece, and 26.1 percent in Spain. https://ec.europa.eu/eurostat/databrowser/view/tipsun20/default/table?lang=en (last accessed 30 April 2020).
6. The analysis that follows is based on interviews (all names are fictitious), participant observation, covert research, and data from financial newspapers.

References

Admati, Anat, and Martin Hellwig. 2014. *The Bankers' New Clothes: What's Wrong with Banking and What To Do about It*. Princeton, NJ: Princeton University Press.

Basel Committee on Banking Supervision. 2017. Press release 7 December. https://www.bis.org/press/p171207.htm (last accessed 30 April 2020).

Braverman, Harry. 1974. *Labor and Monopoly Capital: The Degradation of Work in the Twentieth Century*. New York: Monthly Review Press.

Carswell, Grace, and Geert De Neve. 2018. "Towards a Political Economy of Skill and Garment Work: The Case of the Tiruppur Industrial Cluster in South India." In *Industrial Labor on the Margins of Capitalism: Precarity, Class, and the Neoliberal Subject*, ed. Chris Hann and Jonathan Parry, 309–35. Oxford: Berghahn Books.

Chong, Kimberly. 2018. *Best Practice: Management Consulting and the Ethics of Financialization in China*. Durham, NC: Duke University Press.

Cushen, Jean. 2013. "Financialization in the Workplace: Hegemonic Narratives, Performative Interventions, and the Angry Knowledge Worker." *Accounting, Organizations and Society* 38(4): 314–31.
Davis-Blake, Alison, and Joseph P. Broschak. 2009. "Outsourcing and the Changing Nature of Work." *Annual Review of Sociology* 35: 321–340.
Fink, Philipp, Martin Hennicke, and Heinrich Tiemann. 2019. "Ungleiches Deutschland Sozioökonomischer Disparitätenbericht 2019." Bonn: Friedrich-Ebert-Stiftung.
Graeber, David. 2018. *Bullshit Jobs*. London: Penguin Books.
Gudeman, Stephen. 2016. *Anthropology and Economy*. Cambridge: Cambridge University Press.
Gupta, Priya S. 2019. "The Entwined Futures of Financialization and Cities." *Cambridge Journal of Economics* 43(4): 1123–48.
Harvey, David. 2007. *A Brief History of Neoliberalism*. Oxford: Oxford University Press.
Ho, Karen. 2005. "Situating Global Capitalisms: A View from Wall Street Investment Banks." *Cultural Anthropology* 20(1): 68–96.
Matos, Patricia. 2012. "Call Center Labor and the Injured Precariat: Shame, Stigma, and Downward Social Mobility in Contemporary Portugal." *Dialectical Anthropology* 36(3/4): 217–43.
Ofstehage, Andrew L. 2018. "Financialization of Work, Value, and Social Organization among Transnational Soy Farmers in the Brazilian Cerrado." *Economic Anthropology* Special Issue: Financialization 5(2): 274–85.
Riles, Annelise. 2010. "Collateral Expertise: Legal Knowledge in the Global Financial Markets." *Current Anthropology* 51(6): 795–818.
Sassen, Saskia. 2001. *The Global City*. Princeton, NJ: Princeton University Press.
Tombs, Steve. 2017. "After the Crisis: Morality Plays and the Renewal of Business as Usual." In *Neoliberalism and the Moral Economy of Fraud*, ed. D. Whyte and J. Wiegratz, 31–43. New York: Routledge.

12

Writing without Fear—or Bylines

Freedom and Frustration among US American Ghostwriters

Deborah A. Jones

Jenna Glatzer counts herself lucky. After ghostwriting thirty-three books, mostly memoirs and a smattering of health and wellness guides, she says "there's really only one project that bugs me I can't take credit for." She does not elaborate, and I am left uncertain as to whether this project is the same as another one she has just told me about, one that she worked on for two years but was not permitted to list on her CV due to a non-disclosure agreement. Not long after Glatzer had completed that book, she received an inquiry regarding preparing a manuscript on a similar topic. The new project sounded intriguing, and Glatzer knew she was qualified to do it, but could not prove she had the experience. The named author of the first book was an academic. Academics, ghostwriters regularly told me, were the worst about sharing credit.

Among the ghostwriters I have interviewed, Glatzer is both highly typical as well as fairly unusual. Like the overwhelming majority of my American or US-based research participants, she is female, university educated, a native speaker of English, and white. She came to ghostwriting as a second career—ghostwriting is never anyone's plan A—and, like many of my interlocutors, she did so after a significant life disruption forced her to re-examine her anticipated path. Although "ghosting" was not her dream job, she speaks enthusiastically about it, explaining that writing "in another's voice" helped her refind her footing after spending three years housebound with agoraphobia. Trained as a stage actress, Glatzer has a good ear for verbal patterning, though she pointed out that a good ghostwriter does not imitate the named author precisely but works to capture their voice while telling their story in an effective and compelling manner. She considers it a "a joy to get to know someone whose life is worth a book," and to occupy their world for a time.

While memoir writers seem to be the most satisfied of ghostwriters (and while there is undoubtedly some bias in my sample, which mostly comprises self-selected volunteers), Glatzer's professed passion for her work is not unique. One of my study's most striking findings has been how much my research participants seem to enjoy and find fulfillment in writing as someone else. They speak of bringing stories that might otherwise go untold into the world; of ensuring important ideas and new discoveries are communicated with clarity; and of empowering people who have contributions to make, but do not have the writing skills (or the standard English) to make them effectively. Once ghostwriters deliver a manuscript, they let go, relinquishing all credit to the named author. And then they move on, unburdened, to the next project. As I speak to Glatzer—eyeing the clock, because I have revisions to attend to on my own languishing journal article—I find myself somewhat envious of the freedom she enjoys. I briefly imagine being able to write without fear of judgment (or having to go through peer review), of being able to dip into different lives and genres, to try on different avatars, and to be paid good money to boot.

But Glatzer was also quite different from many of the ghostwriters I spoke to. First, her clients (the ones she could discuss, that is) included a reality TV star, a disabled athlete turned inspirational speaker, a teen activist whose book with Glatzer became a made-for-TV movie, and five-time Grammy award winner Céline Dion. Top-tier ghostwriters can earn upward of 80,000 US dollars per project, plus royalties. However, the ghostwriters who can command such prices are a small minority, and many of them work for agencies that take a large chunk of the pay. Other ghostwriters I discuss in this chapter are working in far less lucrative genres such as undergraduate term papers or search engine optimized blog posts. Faith-based writers or those working with disadvantaged populations, such as refugees, may only receive small honoraria—or may even volunteer their labor. The median sticker price for a ghostwritten memoir—typically the product of months if not years spent analyzing hours of interviews, transcriptions, and other exchanges with clients—is difficult to pin down. However, my research suggests that the going rate in the United States for a 50,000 to 60,000-word manuscript by a moderately experienced freelancer working with a non-celebrity client (for example, a senior citizen writing a family history) is about US$20,000 in the middle part of the country but 50 percent higher on the coasts, particularly in New York and California. For a manuscript commissioned through an agency, the price is easily double that, though what the "ghost" receives is sometimes much lower.[1]

Another way Glatzer is unusual is that she is quite public both about being a ghostwriter as well as the personal reasons she came to the profession. I approached her precisely because she has been quoted in numerous news stories about ghostwriting, and, unlike many of my interlocutors, is not nervous around researchers. Because she writes publicly about ghostwriting, I can refer to Jenna Glatzer by her actual name; I preserve the anonymity of interlocutors who wish it by referring to them by first-name pseudonyms. Generally, memoir ghostwriters are the most open about their profession because their work is the least stigmatized—in fact, when celebrities are involved, ghostwriting can seem quite glamorous. Meanwhile, ghostwriters of other genres, such as academic essays and articles, are rarely invited to be so forthright about their work, or only agree to do so if their names can be withheld.

Finally, Glatzer is atypical in that she regularly manages to negotiate cover-level credit for her work. By "cover-level credit," I mean that she secures prominent bylines in which she is listed as co-author (e.g., Céline Dion and Jenna Glatzer) or as memoirist (Céline Dion with Jenna Glatzer; Céline Dion as told to Jenna Glatzer)—albeit in a much smaller font. When Glatzer cannot secure cover-level credit, she usually manages to negotiate another form of acknowledgment within the pages of the book, and permission to include the title on her list of completed works. "Credit is normally not a big deal for me," Glatzer elaborates. "A lot of ghostwriters assume they're not getting credit. I assume the opposite. I send a contract assuming I will get credit, and most people go along with it . . . If I'm not getting credit, it's a higher fee [an average increase of $5,000]."

Glatzer acknowledges that part of her success in getting bylines arises from the genres she works in, and consequently the clients she has. "Memoirs are more stylistic," she explains, contrasting the work ghostwriters do to tell life stories with, for example, ghostwriting a how-to book, an academic essay, or a piece of creative writing. With memoir, the named author is presumed the expert in their own history, and the ghostwriter merely someone who helps them tell it more effectively. Having a co-author does not detract from the legitimacy of the named author's story and, in cases in which the named author might be perceived as unreliable (alleged murderer OJ Simpson, for example), it can actually be taken as verifying it. By contrast, the named authors of information-and-analysis driven books are often wary of sharing credit. For academics, doctors, psychologists, businesspeople, and religious leaders, the revelation that they used a ghostwriter might undermine their authority or throw their ownership of ideas into question. Thus, Glatzer has almost always secured credit for the memoirs she has written but been relegated to "editor" on more expository projects, even if the work she did went far beyond what most would consider as editing. Of the thirty-three ghostwriting projects Glatzer has completed, her CV lists only two-thirds of them—and again, this is actually quite a high rate of visibility for a ghostwriter. Among my project participants are people who have secured credit for one in five, ten, twenty, or hardly any of their ghostwritten texts at all.

My ghostwriter interlocutors often tell me that they have done at least one project that "I wouldn't want my name on anyway." Yet they do fret about lack of credit, because an absence of bylines can make it extremely difficult for a ghostwriter to get more work. While more established ghostwriters often acquire projects through colleagues and word of mouth (such referral processes being quite common in professions requiring discretion), a sparse CV can be a real impediment for those just starting out. Like other people developing their businesses, ghostwriters build their careers by demonstrating competence, experience, and, ideally, a roster of clients who sing their praises. Yet the very notion that a ghostwriter should have a client list to share can seem paradoxical. As Glatzer notes, the prevailing assumption is that ghostwriters, by definition, do not receive any form of credit and, further, are to remain invisible once their work is complete. Thus, asking for credit, asking to be seen, can seem like a bold act, and listing one's achievements on, for example, one's freelance website can feel like a betrayal of the ghostwriter–client relationship.

How do you build your career when your brand is being invisible? While ghostwriting can be sensationalized, it is one thing to author Céline Dion's memoir and quite another to admit you write term papers and theses for a living. Most of my ghostwriter interlocutors needed to be quite subtle in how they presented themselves and their work. This was not only because they wanted to protect their clients' reputations and feelings (most US-based ghostwriters are female, and many see their work as an act of care), but because ghostwriting remains stigmatized in some circles. Later in this chapter, I explain how one academic ghostwriter, whom I will call Erin, built her client roster. Like Glatzer, Erin finds meaning in ghostwriting, explaining how it helped her overcome the paralyzing writing anxiety that forced her to abandon her own academic career. As a self-defined "ghost," "tutor," "silent co-author," and "substantive editor," she "helps people not to be lost" and "is the person I needed to have [in graduate school]." But compared to Glatzer, Erin rarely receives credit for what she produces, and she has faced personal and professional difficulties "living in the shadows."

The freedoms and frustrations that ghostwriters find in their profession offer renewed opportunity to consider the complicated relationship between work and self, both as it has existed in the past as well as in the twenty-first century. Ghostwriting initially seems categorically alienating:

the ghostwriter relinquishes their creative work to a named author who claims credit for it, uses that credit to advance their own career, and profits far beyond what they paid the ghost. Yet the scholarly record abounds with illustrations of the "dialogical" and "heteroglossic" (Bakhtin [1934/35] 1981) nature of speech and writing, reminding us that the very notion of single authorship is an illusion. The production of seemingly individual authors is an interactional achievement grounded in social relations, division of labor, and sometimes financial exchange (Putnam 1975; Goffman 1981; Irvine 1996; Tomlinson and Millie 2017; Wolf-Meyer 2020).

The dampening of other voices can be the result of uneven, oppressive power relations, but this is not always the case; people who lend their words to others may have a variety of motivations for doing so. Similarly, while experiences of alienation, or at least unfairness, seem to be a human universal, they are not perceived or experienced in the same way everywhere (Schwimmer 1979). Many scholars have observed their interlocutors enter what seem to be irrational, even exploitative arrangements in order to funnel resources from their work environments into personal projects, or to cultivate relationships they anticipate being useful down the line (Henig and Makovicky 2017; Smith 2019; also, Rajković, Santos et al., and Smith, this volume). Likewise, workers may distinguish between work they strongly identify with and work that just pays the bills. Artists, for example, have long sought other means for supporting their crafts, finding fulfillment, frustration, or even relief in their "day jobs," depending on the nature of the employment, the compensation, and when and how it takes them away from their "real work" (Schwimmer 1979; Gerber 2017). Although not all ghostwriters identify as artists, for some, ghosting becomes an avenue to a creative life, whether because it offers financial support or because writing as someone else is itself a creative challenge. For others, ghosting offers the chance to set one's own hours or to work remotely—serious perks if you are, like many of my interlocutors, in a caregiving position, managing a chronic illness, or living somewhere employment opportunities are limited.[2]

In the next section, I situate ghostwriting within the neoliberal economy and its burgeoning market for outsourced linguistic labor, showing how ghostwriters and their clients (who may or may not also be the named authors of texts) often find themselves in a symbiotic relationship. This symbiosis affects how ghostwriters perceive their work, and they can find ghosting collaborative, caring, personally fulfilling, and financially advantageous—even when they are not receiving credit for anything they write. I then provide an extended case study of the woman I call Erin. Erin's story will both affirm and complicate some of what I lay out in the section prior. My objective is to capture the range of feelings that my ghostwriter interlocutors can and do have about what is, for most of them, an unexpected career path, but one they often enjoy. Ultimately, I argue that we must be cautious about what we presume selling authorship or relinquishing credit actually represents to those who do it. This not to say that ghostwriting is never exploitative or alienating, nor that lack of credit is not a serious problem for some. However, when ghostwriters feel frustrated with their profession, it is not necessarily because they have been denied a byline.

This study is based on e-mail or direct messaging exchanges with seventy-two ghostwriters working in English; forty-one interviews with specifically American and/or US-based ghostwriters; an analysis of English and some German-language media related to ghostwriting (advertisements, news articles, agency blogs, freelance business development tips); and participant observation in online forums where writers trade tips about potential projects, where to publish, and how to handle pricing, contracts, and difficult clients. Although I secured several interviews by directly contacting ghostwriters and ghostwriting agencies with established online presence, the majority of my interlocutors were self-selecting participants who replied to queries I posted on social media and job boards. Most of my interlocutors cited "word of mouth" or referrals from other ghostwriters as the way they generated most of their business. However, because ghostwriters tend to work remotely, many regularly browse internet forums for professional community, or receive "pings" from job boards that alert them to potential opportunities. Thus, when I placed advertisements seeking interviews, my would-be interlocutors received my invitation.[3] Suddenly, I was flooded with messages from ghostwriters eager to talk about their work—and curious about what else I was finding.

Language as a Commodity? Ghostwriting in the Twenty-First Century

In the final chapter of their book *Language, Capitalism, Colonialism*, Monica Heller and Bonnie McElhinny (2017) locate several linguistic trends in the contemporary economy that seem to bump up against each other. These include: the importance of communicative labor and the increasing tendency to outsource it (to overseas call centers, for example; see also Awal, this volume); the treatment of language skills as less a personal quality than an asset to be managed (consider the explosive growth of standardized tests like CELTA and TOEFL that measure and certify English language abilities for the marketplace); and an emphasis on the "authenticity" of goods and workers, both of which are now subject to brand management. (On "personal brands" and their role in job seeking and hiring, see Gershon 2016, 2017.)

Ghostwriting, defined here as composing original texts in another's voice, in a situation in which some notion of "single authorship" is expected or valued, such that the named author benefits from claiming credit, would seem to exist at the confluence of these trends.[4] Memoir publications, for example, have surged in the anglophone world since the 1990s (Yagoda 2009), and many of them are ghostwritten. Digitalized labor and self-publishing platforms have democratized who can tell their story (and seek assistance in doing so), and my ghostwriter interlocutors took pride in helping communicate the experiences of populations previously less heard. Personal narrative has also come to play a key role in the business sphere, where books offering origin stories and lessons learned have become key tools for branding. Although they rarely sell well, such books serve as credentials that elevate the named author's profile and offer access to lucrative lecture circuits. Shorter texts, such as search-engine-optimized blog posts hosted on a personal website, and "thought leadership" columns published on content consolidators like Huffington Post, Medium, and even Forbes, have become important to small-business owners and freelancers trying to increase their visibility or direct traffic to their websites. Blogs primed for Google's ever-changing algorithms can be purchased through bulk content providers or commissioned via job boards or work distribution platforms (cf. Gershon and Cefkin, this volume.) For those seeking more personal attention, there are now dozens of freelancers and boutique ghostwriting agencies offering bespoke texts and social media management. There are even at least two venture-capital backed start-ups specializing in book-length manuscript development: Scribe, based out of the tech-hub Austin, Texas; and Reedsy, a London-based platform for hiring writing professionals, which was developed, in part, through a European Union Horizon 2020 grant.

And yet, even if ghostwriting is a growing field, it is not a new one. Business executives have long relied on others to write their letters and speeches. Students have long paid others to compose their term papers. Likewise, junior researchers regularly relinquish credit to senior academics in exchange for financial support, letters of reference, or the promise of future opportunities (see Gupta 2014, and Sukarieh and Tannock 2019, on the role—and plight—of foreign research assistants). In American evangelical movements, the tradition of scripting testimony (accounts of how one's life has been touched by God), or hiring a ghostwriter to do so, goes back decades, if not longer.[5] Although more families are now having ghostwriters compose "legacy books" in a loved one's name, helping the elderly document their memories is not a new practice. All of this reminds us that language has never been divorced from political economy and, in fact, it has long been an object of exchange. As linguistic anthropologist Judith T. Irvine concisely put it, talk is *not* cheap (Irvine 1989, emphasis mine).

Heller and McElhinny are not concerned with ghostwriting per se, but they certainly acknowledge the history of redistributing linguistic labor, observing that "secretaries and stenographers . . . telephone operators . . . translators, interpreters, and scribes" have long provided "crucial services." "What is new," they suggest, is that "these processes are not only intensified by [global] competition, but the elements of linguistic form and linguistic practice that compose them are increasingly amendable to being treated as commodities—that is, as resources available for exchange, and measurable (perhaps with some difficulty) in terms of money" (Heller and McElhinny 2017: 242–43). Such observations ring true if we consider that much of the anglophone ghostwriting market turns upon what Michael Silverstein (1996) called "monoglot standard," an ideology that posits only one variety of a language can be correct, and if there are multiple varieties, some are more prestigious than others. Monoglot standard not only drives clients unsure of their own standard language skills to seek ghostwriters, but also informs who can become a ghostwriter and how much they can charge for their services. It is no coincidence that the majority of my American interlocutors are white, native speakers of English, and with Anglo names—that is, people who not only sound like they control the standard, but look the part as well (Rosa 2019). Globally, texts written by native English speakers from North America and Britain are more expensive than those written by native English speakers from India or Kenya, and not only because of the differences in the cost of living. Because clients, in hiring a ghostwriter, are also purchasing a voice, standard language competence and dialect prestige are evaluated by ghosts and clients alike as assets to be acquired or leveraged, rather than individual traits.

We might also see the commodification of language in how ghostwritten texts can be bought or sold through online forums with the aid of electronic payment systems. Recent years have seen numerous exposés about "essay mills" in former British colonies that crank out term papers for lazy undergraduates in the anglophone center. Such investigations reveal sweatshop-like conditions, serialized work, and an economic race to the bottom. The Africans and South Asians composing the essays often have advanced degrees in their own countries, but limited job opportunities and low wages force them to turn to ghostwriting. One can observe a somewhat similar trend in the United States, where, at the domestic level, both the supply of and the demand for ghostwriters has been driven by the casualization of labor. As newspapers have folded and tenure lines evaporated, journalists and academics have sought other writing and research projects to make ends meet. Meanwhile, business professionals who, a generation ago, might have spent decades at the same firm have been forced into freelancing. Often, this means devoting substantial time to drumming up business without the aid of administrative support or a marketing team. Ghostwriters and other contract-based content producers step in to fill that gap.

There is also a symbiotic relationship between those who buy and sell ghostwritten academic work. US students and recent graduates facing bleak employment prospects and staggering educational debt described taking on others' term papers (or even completing entire online classes) to make ends meet. Likewise, degree-seekers sometimes hire ghostwriters to complete coursework for a class they deem non-essential or too time consuming. For example, I interviewed one woman who was bankrolling her own education by writing term papers for international engineering students who struggled with required courses in the social sciences and humanities.[6] Other academic ghostwriters pointed out that their clients were buying essays because, by outsourcing some of their coursework, they could "take" the maximum number of credits each term and then graduate early. In the United States, finishing a single semester early can save a student several thousand dollars, and so paying for a ghostwriter can be financially (if not ethically) quite prudent.

This does not mean that ghostwriting clients are never lazy or vain. However, once ghostwriting is situated within the contemporary economy, it becomes clear that the reasons why one would purchase ghostwritten content can be quite complex. Likewise, my ghostwriter interlocutors who worked as ghostwriters described a variety of motivations for and feelings about writing as someone else. Generally, those who came to ghostwriting in a state of financial desperation and who really wanted to be producing their own, credited publications were the most frustrated. However, others did ghostwriting alongside (or as a means of financing) their own writing, or claimed to be happy being full-time ghosts.

Although none of my interlocutors initially set out to become ghostwriters, almost all were put off by the suggestion that ghostwriting was a career only pursued out of desperation, or that being required to relinquish authorship automatically amounted to exploitation. My interlocutors were quick to point out the collaborative nature of their work. Ghostwriters typically develop memoirs, religious testimony, and other personal narratives on the basis of interviews with the named author and others close to them, filling in contextual gaps (relevant historical dates and details, for example) as needed. My study participants also observed that by the time a client seeks a ghostwriter, they may have been trying to write on their own for quite some time and have extensive notes and drafts prepared.

Nearly a quarter of my interviewees had composed or heavily edited texts for medical doctors and researchers (four specialized in this area), producing: texts including articles for peer review; health management books; blog and Twitter posts; and pharmaceutical chat-bot scripts. All insisted that even though they were relinquishing credit to named authors, their named authors remained the real experts in their subject matter. Like the memoirists, medical ghostwriters saw themselves as communicating their named authors' ideas as effectively as possible, often for the benefit of patients, because they believed in their clients' work.

Thus, ghostwriters often saw their work as not only collaborative, but caring. This was the case even when ghostwriters did produce much of original content. For example, one business ghostwriter described her work as "helping people get to where they need to be." She was particularly committed to working with women, who, she argued, face more scrutiny and skepticism of their abilities, and therefore need to devote extra time to making themselves both visible and visibly competent. Her proudest ghostwriting achievements were researching and writing a book credited to her client that is now on multiple business school curricula, and helping that same client master a voice for email and social media that the client could eventually reproduce herself. Academic ghostwriters also tended to do a combination of content production, tutoring, and handholding. Erin, whose case we will examine more closely in the next section, described drafting (but not sending) emails to professors for a PhD candidate client who was struggling to keep his dissertation committee afloat. "The word 'together' is so comforting," Erin explained, "as in, we'll get through this together."

Although my interlocutors were invested in the success of their named authors, they also described ghostwriting as "personally fulfilling" and "a creative outlet." For those doing expository writing, ghosting was an opportunity to learn about new subject matter and amplify meaningful ideas. Evangelical ghostwriters described their work as a means of growing closer to God and his miracles. Creative writers often saw ghosting as a skill-building exercise. Crafting someone else's personal narrative, job application, or social media posts was a challenge in capturing a voice and creating a character. And it paid. For several of my interlocutors, ghostwriting was a ticket to living the writing life, albeit without named authorship, but also without the pressures that named authorship can bring.

In sum, at first glance, ghostwriting in the twenty-first century seems to encapsulate some of the most distressing trends of the neoliberal marketplace. Following Heller and McElhinny, ghostwriting regularly involves the outsourcing of communicative labor, often for low pay and limited contracts, to populations who have lost, or never had access to, more stable work environments. Racist language ideologies that rank white North

American and British English above African and Asian English not only drive the ghostwriting market, but also shape who can actually make a living from it. Finally, the recent explosion of ghostwritten texts reflects the trend of treating both language skills and authenticity as assets to be managed. And yet, my ethnography suggests that at least some ghostwriters find real purpose, even enjoyment, in their work. Certainly, it matters how much choice ghostwriters feel they have in choosing their projects, and how much creative freedom they experience in executing them. Pay is important, as are reasonable deadlines. Generally, the biggest predictor of whether a ghostwriter will feel satisfied with their work is whether they experience a positive personal relationship with the client and a sense of investment in elevating the named author and/or their ideas.

That said, positive relationships could also make questions of credit quite tedious. On the one hand, ghostwriters who relinquished authorship were often willing to do so precisely because they understood that claiming credit could hurt their named authors. On the other hand, almost all of my interlocutors could describe a case in which they felt "hurt" or "burned" by a client or named author who refused to acknowledge their assistance in any way or serve as a future reference. In the next section, we will consider how academic ghostwriter Erin's business and life more generally were affected by such situations.

Erin: From Graduate Student to Ghost

Erin came to ghostwriting after, in her own words, "crashing and burning out of" a graduate program in the humanities. I knew her at the time, and can attest that her intelligence, potential as a researcher, and skill as an educator were never in question. (Erin and I reconnected as part of this project; she was one of its earliest inspirations and supporters.) She shone in the classroom, both as a student and as a teaching assistant. Privately, however, she was juggling several personal challenges, including her mother's deteriorating health, and ongoing insecurity about her working-class background—while most of her peers had degrees from elite institutions, Erin had put herself through a regional state college. She was thankful the graduate program had taken a chance on her, even granting her a special scholarship. Yet ironically, their generosity increased the pressure she felt to prove herself, making her feel ashamed to ask for help. Over time, her impostor syndrome grew paralyzing, to the point that she was failing to complete required assignments. It was not that Erin was not writing or not attending classes and seminars; she was failing to submit her work for evaluation. After racking up a string of "incompletes," she lost her funding and was dismissed from the university without even a master's degree.[7]

This was during the Great Recession, when, Erin recalls, "it was difficult to find a job washing dishes." To make ends meet, Erin cleaned houses, worked for a landscaper, and returned to nannying, which was one way she had made money before graduate school. She also tutored her sister's college-age friends as well as the children she babysat, and through this developed a network of clients. However, she was struggling to pay the rent and felt uncertain about her future, so when the time came to renew her lease, she gave up her apartment and slept on the couches of her few loyal friends (most of her social network had disappeared with her scholarship). One of those friends was working on their doctoral dissertation and having a very difficult time. This friend had produced a draft, but their adviser and committee members were not pleased with it and had ordered a complete overhaul. Erin saw that her friend was deeply discouraged and so offered to help them in exchange for a place to stay. In the end, Erin redeveloped the entire thesis, strengthening the theoretical framework based on what had already been written, tightening the body chapters, and then having her friend act as a proofreader and fact checker. Erin even wrote the acknowledgments (in which she thanked herself) and managed communication with her friend's committee. Soon, Erin found herself doing more writing and editing tasks for other graduate students. Some dissertators hired her to manage their bibliographies (both formatting and finding appropriate references); others sought organizational and stylistic assistance; and a few even had her sketch the first drafts of their chapters. Similar to memoir ghostwriters, Erin and other academic ghosts regularly pointed out that the named authors had all their ideas in their heads but struggled to make the jump to paper. The difference, they observed, is that academics in the social sciences and humanities are expected to be good at organizing and communicating their thoughts without much external assistance, whereas people who work in other disciplines are not expected to have such skills.

As her clients climbed the academic ranks, so did Erin. When they went on the job market, she refined their cover letters, formatted their CVs, and edited their presentations to the hiring departments. Once they were hired, she coaxed dissertation chapters into articles and then full monographs. She wrote letters of reference for her clients' undergraduates (for internships and study abroad programs, for example) so that the clients could stay focused on what she calls "CV-able" tasks. When the clients went up for tenure, Erin helped them write their reports and assemble their portfolios. The irony that Erin, who had failed out of her own graduate program, was doing the work of an assistant, soon-to-be associate professor was not lost on either her or her clients. Her lack of credentials, she explained, made her "a complete liability" but also "very safe," because "no one is ever going to believe I had anything to do with this."

Over the course of our conversations, Erin occasionally seemed a bit wistful: "I realize now that I could have done it [the PhD]." But she also emphasized that she had not entered the academy primed for its demands. It was not just that she felt academically underprepared; "I wasn't raised to advocate to myself, to do anything for [to prioritize] myself, and graduate school was exactly about that." What Erin had been raised to do, she said, was help others, so it made sense that she became a nanny and a ghost. By the time we spoke, Erin had been doing what she calls "co-authoring" and "substantive editing" for a decade. She had been called back to her hometown to care for her mother, who was suffering from a neurodegenerative disease. She still works with academics but recently built a larger and more lucrative business tutoring students from a nearby university—specifically, shepherding first-years through the university's notorious first-year composition program. She charges $1,500 for a semester's work of support, and typically works with students via a combination of video conferencing and Google Docs, less to maintain distance from clients than because her caregiving demands require flexibility. Although she does have some long-term undergraduate clients, and while she has composed entire papers for students "in a jam," she says her goal is to provide her students with enough guidance that they will be able to work independently down the line.

When I asked Erin about the ethics of providing what US universities often term "unauthorized aid" to undergraduates, she admitted she "crosses the line all the time." However, she also observed that what constitutes academic honesty is not consistent over the course of educational experience. Many students are surprised to find out that practices that were perfectly permissible in high school (not to mention graduate school), such as having a friend, family member, or even teacher advise them on their writing, can be grounds for expulsion in the undergraduate years. Like other academic ghostwriters I interviewed, she noted that many students turn to "unauthorized" assistance not because they are lazy, but because they are in over their heads, and the reasons why they are struggling might not be entirely their fault. For example, Erin observed that low pay, large class sizes, and short-term contracts meant there was a lot of staff turnover in the mandatory composition program; as a result, the instructors were not necessarily experienced or even interested in teaching first-year writing. She also railed against the "minimalist tutoring" philosophy that pervades US university writing centers, leaving students who actually do seek assistance with vague (if any) advice and little reassurance.[8] Finally, Erin condemned the rise of "academic integrity" offices that rush to discipline undergrads for missteps rather than teaching them how to avoid them in the first place. Erin sees her own work as compensating for the education her students either lacked upon arriving at the university or have since been denied. "I learned everything ten steps too late," Erin reflected, "but at least now I can share what I know."

As we spoke, I caught glimpses of the Erin I knew years ago, the woman whose analytical instincts, formidable verbal skills, and passion for social justice issues first brought her to graduate school. On the one hand, her talents seemed wasted as a ghostwriter, and I wondered what kind of academic career she might have had if things had turned out differently. On the other hand, Erin spoke with a strong sense of purpose. She had finally overcome her writing anxiety and impostor syndrome, or at least found a way to manage it. She listed her attributes: "I have a good sense of the big picture"; "I know where to put the little pieces"; "I'm a good listener"; "I'm good at meeting other people's deadlines"; "I'm comfortable in someone else's skin." I commented that there were certainly times when I could have used someone like Erin in my academic life. Erin pointed out that I was not her typical client, because most of her graduate and postdoctoral clients were male. She theorized that this was because "men hole up" while women "reach out," seek support from colleagues, or join writing groups. Men, she suggested, "lean on women." She described how her work involved offering "emotional support" to her male clients, "telling them they're good scholars, and why."

Like many other women who have labored behind the scenes of the ivory tower, Erin has struggled to be paid or acknowledged. Partly because of her own lack of an advanced degree and partly because so many of her early clients were low-income graduate students, Erin set her prices below market, or underreported her hours. Even then, her clients were slow to settle up, and Erin was reluctant to "go debt collecting." Like other ghostwriters I spoke to, Erin claimed to not care much about authorship but did expect some form of reciprocity. She understood quite well why her academic clients hid or understated her contributions, but she was frustrated when not listed at all in the acknowledgment section of a dissertation, even for something as innocuous as "copyediting." ("Copyediting" was how Erin and her clients sometimes framed her services, even if it was evident to both of them that she was doing much more. My interlocutors often noted that part of their job is reaffirming the story the named author is telling themselves about why they are paying for external support.) Erin observed that academics use acknowledgment sections as a means of networking, playing up support from bigger named scholars, because doing so suggests that those scholars found their work worthy of attention. Closer colleagues, such as members of one's cohort, tend to be listed in a line (often alphabetized, so as not to offend), even if they were actually the ones who were the most engaged in reading drafts and providing feedback. Erin, if mentioned at all, tended to be listed apart from this group. She also was not invited to post-defense celebrations. Again, she understood why she needed to remain behind the scenes but recalled feeling hurt when clients who had used her services did not even follow up to tell her how the defense had gone. This particularly stung when the client received accolades for work that Erin had helped develop, and if she only heard about this second hand. Overall, Erin stressed, it was not the lack of a byline that bothered her, but the exclusion. In academia, graduate school relationships become community for decades to come. Erin was written out of the story, even when she was involved in writing it.

Although she finds it less stimulating, Erin describes working with undergraduates a relief because the price, nature, and duration of the services she is offering is much clearer. She has also been developing business writing services (cover letter editing, CV formatting, helping clients "package" themselves for prospective employers) to help her expand and diversify her client base. Business writing is also less stigmatized, and Erin would like to be able to be more public about her profession. My interlocutors who did or had done academic writing reported difficulty talking about their work with family, friends, and even academic clients. (Someone who wants to believe they are only contracting copyediting services does not want to hear you have written term papers.) Admitting to being a ghostwriter can also make dating difficult, as explaining why one makes a living writing as someone else often requires telling backstories one might rather not share right away. And of course, ghostwriting leaves gaps in one's CV, which makes it difficult to move into another field. Now in her mid-thirties, Erin lives in her childhood home, is paid in large part under the table, and has only a BA to her name. "The neighbors, they see a good daughter and granddaughter. But everything else I've accomplished is invisible."

"I think what I've done is a positive good," Erin pivots again, reminding me, as ghostwriters often do, of the challenges and injustices that lead clients to seek help and the opportunity ghostwriters have to elevate people and ideas. Invisibility is part of the job, she affirms; it is not just something that clients insist on, but something that ghostwriters are often happy to give. Yet Erin draws a line between the contractual invisibility that denies her authorship and the broken social relations that erase her in spaces beyond the page. If Erin has experienced alienation, or another loss of identity, it seems not to be merely because she has relinquished bylines, but because she has been cut off by people she invested in. For some ghosts, the object of their labor is not so much the texts they write, but the people they care for.

Conclusion: A Tale of Two Ghosts

The two ghostwriters whose stories I have told have much in common. Both Erin and Jenna Glatzer came to ghostwriting after experiencing life interruptions that forced them to rethink their intended career paths. Both had to balance significant personal challenges that made holding a traditional 9-to-5 job difficult, and made remote, contract-based work appealing. Each found clients they enjoyed working with and were pleased to empower. Both described finding freedom in writing as someone else, and pleasure in learning about different lives and subject matter.

But they also have significant differences—differences perhaps best reflected in how I refer to these women throughout this chapter. Glatzer, whom I introduced by her real name, regularly receives cover-level credit for her work on memoirs. She has a strong internet presence and is regularly quoted in articles on ghostwriting. By contrast, Erin is a pseudonym. The academic work Erin does is stigmatized, and if I were to use her real name, both she and her named authors could quickly come under scrutiny. Erin's internet presence is comparatively scant; she acquires clients primarily through word of mouth. At one point in our interview, she referred to herself as a name on a slip of paper passed between friends at a bar, "like a hooker." When acknowledged, Erin's contributions are often minimized as copyediting. Glatzer has also faced such erasure, but far less often and in exchange for higher pay. Most of Glatzer's named authors are people who are not particularly vulnerable to what one might call "ghost-busting." As such, Glatzer's clients tout her services, and Glatzer herself has been able to write about her experiences as a ghostwriter. She has no shortage of bylines. Ghostwriting is a professional identity she proudly and loudly claims.

These differences have significant repercussions. Despite battling agoraphobia, Glatzer has been able to move on with her life. Erin, a decade out from her stint in graduate school, has had difficulty re-establishing herself. Ghostwriting became a lifeline for her, a way to prove her academic competence despite her failures. It was also a means of managing some very challenging family responsibilities. Long term, however, the lack of bylines has made it difficult for her to move into another sort of writing or research career.

"Not getting any credit is hard, it really is," Erin wrote me recently. "Especially for someone coming from academia," she continued, pointing out that in the university system "you don't get money, you get credit," and "people get ridiculously excited to be mentioned in a footnote." I had followed up with Erin to fact check some of the details in this chapter, and we came to speak about the impact the pandemic had had on her client roster, which included dissertators and precariously employed junior scholars. Once again, Erin found herself undercharging clients and scrambling to fill the gaps in her income. On the other hand, she was benefiting from an uptick in work consulting on job and university applications. She had no plans to change careers: "I love helping people achieve their dreams. I love contributing to knowledge, even without the credit. I read the praise of scholars about words I have written, and I feel immensely proud. I love the freedom of being able to work on others' projects without the emotional baggage that comes with working on my own."

Erin ended her note to me with reference to this very chapter, which she read, commented on, and now ultimately provides its conclusion: "Ghostwriting is, as your article well documents, complicated emotional and intellectual work."

Acknowledgments

I would like to thank the Max Planck Institute for supporting an unconventional project; my MAX-CAM colleagues for hearty debate about authorship, alienation, credit, and care; and most importantly, the dozens of ghostwriters who gave their time to this study. I hope they will find this chapter resonates with their experiences.

Deborah A. Jones is a research fellow at the Max Planck Institute for Social Anthropology in Halle (Saale), and an affiliate of the Max Planck–Cambridge Centre for Ethics, Economy, and Social Change. Trained in linguistic anthropology, she specializes in the study of language, ethics, and political economy. Jones conducts research in Ukraine, the United States, and among digital communities.

Notes

1. These prices are typically for the manuscript only, not publishing or printing. At the time of writing, the going rate for a non-celebrity ghostwritten-memoir manuscript was between $15,000 and $35,000, though I encountered several memoirists, especially those doing faith-based writing, who charged much less, and some agency owners who reported much, much higher fees. The average number of book projects a memoirist was completing in a year was three, though this again varied tremendously depending on the size and cost of the project, and whether ghostwriting was a primary or secondary source of income.

2. I did not ask my interlocutors directly about health conditions, caregiving responsibilities, citizenship status, or eligibility to work locally, and so I do not have specific statistics as to what percentage were navigating such challenges. Those who did reveal such personal details tended to do so when I asked them how and why they came into ghostwriting.
3. Two forums proved particularly useful for recruitment: first, the "Binders" women's and non-binary writing support groups on Facebook, which are moderated, invitation-only, and tend to attract people who [aspire to] publish in professional venues, or assist those aiming to do so; and second, the legendary American online classifieds board Craigslist. My Craigslist contacts worked in a large variety of often lower-paid genres, particularly academic, business, and faith-based writing. My research does not suggest that Craigslist is where most ghostwriting transactions take place. However, it was a fruitful recruitment site because it is one of the few remaining spaces for US writers and clients to connect anonymously and without tedious bidding processes, user fees, or credibility-building exercises. Although one can post or reply to "global" jobs on Craigslist, the metro-area organization of the board means that many opportunities are local and paid at locally appropriate wages. In short, Craigslist is a space in which US-based ghostwriters can avoid the competition and audit culture that characterizes newer work distribution platforms.
4. For the purposes of this study, ghostwriters are people who: (1) develop texts for clients in a way that goes substantially beyond what most would consider "editing" or "giving feedback"; (2) are by definition not credited with primary authorship, and often completely relinquish authorship rights to their client and/or named author through a non-disclosure agreement or other legal contract; (3) write as someone else, not merely for or on behalf of someone else, in a context in which some notion of "single authorship" is expected or valued; and (4) may pass themselves off as the named authors, but moreover, the named authors pass off ghostwritten work as their own, effectively purchasing, and claiming for themselves, competence, creativity, and time spent.
5. I have been able to trace the use of ghostwriters by one US Christian publication to the 1940s. The magazine recruited housewives to ghostwrite accounts of miracles witnessed by community members. It still relies almost exclusively on female ghostwriters, but now recruits them via an annual essay contest.
6. US undergraduate education traditionally follows a "liberal arts" model. Students are required to take courses in a variety of disciplines over four years; they are also asked to complete courses that prepare them for living and working in a diverse world. This holistic approach has recently come under fire from those concerned about soaring educational costs and reducing time-to-degree.
7. Doctoral programs in the United States typically involve two to three years of coursework followed by comprehensive exams, which allow one to achieve PhD candidacy. Having a master's degree does not exempt one from these exams, nor can one opt out of coursework; as such, first-year PhD students may or may not have prior graduate-level experience.
8. Designed to "make the student do all the work" (Brooks 1991) in the interest of producing better writers rather than better papers, the philosophy encourages tutors

not to write on the student's draft but to have the student read their work aloud and locate errors, disfluencies, and missing transitions themselves. This strategy can backfire when a student requires real assistance with grammar, structure, or style.

References

Bakhtin, Mikhail. (1934/35) 1981. "Discourse in the Novel." In *The Dialogic Imagination: Four Essays*, ed. Michael Holquist, trans. Caryl Emerson and Michael Holquist, 259–422. Austin: University of Texas Press.

Brooks, Jeff. 1991. "Minimalist Tutoring: Making the Student do all the Work." *Writing Labe Newsletter* 15(6): 1–4.

Gerber, Alison. 2017. *The Work of Art: Value in Creative Careers.* Palo Alto: Stanford Unversity Press.

Gershon, Ilana. 2016. "'I'm Not a Businessman, I'm a Business, Man': Typing the Neoliberal Self into Branded Existence." *HAU* 6(3): 223–46.

———. 2017. *Down and Out in the New Economy: How People Find (Or Don't Find) Work Today*. Chicago: University of Chicago Press.

Goffman, Erving. 1981. *Forms of Talk*. Philadelphia: University of Pennsylvania Press.

Gupta, Akhil. 2014. "Authorship, Research Assistants, and the Ethnographic Field." *Ethnography* 15(3): 394–400.

Heller, Monica, and Bonnie McElhinny. 2017. *Language, Capitalism, Colonialism: Toward a Critical History*. Toronto: University of Toronto Press.

Henig, David, and Nicolette Makovicky, eds. 2017. *Economies of Favour after Socialism*. Oxford: Oxford University Press.

Irvine, Judy. 1989. "When Talk Isn't Cheap: Language and Political Economy." *American Ethnologist* 16(2): 248–67.

———. 1996. "Shadow Conversations." In *Natural Histories of Discourse*, ed. Michael Silverstein and Greg Urban, 131–59. Chicago: University of Chicago Press.

Putnam, Hilary. 1975. *The Meaning of "Meaning."* Minneapolis: University of Minnesota Press.

Rosa, Jonathan. 2019. *Looking Like a Language, Sounding Like a Race: Raciolinguistic Ideologies and the Learning of Latinidad*. Oxford: Oxford University Press.

Schwimmer, Erik. 1979. "The Self and the Product: Concepts of Work in Comparative Perspective." In *Social Anthropology of Work*, ed. Cheryl Wallman, 287–315. London: Academic Press.

Silverstein, Michael. 1996. "Monoglot 'Standard' in America." In *The Matrix of Language: Contemporary Linguistic Anthropology*, ed. D. Brenneis and R. Macaulay, 284–306. Boulder, CO: Westview Press.

Smith, Rachel. 2019. "Be Our Guest/Worker: Reciprocal Dependency and Expressions of Hospitality in Ni-Vanuatu Overseas Labour Migration." *Journal of the Royal Anthropological Institute* 25(2): 349–67.

Sukarieh, Mayssoun, and Stuart Tannock. 2019. "Subcontracting Academia: Alienation, Exploitation and Disillusionment in the UK Overseas Syrian Refugee Research Industry." *Antipode* 51(2): 664–80.

Tomlinson, Matthew, and Julian Millie, eds. 2017. *The Monologic Imagination*. Oxford: Oxford University Press.
Wolf-Meyer, Matthew. 2020. "Facilitated Personhood." *Journal of the Royal Anthropological Institute* 26(1): 167–86.
Yagoda, Ben. 2009. *Memoir: A History*. New York: Riverhead Books.

Afterword

GERD SPITTLER

Work is more than just an economic category: it concerns the worker as a human person. A recent volume of papers, based on a conference held in 2019 at the Collège de France in Paris to mark the centenary of the International Labor Organization (ILO), is devoted primarily to work in the age of neoliberalism and the digital revolution (Supiot 2019). It also has sections devoted to "pays émergents" such as China, Korea, India, South America, "le vieux monde industriel," and African countries such as Mali, Senegal, and Niger. Most of the authors are lawyers aiming to formulate laws for "decent work" in the context of a global economic order in which wage labor is declining and self-employment is on the rise. Their articles reveal the extent to which work is determined by legal norms. Today, the main task is to set up new standards to protect workers against the neoliberal deregulation of the labor market. Most authors follow a specifically French tradition that privileges a strong state to regulate labor relations, in contrast to (neo)liberal laissez-faire ideology. The social scientist questions how far these sometimes subtle legal debates correspond to reality, particularly when it comes to the Global South. The ILO refers to anything that deviates from the European norm as "atypical work," but it is the task of anthropologists to draw attention to the autonomous character of work on other continents.

Anthropology and history have a long tradition of research into the semantics of work (Spittler 2016a). Words such as entrepreneur, freelance, leisure, unemployment, and work itself are not simply words but are terms that have a history, often a contested history, as Werner Conze showed in a justly celebrated article on the concept of work in Europe (Conze 1972). But the scope and method of a comparative semantics of work need to be considered carefully. According to Thomas Sokoll, reflecting on a recent significant contribution: "To put it bluntly, most of the contributions in this volume go far beyond the heads—or rather, beyond the bodies and hands—of those affected. What work consists of in concrete terms and what exactly happens at the workplace—we learn almost nothing about that" (Sokoll 2016: 407, my translation). In my own contribution to this volume, I too argued that public discourses on work must be distinguished from its actual practice (Spittler 2016b). This practice includes "working speech," which can only be investigated through an ethnographic approach: ideally a combination of participation, observation, and interviews.

Katherine Miller's fieldwork in Hunza Valley in Pakistan lasted seventeen months. She conducted interviews, but she also helped in the performance of agricultural tasks, in addition to accompanying and observing the farmers. She asked them questions while they were working, and learned that their work was far more than just a rational and useful activity. Although the work was laborious, it gave them pleasure and aesthetic perceptions of their surroundings. Work was marked by conversations, laughter, and flirting. From a methodological point of view, Miller's chapter makes it clear that it is not enough to compose a discourse on work, but that participation in its practice, including conversations carried on during the activity, brings new insights.

Olivia Angé observed women in the Argentinian province of Jujuy who produce miniatures (*miniaturas*). She helped to produce them, accompanied women to the market, took part in their conversations, and sold miniature clay pots herself. These women do not behave in the manner of a *homo oeconomicus*. In order to be successful, they need *fuerza*, *suerte*, and *ánimo*. They obtain these through their relationship to Saint Anne, in whose honor a big festival is held on 26 July. Santa Ana is the patron saint of work; she works hard herself, and teaches this work ethic to her devotees.

Having formerly worked as an intern in a TV company in Ghana, Anna-Riikka Kauppinen subsequently conducted fieldwork there for her PhD. She participated in discussions, visited her colleagues at home and during their leisure activities, and made friends. The strong work ethic of these young professionals is based on the principle of excellent work being an end in itself. This is unusual. Kauppinen contrasts this work ethic with other models that conflict with this ethic. The work ethic of President Nkrumah also underlined the value of work, but only when it was performed for society as a whole; otherwise, it was a bourgeois conception. Some colleagues and superiors work in order to become "big men" with political connections. Last but not least, the work ethic of the young media professionals contrasts with the ethic of their relatives, who expect a return for the family after helping to finance their education.

In a chapter based on interviews and participant observation, Santos and his colleagues discuss the "996 schedule" (working from 9 in the morning to 9 in the evening, for six days a week) among IT programmers and taxi drivers in China. They find that this schedule mixes pre-existing values of entrepreneurship and industriousness with new neoliberal ideologies of work, but they pay less attention to the former than they do to the latter.

Johannes Lenhard investigates "venture capital investors" in Germany, England, and the United States. He has immersed himself personally in this business world, not only conducting interviews but also observing interaction at work, and taking part in meetings. What makes this activity so interesting is that the potential investors are not dealing with functioning companies, but rather with vague embryonic ideas. Emotions, sympathies, and trust therefore play an important role in decision taking. Lenhard finds that libertarian narratives dominate discussions with clients: the emphasis is on novelty, innovation, increasing democracy, decentralizing power, destruction of the old, and freedom from the state, combined with domination of the market.

The book is subtitled "Chimeras of Freedom in the Neoliberal Area." Most chapters interpret work in the context of neoliberalism. But how dominant and how novel is this neoliberalism compared with other economic models? While the venture capital investors studied by Lenhard clearly represent a neoliberal ideology, in other contributions the neoliberal traits are mixed with other elements. This embedding is described in the detailed ethnographies, but it might be better theorized. For example, the household plays a role in several chapters. It appears in the guise of the family in discussions of the work–life balance (Santos et al., Kauppinen). It is treated by several authors as an economic institution (Miller, Angé, Smith, Kauppinen), but only Terpe offers theoretical elaboration, by engaging with Max Weber and Karl Polanyi. As I have shown elsewhere (Spittler 2011; Spittler 2016a: Ch. 6), the study of householding in human history deserves closer attention. Households as economic units play an important role today in the Global South as a form of survival economy. This can also be said of Eastern Europe after the end of socialism (Gudeman and Hann 2015). The household persists as an economic unit in modern family enterprises and in the IT sector (Huber 2012). The family economy cannot be viewed from an evolutionist perspective as belonging to the past, any more than the neoliberal economy can be viewed as the *non plus ultra* of modernity.

A similar argument can be made concerning the relationship between human beings and the objects of their work (Spittler 2003). When we speak of working with tools and materials, we seldom conceive of this as interaction, but rather as instrumental action. This conception of work as the transformation of objects has a long tradition in the West. But ethnographic case studies show an interaction between workers, instruments, and objects of work. If work is conceived as interaction rather than one-sided action, then the objects towards which work is directed are more than passive objects that can be manipulated at will. Rather, they possess autonomy and self-will. Many societies regard not only animals and plants but also non-organic things as being animated and self-willed. In his famous essay *The Gift*, Marcel Mauss (2016) treats the character of things as subjects.

He devotes a section to "the spirit of the thing given" as the basis for the exchange of gifts. But neither Mauss nor his successors took this spirit into account with regard to people's interactions with the tools and materials with which they work. The word *matière* derives from *materia*, meaning "matter." In a later essay, Mauss (2006) shows that it used to be regarded by craftsmen as animated, while our modern notions are based on a new opposition between mind and matter that spread to the rest of Europe from France and England.

But has the idea of work as interaction really disappeared today, or does the instrumental view prevail only due to the prejudices of social scientists? For Bruno Latour there is no traditional–modern dichotomy (Latour [1991] 1993). Things always were, and still are, actors in a socio-technical system (see also Suchman 1987, 2005). For most of the contributors to this book, too, work is more than an instrumental activity. "*C'est un régime de travail réellement humain* [It is a truly humane work regime]," as Alain Supiot would say, echoing the founding charter of the ILO (Supiot 2019). It is "work" and not just "labor," as Chris Hann remarks in the Introduction. It involves feelings and ethical judgments. Several chapters refer to joy and pleasure as elements of the work process (Miller, Angé, Kauppinen, Santos et al.), but they do so in the context of relations between the workers and not interactions between workers and objects. Katherine Miller and Olivia Angé come closest to the latter. Miller describes the effect of surroundings on workers: "the beauties of the place: the pleasant shade, the warm gold of the apricots, and the sound of water trickling in the irrigation channels". And according to Angé, the miniatures produced by the women are not really animated, but their work is significantly influenced by Saint Anne.

A central theme of the whole volume is the relation between work and freedom. The authors oscillate theoretically between Foucault (individual freedom) and Polanyi (responsible freedom). It is a pity that only Terpe engages closely with Max Weber, whose importance for the anthropological study of work I have outlined elsewhere (Spittler 2008). In *The Protestant Ethic and the Spirit of Capitalism*, Weber (2002a) postulates the psychological needs of people who are unable to bear the uncertainty of predestination, and who seek to ensure salvation for themselves by leading disciplined lives. But this mechanism is inadequate as an explanation for the rise of modern capitalism. In a later article titled "The Protestant Sects and the Spirit of Capitalism" (2002b), Weber's argument is more sociological. Here he studies how organizational structure (marked by voluntary membership, a responsible lay congregation instead of an authoritarian hierarchy, and an uncompromising individual discipline) enables the establishment of a systematic conduct of life (*Lebensführung*). Life can be conducted in many different forms. For Weber, its rationalization by the

Protestants was a unique historical achievement. However, it was hardly a step forward in the ethical evolution of man. In Weber's view, the establishment of systematic ethical constraints on economic behavior remained elusive and improbable.

Finally, although the majority of the authors in this book are anthropologists, and non-European contexts feature prominently, it is instructive to note that the theory building with which they engage is confined to Euro-American scholarly traditions. This reflects the current state of the social sciences. Should we make more effort to learn from the South, not only ethnographically but also theoretically? In recent years, many contributors to the postcolonial debates in the United States and Europe have called for the decolonization of the humanities and the social sciences, for example with regard to Africa. I too think it is time to rethink basic categories. Decolonizing African studies is a first step, but it cannot be the last. Decolonizing often means not so much a new epistemology as a critique of colonialism. It tends to portray Africans not as agents of their destiny but as the victims of slavery and colonialism. What we need is not an epistemology of the South but rather theories that go beyond North and South—theories that can integrate all points of the compass. These theories are very difficult to formulate. Ethnography cannot replace them, but it has to play an important part in the process of renewing the social sciences. Participant observation, looking for "the native's point of view," may sound old fashioned. But it remains the best way to challenge established categories.

Gerd Spittler is professor emeritus of social anthropology at Bayreuth University. His publications on work include *Founders of the Anthropology of Work* (1998); *African Children at Work* (with M. Bourdillon, 2012); *Anthropologie der Arbeit* (2016); and the chapter "Work – Transformation of Objects or Interaction between Subjects" (2016). He has been a fellow at the Institute for Advanced Study, and the IGK International Research Center "Work and Human Life Cycle in Global History," both based in Berlin, and at the Institut d'Études Avancées at Nantes.

References

Conze, Werner. 1972. "Arbeit." In *Geschichtliche Grundbegriffe: Historisches Lexikon zur politisch-sozialen Sprache in Deutschland*, ed. Otto Brunner, Werner Conze, and Reinhart Koselleck, 1154–1215. Stuttgart: Klett.

Gudeman, Stephen, and Chris Hann, eds. 2015. *Oikos and Market: Explorations in Self-sufficiency after Socialism*. New York: Berghahn Books.

Huber, Birgit. 2012. *Arbeiten in der Kreativindustrie: Eine multilokale Ethnographie der Entgrenzung von Arbeits- und Lebenswelt.* Frankfurt: Campus.
Latour, Bruno. (1991) 1993. *We Have Never Been Modern.* Cambridge, MA: Harvard University Press.
Mauss, Marcel. (1939) 2006. "Conceptions Which Have Preceded the Notion of Matter." In *Techniques, Technology and Civilisation by Marcel Mauss,* ed. Nathan Schlanger, 141–46. New York: Durkheim Press / Berghahn Books.
———. (1923–24) 2016. *The Gift.* Expanded Edition. Chicago, IL: HAU Books.
Sokoll, Thomas. 2016. "Kommentar: Alteuropäisches Erbe, moderne Ausprägung und postmoderne Verwerfungen im Arbeitsbegriff." In *Semantiken von Arbeit: Diachrone und vergleichende Perspektiven,* ed. Jörn Leonhard and Willibald Steinmetz, 393–409. Cologne: Böhlau Verlag.
Spittler, Gerd. 2003. "Work – Transformation of Objects or Interaction with Subjects?" In *Exploitation and Overexploitation in Societies Past and Present,* ed. Brigitta Benzing and Bernd Herrmann, 327–38. Münster: Lit. [Reprinted 2016 in: Andreas Eckert, ed. *Global Histories of Work,* 169–82. Oldenbourg: de Gruyter.]
———. 2008. *Founders of the Anthropology of Work: German Social Scientists of the 19th and Early 20th Centuries and the First Ethnographers.* Berlin: Lit.
———. 2011. "Transformation of the Family Economy in Africa: From Pioneers to Survivors." In *Families, Ties and Care: Family Transformation in a Plural Modernity,* ed. Hans Bertram, 521–36. Opladen: Barbara Budrich.
———. 2016a. *Anthropologie der Arbeit: Ein ethnographischer Vergleich.* Wiesbaden: VS Verlag für Sozialwissenschaften.
———. 2016b. "Arbeit zur Sprache bringen – ethnographische Annäherungen." In *Semantiken von Arbeit: Diachrone und vergleichende Perspektiven,* ed. Jörn Leonhard and Willlibald Steinmetz, 147–66. Cologne: Böhlau Verlag.
Suchman, Lucy. 1987. *Plans and Situated Actions: The Problem of Human–Machine Communication.* Cambridge: Cambridge University Press.
———. 2005. "Affiliative Objects." *Organization* 12(3): 379–99.
Supiot, Alain, ed. 2019. *Le travail au XXIe siècle: Livre du centenaire de l'organisation internationale du travail.* Ivry-sur-Seine: Ed. de l'Atelier.
Weber, Max. (1904) 2002a. *The Protestant Ethic and the Spirit of Capitalism,* ed. Stephen Kahlberg. Los Angeles: Roxbury.
———. (1906) 2002b. "The Protestant Sects and the Spirit of Capitalism." In *Max Weber: The Protestant Ethic and the Spirit of Capitalism,* ed. Stephen Kahlberg, 127–47. Los Angeles: Roxbury.

Index

Accra, Ghana
ethnography in, 127n1
private media of, 108–28
professionalism in, 109–10
salary in private media of, 109
white-collar work in, 110–12
work for men in, 18–19
adulthood, gendered notions of, 126
adwuma, 117–18
affect, 93–97
affective practices, 18, 90, 91, 102–3
class and, 95
of women, 97–100
Africanist anthropology, 111
ethnography in, 124
Aga Khan Development Network (AKDN), 54, 57–58, 59, 65
Aga Khan Rural Support Programme (AKRSP), 52, 54–55, 57–58
Airbnb, 209, 223
Akerlof, George, 43n3
alasitas, 75, 85n7
alienation, 31, 93, 113–14, 262, 272
Allen, Catherine, 77, 80
Altit Town Management Society (ATMS), 57, 61–62
altruism, self-interest *vs.*, 41–42
amántse, 62–63, 64
Andes mountains, Argentina
capitalism in, 83–84
ethics of work and freedom in, 70–86
ánimo, 79
Anne (Saint), 70–71, 73, 86n15
celebration of, in Humahuaca, 74–80
money of, 85nn8–9
anthropology
Africanist, 111, 124
ghostwriters and, 21–22
work and ethics in, 1–22
See also work; work ethic
Argentina, 70–84, 85n4
cosmology in, 18
Asante kingdom, 113
ATMS. *See* Altit Town Management Society
attitude, social order and, 94–96
authorship
Guyer on, 19
partial, 122
self-realization and, 124
work, excellence and, 121–25
See also ghostwriters
autonomy, 232
of labor, 159
in neoliberalism, 215–16
post-colonial state and, 112–14
precarity, affect, and, 93–97
relational, 93–94
in work distribution platforms, 215
of work process, 122

bagh, 65
banks, 242, 244, 252. *See also* finance; money
Basel Committee on Banking Supervision, 256n1
Basel III framework, 241
Bedürfnisse, 188
beneficio, 82–83
Benkler, Y., 203
Berlin, Germany, 242–45, 249–51
Bhutto, Zulfikar Ali, 53
Binders, Facebook group, 275n3
bishilian, 139
blackbirding, 33, 38, 44n8
Bloch, Maurice, 7
blue-collar workers, 5–6, 20, 223
management *vs.*, 14
boredom, 91

bottom line, 222
for VCs, 226–27
Brentano, Lujo, 32
Bücher, Karl, 8–9
Burushaski language, 64, 67n1
ByteDance, 137, 143, 154n5

call centers, North Indian, 104–5n1
class and, 97–100
friendship and precarity at, 89–105
social death in, 93
Calvinism, 186
Cant, Alanna, 84
capitalism, 13–14
Andean, 83–84
desires under, 188
finance, 242
freedom in, 186, 192
labor under, 30, 162–63
needs under, 188
overwork and, 132–55
patriarchal society and, 103
platform, 221
social reproduction linked to, 116–17
Streeck on, 188, 197–98
wage labor and, 41
Weber on, 185–86
work ethic under, 183–85
work under, 162–63
See also specific topics
Capitalism, Socialism, and Democracy (Schumpeter), 235
Carbonella, August, 175
categorical imperative, 160
Catel, Robert, 158
Catholicism, 73–74
in Argentina, 70–84
Chengdu, China, 142–43
China, 154n6, 209–10
work ethic in, 141–42
work in, 19
work-life balance in, 132–55, 138
class
affective practices and, 95
call-center work and, 97–100
hierarchy and, in workplace, 90
in India, 91–92
See also middle-class
climate charge, 11, 187–88
Coase, Ronald, 14, 202–3, 205, 210, 216, 217n1k
Colin, Nicolas, 234
collective labor, 17, 37
household, 58–59
in Hunza Valley, 52–60
in New Hebrides, 35–36
colonial era
commoditized contractual labor in, 32–34
in India, 90–91
work in, 29
colonialism, 282
French, 35–36
Committee for the Protection and Defence of Indigenous Populations, 35
commodification
of language, 265–66
of work, 30–32, 162–63, 175
commodities
gifts *vs.*, 41–42
labor as gift and, in Vanuatu, 38–41
labor *vs.*, 32
workers as, 44n13
consumption
in Indian culture, 103
pleasure and, 65
contest mechanisms, for design of work, 206–7
Convention 169 on Indigenous and Tribal Peoples, 71–72
Convention People's Party (CPP), 113
conviviality
creativity and, 97–100
personhood in, 103
Conze, Werner, 278
cordillera, 70–71, 72, 85n4
corvée, 35, 44n12, 53, 56
cosmology, in Argentina, 18
cost optimization, 24–247, 243
counterhegemony, 161
countermovement, 17, 20
against socialism, 158–77
in Yugoslavia, 162–63, 175
Covid-19, 2, 11, 154n3
CPP. *See* Convention People's Party
Craigslist, 275n3
creative destruction, 233, 235

creativity, conviviality and, 97–100
crowdfunding, 205–6
Cruz, Doña, 74, 80
Čukić, Branislav, 167–68

Declaration of Philadelphia, 43n4
decolonization, 282
deregulation
  Foucault on, 159–60
  in neoliberalism, 175–76
  Polanyi on, 159–60
desires, 188
deskilling, 246
development policy, participation in, 57–58
dharma, freedom as, 91
Didi app, 19, 148–50
digitization
  entertainment industry and, 127n11, 128n14
  financial services and, 242
  technology promoting, 12, 14
  VCs and, 222–36, 236nn1–2
  work distribution changed through, 203–8
  working from home through, 2–3, 21, 22
  work-life balance and, 133, 193
  See also technology company; work distribution platforms
Dion, Céline, 259, 261
distribution, 162–63
  according to work, 168
  scaling and, 76–78
  See also work distribution platforms
divided masters, 225
double movement, 159, 161
Douglas, Mary, 185
drivers, e-hailing
  algorithmic, 148–50
  conventional taxi drivers *vs.*, 148–50
  996 schedule and, 151–53
due diligence, 231
Durkheim, Émile, 15, 30–31
  on ethical unfreedom, 136

economic ethic
  freedom and, 183–87
  in Halle, Germany, 189–97
economics, ethics *vs.*, 71
economy
  closed household, 8
  household, 2–3
  market, of China, 132–33
  moral, 9–10, 110–11
  natural, 28
  platform, 20–21, 133
  of 2010s, 140
  See also specific topics
Economy and Society (Weber), 199n1
e-hailing drivers, 149
embeddedness, 159
emic concepts, 6–7
emotional labor, 89, 92
  women and, 90, 93
emplacing, 166
employment contracts, 93
Engels, Friedrich, 186
entrepreneurial self, 232, 240, 248, 252, 255
  in neoliberalism, 202–3
entrepreneurship
  freedom and, 241–42
  in Ghana, 114
Epi Island, 37–38
  plantations on, 33
ethical self, 3, 14, 15–16, 58
ethical tension, 222, 225
ethical unfreedom, 136
ethics, 199n2
  economics *vs.*, 71
  proletarian, 160
  of work, 1–22, 49–66, 70–86, 111
  See also work ethic
etic concepts, 6–7, 8
excellence, work, and authorship, 121–25

Facebook, 221, 234, 235, 275n3
Fajans, J., 28
family
  money *vs.*, in Ghana, 116–17
  professionalism and, 141
  See also household
fascism, 204–5
fenziqian, 146
fiduciary duty, 21
finance
  capitalism, 242

finance *(cont.)*
ethnographies of, 223–26
See also venture capital
financial crisis of 2007, 240
financial freedom, 19, 151
Firth, Raymond, 7
forced labor, 35–37
Forced Labor Convention, 37
Fordism, 2, 4, 10, 14, 96, 158
formal sector, 110
Foucault, Michel, 14–16, 18–19, 86n16, 281
on deregulation, 159–60
on freedom, 90, 136
on liberation, 160–61
on neoliberalism, 160
Fourier, Charles, 8, 13, 14
France, colonies of, 35–36
freedom, 15, 281
in capitalism, 186, 192
as *dharma*, 91
dialectics of, 132
economic ethic and, 183–87
entrepreneurial, 241–42
ethics of work and, in the Andes, 70–86
ethnography of work *vs.*, 136
financial, 19, 151
Foucault on, 90, 136
individualism and, 245
labor and, 55–56
manifestation of, 245–55
money *vs.*, 38–41
morality as prerequisite for, 185
narratives of, 222–26, 228–29, 232–33, 235–36
personal, 134, 135–36, 138, 152, 160
Polanyi on, 132–55, 160, 186–87
positive, 112
service *vs.*, 41
soaring, 229, 232–33
social, 6, 16, 19–20, 134, 135–36, 160
standardization and, 245–55
teamwork and, 247–48
VCs and, 228–33
volunteerism and, 57–61
work and, 12–16, 49–66, 135, 158–77
work ethic and, 183–87
friendship
personhood through, 91
precarity and, at North Indian call centers, 89–105
at work, 100–103
frontline programmer, 154n4
fuerza, 70–71, 73–74, 77, 83
fun, 93–94
mazaq, 59

Gambia, 124
GDR. *See* German Democratic Republic
gender
adulthood and, 126
in workplace, 92
general partners (GPs), 222, 224, 236n1
German Democratic Republic (GDR), 189
German Reunification, 242
Ghana
entrepreneurship in, 114
liberalization in, 118, 127–28n11
neoliberalism in, 126
state socialism in, 112–14
work in, 18–19
Ghaziabad, India, 89–90, 92–95, 100–102
ethnography in, 104–5n1
ghostwriters, 258–60
academic, 266–67, 268–72
anthropology and, 21–22
defining, 264
income of, 274n1
neoliberalism and, 262–68
positive client relationships with, 268
See also authorship
gift
commodity *vs.*, 41–42
labor as, and commodity in Vanuatu, 38–41
labor-time as, 28
The Gift (Mauss), 17, 27, 35, 280–81
gig economy, ethnographies in, 223–26. *See also* digitization; technology company; work distribution platforms
Glatzer, Jenna, 258–61, 274
globalization, 187–88
neoliberalism and, 241–42
gold-plating, 143

Gonda, India, 94–95
Goodman, David, 145
Google, 264
GPs. *See* general partners
Graeber, David, 49, 252
Gregory, Chris, 28, 32–33, 43, 43n2
Greylock Partners, 226
Guangzhou, China, 154n1
Gudeman, Stephen, 85n4
guolaosi, 133
Gupta, Akhil, 93
Gurley, Bill, 237n10
Guyer, Jane I., 29, 43n1, 121–22
  on authorship, 19

Habermas, Jürgen, 199n3
Halle, Germany, 20, 199n7
  work, economic, and social ethics in, 187
hamál, 63
hamsaya, 63
Harrell, Stevan, 142
Haushalten, 184, 195, 199n1
Hayek, Friedrich August, 13–14
  on nationalism, 204–5
health
  health care, 162, 165
  health-care insurance, 158
  health conditions, 111, 283
  See also well-being
Heller, Monica, 263, 265, 267
Hertz, Ellen, 246
hierarchy, 9–10, 89–95, 101–3, 244, 247
  in Asante kingdom, 113
  class and, in workplace, 90
  in Ghanaian media, 118–21
  in secondary school, 94–95
  at work, 102–4
Hochschild, Arlie, 89, 93
home office, 2–3, 12
hospitality, 63
household, 64
  closed, economy, 8
  collective labor in, 58–59
  economy, 2–3
  pleasure in, work, 62
  salaries outside of, 116
  work in, 11
  work *vs.* contributions to, 109
hukou, 141
Humahuaca, Argentina
  celebration of Saint Anne in, 74–80
  material theology in, 83–84
  value creation in, 71–74
human capital, 139
Humphrey, Caroline, 233
Hungary, 17, 22n2
  ethnography in, 16
hunting, 4–5
Hunza Valley, Pakistan, 17, 279
  agriculture in, 51–52
  collective work in, 52–56
  ethnography fieldwork in, 50–52
  moral economy of, 59
  work, ethics, and freedom in, 49–66
hydraulic hypothesis, of Wittfogel, 53

IBM, 214
identification, alienation *vs.*, 113–14
ILO. *See* International Labor Organization
IMF. *See* International Monetary Fund
indenture, 44n7
India
  class in, 91–92
  colonial era of, 90–91
  consumption in culture of, 103
  middle-class subjectivity of, 90
  work for women in, 18
individualism, 24, 182
  freedom and, 245
  in market, 30–31
  See also personhood
informal sector, 110, 121
informal unions, 92
Ingram, John Kells, 32
InnoCentive, 204
international finance, 243
International Labor Convention of 1930, 36
International Labor Organization (ILO), 36, 37, 43n4, 71–72, 278
International Monetary Fund (IMF), 170–71
intrapreneurs, 254–55
investors, 230–31
  emotions of, 225
  ethnographies of, 223–26

Islam
ethical thought of, 64
finance of, 225, 235
Isma'ili, 59–60
IT developers, 137–40, 141
IT workers, 140–44, 152–53
burnout of, 132–34

Jacomb, Edward, 44n9
jamaat khana, 60
jobless growth, 110–11
Jujuy, Argentina, 70
re-ethnicization movement in, 72

Kaggle, 204
Kalanick, Travis, 237n10
Kalberg, Stephen, 185
Kant, Immanuel, 160
Karakoram Highway (KKH), 53
Kasmir, Sharryn, 175
Keane, Webb, 136
Keynes, John Maynard, 10, 15
Keynesianism, 158
Khan, Masood, 57
khidmat, 59–60
khun, 64
Kickstarter, 206
Kindergarten Day, 39–40
kinship networks, caste-based, 101
KKH. *See* Karakoram Highway
knitting, 86n14
Kolla, 18, 70, 71–72
Kragujevac, Serbia, 19
kuti, 58

labor
autonomy of, 159
under capitalism, 30, 162–63
commodification of, 162–63
commoditized contractual, in colonial era, 32–34
commodity *vs.*, 32
communal, 35–37
divisions of, 11
emotional, 89
forced, 35–37
freedom and, 55–56
history of, in Vanuatu, 32–34
linguistic, 265
migrants, 27–42
mock, 163
NGO contracts for non-technical, 57
in oral history narratives, 51
Polanyi on, 32, 172
precarity of, 133
Smith, A., on, 12–13
unions, 113
in Vanuatu, 38–41
wage, 41
work *vs.*, 5
See also work
labor-time, 28
Labour in a Socialist Society (Okore), 112
Laidlaw, James, 136, 229, 233
laissez-faire, 13, 134, 159, 160
Lamen Island, 30, 34, 37–38, 38–41
Lampland, Martha, 162
Language, Capitalism, and Colonialism (Heller & McElhinny), 263
language, commodification of, 265–66
law, morality *vs.*, 31
Leins, Stefan, 224
leisure, 67n6
work *vs.*, 96–97
Lentz, Carola, 124–25
on middle-class, 127n9
Lévi-Strauss, Claude, 76
liberalism, 160
liberalization
in Ghana, 118, 127–28n11
in Yugoslavia, 158–77
liberation, 162
Foucault on, 160–61
of work, 163–67, 175
libertarianism, 6, 21, 231, 233
of VCs, 229–30
limited partners (LPs), 224, 236n1
linguistic labor, 265
LinkedIn, 223
love, work and, 62–65
LPs. *See* limited partners
Lukács, Georg, 13, 16
Luther, Martin, 183
Lyft, 215

Ma, Jack, 132
machine-learning, 137
Mahmood, Saba, 90

Malinowski, Bronislaw, 8, 9, 13, 27–28
Mallard, Grégoire, 35–36
management
 blue-collar worker *vs.*, 14
 risk, 242–43, 246
 self-management, 168, 169
 in work distribution platforms, 212–15
Mankekar, Purnima, 93
manong, 139
market economy
 of China, 132–33
 individualism in, 30–31
 Polanyi's critique of, 134–35
 See also capitalism; laissez-faire
Marx, Karl, 5, 15, 29, 30, 41, 162, 186
 on productivity, 7–8
 on work, 31
masculinity, 112
 in Ghanaian private media, 118–21, 124–25
material theology, 83–84
Mauss, Marcel, 17, 27, 28–29, 35, 41, 42, 63, 280–81
 on law *vs.* morality, 31–32
 on solidarity, 31
Mazzucato, Marina, 237n13
McElhinny, Bonnie, 263, 265, 267
Mechanical Turk, 201, 203–4, 209, 214
media, private
 of Accra, 108–28
 men *vs.* women in, 122–23
 salary in Ghana, 109
Meillassoux, Claude, 116
Melanesia, 27–28, 32–34
 exchange in, 30
memoirs, 258–60, 264
men
 private media, wealth accumulation and, 118–21
 women *vs.*, in private media, 122–23, 128n12
 work for, in Ghana, 18–19
menstrual cycles, temporality of, 102
#Metoo, 128n12
microhydel, 54, 57
middle-class
 global, 125
 Lentz on, 127n9
 professionalism and, 115–16
 subjectivity of India, 90
 work of, 114–18
migration, 66
Milošević, Slobodan, 176
miniaturas, 67n5, 86n10, 279
 crafting, as self-making, 81–83
 exchange of, 75–78
 production of, 70–86
 work of crafting, 79–81
minimum wage, 1
Mirs of Hunza, 55, 59
 route politics of, 53
mock labor, 163
mohabat, 62–63
money
 family *vs.*, in Ghana, 116–17
 freedom *vs.*, 38–41
 in private media, 127n2
 of Saint Anne, 85–86nn8–9
 work, and middle-class, 114–18
monoglot standard, 265
monopolies, 222, 224
 VCs on, 233–34
moral economy
 of Hunza Valley, 59
 of work, 72–73, 114–15
 See also economic ethic; economy
moral experience, 49, 66
morality
 freedom and, 185
 Mauss on law *vs.*, 31–32
motivation, employee, 245–47
Munro, Doug, 43–44n6
mutual aid, 62

nanny state, 158–59
The Nation (Mauss), 35
National Democratic Congress (NDC), 120–21
natural economy, 28
NDC. *See* National Democratic Congress
nearshore financial services, 240–44, 249, 253
needs, under capitalism, 188
neoliberalism, 6, 15, 17, 21, 58, 111–12, 114, 133, 159, 240, 278
 autonomy in, 215–16
 deregulation in, 175–76
 entrepreneurial self in, 202–3

neoliberalism *(cont.)*
era of, 10–12
Foucault on, 160
in Ghana, 126
ghostwriters and, 262–68
globalization and, 241–42
subjectivity in, 14, 247–48, 251–52
work distribution platforms and, 201–2
workers in, 94
New Hebrides, 35–36
New Patriotic Party (NPP), 120–21
New Rural Social Pension Scheme, 155n8
NGO. *See* non-governmental organization
996 schedule, 132–33, 135–36, 137–38, 142, 143, 279
e-hailing drivers and, 149, 151–53
work-life balance and, 146
Ni-Vanuatu, 27–42
Nkrumah, Kwame, 19, 113, 279
non-governmental organization (NGO), 54
non-technical labor contracts for, 57
non-work, 169–72
NPP. *See* New Patriotic Party

obligation
moral, 149
self-realization and, in work, 110–12
offshoring, 241
Okore, Anoma, 112
"On Freedom" (Polanyi), 134, 135
Ong, Aihwa, 93
oral history, 51
Orbán, Viktor, 16, 17, 22n2
outsourcing, 262–63
overtime
white-collar professionals and, 152n1
work, 133, 139
overwork, capitalism and, 132–55
ownership, of work and life, 140–44

Pachamama, 73–74
Pakistan-China relations, 66
palava, 109
Palikula, 34, 38
participation, in development policy, 57–58
patriarchal society, capitalism and, 103
peasant studies, 9–10
peer-to-peer work exchange, 206, 208
personal freedom, 134, 160
social freedom *vs.*, 135–36, 151–53
of taxi drivers, 146–47
work and, 138
See also freedom
personhood, 14, 19
in conviviality, 103
through friendship, 91
pinyin system, 154n2
plantations, 33
economy of, 29
platform capitalism, 221
pleasure
consumption and, 65
in household work, 62
work *vs.*, 49, 66
See also fun
Polanyi, Karl, 13, 15, 16–17, 41, 49–50, 66, 162, 182, 192, 280–81
on countermovement, 19–20
on deregulation, 159–60
on double movement, 153, 161
on freedom, 132–55, 160, 186–87
on labor, 32, 172
on market economy, 134–35
on social ethic, 193–94, 197–98
on socialism, 134
political economy. *See* capitalism; neoliberalism; *specific topics*
Popper, Karl, 6
post-colonial state, autonomy and, 112–14
Pradesh, Uttar, 104–5n1
precarity, 11, 112
affect, and autonomy, 93–97
friendship and, at North Indian call centers, 89–105
of labor, 133
prestation, 17, 27, 28–29, 41, 42
communal work and, 35–38
private media
hierarchy in Ghanaian, 118–21
masculinity in Ghanaian, 118–21, 124–25
men *vs.* women in, 128n12

money in, 127n2
wealth accumulation, and men, 118–21
private sector, 110, 116, 118, 127n10
process-driven work, 245–55
productivism, in Yugoslavia, 163, 175
productivity, 7–8
professionalism, 127n2
family and, 141
in Ghana, 109–10
middle-class and, 115–16
salary and, 110–11
profit, 14
proletarian ethics, 160
proletariat, 4
The Protestant Ethic and the Spirit of Capitalism (Weber), 125, 183–84, 281
Protestantism, 41
work ethic of, 20, 83, 182–84, 189–91
"The Protestant Sets and the Spirit of Capitalism" (Weber), 281
protocols of recognition, 60–61

Qoyllur Rity pilgrimage, 80
Qur'an, 64

rajaáki, 53, 55, 57, 58–59
reciprocity, 65
Recognized Seasonal Employer (RSE), 28, 38
redistribution, in Yugoslavia, 162–64, 166
re-ethnicization movement, 72
Reformation, 187
relational autonomy, 93–94. *See also* autonomy; personhood
religion, 41, 60
in Argentina, 70–84
Protestantism, 14, 20, 83, 182–84, 189–91
workism as, 133
See also Catholicism; cosmology; Islam
remote work, 207
reputational effects, 21
responsibility
individualized, 196–97
social, 196–98
restructuring, 243
Riles, Annelise, 246
risk management, 242–43, 246
Robbins, Joel, 71
rom (clan), 58, 63, 67n3
Rosenblat, Alex, 155n10
route politics, 53
RSE. *See* Recognized Seasonal Employer
Rudnyckyj, Daromir, 225, 235

salary
outside of household, 116
in private media industry of Ghana, 109
professionalism and, 110–11
of taxi drivers, 145
of women, 101–2
Samasource, 209
sanctions, 67n3, 101
The Savage Mind (Lévi-Strauss), 76
scaling, distribution and, 76–78
Schumpeter, Joseph, 233, 235–36
Scribe, 264
secondary school, hierarchy in, 94–95
self-employment, 190–91
self-interest, altruism *vs.*, 41–42
self-making, *miniaturas* as, 81–83
self-protection, 19–20
self-realization, 19, 125, 253
authorship and, 124
obligation and, in work, 110–12
work as, 108–28
Serbia, 167, 170, 173
service, freedom *vs.*, 41
sexual harassment, 97–98
shareholder mentality, 251–52
Shenzhen, China, 132, 137, 141, 143
shuasís, 61
Shyrock, Andrew, 63
sick leave, 103
Silicon Valley, 223, 226, 228
Silverstein, Michael, 265
Smith, Adam, 49
on abstract labor, 12–13
social death, 93
social debt, 182
social ethic, 187
in Halle, Germany, 189–97
Polanyi on, 193–94, 197–98
social freedom, 66, 134, 160, 186
personal freedom *vs.*, 135–36, 151–53
self-protection as, 19–20
of taxi drivers, 149

Social Insurance Law, 155n8
socialism, 10–11, 17
  countermovement against, 158–77
  late, 174
  Marxist-Leninist-Maoist, 10
  Polanyi on, 134
  state, in Ghana, 112–14
  utopian, 14
  work in, 163–67
  in Yugoslavia, 15, 19–20, 161–67, 174–75
social media platforms, 137
social order, and attitude, 94–96
social protection, 158
social question, 165, 170
social reproduction, capital linked to, 116–17
social responsibility, 196–98
social security, 155n8
Society for the Study of Work, 22n1
SOE. *See* state-owned enterprise
Sokoll, Thomas, 278
solidarity, Mauss on, 31
Solidarnošć, 175
Sopranzetti, Claudio, 161
Soviet Union, 10
S&P500, 237n7
Spittler, Gerd, 7, 43n5, 49–50
  on work, 52
Spronk, Rachel, 115–16
staff, non-scientific, 1–2
standardization, freedom and, 245–55
start-ups, 221, 223, 231
state-owned enterprise (SOE), 144, 155n7
Streeck, Wolfgang, 182, 184
  on capitalism, 188, 197–98
subjectivity, 136
  middle-class, of India, 90
  in neoliberalism, 14, 247–48, 251–52
  of workers, 93
suerte, 70–71, 73, 77, 83
sukúyo, 50, 63
Svetlost, 170, 173

Tamil Nadu, India, 101
Tanna Island, 37
TAO. *See* Taxi Administration Office
Task Rabbit, 203, 223
Taxi Administration Office (TAO), 145
taxi drivers, 144–47
  e-hailing drivers *vs.*, 148–50
  personal freedom of, 146–47
  salary of, 145
  social freedom of, 149
  social life of, 147
teamwork, 243
  freedom and, 247–48
technology, work and, 208
technology company, 215
  Didi Chuxing "Didi," 144
  Tencent, 137–41
  See also digitization; platform capitalism; work distribution platforms
Tencent, 137–41
Thatcher, Margaret, 161
The Theory of Moral Sentiments (Smith, A.), 49
Thiel, Peter, 229, 234
Thomas, Albert, 36
Thompson, Edward Palmer, 164
Thurnwald, Richard, 49–50
Tito, Josip Broz, 162, 164
Topcoder, 203
trabajo, 73
transaction costs, 203
transatlantic slavery, 113
Tribe, Keith, 188
Trobrianders, 27–28
Tuckett, David, 225
TV Central station, 108, 114, 115, 118, 119–21, 126, 127n1
Twitter, 223
2010 landslide, 66, 67n2

Uber, 159, 201, 209, 210, 215, 223, 237n10
unemployment, 242–43
UNESCO. *See* United Nations Educational, Scientific and Cultural Organization
unicorns, 222, 234, 236n2
United Nations Educational, Scientific and Cultural Organization (UNESCO), 72
universal income, 16
Unternehmer, 195
UpWork, 213

Urdu language, 67n1
uyunkosís, 61

value creation, 71–74
Vanuatu, 42
  labor history of, 32–34
  labor in, 38–41
  work in, 29–30
VC. *See* venture capital
Veblen, Thorstein, 9
venture capital (VC), 21, 221–22, 279–80
  bottom line for, 226–27
  capital ownership in, 236n1
  data used by, 227–28
  ethical obligations of, 226–27
  fieldwork on, 222–23
  freedom and, 228–33
  libertarianism of, 229–30
  on monopolies, 233–34
  in sequence of intermediaries, 224
Village Organizations (VOs), 54–55, 57, 59
Virgin of Fatima, 80
vocational training, 192–93
volunteering, 61–62
volunteerism, freedom and, 57–61
VOs. *See* Village Organizations

wage labor, 172
  capitalism and, 41
Wallman, Sandra, 4, 5
Ward, Benjamin, 168
wealth accumulation, 118–21
The Wealth of Nations (Smith, A.), 49
Weber, Max, 14, 20, 83, 125, 182, 190, 192, 280
  on capitalism, 185–86
  Economy and Society, 199n1
  "The Protestand sects," 281
  on work ethic, 183–85, 187, 191, 197–98
WeChat, 140
well-being
  at workplaces, 90, 241
WhatsApp, 223
white-collar work, 5–6, 11–12
  in Ghana, 110–12
  overtime and, professionals, 152n1
Wittfogel, Karl August, 53
women
  affective practices of, 97–100
  in caste-based kinship networks, 101
  emotional labor and, 90, 93
  men *vs.*, in private media, 122–23, 128n12
  salary of, 101–2
  work for, in India, 18
Women's Organizations (WOs), 54–55
work, 278
  autonomy of, process, 122
  under capitalism, 162–63
  in China, 19
  class and call-center, 97–100
  in colonial era, 29
  commodification of, 30–32, 175
  communal, and prestation, 35–38
  of crafting miniatures, 79–81
  definition of, 3–7
  distribution according to, 168
  emancipatory, 112–14
  emotional agility for, 94–97
  ethics of, 1–22, 49–66, 70–86, 111
  ethnography of freedom *vs.*, 136
  excellence, and authorship, 121–25
  freedom and, 12–16, 49–66, 135, 158–77
  friendship at, 100–103
  fun and, 93–94
  in Ghana, 18–19
  hegemony of, 158
  hierarchy at, 102–4
  in household, 11
  household contributions *vs.*, 109
  labor *vs.*, 5
  leisure *vs.*, 96–97
  liberation of, 163–67, 175
  love and, 62–65
  Marx on, 31
  of middle-class, 114–18
  moral economy of, 72–73, 114–15
  non-work and, 169–72
  obligation and self-realization in, 110–12
  overtime, 133, 139
  ownership of life and, 140–44
  personal freedom and, 138
  pleasure *vs.*, 49, 66
  problematizing, 202–5

work *(cont.)*
process-driven, 21
remote, 207
as self-realization, 108–28
in socialism, 163–67
Spittler on, 52
technology and, 208
in Vanuatu, 29–30
wage, 38–39
white-collar, 5–6, 11–12, 110–12, 152n1
for women in India, 18
in Yugoslavia, 163–67, 172–75
workaholism, 133
work-based society, 16
work distribution platforms
analysis framework, 205–15
autonomy in, 215
biases in, 211
control, management, and authority in, 212–15
dispute settlement in, 213
neoliberalism and, 201–2
open-call systems, 203–5, 212, 215–16
reputation mechanisms in, 213–15, 218n9
screen names in, 218n4
sustained connections in, 210
work design and, 206–9
work dissemination in, 209–12
workers, 32
blue-collar, 5–6, 223
as commodity, 44n13
contingent, 3
key, 3
in neoliberalism, 94
neophyte, 92
seasonal, 40–41
self-management of, 168, 169
subjectivity of, 93
work ethic, 3, 15–16, 28
under capitalism, 183–85
Chinese, 141–42
freedom and, 183–87
in Halle, Germany, 189–97
of Protestantism, 20, 83, 182–84, 189–91
Weber on, 183–85, 187, 191, 197–98
work-life balance, 8
in China, 132–55, 138
dialectics of personal and social freedom *vs.*, 151–53
fixed schedule for, 146
996 schedule and, 146
workplace
gender in, 92
hierarchy and class in, 90
sexualization of, 97–105
WOs. *See* Women's Organizations

Xi'an, China, 144–47

Yugoslavia, 158–77
commodification of labor in, 162–63
Communist Party in, 161–62
countermovement in, 162–63, 175
IMF and, 170–71
liberalization in, 158–77
non-work in, 169–72
productivism in, 163, 169–72, 175
redistribution in, 162–64, 166
socialism in, 15, 19–20, 161–67, 174–75
work in, 163–67, 172–75

Zaloom, Caitlin, 225
Zastava car plant, 19, 167–68, 171–76

www.ingramcontent.com/pod-product-compliance
Ingram Content Group UK Ltd.
Pitfield, Milton Keynes, MK11 3LW, UK
UKHW021836100926
8556IPUK00004B/378